Corporate Links and Foreign Direct Investment in Asia and the Pacific

T0340357

Corporate Links and Foreign Direct Investment in Asia and the Pacific

edited by

Edward K.Y. Chen

and

Peter Drysdale

Routledge
Taylor & Francis Group
NEW YORK AND LONDON

in association with

The Pacific Trade and Development Conference Secretariat
The Australian National University
Centre of Asian Studies, The University of Hong Kong

First published 1995 by Westview Press
in association with
The Pacific Trade and Development Conference Secretariat
The Australian National University

Published 2018 by Routledge
605 Third Avenue, New York, NY 10017
4 Park Square, Milton Park, Abingdon, Oxon OX14 4RN

Routledge is an imprint of the Taylor & Francis Group, an informa business

Copy edited by Beth Thomson
Index by Suzanne Ridley
Typeset by Minnie Reis

ISBN 13: 978-0-8133-8973-8 (pbk)

Contents

Tables

Figures

Participants

Dr Florian A. Alburo
University of the Philippines,
The Philippines

Dr C. Fred Bergsten
Institute for International Economics,
United States

Dr Alan E. Bollard
Commerce Commission,New Zealand

Mr Gordon de Brouwer
The Australian National University,
Australia

Mr Javier Guzman Calafell
International Economic Affairs, Mexico

Mr Giovanni Capannelli
Hitotsubashi University, Japan

Professor Richard E. Caves
Harvard University, United States

Dr Lawrence L.C. Chau
School of Economics and Finance,
United States

Professor Edward K.Y. Chen
The University of Hong Kong,
Hong Kong

Dr Po-Chih Chen
Taiwan Institute of Economic Research,
Taiwan

Dr Tain-Jy Chen
Chung-hua Institution for Economic
Research, Taiwan

Dr Leonard Cheng
Hong Kong University of Science and
Technology, Hong Kong

Professor Chia Siow Yue
National University of Singapore,
Singapore

Dr Yun-peng Chu
Fair Trade Commission,
Republic of China

Professor Rolf D. Cremer
Department of Economics,
New Zealand

Professor Wendy Dobson
University of Toronto, Canada

Professor Peter Drysdale
The Australian National University,
Australia

Professor Dennis J. Encarnation
Harvard University, United States

Professor H. Edward English
Carleton University, Canada

Professor Carlo Filippini
Bocconi University, Italy

Dr John Frankenstein
The University of Hong Kong,
Hong Kong

Professor Ross Garnaut
The Australian National University,
Australia

Professor Gary Hamilton
University of Washington,
United States

Dr Farid Harianto
University of Toronto, Canada

Dr Hal Hill
The Australian National University,
Australia

Sir Frank Holmes
National Bank of New Zealand,
New Zealand

Mr Ralph Huenemann
University of Victoria, Canada

Professor Motoshige Itoh
University of Tokyo, Japan

Dr Satish C. Jha
Asian Development Bank, India

Professor Yongwook Jun
Chung-Ang University, South Korea

Dr Mingsarn Kaosa-ard
Thailand Development Research
Institute Foundation, Thailand

Professor Kiyoshi Kojima
Suguradai University, Japan

Professor Akira Kohsaka
Osaka University, Japan

Professor Lawrence B. Krause
University of California, San Diego,
United States

Mr C.H. Kwan
Nomura Research Institute, Japan

Ms Ying-Hua Ku
Chung-Hua Institution for Economic
Research, Taiwan

Professor Y.Y. Kueh
Lingnan College, Hong Kong

Ms P.K. Lau
Hong Kong Polytechnic, Hung Hom,
Kowloon

Dr Lee Tsao Yuan
Institute of Policy Studies, Singapore

Mr Edward Leung
Hong Kong Trade Development
Council, Hong Kong

Dr K.W. Li
City Polytechnic of Hong Kong,
Hong Kong

Dr Justin Lin
Department of Rural Economic
Development, China

Mr Meng-Chun Liu
Chung-Hua Institution for Economic
Research, Taiwan

Professor Mark Mason
Yale University, United States

Professor Corrado Molteni
Bocconi University, Italy

Professor S.J. Nicholas
The University of Melbourne, Australia

Professor Mee-Kau Nyaw
The Chinese University of Hong Kong,
Hong Kong

Dr Juan J. Palacios
University of Guadalajara,
Mexico

Dr Mari Pangestu
Centre for Strategic and International
Studies, Indonesia

Mr Steve Parker
The Asia Foundation, United States

Professor Hugh Patrick
Columbia University, United States

Professor Peter A. Petri
Brandeis University, United States

Mr Graeme Pirie
Asia–Pacific Economic Cooperation
Secretariat, Singapore

Mr Jun Shibata
University of Tokyo, Japan

Professor Denis F. Simon
Tufts University, United States

Dr Hadi Soesastro
Centre for Strategic and International
Studies, Indonesia

Dr Devinda Subainge
World Bank, United States

Dr Yun-Wing Sung
Chinese University of Hong Kong,
Hong Kong

Ms Tomoko Takahashi,
FAIR, Japan

Professor Moktar Tamin
University of Malaya, Malaysia

Dr Min Tang
Asian Development Bank,
The Philippines

Mr John Chun-Wah Tsang
Assistant Director General of Trade,
Kowloon

Professor Shujiro Urata
Waseda University, Japan

Professor Ricardo Vicuna
Ministry of Foreign Affairs, Chile

Professor Ryuhei Wakasugi
Yokohama National University, Japan

Dr D.D. Wang
The University of Hong Kong,
Hong Kong

Mr Tony Waters
University of California, Davis,
United States

Professor Maria Weber
Bocconi University, Italy

Ms Anissa Wong
Industry Department, Hong Kong

Ms Teresa Wong-Kwong
The University of Hong Kong,
Hong Kong

Professor Wu Rong-I
Taiwan Institute of Economic Research,
Taiwan

Dr Eugenia Yakovleva
Institute of World Economy and
International Relations, Russia

Dr Vladimir Yakubovsky
Visiting Fellow, Japan Centre for
Economic Research, Japan

Professor Ippei Yamazawa
Hitotsubashi University, Japan

Dr Soogil Young
Korea Transport Institute,
South Korea

Dr Zhu Naixiao
South China Normal University,
China

Preface

The Asia Pacific economies have enjoyed high growth rates over the past several decades. The East Asian 'economic miracle' began with Japan and was carried forward with the export-oriented industrialisation strategies of the four little 'dragons' — Hong Kong, South Korea, Singapore and Taiwan. It has come to encompass the other East Asian economies, including China, over the last decade or so. The transmission of economic growth throughout the East Asian region has been powerful.

One important mechanism for such transmission has been foreign direct investment. An earlier PAFTAD volume, *Direct Foreign Investment in Asia and the Pacific*, explored the role of foreign direct investment in Asia Pacific development and growth at the end of the 1960s. A number of other studies have examined the impact of direct investment on the regional economy. However, there has been less research on corporate strategies and firm-level behaviour in multinational corporate operations in the region. For this reason, PAFTAD 21 chose to focus on corporate links and foreign direct investment in Asia and the Pacific as its central theme.

This volume is a collection of the edited papers presented at the Twenty-First Pacific Trade and Development (PAFTAD) Conference held in Hong Kong in June 1994. The Centre of Asian Studies, an integral part of the University of Hong Kong, was very pleased to act as host for the conference. Despite the fact that Hong Kong scholars have been participating in PAFTAD activities for a long time, this was the first time that the conference was held in Hong Kong. We would like to express our gratitude to the Hong Kong government for its most generous financial support of the conference. In particular, thanks are due to Mr Brian T.H. Chau, Secretary for Trade and Industry, for his assistance throughout the preparations for the conference. We also thank the Governor of Hong Kong, Mr Christopher Patten, for his presence at the conference and for officiating at the opening ceremony. His opening address was much more than ceremonial, and contained a mixture of his personal insights and experience relating to the issues discussed throughout the conference.

The PAFTAD Conference and this volume would not have been possible without the consortium of funders from around the region. We are grateful to the Asian Development Bank, the Asia Foundation, the Australian National University, the Ford Foundation, the Kansai Federation of Economic Organisations, the Korea Development Institute, the Rockefeller Brothers Fund, the Taiwan Institute of Economic Research and the Tokyo Chamber of Commerce for their continuing support for the work of PAFTAD over many years.

We would like to acknowledge the efficient assistance provided by the PAFTAD Secretariat in Canberra and the advice given by the International Steering Committee. We are also very grateful to the local organising committee members, Dr Lawrence L.C. Chau, Dr Sung Yun-Wing and Ms Teresa Y.C. Wong, for their hard work and guidance. Credit also goes to Ms Mely Caballero-Anthony, Conference Secretary, who was responsible for overseeing the logistics of the conference preparations.

The volume was edited at the PAFTAD Secretariat at the Australian National University. Ms Beth Thomson has done an excellent job in editing the original papers for publication and Ms Minni Reis an equally fine job in designing and typesetting the manuscript.

We trust that you agree that the volume makes a valuable contribution to understanding of the role of foreign direct investment and corporate links in the process of Asia Pacific economic development.

Edward K.Y. Chen and Peter Drysdale
November 1994

1 Introduction and overview ——

Hadi Soesastro

The setting

Some of the most interesting developments that have taken place in recent years in the Asia Pacific region have been in the field of foreign direct investment (FDI). Intraregional FDI flows have increased dramatically over the past 10 years or so. The stock of FDI in the ASEAN countries excluding Brunei (Indonesia, Malaysia, the Philippines, Thailand and Singapore) is estimated to have increased by about 14 per cent annually in 1980–92. The average increase in the stock of FDI in China over the same period was 15 per cent per annum. The rate of increase has been even higher in recent years: about 25 per cent annually for 1988–92. In terms of approvals, reports indicate that inward FDI flows to China increased sharply in 1993. This suggests that there may have been significant diversions of investment to China from other destinations, particularly the ASEAN countries. In the three Asian NIEs (Hong Kong, South Korea and Taiwan) the rate of increase in the FDI stock was on average 22 per cent per annum in 1980–92. The stock of FDI in the whole of developing East Asia (China, the Asian NIEs, Indonesia, Malaysia, the Philippines and Thailand) may have increased by as much as US$130 billion during this period.

Japan was, of course, the main source of FDI to developing East Asia. Based on balance of payments data, during the period 1985–92 cumulative outward flows of Japanese FDI amounted to about US$220 billion. The United States is still the main destination of Japanese FDI, most of it in non-manufacturing activities. In contrast, the bulk of Japanese FDI in East Asia continues to be directed at manufacturing activities. In other words, East Asia has received a substantial share of Japan's total direct investment in manufacturing.

Traditional sources of direct investment, namely the United States and Europe, continue to be important for the East Asian region. There has also been a rapid increase in new sources. The Asian NIEs' stock of FDI in East Asia, most of it in ASEAN countries and China, increased by close to US$40 billion in 1980–92. This means that about one-third of the total increase in the stock of FDI in East Asia during this period

1

originated from the Asian NIEs. A rise in cross-investment is another interesting feature observed in the region. The stock of FDI from developing East Asia in the United States could now amount to about US$10 billion, most of it of recent vintage. Thus, the FDI picture in the Asia Pacific region is characterised not only by a dramatic rise in the volume of direct investment, but also by shifts in the destinations and sources of FDI flows.

The immediate issues that arise from this brief review are the sustainability of these rates of increase, the pattern of distribution of FDI flows across countries in the region, and the likely implications of the changing structure of FDI sources on trade and other cross-border activities of the regional economies. The relevance of these questions, from a regional point of view, rests on a recognition that FDI flows have been responsible for the economic dynamism of the region and in particular the high rates of growth experienced by developing East Asia. In addition, intraregional FDI flows have contributed significantly to the deepening of regional economic interdependencies and the market-driven integration of regional economies. However, in the political economy realm, deepening of interdependence is not always good news. The creation of regional production networks that could in turn alter the geo-economics of the Asia Pacific region may have serious politico-security implications.

Direct investment flows in the region have been influenced by push and pull factors that have changed over the years. Peter Petri in chapter 3 of this volume identifies four waves of FDI flows into developing East Asia in the postwar period. The first wave, which took place in the 1960s and early 1970s, was motivated by protected local markets and the first major yen revaluation. Investment was concentrated mainly in joint ventures in textiles and household electrical equipment. The second wave, in the 1970s, was spurred by the region's bright prospects and the availability of low-cost capital. This wave of investment included import substitution projects in basic industries and the creation of American export platforms in consumer electronics and semiconductors. The third wave, involving the relocation of labour-intensive industry from Japan and the Asian NIEs to ASEAN, resulted essentially from the appreciation of the yen and several NIE currencies in the mid 1980s. This push coincided with a major pull: the significantly improved investment climate in ASEAN countries, which boosted their export capacity.

The story of these first three waves, particularly the third, has often been told. It is the fourth wave that will draw the attention of those interested in the region. Petri identified this as involving a massive foreign investment boom in China. He thought that it may be the most significant wave of investment yet in terms of its geo-economic implications for the region. There is as yet disagreement as to whether this latest wave of investment will cause a major diversion of investment, from the ASEAN region in particular, as investors are attracted to China's huge domestic market. Should ASEAN countries attempt to minimise the threat of diversion by introducing even more liberal investment regimes? If this proves insufficient, what strategy should the ASEAN countries adopt?

An alternative view suggests that this fourth wave may be characterised not so much by a shift in destination as a major change in the origin of FDI flows in the region. This is seen in the increase in capital movements initiated by Overseas Chinese, as manifested in FDI flows from the Chinese economies of Hong Kong and Taiwan. These flows are not, however, going exclusively into China but to a significant degree into ASEAN countries as well. Similarly, it can be argued that the main source of the FDI boom in China could well be Japan.

Yet another scenario postulates that the fourth wave of FDI flows originated in Japan and is undertaken for strategic considerations, but based on a product rather than a market orientation. This scenario, proposed by Ken'ichi Imai at an earlier Pacific Trade and Development Conference, suggests that the fourth investment wave differs from the third in that it is driven, not by the major currency realignments of the 1980s, but rather by the globalisation of Japanese production activities involving new cutting-edge technologies, such as fibre optics. These manufacturing activities on the technological ascendancy curve can be undertaken outside Japan, but with Japan retaining production of core technologies. As the ASEAN countries and China continue to upgrade their technological capability, they will be able to participate in such production networks, together with the Asian NIEs. This scenario sees both a further consolidation of the East Asian regional production network with Japan at its core and simultaneously an elevation of this network to higher technological levels, thus giving support to the 'flying geese' paradigm.

Predicting what might constitute the fourth wave of FDI necessarily involves some speculation. However, in view of the possible significant longer term geo-economic implications, this is both a useful and necessary exercise. Discussion at the Twenty-First Pacific Trade and Development Conference provided important insights into the major factors influencing the direction of changes in the nature and structure of FDI flows in the Asia Pacific region.

The actors

Investment in the Asia Pacific region is undertaken by many investors, each acting on the basis of some guidance or rules. An important feature of the region today is the active involvement in cross-border activities, including FDI, not only of multinational enterprises (MNEs) but also of small and medium sized enterprises from Japan or the Asian NIEs. Firms from developing economies, such as the ASEAN countries, have also entered the picture.

Richard Caves reminded the conference that transaction cost theory sees the MNE as an economic agent that internalises decisions about resource allocation. Such internalisation will be manifested in either a horizontally or vertically integrated firm with activities that spill across national boundaries. To increase our understanding of the behaviour of these actors, Caves suggests in chapter 2 that the process of gross turnover of business units be examined more closely. Business units, he says, undergo processes of birth, expansion, contraction and demise. It has been observed, among other things, that in manufacturing industries infant mortality rates are high, but that there is a correlation between the rates of entrance and exit of firms.

This raises the question of the adaptability of business units to a changed environment, and whether the capability to transform differs across cultures, countries or regions, or sectors. In response to adverse changes in the environment, it has been observed that subsidiaries of MNEs do often restructure and change their roles, rather than opting for exit. Anecdotal evidence was also given about the greater stability, even in bad times, of Thai–Japan joint ventures compared with, say, Thai–Taiwan joint ventures.

In chapter 12, Tain-Jy Chen et al. examine the direct investment patterns in high-wage and low-wage countries of Taiwan's larger firms. As might be expected, Taiwanese FDI in low-wage countries, such as Thailand, is undertaken mainly for defensive purposes, namely to cut production costs and restore the firm's competitiveness in the export market. FDI in high-wage countries, on the other hand, is primarily for the purpose of expanding markets. It is interesting to note the extent to which the behaviour of large Taiwanese firms has *not* been significantly influenced by government policy, particularly with respect to locational decisions.

MNEs and other business units constantly make investment decisions in conditions of uncertainty. Multinational corporations use their proprietary assets to compensate for the uncertainty of the environment in which they operate. Although the imputed value of a firm's proprietary assets may itself suddenly change, it has been observed that MNEs are more likely to be risk takers than other business units. In contrast, small and medium sized enterprises, which are much less able to spread risks, may simply follow others in their investment location decision. The large-scale migration of Japanese small and medium sized enterprises — the supporting industries — to Thailand in the late 1980s essentially followed the successful relocation there earlier on of their subcontractors. At an earlier Pacific Trade and Development Conference, Paul Krugman pointed to the importance of this demonstration effect. The 'new economic geography' would also predict why such clustering or agglomeration occurs. Still needing explanation, however, is why this has not equally been the case in Indonesia. Specifically, why has not Indonesia been able to attract investment by small and medium sized enterprises?

The emerging networks

The case of Greater South China, described so well by Yung-Wing Sung in chapter 4, provides one example of a subregional cluster. It involves investment, mainly in Guangdong, by small and medium sized enterprises from Hong Kong and, to a lesser extent, Taiwan. In fact, a very large proportion of Hong Kong's total FDI in China is in Guangdong, most likely due to proximity and cultural factors. This subregional production network is definitely market driven, and has developed in response to China's policy of opening up its economy. It remains to be seen whether this situation can be replicated elsewhere in the region and how effectively the clustering of economic activities can be influenced by policy. The 'growth triangles' of the ASEAN region — SIJORI (involving Singapore, Johor in Malaysia and Riau in Indonesia), IMT (Indonesia, Malaysia and Thailand) and EAGA (the East ASEAN Growth Area, involving eastern Malaysia, southern Philippines, Brunei and eastern Indonesia) — were initiated (or sponsored) by governments, basically to attract FDI. The success of the growth triangles in achieving this goal will depend on whether the complementarities that exist among their constituents produce locational advantages.

The ASEAN Free Trade Area (AFTA) is also intended to attract investment flows to the ASEAN region as a whole. While the movement of goods has become less constrained, factors cannot as yet move freely. It is hoped that a larger, single, freer ASEAN market will allow greater economies of scale to operate. Within the region, the distribution of FDI will be affected by the way in which investors perceive differences in comparative advantage among the ASEAN countries. The new patterns of division of labour emerging in the ASEAN region are a part of those developing in the wider Asia Pacific region.

In chapter 9, Motoshige Itoh and Jun Shibata study the emerging division of labour and operations of Japanese firms in the Asia Pacific region, focusing on the electrical machinery industry. This industry, while dynamic, has special characteristics that make it more suited to the globalisation of production than other industries. The impact of the emerging division of labour on the operations of Japanese firms in other industries therefore remains inconclusive at this stage.

In the production of VCRs, for example, the parent firm is usually involved in a number of production and assembly stages. This would suggest that the business network will be dominated by the parent company. In the automotive industry, on the other hand, the parent firm is usually involved only in the production of large parts and final assembly. This opens the possibility for firms to develop partnerships or other types of strategic alliances. Gary Hamilton and Tony Waters argue in chapter 5 that although the organisational modes in the automotive sector have evolved from an internalised structure to global networks, the parent firm retains control of the links in the production chain because the network is producer rather than buyer driven. Even within the electrical machinery industry, different types of corporate links or business networks can develop, suggesting that corporate links may not be as sector specific as previously thought. They may be specific to the operations of the 'network firm', that is, the firm that manages and coordinates the network. This will need to be substantiated by further research.

While modes of operation may vary, Denis Fred Simon and Jun Yongwook are of the opinion that Japanese firms investing abroad do in general have a common strategic objective: the creation of regional sources of competitive advantage that will strengthen their position both in the international marketplace and at home. They argue in chapter 10 that Japanese firms have increasingly come to view their counterparts in many Asian economies as actual or potential partners. This indicates that the development and consolidation of regional production networks by Japanese firms is likely to

5

continue. Simon and Jun give a number of interesting examples of the various kinds of business networking engaged in by Japanese firms.

Networking can be of the internal or external kind. Internal networking is undertaken when control, usually through ownership, is considered important. External networking refers to the use of 'bonding' mechanisms of a non-equity type, such as licensing, supplier or original equipment manufacturer (OEM) contracts, subcontracting, or strategic alliances. The different network structures can be either functionally based (through marketing or manufacturing) or even culturally linked. In the more competitive and uncertain environment in which firms operate today, networking enables companies to enhance constantly their access to complementary assets and partners with high value-added.

This trend has a number of possible implications. Some see the emergence of two major production and business networks in the Asia Pacific region, one Japanese and the other Chinese. The latter refers to the cross-border production linkages formed by Overseas Chinese capital, especially with mainland China. Although any Japanese network will most likely be based on technology, it is much more difficult to define the basis of a Chinese network. The notion of a community of Overseas Chinese linked by culture is questioned, especially by the younger generation of Southeast Asians of Chinese ancestry. It can be argued that within each society Overseas Chinese are likely to have a sense of common identity based on their minority status. It is also apparent that particular business practices attributed to the group are often not clearly formulated or transparent, although in practice they seem to have worked well. It has often been suggested that Chinese networks are essentially based on trust. Alternatively, however, they may be based on forms of financial relations.

Further, more precise study is needed to determine whether Japanese or Chinese business networks in the Asia Pacific region are unique to that region or, indeed, unique to Japan and China — if they exist at all as distinct entities. It is also unclear whether these networks have changed over time. There are no compelling reasons to predict that these two major networks are bound to collide with each other. Japanese direct investment in East Asia is not at present concentrated in Southeast Asia, and will probably be directed to China in increasing amounts; a significant amount of FDI from Hong Kong and Taiwan, meanwhile, continues to flow into ASEAN. What we may be seeing is the emergence of two layers of regional production networks, with that of Japan having a higher technological content.

Implications for trade and beyond

The changing nature of direct investment in the Asia Pacific region and the emergence of production networks are believed to have an impact on trade. Petri shows that there is a virtuous circle of investment, trade and growth in the region. The basis for this observation is that outward-oriented trade and investment policies have stimulated trade and attracted FDI, in turn encouraging governments to sustain policies that are favourable for international linkages.

Some believe that this trade–investment nexus may not have existed in the past when FDI inflows — into a number of ASEAN countries, for example — were meant to substitute for imports. Statistics show, however, that for the most part there were no significant reductions in imports, but rather a shift in industrial structure from finished products to capital goods and intermediate inputs. FDI flows into ASEAN in the 1980s were definitely trade creating. In Indonesia, for example, about 70 per cent of direct investment projects undertaken since the latter part of the 1980s have been export oriented. A causal relationship can be established from this observation. If, in the future, non-equity arrangements become the preferred mode of investment, the trade–investment nexus will tend to be weakened.

The creation of regional production networks in East Asia has many interesting implications for trade relations in the region. Intraindustry and intrafirm trade have generally increased. Developing East Asia's trade with major partners (the United States and Europe) has increased steadily, as has the trade imbalance in favour of East Asia. The imbalance between Japan and East Asia in Japan's favour has also risen, as is to be expected given that Japan uses East Asia as an export platform. If further globalisation of Japanese firms results in a different mode of operation, this imbalance may no longer be an issue. However, developments in this area need to be monitored closely; their political–economic implications should not be overlooked.

Concern has been expressed at Japan's relatively low levels of manufacturing imports from East Asia, including parts produced by Japanese subsidiaries. This deserves further, more detailed study. The slowdown of the Japanese economy in recent years may be partly responsible for this trend, but other factors — structural or policy — cannot be ignored. Chia Siow Yue shows in chapter 11 that Japanese firms can make greater use of international procurement centres, such as those in Singapore, to promote the import of parts and components from the region.

The low levels of direct investment in Japan have also received attention, perhaps largely because of the huge imbalance in bilateral FDI flows between Japan and the United States. There is no economic reason why there should be a balance in this relationship, although there is some evidence to suggest that an increase in American FDI in Japan could raise the level of US exports to Japan. Ryuhei Wakasugi in chapter 6 and Mark Mason in chapter 7 both show that while the Japanese government has taken measures to liberalise investment and encourage inflows of FDI, a number of serious impediments to investment still remain. The immediate removal of these impediments and the provision of greater incentives, including subsidies from the Japanese government, are unlikely to have a significant effect on flows of FDI to Japan. Yet it appears that the international community expects Japan to take such steps, to show its political will and its resolve to make Japan a 'normal' country. The situation may change as Japanese companies continue to globalise — and they will be forced to do so as competing networks proliferate, not only in the Asia Pacific region but also globally.

Beyond these issues, there is also a need to study in greater depth the implications for technology transfer of changes in the nature and magnitude of FDI flows in the region, and of the creation of production networks. While the role of government is important in efforts to upgrade human capital and skill, Juan Palacios argues in chapter 8 that technology transfer in the electronics industry has essentially been market driven, that is, driven by market competition. The increase in spin-offs observed in Guadalajara, for instance, supports the hypothesis that direct investment is an effective channel for technology transfer. This conclusion may not be generalisable to other industries. It is, indeed, not immediately clear which technologies have been transferred, and whether more advanced technologies tend to be transferred more readily to import-substituting than to export-oriented activities. However, the question is whether this should matter.

In closing it would be stimulating for further deliberations to repeat the provocative question raised during discussions at the Twenty-First Pacific Trade and Development Conference: what are the effects of emerging production networks and corporate links on consumer welfare in the Asia Pacific region?

2 Growth and decline in multinational enterprises: from equilibrium models to turnover processes

Richard E. Caves

Our understanding of the multinational enterprise (MNE) as an economic agent comes from transaction cost analysis, which demonstrates how the MNE internalises decisions about resource allocation that could occur instead as arm's-length transactions. This powerful theory, first applied to vertically integrated firms, explains equally well why multiactivity firms spill across national boundaries, and what their existence implies for levels and patterns of production and international trade in goods, services and technologies.

Like most of standard microeconomics, the transaction cost theory is static; that is, it predicts or explains positions of equilibrium in which no agent wishes to alter any of its economic choices, or it predicts how the agent will adjust following some exogenous disturbance in the economic environment ('comparative statics'). We apply the body of theory to actual economic agents in whatever setting we find them — in or out of equilibrium, still adjusting to past disturbances, and starting to cope with today's perturbations. At least when analysing statistical samples, economists usually apply equilibrium models to disequilibrated situations with impunity, controlling for displacements from equilibrium where they can and otherwise assuming that they represent random noise. These theoretical and empirical procedures have yielded a useful and satisfying body of knowledge about the MNE. Our major empirical conclusions about MNEs' behaviour probably suffer no serious errors or distortions due to this procedure.

Nonetheless, by applying mainly static models to ever-changing data we might have missed some opportunities for a deeper understanding of the MNE. In this chapter I demonstrate two specific shortcomings in static approaches to the analysis of MNEs.

1   A number of puzzles lurk in the empirical research on MNEs that can be resolved once we recognise that static models have been applied to systematically changing data without filtering the processes of change.

2   The business units that we study undergo systematic processes of birth, expansion, contraction and demise that are not well addressed by the standard

static theory. Rich opportunities for understanding these processes of change are being exposed by empirical research on the gross turnover of enterprises and business units, and by theoretical models of the turnover process.

In the first section of this chapter we summarise empirical and theoretical evidence that has recently accumulated on change and turnover in the distribution of firms in national markets. We then relate that evidence and models to findings in the empirical literature on MNEs and conclude with an effort to identify unexploited opportunities for research on multinationals.

Although the analysis is general, it has important applications to the Asia Pacific area. Japan has recently grown into a major foreign direct investor, and the fates of its recently founded subsidiaries support significant findings about turnover. Offshore assembly operations in East and Southeast Asia incur few sunk costs, and for that reason might be expected to show high turnover and mobility. Multinational businesses originating in Asian developing countries probably face high levels of organisational and commercial risks as they first venture abroad.

Turnover of firms: new evidence and theory

Industrial economists have long been interested in the turnover of firms, but they could work only with truncated samples of the largest industrial firms while comprehensive data lay locked away in the world's census bureaus. In the past decade researchers have at last gained the keys to those locks. Most of the important research is hence quite new, as are the important theoretical contributions. Because the theory seems useful more for organising empirical evidence than for testing hypotheses, we review selected evidence first.

New evidence on business units' turnover

The population of firms that make up an industry is observed over some period of time. Some firms apparently enjoy favourable changes in their costs or capabilities and increase their market shares; others suffer impairments and give up shares. The changes in fortune and the resulting growth or shrinkage tend to coincide in time: at the beginning of a decade one cannot predict which firms (of a given size) will grow and which will shrink. Even in the short run (year to year) there is not on average much persistence in firms' growth rates. A business unit holding a large market share at the outset is more likely subsequently to lose than to augment it; a firm with a small share, unless it exits, is more likely to gain. More churning goes on among the small firms in an industry than among the large ones, but even the leaders are on average likely to lose their positions eventually.

Entrants come on the scene. Not a few of them discover that their cost levels are high or their capabilities inferior, and their exits give rise to high rates of infant mortality. Luckier entrants whose productivity levels equal or exceed the typical incumbent's survive and grow. Sufficiently unproductive incumbents, of whatever age, exit. Indeed, among markets, those with high (gross) rates of entry tend also to show high rates of exit.[1] This pattern is squarely opposed to what we might expect when turnover is ignored: firms enter a market (if it is growing) or exit (if it is shrinking), but never do both at the same time. An ecological pattern is evident whereby an accelerated rate of exit from a market in the recent past speeds the current rate of entry, just as the recent rate of entry speeds exit (in large part due to infant mortality). The surviving entrants of a given cohort prosper and grow. However, taking exits and survivors' growth together, it is not clear whether the market share initially claimed by a given cohort of entrants subsequently expands or contracts. The faster an industry is growing, and the more uncertain are market conditions (for example, the more variable is market demand), the more does growth in supply capacity come from entrants, and the less from expansion by firms already present.

Besides the building of new plants by newly created firms and the shutting down of facilities by exiting firms, turnover also includes the entry of firms established in other markets that buy control of firms or plants in this market, and the exit of firms that sell their plants to these entrants or to others. The relative occurrence of plants opened and closed and plants bought and sold varies greatly from industry to industry. Concentrated industries and industries whose firms deploy complex bundles of proprietary assets see many changes in plant control; more opening and closing of plants occurs in unconcentrated industries or industries with simpler firms.

These processes of turnover are important for an industry's productivity. Shrinking and exiting units commonly show low and/or declining productivity. Productivity on average is increasing for incumbents that are growing, and surviving entrants quickly match the average productivity of incumbents. Changes in the control of ongoing business units (mergers, sell-offs) also affect productivity, because business units whose productivity is slipping are more likely to undergo changes in control, and their productivity typically revives for several years after the change (Lichtenberg and Siegel 1987; Baldwin and Caves 1991).

Several structural differences among industries are closely associated with differences in these turnover processes. Rapid growth of productivity in an industry is associated with more churning in its population of firms. Concentrated industries and industries with heavy sunk costs of production tend to have less turnover, although with respect to concentration the difference is largely between the least concentrated industries and the rest. Industries, including the concentrated ones, in which firms undertake heavy (and apparently uncertain) investments in proprietary assets, intangibles, goodwill and the like tend (with exceptions) to undergo more turnover, and the fluctuating market values of their incumbent firms can be read as fluctuating values imputed to these proprietary assets (Cockburn and Griliches 1988; Lustgarten and Thomadakis 1987).[2]

Theoretical models explaining turnover processes

Several new theoretical models stand ready to explain one or another aspect of these turnover processes. They will be surveyed here selectively. Their main uses are two.

11

First, they address the task of explaining how these empirical patterns could emerge from the behaviour of firms that are rational actors, so we can understand what structural conditions and economic uncertainties must be present in order to explain the patterns observed empirically. Second, they supply corollary predictions that fortify our analysis of the data: if empirical pattern A is observed, then pattern B should also be evident.

Jovanovic (1982) focused on the potential entrant firm's ignorance of the costs that it will incur if it enters. Specifically, each entrant is assumed to know the variance of the distribution of firm-specific efficiencies from which it will draw, but not the mean that pertains to its own as yet untested abilities. Upon entering (and paying an unrecoverable fixed cost) the firm learns its capability. The entrant that finds itself a washout exits promptly. The entrant who can match the incumbents survives and grows. The size distribution of firms at any time will depend on the distribution of efficiency levels and the growth that firms undertake conditional on whatever cost advantages they possess.

A significant corollary of this model (emphasised by Lippman and Rumelt 1982) is that incumbent firms that have survived their infancy should earn excess profits, as they must in equilibrium in order to offset the losses of the defunct infants and yield normal expected profits to all resources devoted, successfully or not, to the industry. Other corollaries are equally helpful in explaining the empirical patterns. Hazard rates (the proportion of survivors who exit in a given period) that are higher for younger and smaller firms are consistent with mean-regression processes but also with a greater longevity for the larger and older firms. The higher the cost of entry (or the barriers to entry), the lower is the turnover of incumbents, and the longer are their expected lifespans (Hopenhayn 1992).

If Jovanovic's model illustrates the role of uncertain investments by entrants, other models do the same for incumbents' decisions. A mechanism of 'active learning' was proposed by Ericson and Pakes (1989), whereby incumbents invest in research or exploration activities that have uncertain outcomes. The firm investing successfully prospers and expands, while the unsuccessful one suffers a loss, contracts and perhaps exits. Whereas the models of Jovanovic (1982) and others mostly generate a stable limit distribution of firm sizes from a continuum of firms, Ericson and Pakes' model involves a small number of (Cournot) competitors and allows concentration to fluctuate and the size distribution's shape to vary over time.[3] In a simulation model constructed in the same spirit, Nelson and Winter (1978) pointed out that the concentration of such a firm-size distribution increases with the variance of returns to investments in innovation; it also increases (paradoxically) with the 'vigour' of competition, in that the more aggressively a successful firm expands and displaces its rivals, the more concentrated does the industry become.

Finally, turnover of firms can result from exogenous technical change that drives established units, if they cannot retrofit current advances, down the productivity ranking of an industry's firms until they either exit or reinvest. Recurrent shocks to input prices cause firms to select production technologies that might be optimal for current factor prices but not all future price sets, so that efficiency levels will subsequently be dispersed (Førsund and Hjalmarsson 1987; Lambson 1991). Models that invoke capital vintages to explain the turnover of firms have, of course, long been with us; the striking feature of recent empirical work is the extent to which it associates the turnover of firms with infant mortality rather than technological ageing, suggesting that uncertainties about outcomes are more important than the certainties of industrial geriatrics.

We note that these theoretical models replace an older tradition of research on random processes in firms' growth associated with Gibrat's Law, the hypothesis that growth rates are independent of firms' initial sizes. This hypothesis implies that the concentration of the firm-size distribution increases without limit, a prediction ultimately rejected by statistical research. Although growth's independence of size often is not rejected for samples of large firms (not necessarily direct competitors in the same industry), comprehensive data always show greater variance of growth rates (and higher exit rates) for smaller firms, consistent with a churning but stable size distribution of competitors (see, for example, Evans 1987).

An independent and less formal theoretical explanation has surfaced for the productivity gains that accompany changes in the control of business units and the fluctuating values imputed to firms' proprietary assets (so important for understanding the MNE). The literature on MNEs identifies their international expansion with firms' distinctive proprietary assets, and their varying successes with the diverse qualities of these assets. The assets might represent goodwill possessed by the firm, but they also represent capabilities or routines that the firm's team of members can perform. Because the assets are ill-defined and subject to moral hazard when shared between firms, they are not readily bought and sold except through a change in the control of the firm. Because they are 'lumpy' or intangible and have multiple uses, they tend to be found in the hands of firms that are large and diversified. These assets are subject to recurrent shocks that change the configuration of other assets with which they are used or the markets in which they prove most productive. The shocks also change their imputed market values. This characterisation of proprietary assets taken from the literature on MNEs suffices to explain why and where turnovers of corporate control are most productive (that is, increase the value of the assets conveyed) and why market shares and firms' valuations tend to be unstable in markets where these assets are important.

Applications to research on the multinational enterprise

Interpreting the growth of multinational firms

Much research on the expansion of multinational companies centres on the genesis of their proprietary assets and the subsequent exploitation of those advantages. Although we cannot readily test hypotheses about how these assets arise in the national economy, we know that a burst of rapid economic growth in an industrial nation casts up a group of successful companies that subsequently float their expansion into multinational status on these assets. The growth of US-based multinationals after World War II, the expansion of European multinationals following Europe's successful recovery and the growth of Japanese multinationals after Japan's period of spectacular growth strongly support this hypothesis (UNCTC 1988, pp. 28–31, 74–80). For Japan it has been feasible to test this hypothesis statistically. Drake and Caves (1992) demonstrated that research and development outlays in Japan over time came to support the expansion abroad of Japan-based MNEs, and that proprietary assets in the form of differentiated products also evolved into effective bases for investment abroad. The growth rates of large corporations based in a given country tend to be closely aligned with the growth of that national economy, although to an extent that increases with the economic size of the country (Caves 1990).

Other aspects of the multinational's expansion process can be traced in differences between firms in their endowments of assets. We expect that foreign direct investors will have accumulated assets that can generate profits from such ventures. The first statistical test of differences between multinational and purely domestic firms flagged only differences in their sizes and not in their traceable investments in proprietary assets (Horst 1972). This result is not implausible because the fixed cost associated with foreign investment favours firms with a large accumulation of assets, and size (within industry) is itself a proxy for the accumulation of commercially valuable assets. However, more recent investigations have demonstrated the separate roles of intangible-asset stocks and broad product lines (Grubaugh 1987a).

Especially revealing about the sequential growth process is the interrelation between firms' exports and their foreign investment decisions. The static neoclassical model predicts that the firm will choose the more profitable means (or combination) of local production and exporting from another source to serve any given market. This model leads us to expect that exporting and foreign investment will be substitutes, with their balance controlled by their relative cost effectiveness (Horst 1971). That result is indeed confirmed in statistical studies that control properly for the sources of disturbance that drive this substitution relationship (see, for example, Grubert and Mutti 1991). However, the hypothesis regularly fails when applied (with few or no controls) to the relation between foreign sales and exports for firms or sectors over time. That 'cut' through the data is apparently dominated by developmental and learning processes, whereby export sales pave the way for foreign investments and successful foreign investments reveal profitable exporting activities. Positive relationships between exporting and foreign investment, apparently inconsistent with substitution, have accordingly appeared in a wide range of intertemporal studies, including Bergsten, Horst and Moran (1978, ch. 3), Martin (1991), Drake and Caves (1992) and Heiduk and Hodges (1992).[4]

More and Caves (1994) uncovered particularly clear evidence of the difference between static and developmental relationships between exporting and foreign investment in their study of the determinants of the growth of royalty payments received by US multinational companies from their subsidiaries. Their analysis was conducted both across a sample of host countries (for all industries) and across a sample of industries (for all host countries). Among industries the rates of growth of US foreign investment stocks apparently varied little, while among countries they varied greatly. Consequently, among sectors the growth of royalty payments and the growth of intrafirm exports from the US parents appear to be substitutes, while among countries they appear to be complements. That is, for host countries whose stocks of US foreign investment are growing rapidly (slowly), both intrafirm exports and royalties from sales of locally made goods embodying the parents' intangibles are growing rapidly (slowly).

Several lines of research support the hypothesis that firms grow into multinationality through a series of steps that maximises expected value by accumulating experience and other resources along the way. Exporting activity, as already mentioned, is one source of specific low-cost learning for potential foreign investors (Denis and Depelteau 1992). Multinational expansion commonly proceeds through a series of host countries starting with the nearest and/or most familiar (Horst 1972), an effect seen especially in unilingual English-speaking countries and in one-time colonial empires. The expansion process also uses experience gained in one host to support investment in similar hosts (Benito and Gripsrud 1992). The choice between entering a foreign market by acquiring an existing business and by constructing a new plant is made with an eye to minimising the costs of inexperience[5] or making repetitious use of a systematised procedure (Caves and Mehra 1986; Zejan 1990). Firms proceeding through a series of such incremental steps have emerged more successful than those that take discrete jumps (Newbould, Buckley and Thruwell 1978; Buckley, Berkova and Newbould 1983). On the other hand, no difference in performance was found between firms that acquired existing firms and those that built new plants — consistent with the expectation that each investor sought to use the mode most effective to its particular situation (Buckley, Berkova and Newbould 1983).

Implications for cross-sections of MNEs

These evolutionary features of MNEs' expansion processes hold many implications for cross-sections of firms observed at a point in time and cross-section variations in their growth rates. Recall the prevalence of the process of regression to the mean found in general distributions of companies' sizes and/or growth rates. This implies that growth will not be highly persistent for individual firms, that initially large companies will tend subsequently to grow more slowly, and that no simple relationship will prevail between size and profitability (although growth and profitability should be positively related). Thus firms expanding internationally tend to grow faster than their peers (Cantwell and Sanna-Randaccio 1993), but growth might if anything be negatively related to the extent of multinationality attained at a point in time. Firms seem to grow in parallel domestically and internationally (Blomström and Lipsey 1991; Jeon 1992), consistent with the exploitation of their proprietary assets wherever possible. As expected, their growth shows some, but not much, continuity (Tschoegl 1983; Kumar 1984).

The perspective of random growth and size changes provides various predictions about the population of the world's MNEs. In steady state the largest MNEs should be growing less rapidly than their smaller brethren. This hypothesis first came to be tested from an opposite perspective — the 'American challenge' that large US-based MNEs would eventually swamp their European market rivals. Rowthorn and Hymer (1971) found to their surprise that for the decade 1957–67 no positive size–growth relation existed, and indeed a negative one prevailed through most of the range of firm sizes that they observed. Only for the very largest firms did their hypothesis appear to hold (see also Buckley, Dunning and Pearce 1978, 1984). Droucopoulos (1983), revisiting their analysis with the data extended to 1977, concurred that the generally negative size–growth relation gives way to independence between size and growth only for a small number of the largest firms.[6] What we know about the size–growth relation for MNEs is thus largely consistent with our expectation about stable size distributions of firms.

Other comparisons of firm size and growth have contrasted MNEs with large domestic firms. Kumar (1984), who compared UK MNEs with their domestic brethren, found the MNEs larger but on average less profitable and slower growing. Siddharthan and Lall (1982; see also Cantwell and Sanna-Randaccio 1993) found that, with initial size controlled, the growth of 125 large US firms decreased with initial size and initial degree of multinationality but increased with profitability, access to scale economies in their industry, and opportunities for intangibles-based diversification of their activities.[7]

The average profitability of MNEs is usually found to exceed that of domestic firms (refer to Benvignati 1987, for example)[8] — presumably because of rents to the proprietary assets that fostered the firms' multinational development — and increases in multinationality are accompanied by increases in profit (see, for example, Grant 1987). However, profitability usually displays no positive relation to firm size (Kumar 1984) except that firms in small size-classes can appear unprofitable due to the losses of unsuccessful entrants.[9] Much evidence confirms the expectations that newly founded subsidiaries on average earn low profits (Ågren 1990, on Swedish firms' subsidiaries recently started in the United States) and that the average profits of the survivors increase as they age (Lupo, Gilbert and Liliestedt 1978).

In stochastic growth processes the variability of firms' levels of performance (growth, profitability) holds important implications for their size distributions. The purely statistical research on firm populations associated with Gibrat's Law (mentioned previously) depends for its 'shocking' conclusion — that concentration rises without limit — on the variance of growth rates being independent of firms' sizes. Contradicting this assumption, a standard empirical result on general size distributions of firms is that the variance of growth rates decreases with the size of the firm. Tschoegl (1983) confirmed this for a sample of large international banks, while finding at least weak evidence that multinationality cuts the variability of their growth rates. One expects, however, that the variance of outcomes for new foreign investments will be high, inflating the variance of profit and growth outcomes for samples consisting of new foreign investors. There is not much evidence on this point, but Mitchell, Shaver and Yeung (1992) confirmed that the risk of failure is reduced for firms that have already achieved multinational status but inflated for firms that are changing (either increasing or decreasing) their multinational presence. There is also evidence (Shaked 1986; Lee and Kwok 1988) that the financial leverage selected by large companies decreases with their degree of multinationality; this is consistent with greater business risks in foreign investments, although the predominance of diversification benefits implies that a positive relation should prevail.[10]

In sum, the evidence seems broadly consistent with several propositions. MNEs are on average more profitable than domestic firms (from rents to their proprietary assets). MNEs and single nation firms are subject to the same turnover and mean-regression processes. MNEs seem to draw from more risky distributions on average, however, and this could explain a widened dispersion of firm sizes and greater turnover of firms (initially) in any given size-class.

Multinationality and seller concentration

A final aspect of the distribution of MNEs' sizes that calls for clarification is the positive correlation between the prevalence of MNEs and the level of seller concentration regularly observed in industrial markets. This correlation has been the subject of much contention. Caves (1971) argued that the factors promoting MNEs also give rise to barriers to entry that limit the number of firms occupying a market. High levels of advertising and R&D, the prime suspects, can be associated with entry barriers either because they are themselves subject to scale economies or because they can provide large and enduring advantages to first movers over later entrants to a market. The positive correlation among industries between concentration and multinationality need not show that multinationality causes concentration, because common underlying causes are sufficient to account for the correlation. Other researchers, however, have been convinced that the prevalence of MNEs in concentrated industries stems from their opportunity and inclination to use predatory practices against their domestic rivals in both source and host countries. Some have claimed to find a positive causal effect of MNEs' prevalence on concentration even with entry barriers controlled.

These positions might be reconciled by showing that, through random processes and without any overt predation, multinationality could be correlated positively with concentration after entry barriers are controlled. The mechanism (found in Nelson and Winter 1978) goes as follows. In any industry the variance of firms' growth rates increases with the variance of returns to uncertain investments in intangibles such as innovation and customer goodwill. Successful investors find that they can reap rents through expansion into foreign markets, just as they can profitably grow in any market already occupied. The larger the variance, the more multinationality will result, and the more does concentration tend to increase in any given (national) market. Thus, with the structural component of entry barriers controlled statistically in the usual static way (by prevailing average levels of R&D and sales-promotion outlays), the extent of multinational operation proxies the unobserved variance of the distribution of success. Multinational activity and concentration will be associated more strongly than (static) entry barriers would suggest, without conscious or legally culpable predation necessarily being undertaken by the multinationals.

Evidence on the decline and demise of MNEs' operations

While much evidence associates the expansion process of multinational firms with stochastic growth, the evidence on their decline and demise is much less extensive. The theory that proprietary assets serve as the basis for foreign investment implies that turnover will occur in the ranks of MNEs (Boddewyn 1983). The transaction-specific assets, intangibles, competences etc. are themselves subject to depreciation and obsolescence. Technological and organisational innovations can be made obsolete by still newer developments. They can be copied and improved upon by imitators. Serving a market through a foreign subsidiary can lose its advantage over exporting, licensing or some other contractual method when direct investment is no longer the best way to serve the foreign market.

Little research has been done on divestments and exit decisions by MNEs. Among the historical studies, Jones (1986) emphasised the variability of the success of early multinationals based in the United Kingdom; errors in managerial systems were a common source of failure, and successes were owed to strong proprietary assets or, lacking those, participation in cartels (see also Casson 1986). Wilson (1980) analysed divestments recorded in the Harvard Multinational Enterprise Project database, while Torneden (1975) surveyed divestment decisions announced by US *Fortune 500* companies. Neither author calculated hazard rates that can be compared to those reported in studies of turnover in national markets, but both studies indicate that these rates are high. (Torneden reported that, during 1967–71, divestments were 16 per cent of the number of new subsidiaries founded.) Furthermore, both studies present fragmentary evidence on the creation and divestment of foreign subsidiaries over time that is consistent with the high infant mortality noted previously. The mortality rates of subsidiaries appear lower than those reported for populations of domestic establishments, but then the branches of established firms have lower mortality rates than do new firms, and are less sensitive to exogenous shocks that limit new firms' life expectancies (Audretsch and Mahmood 1995).

The most thorough study of exit pertains to Japanese subsidiaries started in the United States and Europe in 1980–90. Yamawaki (1994) discovered that the subsidiaries in the United States most likely to exit during 1991–93 were those initially acquired by merger and diversified from their parents; acquisition by merger also weakly predicted exit by subsidiaries in Europe. Presumably, business units previously transferred in the market for corporate control are subject to less organisational integration with the acquiring enterprise than subsidiaries newly begun, and less adjustment cost when they are detached.

Other hypotheses tested about factors explaining divestment decisions have similarly been chiefly organisational, a fact that might reflect the orientation of the researchers more than the potential state of full knowledge. Wilson (1980) concluded that foreign subsidiaries integrated with the parent through intracorporate trade are more likely to survive. Torneden's (1975) findings agree. Wilson also found some evidence that larger subsidiaries and those with more diversified output tend to survive, consistent with the obverse of the infant mortality pattern already noted. Yamawaki obtained this result for Japanese subsidiaries in Europe but not in the United States. Van den Bulcke et al. (1980), comparing exit rates of domestic and foreign business units in Belgium, found evidence suggesting that small (new?) foreign units are at especially great risk. Divested subsidiaries are rather commonly sold off to domestic host country enterprises, consistent with their demise being associated with the random hazards specific to foreign direct investment (Boddewyn, cited in Wilson 1980).[11] Also, divestments of foreign subsidiaries are not concentrated in less developed countries, leaving ample causal room for product market (versus national market) uncertainty as the cause of divestment.[12]

Wilson also tested for company characteristics that could explain divestment, finding some evidence that it follows top executive turnover or a decrease in the earnings reported by the company in the previous year. (That decline might, of course, be partly due to the faltering of the foreign subsidiary.) Torneden's case studies support the executive turnover hypothesis. A limited number of other case studies also agree with this finding. Grunberg (1981) emphasised the interdependence of a foreign subsidiary and the rest of the parent's operations as a deterrent to divestiture, and he stressed the roles of both positive real shutdown costs (negative salvage value) and the less tangible costs stemming from potential losers' resistance to changes in bureaucratic power relationships within the parent firm.

The joint venture is a special type of international business unit whose turnover has been studied extensively. Kogut (1988) showed that hazard rates for joint ventures, whether domestic or international, are quite high. They peak at five to six years, with the mortality rate of international ventures exceeding that of ventures shared by domestic firms. Yamawaki (1994) showed that hazard rates are higher for partly owned than for fully owned Japanese subsidiaries, and Gomes-Casseres (1987) that over the long run US multinationals had sold or liquidated partly owned subsidiaries at about twice the frequency of wholly owned subsidiaries. What factors explain the high rates of gross turnover? Franko (1971) first pointed to the governance costs and problems of opportunism that arise in the relations between partners, often bringing the life of a joint venture to an end. The implication was drawn that joint ventures frequently fail because they were mistakes in the first place. As Gomes-Casseres pointed out, that story carries the unsatisfying implication that joint venture partners sign up in ignorance of the hazards that lie ahead. It is true that one does not always anticipate the ways in which a business partner might cheat, but one certainly tries. It would be attractive to test an explanation resting on news (good or bad) that is revealed to the joint venture partners after they have committed resources to the venture.[13]

Nonetheless, Franko's empirical evidence offered solid support for his 'mistakes' hypothesis.[14] Only limited tests can be found of the hypothesis that joint ventures arise to carry out uncertain and/or probably short-lived activities. A good example is the conclusions of Agarwal and Ramaswami (1992) about how the characteristics of MNEs and host countries interact to explain the selection of joint venture organisations.

Kogut (1988) tested several hypotheses about joint ventures' survival. Some of them predict that certain ownership configurations — such as one partner holding a dominant share — insulate joint ventures from disagreements or shifts in the partners' interests. Other hypotheses hold that joint ventures seek to create or exploit proprietary assets that themselves are specialised and subject to obsolescence, eventually bringing down the joint venture when they decay. Although none of these was confirmed in the statistical tests, one suspects that they should not be written off. In particular, the vulnerability of joint ventures to proprietary assets' obsolescence is consistent with their apparently high hazard rates relative to parent (or other large) firms, which commonly hold portfolios of such assets and hence can survive the demise of any one of them.

Another potentially short-lived international business venture is the offshore processing unit that assembles or processes inputs (mostly imported) and exports the output to its overseas parent or elsewhere. With their low sunk costs, such subsidiaries can readily be relocated in response to changing prices (for example, a change in host country wages). Their footloose status adds to the bargaining power of the MNE and reduces that of the host government. Flamm (1984) modelled the partial adjustment process that might be observed if changes in local unit labour costs indeed provoke substantial relocation. He found that the foreign investor's response to local wage changes is somewhat elastic and occurs quickly.

Is there a reason other than temperamental positivism why researchers' attention has stayed away from international divestment? A real phenomenon is probably involved in the sunkenness of foreign investments. To choose foreign investment against other modes of serving a given market is generally to pick the option that has the largest fixed and sunk cost (Anderson and Gatignon 1986). Hysteresis is involved once a foreign investment is in place, as the investor then holds the real option of continuing to choose a positive output from the subsidiary without again incurring the fixed cost. For example, many studies of foreign investment decisions show that host countries' changes in tariffs or other trade or foreign investment policies have tipped the balance in favour of the investment, and this is confirmed statistically in studies that relate flows of foreign investment to current levels of trade restrictions (Caves and Mehra 1986; Drake and Caves 1992). Yet tariffs usually fail to show up as statistically significant determinants in studies seeking to explain the accumulated *stocks* of foreign investment. A sufficient reason is that, subsequent to the initial foreign investment, the inducing policy might be removed without causing the MNE to withdraw its investment; it might remain years later, even if trade liberalisation had cost part of its initial investment.[15]

Summary and conclusions

The analysis of MNEs has been well served by two bodies of standard economic theory: transaction cost analysis, which explains the MNE as a displacer of market transactions with internal coordination; and location theory, which explains equilibrium patterns of production and trade. To be well served, however, is not to be fully served. This chapter has argued the relevance of recent developments in the analysis of change and turnover in business populations (both theory and evidence). Patterns of entry and exit and the churning of units within more or less stable size distributions characterise all business populations. New theoretical models explain those processes, showing how they can result from actions by intendedly rational firms making costly investments that have uncertain outcomes.

Much evidence on MNEs and their growth and decline can, it turns out, be reconsidered fruitfully in light of turnover processes, even if turnover is alien to the standard economic theory of multinationals. Findings about changes over time in MNEs' prevalence and activity patterns in particular call for analysis in terms of learning, experimentation and random realisations. Lines of research involving cross-sections of MNEs need to recognise that statistical associations in these cross-sections are often driven by these dynamic patterns.

Research on MNEs can be improved if researchers merely heed these warnings when applying standard theory to the data. Better still, empirical research on the dynamics of general business populations can be screened for research designs applicable to MNEs. We close by suggesting some such lines of research. Research on divestment and exit has been seriously neglected. We know a lot about determinants of (equilibrium?) market shares held by MNEs, and about the processes by which firms grow into these equilibriums. We do not know much about how long MNEs persist or how frequently they expire. Do their shares in national markets churn more than those of competing domestic firms? Are the imputed values of their proprietary assets subject to as much fluctuation as those of their domestic brethren, or does the MNE's geographic diversification serve to spread this risk?

The meagre stock of research on decline and exit can be supplemented in other ways. We know that firms on average profit from exploiting their proprietary assets through foreign investment. How much of this profit is pure rent to the assets? How much represents the risk premium that (risk neutral) successful firms must in the long run earn in order to offset the losses of those who fail? A closely related question is how much of the apparent longevity of many MNEs (or of their individual foreign subsidiaries) is due to persistent rent streams, and how much purely to hysteresis effects, that is, profits that are 'subnormal' but not low enough to warrant exit.

Knowledge about hazard rates for foreign subsidiaries would be especially valuable. Are these high in product or national markets where entrants' successes are *a priori* likely to be especially risky or uncertain? Do they involve high levels of infant mortality, as seen in the turnover of establishments in domestic markets? Or is the mortality of foreign direct investment more related to MNEs' proprietary assets' becoming obsolete? Are the much noted batches of imitative and reactive foreign investment differentially subject to subsequent reverses, as some obvious theoretical considerations suggest that they might be?

Although a disproportionate debt is owed to scholars of business administration for what we do know about MNE turnover, they bring a problematical mind-set to research on turnover, namely, that every exit or sell-off reveals a mistake. While mistakes do occur, and managers share with the rest of humankind the difficulty of admitting them, many exits and failures are surely just the luck of the draw. Business normative problems certainly include estimating the probability distribution correctly beforehand, and when necessary cutting one's losses optimally later on. A bet that looks better than fair but turns out badly might be an occasion for railing against cruel fate, but it does not call for a change in investment behaviour.

There are also implications for public policy (and its study) that have so far been neglected in this paper. The turnover and random realisations of uncertain outcomes bring MNEs into contact with public policy in many ways, and both firms and policy makers need to recognise the prevalence of random outcomes. MNEs that are planning investments in particular nations or provinces commonly foment what look like Bertrand auctions among job-hungry governments for the provision of infrastructure and tax breaks. Would governments jump so readily into that game if they focused on the probability that still other investors will come around tomorrow? Similarly, disinvestments and withdrawals that are easily portrayed as evasions of legal responsibility might instead be responses to bad market outcomes. The most important implication for public policy probably lies in taxation and, more generally, the efforts that national governments make to intercept rents and quasi-rents on their way into foreign pockets. A pure rent by definition is there for the taking, and its capture will not change the future behaviour of rational investors. Many surpluses, however, are likely to be quasi-rents in whole or in part. Their capture tends to scare off future investors to degrees that depend on just the uncertainty about realisations that we have described.

Notes

1 These patterns appear consistently in data on manufacturing industries in several industrialised countries. The most comprehensive study is Baldwin (1995), which is based on Canadian data. Other well-known studies include Dunne, Roberts and Samuelson (1988), Evans (1987), Gort and Klepper (1982), and papers by Schwalbach, Sleuwaegen and Dehandschutter, and Dunne and Roberts in Geroski and Schwalbach (1991).

2   Besides births and deaths, changes in the control of ongoing business units (mergers, sell-offs) play a role in the turnover process because business units whose productivity is slipping are more likely to undergo changes in control, and they typically take some time to recover after the change.

3   Somewhat similar is the model of Klepper and Graddy (1990), interesting in this context because it seeks to explain a specific set of facts about the changes in the number of firms in an industry over its long-run trajectory of development from innovation to maturity. Model and evidence exhibit one glaring incongruity: the authors must assume that new entrants come from some unrenewed queue of potential entrants given at the outset; this non-renewal seems to clash with the random processes of search and discovery that otherwise underlie the model.

4   Similarly, positive correlations regularly emerge between firms' exports and the sales of their foreign subsidiaries when no controls are imposed for the firms' levels of international development or the relative costs of these competing modes of expansion (Lipsey and Weiss 1984).

5   For example, novices are more likely, *ceteris paribus*, to choose a joint venture, especially one in which they hold a minority stake (Franko 1989).

6   Droucopoulos found unusual results for 1972–77 involving a positive size–growth relation for about one-third of the largest firms. One wonders whether this was due to the effect of the 1973 oil price inflation on the nominal sales of the large international oil companies.

7   Also relevant, though hard to generalise, are Shapiro's (1980) results on foreign subsidiaries and domestic firms in Canada, where US MNEs surely have their maximum advantage over other MNEs. US subsidiaries accordingly are more profitable than either domestic firms or the subsidiaries of non-US MNEs. They are probably more mature (on average), however, and hence slower growing. Shapiro's results clearly demonstrate mean regression.

8   Benvignati tested the dependence of business units' profitability on their own multinationality (positive effect) and on the multinationality of their (diversified) parents (no effect). Of the putative sources of business units' proprietary assets, sales-promotion outlays have an independent positive influence on profitability, but research outlays do not.

9   This summary has not distinguished between samples of firms drawn from assorted single countries and those with diverse nationalities. Among firm samples drawn from developed countries, there is no evidence that these stochastic growth processes vary with nationality. Similarly, various studies have found profitability negatively related to multinational status in settings where multinationals have recently been expanding, so that shake-out processes are under way (references cited in Caves 1982, p. 35).

10   The result is not without its complicating factors. Multinationals naturally exhibit higher levels of R&D and sales-promotion outlays than do large domestic firms, and Lee and Kwok (1988) argued that these should increase the agency cost of debt and reduce leverage. Also, the intertemporal variance of cash flows is indeed lower for multinationals than for domestic firms, which should reduce expected bankruptcy costs and increase the use of leverage.

11 Wilson reported that in 1951–75, 48 per cent of divested subsidiaries were sold while 42 per cent were liquidated (with the balance unknown or expropriated). Of course, some subsidiaries may be sold not because their performance is unsatisfactory or failing but because a buyer offers an attractive price. The assumption implicit in this literature, however, is invariably that a divestment represents a failure. It contrasts with an economist's expectation that a business asset will change hands when a buyer with a higher reservation price comes along; that the potential seller is running a loss is neither necessary nor sufficient to satisfy this condition.

12 For a chronicle of failed foreign investment in the United States, see Glickman and Woodward (1989, pp. 129–35).

13 Gomes-Casseres showed that joint ventures of US multinationals had reverted to sole ownership less frequently in those countries and sectors where joint ventures are most commonly used by all foreign investors. This is inconsistent with a simple 'mistakes' hypothesis.

14 Franko found that joint ventures' hazard rates are higher where MNEs market products of standardised quality and design worldwide, while MNEs' tolerance of joint ventures is greater where their host country operations are highly independent (for example, involving non-traded goods). Also, the abandonment of joint ventures occurs when the MNE 'outgrows' them in developing a coherent international organisational structure. These patterns are all clearly consistent with a 'mistakes' hypothesis and only arguably consistent with the hypothesis that terminations represent bad outcomes for ventures subject to *ex ante* uncertainty.

15 We also take note of Grubaugh (1987b), who sought to model the expansion of multinational firms in terms of an initial threshold investment that takes them to, say, 10 per cent of their activities outside their home country, possibly followed by incremental expansions built on that base. The statistical analysis does not obtain very cogent results, but the model is consistent with extensive evidence that initial foreign investments provide the MNE with packages of options that can be exercised on receipt of further favourable news.

References

Agarwal, Sanjeev and Sridhar N. Ramaswami 1992, 'Choice of Foreign Market Entry Mode: Impact of Ownership, Location and Internalization Factors', *Journal of International Business Studies*, 23, First quarter, pp. 1–27.

Ågren, Lars 1990, *Swedish Direct Investment in the United States*, Stockholm: Institute of International Business, Stockholm University.

Anderson, Erin and Hubert Gatignon 1986, 'Modes of Foreign Entry: A Transaction Cost Analysis and Propositions', *Journal of International Business Studies*, 17, Fall, pp. 1–26.

Audretsch, David B. and Talat Mahmood 1995, 'New Firm Survival: New Results Using a Hazard Function', *Review of Economics and Statistics* (forthcoming).

Baldwin, John 1995, *The Dynamics of Competition*, Cambridge: Cambridge University Press (forthcoming).

Baldwin, John and Richard E. Caves 1991, 'Foreign Multinational Enterprises and Merger Activity in Canada', in Leonard Waverman (ed.), *Corporate Globalization through Mergers and Acquisitions*, Calgary: University of Alberta Press, pp. 89–122.

Benito, Gabriel R.G. and Geir Gripsrud 1992, 'The Expansion of Foreign Direct Investments: Discrete Rational Location Choices or a Cultural Learning Process?', *Journal of International Business Studies*, 23, Third quarter, pp. 461–76.

Benvignati, Anita M. 1987, 'Domestic Profit Advantages of Multinational Firms', *Journal of Business*, 60, July, pp. 449–61.

Bergsten, C. Fred, Thomas Horst and Theodore H. Moran 1978, *American Multinationals and American Interests*, Washington DC: Brookings Institution.

Blomström, Magnus and Richard E. Lipsey 1991, 'Firm Size and Foreign Operations of Multinationals', *Scandinavian Journal of Economics*, 93(1), pp. 101–7.

Boddewyn, Jean J. 1983, 'Foreign Direct Divestment Theory: Is It the Reverse of FDI Theory?', *Weltwirtschaftliches Archiv*, 119(2), pp. 345–55.

Buckley, Peter J., Zdenka Berkova and Gerald D. Newbould 1983, *Direct Investment in the United Kingdom by Smaller European Firms*, London: Macmillan.

Buckley, Peter J., John H. Dunning and Robert D. Pearce 1978, 'The Influence of Firm Size, Industry, Nationality, and Degree of Multinationality on the Growth of the World's Largest Firms, 1962–1972', *Weltwirtschaftliches Archiv*, 114(2), pp. 243–57.

_____ 1984, 'An Analysis of the Growth and Profitability of the World's Largest Firms 1972 to 1977', *Kyklos*, 37(1), pp. 3–26.

Cantwell, John and Francesca Sanna-Randaccio 1993, 'Multinationality and Firm Growth', *Weltwirtschaftliches Archiv*, 129(2), pp. 275–99.

Casson, Mark 1986, 'Foreign Divestment and International Rationalisation: The Sale of Chrysler (UK) to Peugeot', in John Coyne and Mike Wright (eds), *Divestment and Strategic Change*, Oxford: Philip Allan, pp. 102–39.

Caves, Richard E. 1971, 'International Corporations: The Industrial Economics of Foreign Investment', *Economica*, 38, February, pp. 1–27.

_____ 1982, *Multinational Enterprise and Economic Analysis*, Cambridge: Cambridge University Press.

_____ 1990, 'Growth of Large Enterprises and Their Market Environments', in Peter de Wolf (ed.), *Competition in Europe: Essays in Honour of Henk W. de Jong*, Dordrecht: Kluwer, pp. 61–83.

Caves, Richard E. and Sanjeev Mehra 1986, 'Entry of Foreign Multinationals into U.S. Manufacturing Industries', in Michael E. Porter (ed.) *Competition in Global Industries*, Boston, MA: Harvard Business School Press, pp. 449–81.

Cockburn, Iain and Zvi Griliches 1988, 'Industry Effects and Appropriability Measures in the Stock Market's Valuation of R&D and Patents', *American Economic Review*, 78, May, pp. 419–23.

Denis, Jean-Emile and Daniel Depelteau 1985, 'Market Knowledge, Diversification, and Export Expansion', *Journal of International Business Studies*, 16, Fall, pp. 77–89.

Drake, Tracey A. and Richard E. Caves 1992, 'Changing Determinants of Japanese Foreign Investment in the United States', *Journal of the Japanese and International Economies*, 6, September, pp. 228–46.

Droucopoulos, Vassilis 1983, 'International Big Business Revisited: On the Size and Growth of the World's Largest Firms', *Managerial and Decision Economics*, 4, December, pp. 244–52.

Dunne, Timothy, Mark J. Roberts and Larry Samuelson 1988, 'Patterns of Firm Entry and Exit in U.S. Manufacturing Industries', *Rand Journal of Economics*, 19, Winter, pp. 495–513.

Ericson, Richard and Ariel Pakes 1989, An Alternative Theory of Firm and Industry Dynamics, Working paper, Yale University.

Evans, David S. 1987, 'The Relationship between Firm Growth, Size, and Age: Estimates for 100 Manufacturing Industries', *Journal of Industrial Economics*, 35, June, pp. 567–81.

Flamm, Kenneth 1984, 'The Volatility of Offshore Investment', *Journal of Development Economics*, 16, December, pp. 231–48.

Førsund, Finn R. and Lennart Hjalmarsson 1987, *Analyses of Industrial Structure: A Putty-Clay Approach*, Stockholm: Industrial Institute for Economic and Social Research.

Franko, Lawrence G. 1971, *Joint Venture Survival in Multinational Corporations*, New York: Praeger.

_____ 1989, 'Use of Minority and 50-50 Joint Ventures by United States Multinationals during the 1970s: The Interaction of Host Country Policies and Corporate Strategies', *Journal of International Business Studies*, 20, Spring, pp. 19–40.

Geroski, P.A. and J. Schwalbach (eds) 1991, *Entry and Market Contestability*, Oxford: Blackwell.

Glickman, Norman J. and Douglas P. Woodward 1989, *The New Competitors: How Foreign Investors Are Changing the U.S. Economy*, New York: Basic Books.

Gomes-Casseres, Benjamin 1987, 'Joint Venture Instability: Is It a Problem?', *Columbia Journal of World Business*, 22, Summer, pp. 97–102.

Gort, Michael and Steven Klepper 1982, 'Time Paths in the Diffusion of Product Innovations', *Economic Journal*, 92, September, pp. 630–53.

Grant, Robert M. 1987, 'Multinationality and Performance among British Manufacturing Companies', *Journal of International Business Studies*, 18, Fall, pp. 79–89.

Grubaugh, Stephen G. 1987a, 'Determinants of Direct Foreign Investment', *Review of Economics and Statistics*, 69, February, pp. 149–52.

_____ 1987b, 'The Process of Direct Foreign Investment', *Southern Economic Journal*, 54, October, pp. 351–60.

Grubert, Harry and John Mutti 1991, 'Taxes, Tariffs and Transfer Pricing in Multinational Corporate Decision Making', *Review of Economics and Statistics*, 73, May, pp. 285–93.

Grunberg, Leon 1981, *Failed Multinational Ventures: The Political Economy of International Divestments*, Lexington, MA: Lexington Books.

Heiduk, Günter and Ulrike W. Hodges 1992, 'German Multinationals in Europe: Patterns and Perspectives', in Michael W. Klein and Paul J. J. Welfens (eds), *Multinationals in the New Europe and Global Trade*, Berlin: Springer-Verlag, pp. 164–90.

Hopenhayn, Hugo A. 1992, 'Entry, Exit, and Firm Dynamics in Long Run Equilibrium', *Econometrica*, 60, September, pp. 1,127–50.

Horst, Thomas 1971, 'The Theory of the Multinational Firm: Optimal Behavior under Different Tariff and Tax Rules', *Journal of Political Economy*, 79, September, pp. 1,059–72.

_____ 1972, 'Firm and Industry Determinants of the Decision to Invest Abroad: An Empirical Study', *Review of Economics and Statistics*, 54, August, pp. 258–66.

Jeon, Yoong-Deok 1992, 'The Determinants of Korean Foreign Direct Investment in Manufacturing Industries', *Weltwirtschaftliches Archiv*, 128(3), pp. 527–42.

Jones, Geoffrey 1986, 'The Performance of British Multinational Enterprise, 1890–1945', in Peter Hertner and Geoffrey Jones (eds), *Multinationals: Theory and History*, Aldershot: Gower, pp. 96–112.

Jovanovic, Boyan 1982, 'Selection and the Evolution of Industry', *Econometrica*, 50, July, pp. 649–70.

Klepper, Steven and Elizabeth Graddy 1990, 'The Evolution of New Industries and the Determinants of Market Structure', *Rand Journal of Economics*, 21, Spring, pp. 27–44.

Kogut, Bruce 1988, 'A Study of the Life Cycle of Joint Ventures', in Farok J. Contractor and Peter Lorange (eds), *Cooperative Strategies in International Business*, Lexington, MA: Lexington Books, pp. 169–85.

Kumar, Manmohan S. 1984, 'Comparative Analysis of UK Domestic and International Firms', *Journal of Economic Studies*, 11(3), pp. 26–42.

Lambson, Val Eugene 1991, 'Industry Evolution with Sunk Costs and Uncertain Market Conditions', *International Journal of Industrial Organization*, 9, June, pp. 171–96.

Lee, Kwang Chul and Chuck C.Y. Kwok 1988, 'Multinational Corporations vs. Domestic Corporations: International Environmental Factors and Determinants of Capital Structure', *Journal of International Business Studies*, 19, Summer, pp. 195–217.

Lichtenberg, Frank R. and Donald Siegel 1987, 'Productivity and Changes in Ownership of Manufacturing Plants', *Brookings Papers on Economic Activity: Microeconomics*, 3, pp. 643–73.

Lippman, S.A. and R.P. Rumelt 1982, 'Uncertain Imitability: An Analysis of Interfirm Differences in Efficiency under Competition', *Bell Journal of Economics*, 13, Autumn, pp. 418–38.

Lipsey, Robert E. and Merle Yahr Weiss 1984, 'Foreign Production and Exports of Individual Firms', *Review of Economics and Statistics*, 66, May, pp. 304–8.

Lupo, L., A. Gilbert and M. Liliestedt 1978, 'The Relationship between Age and Rate of Return of Foreign Manufacturing Affiliates of U.S. Manufacturing Parent Companies', *Survey of Current Business*, 58, August, pp. 60–6.

Lustgarten, Steven and Stavros Thomadakis 1987, 'Mobility Barriers and Tobin's q', *Journal of Business*, 60, October, pp. 519–37.

Martin, Stephen 1991, 'Direct Foreign Investment in the United States', *Journal of Economic Behavior and Organization*, 16, December, pp. 283–94.

Mitchell, Will, J. Myles Shaver and Bernard Yeung 1992, 'Getting There in a Global Industry: Impacts on Performance of Changing International Presence', *Strategic Management Journal*, 13, September, pp. 419–32.

More, Anand and Richard E. Caves 1994, 'Intrafirm Royalties in the Process of Expansion of US Multinational Enterprises', in V. N. Balasubramanyam and David Sapsford (eds), *The Economics of International Investment*, Aldershot: Edward Elgar, pp. 65–84.

Nelson, Richard R. and Sidney G. Winter 1978, 'Forces Generating and Limiting Concentration under Schumpeterian Competition', *Bell Journal of Economics*, 9, Autumn, pp. 524–48.

Newbould, G.D., P.J. Buckley and J.C. Thruwell 1978, *Going International: The Experience of Smaller Companies Overseas*, Somerset, NJ: Halsted Press.

Rowthorn, Robert with Stephen Hymer 1971, *International Big Business, 1957–1967: A Study of Comparative Growth*, Cambridge: Cambridge University Press.

Shaked, Israel 1986, 'Are Multinational Corporations Safer?', *Journal of International Business Studies*, 17, Spring, pp. 83–106.

Shapiro, Daniel M. 1980, *Foreign and Domestic Firms in Canada: A Comparative Study of Financial Structure and Performance*, Toronto: Butterworths.

Siddharthan, N.S. and Sanjaya Lall 1982, 'The Recent Growth of the Largest U.S. Multinationals', *Oxford Bulletin of Economics and Statistics*, 44, February, pp. 1–13.

Torneden, Roger L. 1975, *Foreign Disinvestment by U.S. Multinational Corporations: With Eight Case Studies*, New York: Praeger.

Tschoegl, Adrian E. 1983, 'Size, Growth, and Transnationality among the World's Largest Banks', *Journal of Business*, 56, April, pp. 187–201.

UNCTC (United Nations Centre on Transnational Corporations) 1988, *Transnational Corporations in World Development: Trends and Prospects*, New York: United Nations.

Van den Bulcke, D. et al. 1980, *Investment and Divestment Policies of Multinational Corporations in Europe*, New York: Praeger.

Wilson, Brent D. 1980, The Disinvestment of Foreign Subsidiaries by U.S. Multinational Companies, DBA thesis, Harvard Business School.

Yamawaki, Hideki 1994, Exit of Japanese Multinationals in U.S. and European Manufacturing Industries, Working paper, Catholic University of Louvain.

Zejan, Mario C. 1990, 'New Ventures or Acquisition: The Choice of Swedish Multinational Enterprises', *Journal of Industrial Economics*, 38, March, pp. 349–55.

3 The interdependence of trade and investment in the Pacific —

Peter A. Petri

Since the mid 1980s East Asia's international linkages have grown noticeably stronger.[1] The region's share of world trade and investment has increased, and more of these flows now involve regional partners. The acceleration of foreign direct investment (FDI) in the region is especially important, and several East Asian nations have joined the exclusive list of countries that are the world's major sources of FDI. Growth, trade and FDI have reinforced each other, helping to fuel a remarkably long and broad economic expansion in East Asia, despite global recession. Many countries are now looking to the East Asian 'trade–investment nexus' to find solutions to their own economic problems. An important purpose of this chapter is to analyse how this mechanism has worked.

East Asia's growth and economic integration is explained in large part by the region's outward-oriented economic policies and its high rates of investment in human and physical capital (World Bank 1993). But the unusual speed, diffusion and geographic concentration of economic progress also suggest that these conventional determinants have been amplified by various reinforcing mechanisms, including economies of scale in certain industries and types of transactions, externalities in the development of new technologies and lines of business, and positive feedback between economic policies and the economic environment. Some of these 'amplifiers' will be explored and tested in this study.

The chapter begins by reviewing aspects of a new theoretical literature on the clustering of economic activities that provides insight into recent regional developments. It then examines the acceleration of the intraregional mobility of goods and capital. Following this, simple econometric analysis is conducted on interactions between trade and investment.

The author gratefully acknowledges help from the Japan External Trade Organisation's New York Office with foreign direct investment data, and the many constructive comments received from discussants and other participants at PAFTAD 21.

Conceptual issues

It has been observed that the time required to achieve substantial changes in national income has steadily diminished over the centuries (World Bank 1991). The income growth attained by England in 58 years in the late 18th century was achieved in only 34 years by Japan in the late 19th century and in just 10 years by China in the 1980s. One plausible explanation for this phenomenon is that the factors required for growth — knowhow, equipment and capital — have become more broadly available and more mobile.[2]

International linkages, principally through trade, have played an important role in all of East Asia's economic 'miracles', although the precise channels of linkage have varied. Recently, the scope of international economic linkages has expanded dramatically to include catalytic factor flows, such as direct investment, portfolio investment, consultancy, management agreements, corporate tie-ups and a host of other commercial interactions.

Perhaps even more than trade, international factor mobility depends on what might be called the 'hardware' and 'software' of international linkages. The hardware includes the transportation and communications infrastructure required for coordinating production and trading activities. The software (which is probably more important) includes the policy framework of international transactions as well as the knowhow accumulated by individual agents through doing business abroad. This includes information on foreign business opportunities and practices as well as these agents' long-term investments in reputations and networks of contacts in particular foreign economies.

The key point is that both the hardware and software of East Asian linkages appear to have improved rapidly in recent years. The costs of regional transactions — transport, communications, information and so on — are typically subject to economies of scale and have fallen sharply with the explosive growth of East Asian transactions. Businesses have acquired wide-ranging experience and developed powerful contacts for executing international projects. The networks of Overseas Chinese have played an especially important role in this process, providing a ready conduit for information and financial flows, and even acting as a substitute for commercial legal systems in the transition economies.

These private sector developments have been reinforced by favourable policy changes. Most East Asian governments have reduced barriers to trade and investment, either across the board or at least in special economic zones. In turn, governmental commitment to liberalisation has encouraged further private investment in the hardware and software of regional integration.

The paradigm of increasing factor mobility provides a useful point of departure for interpreting recent East Asian experience. Insights into the implications of factor mobility have recently emerged in the 'new economic geography' literature (Krugman 1991, 1993; Arthur 1994; Graham 1994). Interestingly, related ideas have also emerged in the business strategy literature (Ohmae 1990; Porter 1990). Ohmae enthusiastically defends the assumption of unlimited factor mobility that is critical to the geography literature; Porter's industrial clusters are the practical counterparts of the theoretical results of economic geography models.

Under a fairly wide range of assumptions, the models of the new economic geography predict a rapid clustering of economic activity, even if demand is initially distributed uniformly over space. Clustering is especially pronounced if there are significant economies of scale that are external to firms but localised geographically. An example of such local external economies of scale is access to a large pool of specialised suppliers and workers — requiring many similar firms to be located in the same place. Because of scale effects, an established cluster has a strong 'incumbent' advantage over smaller new clusters.

The theory has less to say about *where* clusters form. Presumably the core advantage of a site depends on conventional factors that make the site attractive when the first investments are made. For example, the primary motives for investing in China may be low wage rates and large potential markets. Local external economies of scale then amplify these advantages as investment begins and the supply of critical inputs and skills expands. As additional people and companies gather in the emerging cluster, the location becomes still more attractive because it now also represents a significant market.

Clustering has intriguing applications in the East Asian context. One implication is that factor mobility and increased trade may have played a critical role in recent East Asian growth by stimulating the development of new economic clusters. The dynamism of several East Asian industries (automobiles in Japan, microcomputers in Taiwan and electronics in Malaysia, for example) and cities is consistent with such clustering and the gains from agglomeration. These issues will be discussed in more depth below in the context of the trade–investment nexus.

Another implication of factor mobility is heightened competition for foreign investment. If the attractiveness of a site to each investor depends on the presence of other investors, then policies that encourage investment may be crucial for getting clusters off the ground (or for warding off competitors). New clusters can form as a result of major shifts in economic gravity (such as the opening of Chinese markets) or simply because of growth. Beyond a certain size, clusters do not get larger, but split and multiply.[3] New clusters can render existing clusters uncompetitive and cause agglomeration economies to unravel. Growth with factor mobility does not always imply geographically balanced expansion; it can also lead to abrupt shifts in industrial location across cities or countries.

These issues are of great practical interest because regional interdependence, especially through investment, is emerging as the dominant fact of East Asian economic life in the 1990s, much as overall export growth did in the 1970s and 1980s. Interdependence is likely to boost regional efficiency and growth, but it may also impose more adjustments on individual countries than they have had to face in the recent past.

Deepening interdependence

A clear implication of the increased mobility of goods and factors (or, equivalently, vanishing borders) is greater economic integration and interdependence. East Asia's expanding intraregional trade and investment provides ample evidence of such trends. Moreover, although the region's international transactions have generally expanded, there is some evidence that intraregional transactions have grown especially fast. This is true even if one controls for the region's growing importance in the world economy. Such an emerging intraregional bias suggests that the mobility of goods and factors may have increased particularly fast within the region.

Trade interdependence

From the late 1940s until the mid 1970s, the share of intraregional trade in East Asia's total trade declined, while the shares of trade with North America and Europe increased (Table 3.1). Due to the legacies of European and Japanese imperialism, East Asia had been exceptionally interdependent before World War II (Petri 1993). After the war, the region's trading system became more diversified, with trans-Pacific trade growing especially fast. Only in the 1970s did the spectacular growth of East Asia's own markets begin to outweigh the development of extraregional ties with Europe and North America.

The more sophisticated measure of interdependence used in the lower half of Table 3.1 and in Figure 3.1, the gravity coefficient measure, shows that the disintegration of

Table 3.1   Measures of regional interdependence (two-way trade), 1938–92

	1938	1955	1969	1979	1985	1990	1992
Intraregional trade as a share of regional trade (per cent)							
North America	0.227	0.334	0.379	0.287	0.330	0.313	0.314
Western Europe	0.461	0.491	0.647	0.664	0.654	0.712	0.711
East Asia	0.671	0.313	0.293	0.332	0.363	0.407	0.453
Pacific region	0.583	0.450	0.566	0.545	0.643	0.649	0.667
Gravity coefficients of intraregional trade							
North America	1.73	1.65	2.09	1.95	1.71	1.84	1.86
Western Europe	1.16	1.23	1.46	1.51	1.58	1.50	1.55
East Asia	4.48	4.45	2.97	2.64	2.05	2.09	2.13
Pacific region	1.89	1.49	1.90	1.91	1.67	1.71	1.69

Source: Petri's estimates.

Figure 3.1   Intensity of regional trade, 1938–92

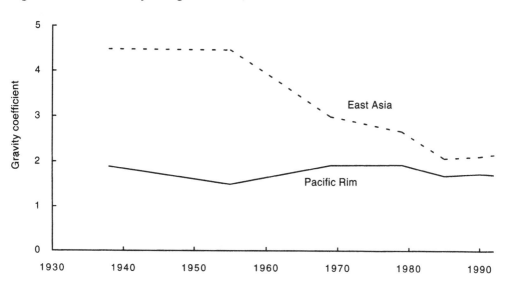

Source: Petri's estimates.

the relatively integrated East Asian economy continued well into the 1980s. Essentially, the gravity coefficient measure reflects those differences in the trade shares of partners that cannot be attributed to the different sizes of the partners. The gravity coefficient has been widely used in the analysis of intraregional trade bias — from early global studies by Linneman (1966) to recent applications to East Asia by Drysdale and Garnaut (1993) — and is calculated by dividing the bilateral trade share of a partner by the partner's share in world trade. A gravity coefficient larger than one indicates that the partner is more important in the bilateral relationship than in global trade, that is, it enjoys a positive bilateral bias. East Asian gravity coefficients are typically larger than one, indicating greater intraregional bias than is found in either Europe or North America.

Had East Asia's intraregional trade expanded simply in proportion to the impressive growth of its markets, then the region's intraregional gravity coefficient would have stayed constant. In fact, though, during most of the postwar period the gravity coefficient of East Asia's intraregional trade has steadily declined. The coefficient was unusually high before and just after World War II (Figure 3.1), and even with its subsequent decline, East Asian interdependence remains somewhat more intense than Pacific-wide interdependence.

Why the postwar decline in intraregional bias? Perhaps the most important factor was the liberalisation of the global economy, spurred by several successful GATT rounds. Another was the region's growing economic maturity, which led to greater acceptance of its products in the West and to improved communications with more distant markets. The similarity of East Asian industrialisation strategies also played a role by forcing countries to look outside for suitable markets. Finally, the United States took a strong interest in postwar East Asia, providing political leadership, economic aid and hospitable markets.

Significantly, as Figure 3.1 indicates, the long decline in East Asia's intraregional trading intensity ended in the mid 1980s. Although small, the upturn since then is nevertheless noteworthy because it stands in sharp contrast with the steep and steady drop of previous decades. The recent increase in intraregional bias is amplified by increased trade within the Chinese economic area (China, Hong Kong and Taiwan), but is present even if that trade is excluded. Moreover, the intensification of regional trade has occurred on top of considerable trade growth attributable simply to the expansion of East Asian markets. The upturn is easy to miss; for example, Frankel (1993) is able to argue that there is no evidence of increasing integration in East Asia because he compares gravity measures for 1980 and 1990, rather than the post-1985 positive trend with the long pre-1985 negative trend.

Investment trends

Developing East Asia has attracted four waves of foreign investment in the postwar period. Each was substantially larger than the preceding one — both absolutely and relative to trade and GDP — confirming the acceleration of the role of investment in regional linkages. The first investment wave, in the 1960s and early 1970s, was focused on joint ventures in textiles and household electrical equipment. These investments were motivated by protected local markets and by the first major revaluation of the yen in the early 1970s. A second wave of investment occurred in the 1970s, stimulated by the region's good economic prospects and the availability of low-cost capital. This wave included import substitution projects in basic industries as well as highly visible American export platforms in such areas as consumer electronics and semiconductors.

The third wave, which began in the mid 1980s, involved the transfer of labour-intensive operations to East and Southeast Asia in the wake of further appreciation of the yen and some NIE currencies. This wave was much larger than the first two: the regional ratio of inward FDI to GDP more than tripled (Figure 3.2; Table 3.2). Initially dominated by Japan, the wave eventually included substantial flows from the NIEs (Wells 1993). Relative to GDP, Singapore and Malaysia attracted the most foreign investment (Table 3.3, col. 4),[4] with Hong Kong and Indonesia in the next tier.

The 'ASEAN wave' is now receding into history. So far this is only partially visible in balance of payments flow data, which show inflows to developing East Asia (excluding China) levelling off at US$16 billion in 1992. But this appearance of stability is misleading. With the exception of China, approvals of new FDI projects in developing East Asia have declined sharply (Table 3.4). Decreases between 1991–92

Table 3.2   **FDI inflows, 1971–92 (US$ million)**

	China	Hong Kong	Taiwan	Indonesia	Malaysia	Philippines	Korea	Singapore	Thailand
1971		32	25	139	100	57	37	115	39
1972		58	36	207	114	83	61	161	69
1973		142	49	15	172	114	159	353	78
1974		79	69	-49	571	161	163	340	188
1975		203	78	476	350	184	69	292	86
1976		129	67	344	381	158	106	231	79
1977		143	48	235	406	208	132	291	106
1978		259	111	279	500	130	169	300	56
1979	100	338	126	226	573	130	172	838	55
1980	200	374	166	180	934	114	16	1,237	189
1981	439	1,089	151	133	1,265	243	135	1,662	294
1982	430	652	104	225	1,397	193	89	1,602	188
1983	634	603	149	292	1,261	247	90	1,136	358
1984	1,257	679	201	222	797	137	133	1,304	408
1985	1,657	-142	340	310	695	64	219	1,047	164
1986	1,876	989	346	258	489	89	436	1,712	263
1987	2,315	3,339	718	385	423	374	602	2,897	352
1988	3,195	2,442	960	576	719	917	871	2,790	1,117
1989	3,393	1,397	1,610	682	1,668	505	758	4,043	1,741
1990	3,487	1,840	2,121	1,093	2,332	530	715	5,263	2,444
1991	4,366	2,025	2,335	1,482	4,073	544	1,116	4,395	2,014
1992	11,156	2,144	2,471	1,774	4,118	228	550	5,635	2,116

Note: Calculated on a balance of payments basis.

Source: IMF, *Balance of Payments Yearbook*, Washington DC, various issues.

(averaged) and 1993 ranged from 20 per cent in Indonesia to 66 per cent in Malaysia, suggesting that there will be large future drops in FDI inflows.

The fourth, and likely most significant, wave involves a massive foreign investment boom in China. The value of approved projects ('contracted' investment) increased from US$12 billion in 1991 to US$58 billion in 1992 and US$111 billion in 1993 (pers. comm., Xiaoning Gao, World Bank). Roughly a quarter of these contracted projects (valued at US$25.8 billion) were realised in 1993. The 1994 figures, while somewhat below these levels, are still huge: in the first quarter alone contracted investments were worth US$20 billion and realised investments US$5.4 billion. Thus Chinese inflows are comparable in size to investment in the rest of developing East Asia at its 1980s peak. Smaller but similarly impressive changes are evident in other transition economies; Vietnam's FDI approvals were worth US$2.8 billion in 1993, up 48 per cent from the average for 1991–92 (Le 1994).

Figure 3.2   East Asian FDI inflows relative to regional GDP, 1971–92 (per cent)

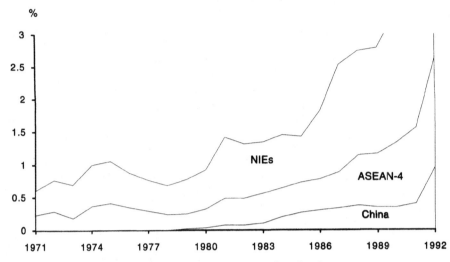

Source: IMF, *Balance of Payments Yearbook*, Washington DC, various issues.

Table 3.3   East Asian FDI stocks, 1988–92 (US$ million, per cent)

	Stock 1988	Inflows 1989–92	Stock 1992	Stock/ GDP 1992 (%)	Growth rate 1988–92 (%)
NIEs	31,702	37,147	68,849	12.1	21.4
Hong Kong	10,285	7,405	17,690	24.0	14.5
Korea	3,700	3,139	6,839	2.5	16.6
Singapore	11,021	18,066	29,087	72.9	27.5
Taiwan	6,696	8,537	15,233	8.4	22.8
ASEAN-4	47,451	49,840	97,291	13.5	19.7
Indonesia	18,844	5,031	23,875	22.0	6.1
Malaysia	7,508	12,191	19,699	40.3	27.3
Philippines	1,619	1,865	3,484	6.9	21.1
Thailand	3,855	8,351	12,206	13.2	33.4
China	15,625	22,402	38,027	9.0	24.9
Total for East Asia	94,778	109,389	204,167	11.9	21.9

Note: Stock 1992 equals stock 1988 plus flows 1989–92. The table updates the most recent comprehensive stock data available (for 1988 from UNCTC 1992) with subsequent balance of payments flow statistics.

Source: UNCTC, 1992; IMF, *Balance of Payments Yearbook*, Washington DC, various issues; World Bank, *World Tables* (data on diskette), Washington DC.

Table 3.4   **Recent changes in FDI approvals, 1991–93 (US$ million, per cent)**

	1991	1992	1993	Change between 1991–92 (ave.) and 1993 (%)
China	11,977	58,124	110,900	216
Indonesia	8,778	10,313	7,632	-20
Korea	1,396	894	880	-23
Malaysia	2,293	2,129	756	-66
Philippines	778	284	362	-32
Singapore	1,698	2,137	2,391	25
Taiwan	1,779	1,461	856	-47
Thailand	4,989	10,024	4,144	-45
Total	33,688	85,365	127,920	115
Total excluding China	21,711	27,241	17,020	-30

Note: Except for China, 1993 data is projected by annualising data for the first 6–9 months of the year.

Source: JETRO, 1994.

The concurrence of the Chinese investment surge and the ASEAN investment collapse may be an example of a new kind of intraregional competition for FDI, fuelled by improved capital mobility.[5] Chinese reforms and progress toward economic and political stability, together with low labour costs and a huge market, have made investment in China very attractive relative to other East Asian sites. In the framework of the new economic geography, China is an ideal site for new clusters of industrial activity. Investors are now flooding to China simply to acquire the option of expanding there later.[6]

These far-reaching changes in investment volumes and destinations are associated with more ambiguous shifts in the source country composition of East Asian investment (Table 3.5). Changes in the source country composition of foreign investment stocks between 1980 and 1988 were very modest; the shares of the United States, Europe, Japan and the NIEs each changed only by one percentage point. But the flow data for 1986–92 (which, unfortunately, are not available in exactly comparable form) show more pronounced changes. The key difference is that the NIEs provided a much higher share of recent flows than in the past.

Do these shifts represent fundamental change in the structure of investment flow sources? This is unclear. The prominence of NIE sources (especially Hong Kong) corresponds to the increased role of China as an investment destination. In 1992, for example, 63 per cent of investments in China came from Hong Kong; a wave of Chinese inflows is thus bound to be accompanied by a wave of Hong Kong outflows. Much of this investment, however, does not originate in the NIEs themselves. A part

Table 3.5   **Distribution of inward foreign investment stocks by source, 1980–92 (per cent)**

Source country	Host country			
	China	NIEs	ASEAN	All East Asia
United States				
1980	16.9	35.6	12.0	20.0
1988	15.8	31.9	13.2	20.7
1986–92	8.0		13.5	
Europe				
1980	14.6	22.4	20.5	19.8
1988	9.5	20.4	26.0	20.5
1986–92	4.4		15.6	
Japan				
1980	5.8	24.1	32.9	24.4
1988	7.2	32.0	28.8	25.5
1986–92	10.2		25.8	
NIEs				
1980	55.8	6.7	24.3	26.0
1988	63.1	6.2	22.3	24.7
1986–92	70.9		29.5	
ASEAN				
1980	0.5	2.1	0.7	1.1
1988	0.8	1.1	1.0	1.0
1986–92	0.8		2.5	
Other				
1980	6.5	9.0	9.5	8.7
1988	3.6	8.4	8.7	7.6
1986–92	5.6		13.1	

Note: See note 1 for geographical definitions.

Source: UNCTC, 1992.

(one-third, according to some estimates) of Hong Kong's investments in China are 'round trip' investments by mainland investors seeking the three-year tax holiday that was available to foreigners until 1994; Hong Kong is also a favourite intermediary for Western investment.[7] Even 'genuine' Hong Kong investment may be highly dependent on third country decisions. For example, American running shoe manufacturers typically operate manufacturing sites in China and ASEAN from the NIEs. Although in the statistics this investment originates in Hong Kong, it in fact represents American corporate decisions.

If, for the sake of argument, 25 per cent of the investment attributed to the NIEs is reallocated to other countries (in proportion to their historical shares), then the source country distribution of recent flows comes to resemble quite closely the distribution of 1988 stocks. In other words, if as little as one-quarter of the NIEs' direct investment is explained by additional demands for intermediation, then there has been very little fundamental change in the source country composition of foreign investment in East Asia. Thus the prominence of investment by Hong Kong and the NIEs could be expected to diminish as China and other emerging economies become more accessible.

The industry composition of foreign investment is relatively stable. The sectoral structure of investment stocks varies predictably across destinations: the primary sector dominates in oil-rich Indonesia, manufacturing in Korea, and a mix of these in other countries (Table 3.6). There is little difference between US and Japanese sectoral investment patterns (see also Dobson 1993). Recent flows have not deviated substantially from these patterns, although there has been a general increase in the share of tertiary investment and, within manufacturing, of electrical equipment. FDI in textiles is declining everywhere; consumer electronics has taken the place of textiles as the 'footloose' industry of the 1990s.

Table 3.6   Distribution of inward FDI stocks (per cent)

	Indonesia (1988)	Korea (1990)	Thailand (1988)	Asia from Japan (1991)	East Asia from the United States (1991)
Primary sector	80.5	0.5	9.2	15.3	23.7
Secondary sector	16.9	67.2	42.8	40.4	36.2
Food, beverages	1.5	4.1	3.6	2.5	2.5
Textiles and clothing	3.5	2.9	4.1	3.9	
Wood and wood products	0.3	1.5		1.0	
Chemicals	3.7	26.7	7.0	6.0	7.3
Metals and metal products	} 5	2.0	4.5	5.7	0.8
Non-electrical machinery		6.0	2.1	3.6	6.1
Electrical equipment		13.4	14.9	9.4	15.0
Transport equipment		7.8	2.6	3.5	1.1
Tertiary sector	2.5	32.1	48.0	44.3	40.1
Construction	0.4	0.5	11.6	1.6	
Trade	1.0	0.7	16.6	8.4	11.3
Finance, insurance		7.7	6.7	9.4	19.6
Transport, communications		0.5	2.6	2.2	
Total	100.0	100.0	100.0	100.0	100.0

Source: UNCTC, 1992; USITC ,1993.

The big changes in regional foreign investment involve not sectoral composition, and probably not source country composition, but rather shifts in the volume and destination of FDI flows. The ASEAN FDI wave is winding down, while the dramatic China wave is gearing up. China's foreign investment stocks are still small, and investment has yet to penetrate much beyond the coastal areas. If liberalisation spreads across China and foreign investment responds as on the coast, Chinese FDI could easily overshadow other direct investment in developing East Asia.

Portfolio capital

Still more spectacular than the growth of FDI has been the recent expansion of international portfolio investment in East Asian stocks and bonds. Between 1988 and 1992, the contribution of net portfolio inflows to the total resource inflows of the developing world grew from 1 to 12 per cent. In 1993, portfolio equity flows to developing countries amounted to approximately US$20 billion, with much of this flowing into Asian markets. This revolution is driven both by the liberalisation of goods and capital markets and by the diversification objectives of investors in developed countries.[8]

The largest emerging stock markets are Asian; the International Finance Corporation ranks Malaysia first, Korea third, Taiwan fourth and Thailand seventh (Hong Kong and Singapore are classified as developed markets). There are now 19 US closed-end funds with assets of US$4.2 billion specialising in East Asia (excluding Japan); 12 were established only in the last four years. Another US$1.8 billion is held in open-end East Asian funds, most of which are also new. And for each US fund launched in 1990 and 1991, seven others were launched in other countries (McCulloch and Petri 1994).

Ultimately, portfolio equity flows into East Asia could become much larger than FDI flows since they do not depend on the complex conditions necessary for direct investment. The benefit to East Asian firms is that foreign purchases reduce the cost of capital and increase market liquidity. By strengthening the stock market, portfolio flows also improve the country's ability to monitor corporate performance and government policy. But portfolio capital flows are volatile; share prices can change rapidly on both domestic and foreign 'news'. Thus the capital mobility implied by portfolio investment also contributes to the competitive pressure faced by individual companies and governments.

Trends in perspective

Even sluggish indicators (gravity coefficients in trade, for instance) are now showing an upturn in East Asian interdependence. In turn, more volatile, expectations-driven variables (portfolio equity investments, for example) have increased greatly. All this suggests a broad acceleration in the movement of technology and capital in East Asia. While these developments are partly the result of positive changes in regional economic policies, their scale and momentum suggests that various indirect mechanisms — such as the development of new industry clusters — are also behind the recent burst of regional growth and economic integration.

These recent trends cannot simply be extrapolated. Because desired capital stocks depend on expectations about the future, investment tends to occur in waves (in response to a sudden change in desired stocks) and is sensitive to changes in policies or trends. The recent wave of investment in ASEAN has tapered off, partly because of bottlenecks, but also because investors achieved their desired configurations of stocks in the wake of the large exchange rate changes of the mid 1980s. Similar mechanisms may also limit the current Chinese boom, which is predicated on continued political stability and reform.

Nor should one exaggerate the effect of recent trends on the region's major political–economic relationships. Despite growing interdependence, East Asia remains closely tied to the United States and other extraregional markets. From the perspective of a typical East Asian economy, trade with the United States is about as important as trade with Japan, or trade with all other East Asian economies combined. Moreover, trans-Pacific trade plays a critical role in the commodity structure of the region's trade. Extraregional markets are especially important for exports of finished manufactures, and thus indirectly for intraregional exports of components and machinery.

The trade–investment nexus

The powerful, dynamic effects of falling trade and investment barriers in East Asia have prompted interesting discussions of a new 'trade–investment nexus'. The argument is roughly this:

1   Outward-oriented trade and investment policies help to stimulate trade and attract direct investment.

2   Direct investment creates additional trade, and trade tends to promote further investment. This mechanism is especially important in the context of liberalised trade and investment policy regimes.

3   Vigorous trade and investment encourages governments to sustain policies favourable to international linkages.

Analyses incorporating some of these arguments are offered in United Nations (1992), UNCTC (1993) and World Bank (1994). The most likely reason for the emergence of such a nexus in recent years is the improved climate for international linkages in both developed and developing countries, or, put in another way, the increased mobility of goods and factors.

While the nexus thesis presumes positive feedbacks between liberalisation and expanding trade and investment, theory suggests that such interactions are not necessarily positive. Some types of foreign investment are stimulated by trade barriers rather than openness. Foreign investment can affect trade positively or negatively. And more intensive interaction with other countries can lead to pressure for protection as well as openness. In East Asia, however, the elements of the nexus have worked predominantly in a positive way. Empirically, trade and investment are positively correlated, and both have been stimulated by policies that encourage openness. The success of these policies has in turn helped to line up political support for further liberalisation: government after government has adopted outward-oriented policies, chiefly motivated by the earlier experience in other countries of economic 'miracles'. Given relatively liberal trade regimes, East Asian investments have become increasingly productive, favouring investments in efficient export sectors rather than inefficient protected industries. The economic pay-offs of these policies have in turn generated international competition in liberalisation; governments now have to match their neighbours in offering a favourable policy environment.

The question of complementarity

Central to the nexus thesis is the idea that contemporary East Asian trade and investment are primarily complements rather than substitutes in bridging international differences in factor endowment. The modern theory of FDI — based on theories of the firm rather than on capital cost differentials — is generally neutral on this issue; it is consistent with either positive or negative correlations between trade and investment.

The effects on trade of investment can be decomposed into effects on trade in various products with different types of relationships to the output of a direct investment project. As summarised in Table 3.7, net exports of products that are produced by the foreign affiliate, that use the affiliate's output as an input (downstream industries) or that are demand substitutes and/or production complements for the affiliate's product will decrease in the home country (and increase in the host country). The net effect on either country's trade will depend on the relative importance of changes in these categories.

Speculation about the likely sign of the trade–investment relationship has varied over time. In the 1960s, proponents of import substitution in developing countries argued that foreign investment in primary commodities limited the growth of alternative industries that were more beneficial to the domestic economy. In recent years, opponents of outward investment from developed countries have warned that FDI will displace exports of the parent industry and possibly related downstream industries, leading to a hollowing out of domestic firms. The current nexus thesis emphasises the possibility that trade will expand as greater capital mobility allows companies to adopt global production strategies, thus leading to increased specialisation worldwide.

What do the data say? The trade–investment relationship can be analysed using microeconomic data reported by parent firms and their subsidiaries, or macroeconomic data on trade and investment flows at an aggregate level. Both types of evidence suggest a positive correlation between foreign investment inflows and trade.

Table 3.7   Effects of foreign production on trade

| Product | Home country | | Host country | |
affected	Exports	Imports	Exports	Imports
Subsidiary's products	–	+	+	–
Downstream products	–	+	+	–
Production complements	–	+	+	–
Demand substitutes	–	+	+	–
Upstream products	+	–	–	+
Demand complements	+	–	–	+
Production substitutes	+	–	–	+

Source: Petri's estimates.

Evidence from firm-level data

Several countries conduct detailed surveys of the export and import behaviour of foreign-affiliated firms. By themselves, these data cannot measure the effects on trade of foreign investment, since an affiliate's domestic purchases and sales can have further trade effects downstream (which would need to be added to the affiliate's own foreign purchases and sales). However, in the case of Japanese-affiliated firms in Thailand, Petri (1992) was able to construct an estimate of the total trade effects of foreign investment by adding downstream trade (calculated using an input–output table) to the direct trade reported by the affiliates. The study concluded that Thailand's exports and imports have increased as a result of the operations of Japanese-affiliated firms.

The effects on trade of foreign investment vary with the age of the investment, that is, with the affiliate's transition from the investment stage of the lifecycle to its mature production stage. This is shown in Figure 3.3, which presents a simulation of the implications for trade and balance of payments of a newly launched affiliate (essentially a composite of the Thai affiliates of Japanese firms established after 1986) in the first four years of its life. The diagram shows that the affiliate brings about a net increase in Thailand's exports and imports from the outset (its foreign sales and foreign input requirements exceed the imports displaced by its local sales). The affiliate even generates a slight positive trade balance by year 4, although the balance of payments impact (which includes returns to foreign capital) remains negative after the initial capital inflow is completed. Both the net trade and balance of payments results are small compared to the various positive and negative effects on exports and imports, which tend to offset each other.

This kind of evidence on the direct and indirect effects on trade of foreign investment is not widely available. However, the direct exports and imports of the

43

Figure 3.3   Effects on trade and balance of payments of $1 of FDI in Thailand

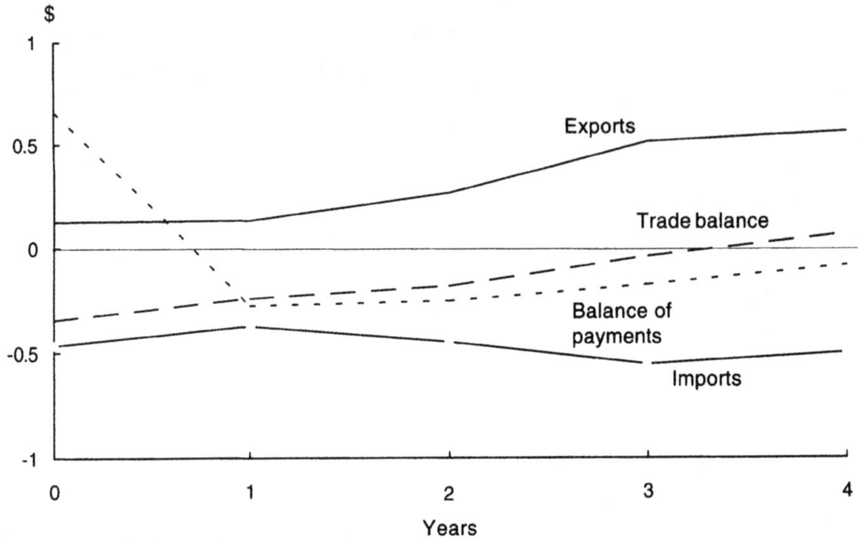

Source: Petri's estimates.

foreign affiliates — which are a large part of the total effect — are often substantial (Table 3.8). One influential line of work has argued, for example, that Japanese-style FDI (as compared with, say, US-style FDI) is especially conducive to the trade-related development of the host economy because it is labour intensive and export oriented (Kojima 1977). The data do not support such a distinction between Japanese and US investment in East Asia (see also Hill and Johns 1986), but do confirm that foreign affiliates generate considerable amounts of trade. For manufacturing firms in East Asia, export/sales ratios are 63 per cent in the case of US affiliates, and 36 per cent for Japanese affiliates (Table 3.8).[9]

In the late 1980s, the export ratios of Japanese affiliates appeared to increase steadily, leading to the hypothesis that a new era of global production systems had dawned. Japanese affiliates were also seen as opening the Japanese market to East Asian manufactures. The recently released 1992 data indicate a reversal of these trends; Japanese affiliates in Asia now export a lower share of their sales than at any time since the investment boom began (Table 3.9). More research is needed on what these changes mean. Perhaps the latest wave of investment into China is again oriented to the local market, or perhaps global recession has temporarily cut exports by Asian affiliates. In any case, recent data do not indicate any significant change in the export orientation of FDI.

Table 3.8 **Sales distribution of Asian affiliates of Japanese and US firms (per cent of total sales)**

	Japanese affiliates			US affiliates		
	Local sales	To Japan	To third countries	Local sales	To US	To third countries
All industries	42.1	29.1	28.7	66.7	14.4	20.1
Manufacturing	63.9	15.8	20.3	36.0	41.0	22.0
Chemicals	78.1	10.3	11.5	76.0	1.0	23.0
Machinery	56.9	13.2	24.9			
Electrical machinery	37.4	29.9	35.7	13.0	60.0	27.0
Transport equipment	92.1	1.5	5.3			

Note: Japanese data are for 1989; US data are for 1988.

Source: Yamazawa et al., 1992; Dobson, 1993.

Evidence from aggregate trade and investment data

Aggregate data also suggest a positive relationship between trade and investment: a country's most important trade partners tend also to be its most important investment partners. This relationship persists even when controlling for differences in a partner's size — that is, there is a significant positive correlation between trade intensity and foreign investment intensity measures across trade partners (Figure 3.4).

To move beyond correlations, more comprehensive models of trade and FDI are needed. In this section, parallel models of trade and investment are estimated in order

Table 3.9 **Sales distribution of Asian manufacturing affiliates of Japanese firms, 1988–92 (per cent)**

	1988	1989	1990	1991	1992
Local sales	59.8	63.9	59.6	54.5	66.1
Export sales	40.2	36.1	40.4	45.5	33.9
To Japan	13.7	15.8	11.8	15.5	15.8
To North America	8.7	6.0	7.6	8.5	3.7
To other countries	17.8	14.3	21.0	21.5	14.4

Source: MITI, 1994.

Figure 3.4   Relationship between FDI and trade intensity

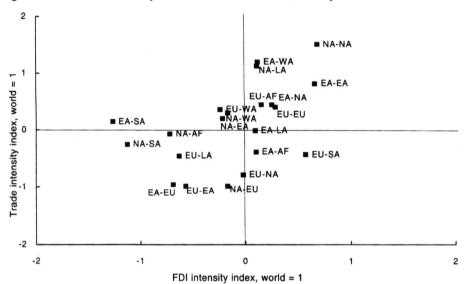

Notes: Home region is listed first, host region second. Constructed from the logs of the gravity coefficients of trade and investment. A positive value for this log index indicates the relationship has above average intensity, a negative value that it has below average intensity.

AF = Africa; EA = East Asia; EU = Europe; LA = Latin America; NA = North America; SA = South Asia; WA = West Asia.

Source: Petri, 1993.

to assess the interdependence of these flows. These models are built in the spirit of Dunning's (1980) eclectic model of FDI, with special emphasis on location-specific characteristics that help to explain why countries attract differing amounts of FDI.[10]

There is no similar, widely accepted model of variations in the volume (rather than composition) of trade across countries, but if such a model were developed from Heckscher-Ohlin and monopolistic competition ideas, it would include determinants such as market size, resource endowments and the policy environment. Thus both the trade and foreign investment regressions estimated below make use of three groups of explanatory variables. The first includes two general characteristics of the host economy: market size and per capita income (Dunning 1980; Dobson 1993; Mody and Shrinivasan 1991). The second includes measures of the two most important resource endowments: human capital and oil. The third includes policy factors that affect international linkages: measures of distortions in macroeconomic policy, trade policy and foreign exchange policy.

Table 3.10   Definitions and sources of variables

Variable	Definition	Source
Trade	Merchandise exports plus imports	*World Tables*
FDI	Balance of payments measures of gross FDI inflows	IMF, *Balance of Payments Yearbook*
Stock	Stock market capitalisation	IFC, *Emerging Markets Handbook*
Population	Millions	*World Tables*
Income	US$	*World Tables*
Enrolment	Primary school enrolment	*World Tables*
Fuel export	Ratio of fuel exports to total exports	*World Tables*
Tariff	Unweighted average of tariff rates	WDR 1991
NTB frequency	Percentage of commodity lines covered by NTBs	WDR 1991
FX premium	Average black market premium on foreign exchange, 1981–90	WDR 1991
Inflation	Average inflation in consumer price index, 1981–90	*World Tables*
Creditworthiness	Survey index of creditworthiness	*Institutional Investor*

Note: Unless otherwise indicated, data are average for 1988–90. *World Tables* refers to the1993 diskette version of the World Bank's *World Tables* database. WDR 1991 refers to the special database constructed by the World Development Report 1991 team.

The principal variables are listed in Table 3.10. To allow for non-linear effects, population and income are introduced with four variables (following Chenery and Syrquin 1975): log income, log population, and their squares.[11] Human capital endowment is proxied by primary school enrolment, and natural resources by the ratio of oil exports to GDP. Physical capital is not introduced explicitly, but is represented by the per capita income variable. Policy indicators include tariffs, non-tariff barriers, the black market premium on foreign exchange and inflation. A data set on 27 low and middle income economies in 1988–90 and 1981–85 is used.[12]

47

Table 3.11   **Determinants of trade/GDP ratios, 1988–90**

	Model 1	Model 2	Model 3	Model 4	Model 5
Constant	1.322	1.463	1.638	1.270	1.259
	(3.45)	(4.02)	(6.37)	(4.79)	(4.18)
Log(pop)	-0.432	-0.458	-0.533	-0.391	-0.388
	(-2.34)	(-3.07)	(-4.43)	(-3.28)	(-2.94)
Log(pop)^2	0.035	0.037	0.045	0.031	0.031
	(1.56)	(2.00)	(3.12)	(2.20)	(2.05)
Log(Y)	0.071	-0.018	-0.024	-0.024	-0.025
	(0.91)	(-0.24)	(-0.44)	(-0.51)	(-0.50)
Log(Y)^2	0.255	0.229	0.238	0.213	0.219
	(5.02)	(5.88)	(7.10)	(6.89)	(6.78)
Enrolment		0.002			
		(0.94)			
Fuel export		2.087	2.296	1.191	1.562
		(2.98)	(4.31)	(1.89)	(2.57)
Tariff		-0.001			
		(-0.25)			
NTB frequency		-0.001			
		(-0.30)			
FX premium		-0.004	-0.005	-0.004	-0.004
		(-2.92)	(-5.08)	(-3.77)	(-3.52)
Log(inflation)		-0.033			
		(-0.83)			
Inward FDI/GDP				0.006	
				(2.62)	
Inward FDI/GDP (early 1980s)					0.008
					(2.07)
Adjusted R^2	0.82	0.90	0.91	0.93	0.92
F	24.40	24.74	44.79	50.61	45.28
SSE	2.04	0.67	0.77	0.56	0.63

Notes: *t*-ratios are in brackets.
          Sample consists of 27 developing market economies.

The determinants of international differences in trade volume are analysed in regressions reported in Table 3.11. Even a model with only population and per capita income variables offers a good explanation of the variance in trade volumes; trade is negatively related to population size (although at a diminishing rate) and positively to income (col. 1). Of the endowment and policy variables, two affect trade significantly: fuel exports (positively) and black market premiums (negatively). Their contribution stands out even more clearly when the noise associated with numerous insignificant variables is removed (col. 3).

Table 3.12   **Determinants of inward FDI/GDP ratios, 1988–90**

	Model 1	Model 2	Model 3	Model 4	Model 5
Constant	5.190	3.713	6.240	-1.195	-6.193
	(1.82)	(1.15)	(2.75)	(-0.34)	(-2.07)
Log(pop)	-1.999	-1.940	-2.450	-0.025	1.605
	(-1.46)	(-1.47)	(-2.31)	(-0.02)	(1.45)
Log(pop)^2	0.198	0.164	0.251	0.048	-0.089
	(1.20)	(1.00)	(1.96)	(0.33)	(-0.80)
Log(Y)	0.402	-0.437	0.012	0.119	0.465
	(0.69)	(-0.63)	(0.02)	(0.28)	(1.38)
Log(Y)^2	0.623	0.564	0.421	-0.657	-1.112
	(1.65)	(1.63)	(1.43)	(-1.35)	(-2.97)
Enrolment		0.016			
		(0.97)			
Fuel export		23.700	18.900	8.500	1.580
		(3.81)	(4.02)	(1.48)	(0.33)
Tariff		0.019			
		(1.02)			
NTB frequency		-0.019			
		(-1.08)			
FX premium		-0.032	-0.022	0.001	0.014
		(-2.38)	(-2.49)	(0.09)	(1.47)
Log (inflation)		0.127			
		(0.36)			
Trade/GDP				4.540	
				(2.62)	
Trade/GDP (early 1980s)					7.838
					(4.86)
Adjusted R^2	0.34	0.57	0.61	0.70	0.82
F	4.30	4.44	7.82	9.64	17.67
SSE	112	53	60	44	27

Notes: t-ratios are in brackets.
Sample consists of 27 developing market economies

The effect of FDI on trade is explored in columns 4 and 5. The theoretical rationale for this variable lies either in its direct effect on trade or in its role as a proxy for the general openness of the environment. The variable appears significantly both in contemporaneous form (col. 4) and in lagged form (that is, when FDI in the early 1980s is used to explain trade in the late 1980s, col. 5).[13] Its coefficient suggests that a \$1 increase in foreign investment flows results in a 60–80 cent increase in trade flows.

The determinants of FDI inflows are analysed in Table 3.12. Here, population and income alone produce a much less satisfactory fit; neither are quite significant at the

10 per cent level. This is not surprising, since not all countries are attractive sites for direct investment, while, by definition, every country has some comparative advantage in trade. Fuel exports and the blackmarket premium again appear as significant determinants, this time of FDI. Once insignificant variables are dropped a reasonably good fit is obtained, suggesting that endowment and policy factors are more important for FDI than trade. Finally, trade affects FDI positively in both contemporaneous and lagged forms (cols 4 and 5). Indeed, with the trade variable included, the fuel export and black market premium variables become insignificant, suggesting that trade captures these effects as well as other dimensions of openness. Its coefficient suggests that a $1 increase in exports plus imports results in a 5–8 cent increase in FDI flows.

The key finding is that trade and FDI significantly affect each other. These results cannot be attributed to simultaneity; they persist when lagged values are used. This interdependence may be causal, as implied in some of the relationships listed in Table 3.7. Or it could be that both flows are affected by similar variables, such as a country's experience with and commitment to international linkages. Lagged FDI has been found to be the most important explanatory factor of current FDI in several previous studies (Dobson 1993; Mody and Shrinivasan 1991).[14] Similarly, lagged trade has often turned up as a significant explanatory variable in time-series trade studies. The one study that has come to our attention on the causal linkage between FDI and trade has found causation flowing from trade to FDI in some cases and from FDI to trade in others (Katseli 1992). Thus, several studies confirm the important role of 'history' in trading and investment relationships, consistent with the hypothesis that learning, experience and relationships accumulated through past trading and investment activities are a critical determinant of current linkages.

The interactions of linkages and policy are explored further in Table 3.13, which presents pair-wise correlations among these variables. In addition to trade and FDI,

Table 3.13   **Correlation of external linkages and protection**

	Trade/GDP	FDI/GDP	Stocks/GDP	Tariffs	NTBs	FX Premium	Inflation
Trade/GDP	1	0.82	0.85	-0.52	-0.35	-0.27	-0.45
FDI/GDP		1	0.60	-0.39	-0.27	-0.18	-0.33
Stocks/GDP			1	-0.51	-0.40	-0.36	-0.42
Tariffs				1	0.52	0.19	0.24
NTB frequency					1	-0.11	0.17
FX premium						1	0.32
Inflation							1
Growth	0.49	0.38	0.52	-0.20	-0.09	-0.48	-0.61

Notes: 10 per cent significance level is 0.26; 5 per cent significance level is 0.32; 1 per cent significance level is 0.45.
         Sample consists of 27 developing market economies.

the table includes a measure of financial openness, the stock market capitalisation/ GDP ratio. Significant positive correlations are found among trade, FDI and market capitalisation. There are also positive correlations among tariffs, the frequency of non-tariff barriers, black market premiums and inflation. Finally, international linkages and distortions are systematically negatively correlated.

East Asia's experience fits neatly into this framework. East Asian economies have consistently pursued less distortionary policies than other low and middle income countries and have built stronger trade and investment relationships. Over time, the experience and investments accumulated through these transactions have helped the linkages become increasingly robust. Hong Kong, Singapore and Malaysia exemplify these relationships; each had a unique approach to policy but kept distortions low, and each was unusually successful in trade as well as in attracting capital. These economies also have an exceptional history of international business experience.

Conclusions

Economic linkages within the Pacific, and particularly East Asia, are becoming broader, deeper and more complex. The increased mobility of capital — particularly intraregionally — is especially important in shaping the region's trajectory of development. This mobility reflects new, liberal trade and investment policies as well as cumulative private investments in international knowhow and business networks.

Increased factor and trade flows have positively affected regional growth. A favourable dynamic appears to link growth, trade, investment and the political economy of outward-oriented policies (the 'trade–investment nexus'). Indeed, the region's most dynamic economies in the 1990s — China and the ASEAN-4 — are those that have made the largest policy changes and received the largest FDI inflows. While the causation is probably two-way, the support of such investments has helped these economies effect major transformations in industrial structure. There is econometric evidence also for positive feedbacks between trade and investment, and for the positive effects of cumulated experience in international transactions.

Many developing countries are now competing to stimulate FDI inflows. This has raised international standards for the liberalisation of trade and investment, helping to make the politics of liberalisation increasingly attractive. For example, Indonesia recently announced a major liberalisation of its FDI regime in order to reverse a recent decline in its investment inflows (Richard Borsuk, *Asian Wall Street Journal*, 3–4 June 1994, p. 1). Additional evidence is offered by the proliferation of special economic zones — areas that have adopted limited but extreme policies of openness (free access to inputs, repatriation guarantees, reduced taxes, abundant infrastructure) specifically to attract foreign investment.

In much of East Asia, these perspectives represent a major turnaround in the policy approach to foreign investment. Japan and Korea, as well as several countries following their example, acquired technology by restricting inward FDI — in effect forcing foreign firms to license their technology to local firms and domestic firms to reverse engineer foreign products. Perhaps the character of labour-intensive production has changed (many labour-intensive operations are now part of more complex production chains), or possibly firms with advanced technologies have become more reluctant to share their knowhow. In any case, foreign investment and international tie-ups appear to have replaced arm's-length approaches to acquiring technology.

While the implications of economic integration are generally favourable, this chapter has also identified areas of potential risk. Factor mobility facilitates the migration of capital and resources to new locations — but this can also mean the decline of previous production sites. Chinese development is an especially important force for change. China's manufacturing boom has led to a decline in manufacturing in Hong Kong and Taiwan, and its investment boom has probably contributed to a decline in FDI in ASEAN. Yet Chinese growth has also generated new opportunities in joint ventures and trade for the whole East Asian region, and especially for Hong Kong and Taiwan. Whether China ultimately emerges as a threat to other East Asian economies or as the engine of regional growth depends on how effectively the region as a whole adjusts to the redeployment of capital.

Notes

1 The geographical definitions used are as follows:

NIEs: Hong Kong, Korea, Singapore and Taiwan;

ASEAN-4: Indonesia, Malaysia, the Philippines and Thailand;

ASEAN: the ASEAN-4 and Singapore;

developing East Asia: China, the Asian NIEs and the ASEAN-4;

East Asia: developing East Asia and Japan;

Pacific region: East Asia, United States, Canada, Australia and New Zealand.

2 Availability is not synonymous with utilisation, and there is little evidence of convergence in global income levels. Nevertheless the possibilities for diffusion appear to be improving.

3 In the mathematical models of the new geography, when demand crosses a certain threshold, the number and location of clusters become indeterminate ('chaotic').

4 The measurement of FDI is highly imperfect; numerous statistical problems remain to be solved (Graham and Krugman 1993).

5 Some observers have blamed the shift of investment funds from ASEAN to China on the lack of loyalty of Overseas Chinese living in other East Asian countries. While the networks of Overseas Chinese make it relatively easy for them to shift funds to new destinations, the dominant motive for such shifts is undoubtedly economic.

6 The ASEAN downturn is not all due to competition from China; inflows peaked in some countries well before the Chinese investment boom began. A critical factor behind the surge was the appreciation of the yen; by the early 1990s companies had adjusted their production sites to the new economic environment.

7   Networks of Overseas Chinese businesses may be providing a 'private legal system' for enforcing contracts in China that would normally be backed by an established legal code in other countries.

8   Since emerging market prices are not highly correlated with prices in developed markets, investors can substantially reduce risk to their portfolios by including emerging market issues.

9   Japanese affiliates do have higher export/sales ratios than US firms in 'all industries' (58 per cent compared with 34 per cent) However, this category includes the sales activities of Japan's major international trading companies, which are not usually engaged in production.

10   Since the data set used contains information on total FDI inflows to various countries, the only determinants of FDI that can be analysed are those that vary across host countries. In particular, no effort will be made to test so-called 'ownership' advantages.

11   This approach was first used by Chenery and Syrquin (1975).

12   The countries are: Argentina, Bangladesh, Brazil, Chile, China, Colombia, Costa Rica, Côte d'Ivoire, Egypt, Hong Kong, India, Indonesia, Kenya, Korea, Malaysia, Mexico, Morocco, Nigeria, Pakistan, Peru, the Philippines, Singapore, Sri Lanka, Thailand, Turkey, Venezuela and Zimbabwe.

13   The lagged form equation reduces the possibility that the coefficient is significant simply because of simultaneity effects, that is, because trade positively affects investment.

14   In the present study as well, including the values of trade and FDI in earlier periods offered sharp improvements in explanatory power. However, the interpretation of such lagged values in the cross-section analysis is problematic; the historical dependent variable could be a proxy for a wide range of country-specific effects not captured by other variables.

References

Arthur, W. Brian 1994, 'Positive Feedbacks in the Economy', *The McKinsey Quarterly*, 1, pp. 1–81.

Chenery, Hollis B. and Moshe Syrquin 1975, *Patterns of Development, 1950–1970*, London: Oxford University Press.

Dobson, Wendy 1993, *Japan in East Asia: Trading and Investment Strategies*, Singapore: Institute of Southeast Asian Studies.

Drysdale, Peter and Ross Garnaut 1993, 'The Pacific: An Application of a General Theory of Economic Integration', in C. Fred Bergsten and Marcus Noland (eds), *Pacific Dynamism and the International Economic System*, Washington DC: Institute for International Economics, pp. 183–224.

Dunning, J.H. 1980, 'Towards an Eclectic Theory of International Production: Some Empirical Tests, *Journal of International Business Studies*, 11, pp. 9–31.

Frankel, Jeffrey A. 1993, 'Is Japan Creating a Yen Bloc in East Asia and the Pacific?', in Jeffrey A. Frankel and Miles Kahler (eds), *Regionalism and Rivalry: Japan and the United States in Pacific Asia*, Chicago, IL: University of Chicago Press.

Graham, Edward M. 1994, Canadian Direct Investment Abroad and the Canadian Economy: Some Theoretical and Empirical Considerations, Washington DC: Institute for International Economics (mimeo).

Graham, Edward M. and Paul R. Krugman 1991, *Foreign Direct Investment in the United States*, Washington DC: Institute of International Economics.

Hill, Hal and Brian Johns 1986, 'The Role of Direct Foreign Investment in Developing East Asian Countries', *Weltwirtschaftliches Archiv*, pp. 355–79.

IFC (International Finance Corporation) 1993, *Emerging Markets Handbook*, Washington DC: IFC.

JETRO (Japan External Trade Organisation) 1994, *JETRO White Paper: Foreign Direct Investment by Japanese Companies and by the Rest of the World*, Tokyo: JETRO.

Katseli, Louka T. 1992, 'Foreign Direct Investment and Trade Interlinkages in the 1990s: Experience and Prospects of Developing Countries', Discussion Paper No. 687, London: Centre for Economic Policy Research.

Kojima, Kiyoshi 1977, *Japan and a New World Economic Order*, Tokyo: Tokyo University.

Krugman, Paul 1991, *Geography and Trade,* Cambridge, MA: MIT Press.

_____ 1993, Complexity and Emergent Structure in the International Economy, Paper delivered at the Conference on New Directions in Trade Theory, October 29–30, Ann Arbor, MI: University of Michigan (mimeo).

Le, Dang Doanh 1994, Economic Reform in Vietnam — Achievements and Prospects, Jakarta: Centre for Strategic and International Studies (mimeo).

Linneman, Hans 1966, *An Econometric Study of International Trade Flows*, Amsterdam: North Holland.

McCulloch, Rachel and Peter A. Petri 1994, Equity Financing of Asian Development, Paper presented at the 6th Biennial Conference of ACAES, Brandeis University, May 16–18 (mimeo).

MITI (Ministry of International Trade and Industry) 1994, Basic Research on Foreign Activity by Japanese Firms [in Japanese], Tokyo: MITI (mimeo).

Mody, Ashoka and Krishna Shrinivasan 1991, Trends and Determinants of Foreign Direct Investment: An Empirical Analysis of US Investment Abroad, Washington DC: World Bank (mimeo).

Ohmae, Kenichi 1990, *The Borderless World*, Homewood, IL: Dow Jones-Irwin.

Petri, Peter A. 1992, 'Platforms in the Pacific: The Trade Effects of Direct Investment in Thailand', *Journal of Asian Economics*, 3(2), pp. 173–96.

_____ 1993, 'The East Asian Trading Bloc: An Analytical History', in Jeffrey A. Frankel and Miles Kahler (eds), *Regionalism and Rivalry: Japan and the United States in Southeast Asia*, Chicago, IL: University of Chicago Press.

Porter, Michael 1990, *The Competitive Advantage of Nations*, New York: Free Press.

UNCTC (United Nations Centre on Transnational Corporations) 1992, *World Investment Directory 1992: Volume I, Asia and the Pacific*, New York: United Nations.

_____ 1993, *World Investment Report 1993*, New York: United Nations.

United Nations 1992, *Economic and Social Survey of Asia and the Pacific, 1992*, New York: United Nations.

USITC (US International Trade Commission) 1993, *East Asia: Regional Economic Integration and Implications for the United States*, USITC Publication No. 2621, Washington DC: USITC.

Wells, Louis 1993, 'Mobile Exporters', in Kenneth Froot (ed.), *Foreign Investment*, Chicago: University of Chicago Press.

World Bank 1991, *World Development Report 1991*, New York: Oxford University Press.

_____ 1993, *East Asian Miracles*, Washington DC: World Bank.

_____ 1994, *Building on the Uruguay Round: East Asian Leadership in Liberalization*, Washington DC: World Bank.

Yamazawa, Ippei et al. 1992, Vision for the Economy of the Asia–Pacific Region in the Year 2000 and Tasks Ahead, Tokyo: Sanwa Research Institute (mimeo).

4 Subregional economic integration: Hong Kong, Taiwan, South China and beyond

Yun-Wing Sung

Greater South China comprises Hong Kong, Macau, Taiwan and the Chinese coastal provinces of Guangdong and Fujian. With the implementation of economic reform in China since 1979, trade and investment flows within Greater South China have intensified. This dynamic region now has a substantial impact on world trade and investment flows.

Table 4.1 shows some basic economic indicators for Greater South China. As the table shows, Taiwan's GDP was more than double that of Hong Kong in 1992. No direct comparison with GDP in Guangdong and Fujian can be made as prices of services in China are much lower than international prices and the GDP of the two provinces is biased downward. A more meaningful basis for comparison is found in the value of exports. Guangdong's exports, of US$33.4 billion, surpassed those of both Hong Kong (US$30 billion) and Thailand (US$32 billion) in 1992. The total exports of the four Greater South China members cannot be used to gauge the exports of this region to the rest of the world because a substantial proportion represents trade within the region.

Fujian is far behind Guangdong in economic strength. In 1992, its exports were only 22 per cent those of Guangdong and its utilised foreign direct investment (FDI) 24 per cent. Most Taiwanese have family links with Fujian, and Taiwan accounts for the bulk of FDI in this province. Even so, the majority of Taiwanese investment in China goes to the economically more dynamic province of Guangdong.

Economically, Macau can be considered an appendage of Hong Kong. This study will therefore concentrate on economic interdependence between southern China, Hong Kong and Taiwan — the 'trio' — and there will no separate discussion of Macau.

In 1979, Beijing greatly increased the autonomy of Guangdong and Fujian, allowing them to manage foreign trade and investment independently and to operate special economic zones. Guangdong operates three such zones: the Shenzhen and Zhuhai zones, which are respectively adjacent to Hong Kong and Macau, and the Shantou Special Economic Zone. Shantou has close links with populations of Overseas Chinese, including a community in Hong Kong that originated in Shantou.

Table 4.1   **Basic economic indicators for Greater South China, 1992**

	Area (sq. km.)	Population (million)	Total GDP (US$ billion)	Per capita GDP (US$)	GDP growth rate (%)	Exports (US$ billion)	
Hong Kong	1,068	5.8	95.6	16,444	5.3	118.6[a]	30.0[b]
Taiwan	35,961	20.8	206.6	10,003	6.5	81.4	
Macau	17	0.4	5.0	13,527	3.1	1.8	
Guangdong	177,901	64.6	41.6	644	19.5	33.4[c]	18.4[d]
Fujian	12,000	31.2	12.5	402	21.7	–	4.1[d]
Total	226,947	122.8	–	–	–	–	

Notes: a   Total exports (including re-exports).
         b   Domestic exports.
         c   Based on data from *China Customs Statistics*.
         d   Based on data from Ministry of Foreign Economic Relations and Trade. Exports from processing operations are calculated according to processing fees rather than output value.

Fujian operates the Xiamen Special Economic Zone, which is located opposite Taiwan.

The opening of China coincided with the emergence of severe labour shortages in Hong Kong and Taiwan and the need for these two economies to restructure. There has been a large-scale movement of export-oriented, labour-intensive industry from Hong Kong to Guangdong, and a similar movement from Taiwan to Guangdong and Fujian. The trade flows generated by Hong Kong investment in Guangdong have been huge. Most of Hong Kong's outward processing activities in China are in Guangdong, and the bulk of their output is imported into Hong Kong for re-export to third countries. In 1992, Hong Kong's re-exports of goods made in Guangdong under outward processing contracts were worth nearly US$36 billion, thus exceeding Hong Kong's domestic exports of US$30 billion.

Greater South China and subregional economic zones

As East Asian countries took measures to liberalise their economies in the 1980s, geographic and market forces brought about the emergence of numerous subregional economic zones. Trade and investment flows between the border areas of neighbouring countries intensified as countries at different stages of economic development sought to take advantage of complementarities in factor endowment and technological capacity (Chia 1993). These subregional economic zones are variously called transnational export processing zones, natural economic territories (Scalapino 1992) and growth triangles (ASEAN terminology).

Apart from Greater South China, examples of subregional economic zones in East Asia include the Tumen River Area Development Project in Northeast Asia, involving the Russian Far East, Mongolia, northeast China, the Korean Peninsula and Japan; the Baht Economic Zone, encompassing Thailand and the contiguous border areas of southwest China, Myanmar, Laos, Cambodia and Vietnam; the Mekong River Basin Project, involving the riparian countries of Thailand, Myanmar, Vietnam, Laos, Cambodia and southwest China; and the three growth triangles of ASEAN, namely SIJORI (Singapore, the Malaysian state of Johor and Riau in Indonesia), the proposed northern growth triangle (western Indonesia, northern Malaysia and southern Thailand) and the proposed eastern growth triangle (Brunei, eastern Indonesia, southern Philippines, and Sabah and Sarawak in eastern Malaysia) (Chia 1993).

Greater South China was East Asia's first and most successful subregional economic zone. The impetus for its formation came primarily from the economic liberalisation of China, and secondarily from the economic liberalisation of Taiwan. Many barriers to the economic integration of the trio remain, the main ones being the remnants of central economic planning in China and Taiwan's ban on direct business links with the mainland. Despite the lack of an overall institutional framework for coordinating economic integration, geographic and cultural proximity and the huge gains to be made from economic complementarity have overcome many of the barriers to closer ties within the region. Private initiatives and market forces have led to intense trade and investment flows within Greater South China. The success of this regional initiative helped stimulate the formation of SIJORI, in 1989.

From 1991 to 1992, utilised FDI in China jumped from US$4.4 billion to US$11 billion, then to US$26 billion in 1993. China's share of total FDI in developing countries was 24 per cent in 1992 and 27 per cent in 1993, making it by far the largest recipient of direct investment among developing countries in these years. In 1993, FDI in China exceeded the combined total for Mexico, Argentina, Thailand and Indonesia, respectively the second to fifth largest recipients of FDI among developing countries.

Guangdong accounts for roughly one-third of cumulative FDI in China. Investment in Guangdong jumped from US$1.8 billion in 1991 to US$3.6 billion in 1992, then to US$7.5 billion in 1993. This was far more than the 1992 figure for FDI in Thailand of US$2.1 billion. China — and Guangdong in particular — attracted so much direct investment in 1993 that capital flows into ASEAN decreased markedly. In 1993, FDI in Malaysia fell by 60 per cent, while investment in Thailand also declined. The drop in FDI reinforced the determination of ASEAN governments to attract investment by setting up the northern and eastern growth triangles. FDI in China dropped by 50 per cent in the first quarter of 1994, partly because foreign investors were concerned about inflation and macroeconomic stability in China, and partly because the ASEAN investment environment had improved.

Overview of the integration of the trio

Even before China initiated its open door policy, the economic ties linking China and Hong Kong were quite strong. The relationship was, however, an asymmetric one: Hong Kong was open to Chinese exports and investment, but China was closed to exports and investment from Hong Kong. In the 1960s, Hong Kong was China's foremost market. China's trade surplus with Hong Kong amounted to around one-fifth of China's total exports, and China used the hard currency thus earned to finance its imports of grain, industrial raw materials and capital goods from developed countries. With economic reform and the open door policy, the relationship between China and Hong Kong has become more balanced and multifaceted, as will be seen later. Since the late 1980s the two economies have become highly integrated, and each is at present the other's main trading and investment partner.

Despite the absence of official ties, economic integration between China and Taiwan has proceeded at a fast pace, largely through the efficient intermediation of Hong Kong. In 1991, Taiwan passed Hong Kong and the United States to become the second largest supplier of goods to China after Japan; Taiwan also overtook the United States and Japan to become the second largest investor in China after Hong Kong. In 1992, China replaced Japan to become the second largest market for Taiwan's exports after the United States.

As a result of both geography and Taiwan's policy of not having direct business links with China, Hong Kong and southern China are much more tightly integrated than Taiwan and southern China. Unlike Taiwan, which has no land links with China, Hong Kong is able to truck semimanufactures to its subsidiaries across the border. Trucking minimises turnaround time, which is crucial in vertically integrated manufacturing. Whether in terms of labour costs, transportation costs or turnaround time, investing in southern China is not very different from investing in Southeast Asia for Taiwan, though the region does offer the advantage of having a common culture.

Although the ties between Hong Kong and Guangdong, Taiwan and Fujian, and Hong Kong and Taiwan are quite close, this is not true of the relationship between Guangdong and Fujian. As both provinces are poor in natural resources and are at a similar stage of economic development, they lack complementarity. Neither are they strong rivals. The two provinces are linked to separate communities of Overseas Chinese speaking different dialects, and this has moderated competition between them for overseas investment.

Integration through cultural affinity

Despite healthy trade and investment flows within the trio, Greater South China lacks institutional integration. This is especially true, of course, of China and Taiwan. Apart from the lack of diplomatic and commercial ties, the three areas most often identified by textbooks as impediments to economic integration are tariffs, controls on factor movements, and exchange risks. On all three counts, the barriers to economic integration in Greater South China are high. Take, for instance, the case of China and

Hong Kong. Even though China will resume sovereignty over Hong Kong in 1997, the Sino–British Agreement specifies that Hong Kong will remain a separate customs territory and that it will continue to have its own currency. Migration from China to Hong Kong will continue to be strictly controlled. It can therefore be argued that, even after 1997, Hong Kong and China will be less institutionally integrated than, say, Greece and Ireland. As members of the European Union, there is complete freedom of movement of goods and factors between these latter two countries. Members of the European Monetary System within the European Union are even more closely integrated owing to their pegged exchange rates. As China is not a member of the GATT and the Chinese currency is not convertible, Hong Kong is institutionally more closely integrated with most Western economies than it is with China.

Though economic theory concentrates on tariffs, migration and exchange risks, geography and culture may be even more important for economic integration. Hong Kong is only half an hour's train ride from China; Taiwan, too, is nearby. Many Hong Kong residents have their ancestral roots in Guangdong, and this province is the prime site of Hong Kong's investment in China. Likewise, Taiwan accounts for most investment in Fujian. This geographic and cultural proximity has enabled businesspeople to find ways around formal barriers to trade and investment. Tariffs, for example, can be evaded through smuggling, which is rampant between Hong Kong and China, and between Taiwan and China. Migration from Hong Kong and Taiwan to China is relatively free, though movement in the other direction is highly controlled. Despite this, illegal immigrants from the mainland often find their way into Hong Kong and Taiwan, attracted by the tight labour markets of these countries. Though the Chinese yuan is not convertible, the Hong Kong currency is circulated widely (if unofficially) in Guangdong, especially in the Shenzhen Special Economic Zone. The Hong Kong government has estimated that 22–25 per cent of the total currency supply, or roughly HK$17 billion (US$2.2 billion), circulates in China (*Hong Kong Economic Journal*, 5 May 1994). A grey market for yuan also existed in Hong Kong for some time. The grey market was turned into an open market in 1993, when China officially permitted visitors to bring 5,000 yuan out of or into China. Many Hong Kong shops for tourists also now accept payment in yuan.

Unilateral policy changes

Unilateral policy changes have played an important part in the integration of the trio. As mentioned earlier, China has tailored its open door policy to build closer links with Hong Kong and Taiwan. Taiwanese businesses enjoy special concessions in China: taxes and import controls on Taiwanese goods are less stringent; a 1988 State Council decree favours Taiwanese over other foreign investment (Sung 1992, p. 8); and local authorities tend to give Taiwanese investors preferential treatment in terms of faster approvals and better supporting services.

Though China is more open to Taiwan than it is to any other country, in the other direction the reverse is the case. Taiwan has gradually liberalised import controls on Chinese products since 1987. The number of items that can be indirectly imported increased from 29 itcms in July 1987 to 90 items in January 1989, 155 items in early 1990 and 1,654 items at the end of 1993 (Yeh 1994, p. 2). Taiwan eased its foreign exchange controls, also in July 1987, and Taiwanese businesses started to invest indirectly in China via subsidiaries established in Hong Kong or elsewhere. When the Taiwanese government gave its citizens permission to visit their relatives in China in November 1987, visits to the mainland soared. In October 1989, Taiwan promulgated regulations sanctioning indirect trade, investment and technical cooperation with China. This policy requires that all trade, investment and visits be conducted indirectly, that is, via Hong Kong or other countries. Taiwan still prohibits investment from the mainland, though it seems that China has invested in Taiwan through its overseas subsidiaries.

On paper, Hong Kong businesses do not receive favoured treatment in China. In reality, though, owing to geographical proximity and kinship links, they do enjoy a significant advantage. Hong Kong investors have been able to obtain concessions from local authorities in Guangdong through the kinship network. It is also easier for Hong Kong Chinese to visit the mainland because they do not need to obtain visas. China is thus more open to Hong Kong than it is to other economies. Hong Kong, of course, is open to the whole world, including China. However, as part of its drive to curb illegal migration, Hong Kong places especially strict controls on visits from China. In a reciprocal arrangement, Beijing also imposes strict controls on visits to Hong Kong.

China plans to abolish favours to Taiwanese and Overseas Chinese investors as part of a reform package designed to help it gain entry to the GATT. However, Hong Kong residents and Taiwanese will continue to enjoy simpler border formalities as well as special informal treatment from local authorities in Guangdong and Fujian.

Trade and investment within Greater South China

International trade statistics are in general available for countries or customs territories but not for provinces. For this reason, the discussion here will focus mainly on trade between China (not Guangdong/Fujian), Hong Kong and Taiwan. Some data on trade between Guangdong and Hong Kong are available, however.

Table 4.2 shows China's contracted inward investment by source country. Hong Kong is by far the largest investor in China, with Taiwan a distant second; the United States and Japan are in third and fourth places. Hong Kong's large share of investment in China conceals its important role as an intermediary. In Chinese statistics, investment from Hong Kong includes investment by the subsidiaries of foreign companies incorporated in Hong Kong. Many multinational companies choose to test the Chinese environment by launching investment from their Hong Kong subsidiaries, thereby taking advantage of Hong Kong's considerable expertise in this area. Chinese enterprises also invest in China from their Hong Kong subsidiaries in order to become eligible for the preferential treatment given foreign investors. There is no reliable estimate of the amount of Chinese capital making this 'roundtrip' via Hong Kong.

Table 4.2   **Contracted FDI in China by source country, 1979–92, US$ million (per cent)**

	1979–90	1991	1992	1979–92
Hong Kong	26,480 (58.5)	7,531 (60.6)	40,502 (69.0)	74,513 (64.0)
Taiwan	2,000 (4.4)	1,392 (11.2)	5,548 (9.4)	8,968 (7.7)
United States	4,476 (9.9)	555 (4.5)	3,142 (5.3)	8,163 (7.0)
Japan	3,662 (8.1)	886 (7.1)	2,200 (3.7)	6,748 (5.8)
Total FDI in China	45,244 (100)	12,422 (100)	58,736 (100)	116,402 (100)

Note: Figures in brackets indicate share of total FDI as a percentage.

Source: *Almanac of China's Foreign Relations and Trade*, China Resources Trade Consultancy Co. Ltd, Hong Kong, various issues.

Table 4.2 includes data up to 1992 only. According to preliminary figures, Hong Kong and Taiwan were the two main investors in China in 1993 as well, accounting respectively for 44 per cent and 19 per cent of utilised FDI (*Economic Daily*, 17 January 1994). However, Taiwan's utilised FDI in China, which grew sixfold in 1993, has increased at a far faster rate than Hong Kong's. If Taiwan further liberalises its economic interactions with the mainland, it seems likely that its investment in China will eventually rival that of Hong Kong; its economy is, after all, more than double the size of Hong Kong's.

Typically, two types of investment projects are found in China, the first utilising China as an export base, and the second geared more towards China's domestic markets. The first type tends to involve small-scale, labour-intensive manufacturing industry, and the second type larger and more capital- or technology-intensive manufacturing and services for the domestic market. Whereas Hong Kong and Taiwan invest in both types of projects, developed countries such as the United States and Japan tend to concentrate on the second type.

In the statistics, these two project types coincide roughly with two categories of FDI. The Chinese data distinguish between 'FDI', in which the foreign investor has legal control of the enterprise, and 'other foreign investment', in which the foreign investor does not. 'FDI' comprises investment in 'three types of foreign-invested ventures' (*sanzi qiye*): fully foreign-owned ventures, joint ventures and cooperative ventures. 'Other foreign investment' includes foreign funding of leasing, processing/ assembly operations, and compensation trade, in which the foreign partner provides China with equipment and receives products in return. This category is considered to constitute commercial credit rather than 'FDI' because the Chinese partner retains control of the operation and (usually) pays for foreign machinery and technical assistance with products or with labour services used in making goods for the foreign partner. In this study, 'foreign investment' includes both 'FDI' and 'other foreign investment' but excludes loans.

The first type of investment project corresponds to processing operations, which are export oriented by definition (they have to export their entire output) and which tend to be labour intensive. The second type corresponds to foreign-invested ventures, which can sell part of their output on the domestic market and which tend to be larger in scale and more capital intensive. However, the correspondence is by no means exact. There are plenty of export-oriented, labour-intensive, foreign-invested ventures, though there are very few large-scale, capital-intensive processing operations. It would be true to say, then, that nearly all processing operations involve the first type of project, and that nearly all of the second type of project involve foreign-invested ventures.

As processing operations are labour rather than capital intensive, their contribution to capital formation is quite small. From 1979 to 1992, the cumulative stock of utilised foreign investment in processing operations was only US$991 million, or 2.6 per cent of cumulative utilised foreign investment in China. The cumulative stock of contracted foreign investment in processing operations, meanwhile, was only US$1,343 million, or 1.2 per cent of cumulative contracted investment. China's statistical system grossly under-reports the amount of foreign investment in processing operations. In Guangdong, the actual amount of utilised foreign investment in processing operations has been estimated to be 14 times higher than the official figure in 1990 and 12 times higher in 1991 (Liu et al. 1992, pp. 34–6);[1] the true shares of investment in processing operations in total utilised foreign investment in Guangdong were 27.9 per cent in 1990 and 27.4 per cent in 1991 rather than the official figures of 2.7 per cent and 3.1 per cent.

The adjusted shares of utilised FDI (investment in foreign-invested ventures) in total investment in Guangdong were 68.4 per cent in 1990 and 70.3 per cent in 1991. Though adjustment for under-reporting does raise the share of processing operations significantly, it is still true that investment in foreign-invested ventures in Guangdong is several times larger than investment in processing operations. What is true of Guangdong is just as true of China as a whole, because Guangdong has over two-thirds of all China's processing operations. If we assume that investment in outward processing operations in other provinces is understated to the same extent as in Guangdong, then this type of investment would have constituted 18 per cent of utilised foreign investment in China in 1991.

Though processing operations are not important in terms of the amount of foreign capital involved, they do contribute significantly to China's exports. In 1990, the exports of processing operations were worth US$25.4 billion, or 40.9 per cent of total Chinese exports (Sung 1991a, p. 23). Given that Hong Kong and Taiwan accounted for the bulk of foreign investment in both processing operations and exported-oriented, foreign-invested ventures, it is no exaggeration to say that investment by these two economies, and especially by Hong Kong, constitutes the backbone of China's spectacular export drive.

Hong Kong's investment in China

Hong Kong's investment in China is highly diversified, covering projects ranging from small-scale, labour-intensive operations to large-scale infrastructure. Much of Hong Kong's investment is concentrated in Guangdong. In 1992, utilised FDI in Guangdong was US$3.6 billion, of which US$3 billion came from Hong Kong. According to official statistics, in 1979–93 Guangdong received one-third of cumulative utilised FDI in China, and Hong Kong accounted for over 80 per cent of this flow. Guangdong was thus the destination of over 40 per cent of Hong Kong's FDI in China. Even if we adjust for the under-reporting of investment in processing operations, Guangdong's share of the value of Hong Kong's utilised foreign investment would still be slightly less than 50 per cent. This is because most processing operations are small, even though their numbers are large.

Hong Kong's investment in Guangdong has transformed Hong Kong manufacturing as well as the entire Hong Kong economy. At present, Hong Kong manufacturing firms employ up to 3 million workers in Guangdong; the manufacturing labour force in Hong Kong, meanwhile, fell from a peak of 905,000 in 1984 to 508,000 in 1993. By moving labour-intensive operations to Guangdong, Hong Kong has been able to concentrate on more skilled processes, such as product design, sourcing, production management, quality control and marketing. Hong Kong manufacturing has thus been able to achieve very high growth in labour productivity in recent years. The expansion of exports from processing operations in Guangdong has also increased demand for services, including entrepôt trade, shipping, insurance, and business and financial services. As a consequence, both the Hong Kong manufacturing sector and the Hong Kong economy have become increasingly more service oriented. In short, Hong Kong has become the economic capital of an industrialised Guangdong.

Before Deng Xiaoping's tour of southern China in early 1992 in support of economic reforms, the largest corporations in Hong Kong were not active investors in China, though small and medium sized enterprises, especially labour-intensive manufacturing firms, were investing there in droves. Deng's tour stimulated a wave of investment by major Hong Kong companies, including listed companies such as Cheung Kong, Hutchison-Whampoa, Sun Hung Kai Properties, New World and Kowloon Wharf, in projects ranging from real estate to infrastructure and commerce.

Hong Kong has become the major centre of funding for Chinese firms. A number of investment funds specialising in China have been established, and these have invested in industry and B shares. In 1992, China approved the public listing of selected state enterprises on the Hong Kong stock exchange. Shares in these firms are popularly called H shares and Red Chips. By the end of 1993, H shares and Red Chips were available for 37 companies with a total capitalisation of US$2 billion, or 6.6 per cent of the capitalisation of the Hong Kong stock market (Jao 1994, p. 4). Small investors, apart from buying Red Chips, have also flocked to purchase flats in Guangdong. As a result of these developments, Hong Kong's already high share of China's contracted foreign investment rose from 61 per cent in 1991 to 69 per cent in 1992 (Table 4.2). This indicates that Hong Kong investors are very sensitive to investment opportunities in China, and that they have been one step ahead of potential investors in other countries. As these investors jump on the China bandwagon, Hong Kong's extraordinarily high share will probably decline.

China's investment in Hong Kong

Hong Kong is the prime destination for China's outward investment. Although precise data are lacking, it appears that China passed Japan in 1993 to become the foremost investor in Hong Kong in terms of cumulative investment. According to press reports, the assets owned by Chinese enterprises and government agencies in Hong Kong were worth US$6 billion in 1984, US$10 billion in 1989 and US$20 billion in 1992. China's investments in Hong Kong are diverse and cover nearly all sectors of the economy: banking, insurance, entrepôt trade, shipping, aviation, real estate and manufacturing. This investment has strengthened the ties between the two countries and enhanced the position of Hong Kong as the gateway to China.

It is even possible that China's investment in Hong Kong exceeds Hong Kong's investment in China. The estimate given above of Chinese assets in Hong Kong (US$20 billion) is likely to be biased downwards because there is an incentive for China's local authorities and enterprises to establish unofficial subsidiaries in Hong Kong in order to evade controls on foreign trade and foreign exchange. In 1979–92, when Hong Kong's cumulative contracted foreign investment in China was worth US$74.5 billion (Table 4.2), its cumulative utilised foreign investment was valued at only US$23 billion. Even the latter figure is grossly exaggerated as it includes investment by subsidiaries of Chinese companies and other multinationals incorporated in Hong Kong. Moreover, officials in planned economies tend to exaggerate economic performance (the 'success indicators' problem). Anecdotal evidence suggests that Hong Kong investors often overstate the value of their investments in China with the connivance of local officials. For example, Hong Kong manufacturers tend to put a high value on outdated machinery that they move to China.

As China continues to liberalise its foreign exchange controls, it can be expected that Chinese capital will increasingly flow into Hong Kong through official as well as unofficial channels. It is natural for Chinese enterprises and investors to move their capital to Hong Kong: Hong Kong offers stricter protection of property rights, and funds can be used much more flexibly there. In 1993, partly owing to an infusion of Chinese capital, real estate prices in Hong Kong soared to record heights, surpassing even those of Tokyo.

China's trade with Hong Kong

It has often been said that Hong Kong and China are each other's main trading partners. While this statement is technically correct, it is also misleading in that it lumps together China's trade with third countries via Hong Kong (Hong Kong's entrepôt trade) with China's trade with Hong Kong itself. The discussion here will be based mainly on Hong Kong statistics because Chinese data fail to distinguish between these two types of trade.

As a large proportion of China's trade is conducted via Hong Kong in the form of entrepôt trade, the data on China's trade by country provide at best an incomplete picture. In the statistics, exports are classified by country of destination and imports by country of origin. In the case of US–China trade, for example, each country counts its exports to the other through Hong Kong as exports to Hong Kong, thus understating their exports to the other. (Imports are not understated because they are traced to the country of origin.) Consequently both countries overstate their bilateral trade deficits or understate their bilateral surpluses. American statistics, however, are closer to the mark. This is because, in the early 1990s, around two-thirds of China's exports to the United States were re-exported through Hong Kong, whereas the corresponding percentage for the United States was only around 20 per cent. In 1992, according to US statistics, the United States had a deficit of US$18 billion in its trade with China; in the same year China claimed a deficit of US$306 million with the United States!

As a result of pressure from the United States, China has since 1993 attempted to clarify the final destination of its exports via Hong Kong. With the ensuing reclassification, China's exports to Hong Kong dropped by 41 per cent, while its exports to the United States, Japan and Germany grew by 97 per cent, 35 per cent and 62 per cent respectively. Despite the reclassification, a substantial portion of China's exports to third countries via Hong Kong is still classified as exports to Hong Kong because China is unable to trace the final destination of all its exports via Hong Kong.

Hong Kong's imports of Chinese goods in 1993 amounted to US$49.8 billion. Of these imports, 94 per cent was re-exported to third countries and only 6 per cent remained in Hong Kong. Though China was easily the foremost supplier of Hong Kong's re-exports, with a share of 58 per cent, it was in fourth place after Japan, the United States and Taiwan in the share of imports retained in Hong Kong (6 per cent). Hong Kong's retained imports from China have declined since 1987. China has been unable to capture the higher end of Hong Kong's market, which has been dominated by Japan. Given the increasing affluence of Hong Kong and the Japanese dominance in vehicles, capital goods, and quality consumer durables and consumer goods, the future of Chinese products in Hong Kong is not bright.

Hong Kong was the largest final market (that is, excluding Chinese re-exports via Hong Kong) for Chinese exports in the late 1960s and early 1970s, to be overtaken by Japan in 1973 and the United States in 1987. China continued to regard Hong Kong as its largest market until 1993, when the reclassification of Chinese goods for re-export took effect. In 1993, Hong Kong's imports from China accounted for 54 per cent of China's exports: 51 per cent for re-export to other countries and 3.3 per cent retained in Hong Kong.

The Hong Kong–Guangdong production network

Hong Kong's investment in processing operations in China, especially in Guangdong, has generated huge trade flows. Table 4.3 shows Hong Kong's trade with respect to outward processing operations in China for 1989–93. In 1993, Hong Kong's outward processing-related imports from China amounted to US$38.2 billion, or nearly 74 per cent of Hong Kong's total imports from China. Guangdong accounted for most of Hong Kong's outward processing-related imports from China, with a stable proportion of 93 per cent in both 1992 and 1993. It can therefore be assumed that Guangdong's share of other trade flows between Hong Kong and China involving outward processing (domestic exports to China, re-exports to China and re-exports of Chinese origin) has also been 93 per cent.

The bulk of Hong Kong's imports involving outward processing are further processed or packaged in Hong Kong for export to third countries. If the processing substantially changes the form or nature of the product, then it is classified as domestic Hong Kong exports, that is, exports of goods made in Hong Kong, and otherwise as re-exports via Hong Kong. In 1992 and 1993, re-exports of Chinese origin involving outward processing exceeded domestic Hong Kong exports. Whereas re-exports of Chinese origin involving outward processing grew by 36 per cent in 1992 and 22 per cent in 1993, domestic Hong Kong exports grew by only 2 per cent in 1992 and declined by 5 per cent in 1993. By 1993, re-exports of Chinese origin involving outward processing were worth US$47.1 billion, compared with domestic Hong Kong exports of only US$28.8 billion. The former figure exceeds the latter by 64 per cent, indicating that the value of the output of Hong Kong manufacturers operating in Guangdong/China exceeds that of domestic Hong Kong manufacturers by a substantial margin.

As mentioned previously, Hong Kong manufacturing industry employs 3 million workers in Guangdong and only half a million in Hong Kong. The gap in employment is thus 6:1, but the gap in exports only 1.64:1. The output gap can be expected to be similar to the export gap because most of the output of Hong Kong manufacturers operating in both Hong Kong and Guangdong is exported. Output provides a more useful basis for comparison than employment, partly because Hong Kong workers are more productive, but also because firms involved in processing operations in Guangdong do not produce exclusively for their Hong Kong partners. Value-added would be the best measure for comparing Guangdong and Hong Kong, but statistics on the value-added of Hong Kong operations in Guangdong are not available. The gap in value-added is probably smaller than the output gap as the value-added of processing operations tends to be quite low.

Adjusting for bias in outward processing trade

In view of the importance of outward processing trade, Hong Kong's trade statistics should be interpreted with care, giving due recognition to the special characteristics of such trade. For instance, the share of China in Hong Kong's trade is biased upwards because Hong Kong's domestic exports to China of semimanufactures are reimported

Table 4.3 Hong Kong's trade involving outward processing operations in China, 1989–93, US$ million (per cent)

	Exports to China			Imports from China		Re-exports of Chinese origin	Total HK domestic exports
	Domestic exports	Re-exports	Total	All China	Guangdong		
1989							
US$ million	4,098	5,757	9,855	14,562	13,601	–	28,731
Outward processing/total trade (%)	(76.0)	(43.6)	(53.0)	(58.1)	–	–	–
1990							
US$ million	4,676	7,125	11,800	18,629	17,592	–	28,999
Outward processing/total trade (%)	(79.0)	(50.3)	(58.8)	(61.8)	–	–	–
Growth over previous year (%)	(14.1)	(23.8)	(19.7)	(27.9)	(29.3)	–	(0.93)
1991							
US$ million	5,195	9,466	14,661	25,400	24,011	28,497	29,732
Outward processing/total trade (%)	(76.5)	(48.2)	(55.5)	(67.6)	–	(74.1)	–
Growth over previous year (%)	(11.1)	(32.9)	(24.3)	(36.4)	(36.5)	–	(2.53)
1992							
US$ million	5,719	12,578	18,297	32,566	30,335	38,733	30,245
Outward processing/total trade (%)	(74.3)	(46.2)	(52.4)	(72.1)	–	(78.3)	–
Growth over previous year (%)	(10.9)	(32.9)	(24.8)	(28.2)	(26.3)	(35.9)	(1.73)
1993							
US$ million	5,835	14,870	20,706	38,160	35,617	47,122	28,815
Outward processing/total trade (%)	(74.0)	(42.1)	(47.9)	(73.8)	–	(80.8)	–
Growth over previous year (%)	(2.0)	(18.2)	(13.2)	(17.2)	(17.4)	(21.7)	(-4.74)

Source: Hong Kong External Trade, Hong Kong Census and Statistics Department, Hong Kong, various issues.

into Hong Kong after processing in China.. Semimanufactures may even be re-exported and reimported several times before final export to third countries. Overall growth rates and values for Hong Kong's exports and imports are thus also biased upwards. From 1978 to 1993, Hong Kong's exports grew at an extremely high average rate of 18 per cent per year. In 1993, Hong Kong overtook Belgium–Luxembourg and the Netherlands to become the world's eighth largest exporter.

Table 4.4 tries to correct for bias introduced by outward processing trade in the values, growth rates and market composition of Hong Kong's exports. The first row shows Hong Kong's domestic exports. Domestic exports to China have grown very rapidly because Hong Kong firms supply their subsidiaries in China with materials and components, some made in Hong Kong. Hong Kong's domestic exports to China grew from negligible amounts in the 1970s to US$8.1 billion in 1993. At 28 per cent of Hong Kong's domestic exports, this put China ahead of the United States as the foremost market for Hong Kong products.

The second row of Table 4.4 shows the corresponding statistics for Hong Kong's adjusted domestic exports, that is, total domestic exports less domestic exports to China involving outward processing (largely semimanufactures). Adjusted domestic exports mainly comprise exports of final goods. Their values and growth rates are naturally less than those of domestic exports. More importantly, the decline in the market shares of the United States and the European Union becomes less steep, with the United States remaining Hong Kong's main market. The 1993 market share of China drops from 28 per cent to 10 per cent. This is still a significant share, and can be attributed to the recent liberalisation of China's import regime, which has allowed Hong Kong to export larger quantities of final consumer goods to China. Table 4.3 shows the impact of import liberalisation on domestic Hong Kong exports from a different angle: the share of outward processing trade in domestic Hong Kong exports to China has declined in recent years.

Despite the increase in exports to China, Hong Kong is unable to supply many of the products required by this market because of its narrow manufacturing base. Hong Kong specialises in a few light consumer industries, namely clothing, textiles, electronics, toys, plastics and watches. Due to the rapid growth in outward processing trade, Hong Kong's share of China's imports rose from an insignificant 0.8 per cent in 1979 to peak at 11.4 per cent in 1990. Hong Kong was then the third largest supplier to China after Japan (14.2 per cent) and the United States (12.3 per cent). However, with the liberalisation of China's trade and the subsequent jump in Taiwanese investment, Taiwan became the second largest supplier, and Hong Kong slipped to fourth place. In 1993, the shares of Taiwan and Hong Kong in China's imports were 15 per cent and 8 per cent respectively.

The third row of Table 4.4 shows the adjusted exports of Hong Kong firms operating in both Guangdong and Hong Kong. These are obtained by adding total adjusted domestic exports to Hong Kong's re-exports of goods from outward processing operations in Guangdong (equivalent in turn to 93 per cent of Hong Kong's re-exports of goods from outward processing operations in China).[2] The values and growth rates of the exports of Hong Kong firms are, of course, much higher than those of domestic exports. More importantly, the United States is clearly the foremost market. The share of the US market declined only slightly from 37 per cent in 1978 to 34 per cent in 1993. The share of the Chinese market was only 3.5 per cent, though this understates the reality because Hong Kong manufacturers in Guangdong can sell part of their output directly in China's domestic market.

The fourth row shows Hong Kong's total exports, that is, domestic exports plus re-exports. In 1993, Hong Kong's total exports to China were worth US$43.3 billion, 81 per cent of which were re-exports of third country goods and 19 per cent domestic Hong Kong exports. The trend for total exports is thus dominated by re-exports. Both the values and growth rates of total exports are very high, with China being the primary market in 1993. The share of outward processing trade in total exports to China declined from 59 per cent in 1990 to 48 per cent in 1993 (Table 4.3). The decline is agai due to China's import liberalisation and the consequent rise in imports of goods not related to outward processing. In contrast to domestic exports, the share of Hong Kong's re-exports in China's imports rose continuously from 1.7 per cent in 1979 to 34 per cent in 1993. This shows that, as import liberalisation has taken effect, an increasingly large variety and quantity of goods from third countries has been re-exported to China via Hong Kong. This is a testament to the efficiency of Hong Kong as an entrepôt. In 1993, Hong Kong's total exports to China accounted for 42 per cent of China's imports.

The fifth row shows Hong Kong's adjusted total exports: total exports less exports to China related to outward processing. The adjustment is intended to avoid double counting. Unlike the case of total exports (which indicated that China had replaced the United States as Hong Kong's foremost market), the United States remains the main market according to adjusted total exports. However, China's 20 per cent share of adjusted total exports in 1993 was still quite high because it had imported large amounts of goods not related to outward processing from third countries via Hong Kong.

To summarise, if we disregard trade in semimanufactures between Hong Kong and China, we find that the United States and the European Union still constitute the largest markets for both Hong Kong products and the exports of Hong Kong firms operating in Hong Kong and Guangdong. However, with import liberalisation China is also becoming an important market for final goods.

Table 4.5 shows exports of Hong Kong firms operating in Hong Kong and Guangdong by commodity. Labour-intensive, footloose industries have a major share of their exports produced by outward processing operations in Guangdong. These include travel goods and handbags (95.4 per cent), toys (94 per cent), miscellaneous manufactures (80.5 per cent) and telecommunications and sound recording equipment (77.9 per cent). The more skill-intensive industries have a smaller proportion of their exports produced in Guangdong. These include office and data-processing machines (36.5 per cent), watches and clocks (33.2 per cent) and electrical machinery and appliances (48.6 per cent). The proportion of textiles and clothing exports produced

Table 4.4   Values, growth rates and market shares of Hong Kong's exports, 1978 and 1993

	Value (US$ million)		Growth rate (%)	Market share (%)												
				United States		China		Japan		European Union						
										All EU		Germany		UK	
	1978	1993	1978–93	1978	1993	1978	1993	1978	1993	1978	1993	1978	1993	1978	1993
Domestic exports	8,690	28,815	8.3	37.2	27.0	0.2	28.4	4.6	4.3	26.7	16.4	10.9	6.3	9.5	4.8
Adjusted domestic exports[a]	8,690	22,983	6.7	37.2	33.9	0.2	10.2	4.6	5.4	26.7	20.5	10.9	7.9	9.5	6.1
Adjusted exports of HK firms in HK and Guangdong[b]	8,690	66,783	14.6	37.2	34.4	0.2	3.5	4.6	6.5	26.7	22.5	10.9	7.7	9.5	5.2
Total exports	11,507	135,174	17.8	30.3	23.0	0.5	35.2	7.7	5.1	21.7	14.9	8.6	5.2	7.4	3.4
Adjusted total exports[c]	11,507	114,480	16.6	30.3	27.2	0.5	20.1	7.7	6.1	21.7	17.6	8.6	6.2	7.4	4.0

Notes: a   Adjusted domestic exports = Domestic exports – Domestic exports to China involving outward processing.
        b   Adjusted exports of HK firms in HK and Guangdong = Adjusted domestic exports + 0.93 x Re-exports of Chinese origin involving outward processing (except to China). 0.93 is the share of Guangdong in Hong Kong's imports from China related to outward processing. The market composition of Hong Kong's re-exports of Guangdong origin involving outward processing is not available, but is assumed to be the same as that of Hong Kong's re-exports of Chinese origin. In 1993, the former was 72% of the latter.
        c   Adjusted total exports = Total exports – Total exports to China involving outward processing.

Source: *Hong Kong External Trade*, Hong Kong Census and Statistics Department, Hong Kong, various issues.

in Guangdong is relatively small owing to quota restrictions; Hong Kong historically has the largest clothing quota in the world.

Hong Kong as an entrepôt

Both outward processing and the decentralisation of China's foreign trade have boosted Hong Kong's trade with China, especially Hong Kong's re-exports of Chinese goods to third countries, and of third countries' goods to China. Decentralisation has vastly increased the number of trading partners in China and raised the cost of searching for suitable trading partners. Intermediation has emerged as a way of economising on the costs involved, and has been primarily channelled to Hong Kong because of its expertise in trading.

In 1993, outward processing accounted for 74 per cent of Hong Kong's domestic exports to China, 42 per cent of Hong Kong's re-exports to China and 74 per cent of Hong Kong's imports from China (Table 4.3). Hong Kong's China-related entrepôt trade not connected to outward processing has also grown rapidly. In 1979, the year China's open door policy was inaugurated, Chinese goods re-exported via Hong Kong constituted only 7 per cent of China's total exports, but this share rose rapidly to reach 51 per cent in 1993. Re-exports of third country goods to China via Hong Kong, which had only a 2 per cent share of China's imports in 1979, had a 34 per cent share by 1993.

Guangdong's trade with Hong Kong

Guangdong's trade with Hong Kong is very large, accounting for the bulk of both Guangdong's total trade and Hong Kong's trade with China. In 1993, Hong Kong's outward processing-related imports from Guangdong were worth US$35.6 billion, or 93 per cent of Hong Kong's outward processing-related imports from China (Table 4.3). Guangdong's exports not related to outward processing (exports from 'general trade') were valued at US$10.2 billion, of which at least 80 per cent (US$8.2 billion) went to Hong Kong. Guangdong should thus account for around 60 per cent (US$13.5 billion) of Hong Kong's imports from China not related to outward processing. Hong Kong's total imports from Guangdong in 1993 would, therefore, be worth at least US$43.8 billion, or 85 per cent of the value of Hong Kong's total imports from China.

In 1993, Hong Kong's exports to China related to outward processing amounted to US$20.7 billion; around 93 per cent of this (US$19.3 billion) would have been destined for Guangdong. On top of this, we have to add a substantial amount that is not related to outward processing. It is safe to conclude that, in 1993, Hong Kong's exports to Guangdong accounted for the vast majority of Guangdong's imports of US$41 billion, and of Hong Kong's total exports to China of US$43.2 billion.

China's trade in services with Hong Kong

Trade in services between China and Hong Kong is of great importance. Conceptually, the re-export margin that Hong Kong earns through entrepôt trade represents the

Table 4.5 **Exports of Hong Kong firms operating in Hong Kong and Guangdong by commodity, 1993,[a] US$ million (per cent)**

SITC commodity		Hong Kong[b]	Guangdong[c]	Total
83	Travel goods and handbags	104 (4.6)	2,170* (95.4)	2,274 (100)
894	Toys	431 (6.0)	6,724 (94.0)	7,155 (100)
899	Miscellaneous manufactures	327 (19.5)	1,347* (80.5)	1,674 (100)
76	Telecommunications and sound recording equipment	1,716 (22.1)	6,041 (77.9)	7,757 (100)
69	Metal manufactures, nes	600 (37.8)	988* (62.2)	1,588 (100)
65	Textiles	2,092 (40.6)	3,057* (59.4)	5,149 (100)
84	Clothing	9,289 51.3)	8,826 (48.7)	18,115 (100)
77	Electrical machinery and appliances	2,930 (51.4)	2,774* (48.6)	5,704 (100)
75	Office machines and automatic data-processing machines	2,229 (63.5)	1,279* (36.5)	3,508 (100)
885	Watches and clocks	1,701 (66.8)	847* (33.2)	2,548 (100)
Subtotal		21,419 (38.6)	34,053 (61.4)	55,472 (100)
All commodities		28,815 (39.6)	43,965 (60.4)	72,780 (100)

Notes: a Ranked in descending order of share of exports produced in Guangdong.
 b Hong Kong's domestic exports.
 c Re-exports of Guangdong origin involving outward processing (taken to be 93.3 per cent of re-exports of Chinese origin involving outward processing).
 * Indicates data on re-exports of Chinese origin involving outward processing are not available. Commodity value is assumed to be equal to 0.933 x 0.729 x Hong Kong's re-exports of Chinese origin of the commodity. 0.729 is the proportion of outward processing trade in re-exports of Chinese origin for this group of commodities, while 0.933 is the proportion of Guangdong in Hong Kong's outward processing trade with China.

Source: Data provided by Census and Statistics Department, Hong Kong.

export of services. However, such services are embodied in the goods sold and are usually recorded in trade statistics as the export of goods rather than services.

Hong Kong exports tourism, transportation, trading, construction, financial and business services to China. However, reliable data are available only for entrepôt trade and tourism. Considering the extent of investment between Hong Kong and China, Hong Kong's exports of financial services to China are undoubtedly substantial. Hong Kong is also the foremost base for China consultancy services. According to *Intertrade* (October 1984, p. 2), half of the foreign law firms in Hong Kong provide legal advice on trade with China.

Hong Kong residents accounted for roughly two-thirds of arrivals and expenditure by tourists in China in the early 1990s. Hong Kong is also the gateway for foreigners visiting China, with many joining package tours organised in Hong Kong. Though China has established a number of direct air links with other countries since 1979, the percentage of non-Hong Kong tourists entering and leaving China via Hong Kong has increased since 1982, to reach 44 per cent and 55 per cent respectively in 1987. This paradox is explained by China's decentralisation of the authority to organise tours of China to provincial and local authorities in the early 1980s. Taiwan's lifting of the ban on travel to the mainland in 1987 led to another jump in the number of non-Hong Kong tourists visiting China via Hong Kong.

In commodity trade, Hong Kong is an important entrepôt and transshipment centre for China. Sung (1992, p. 19) estimates that, in 1990, transshipments of goods from third countries to China via Hong Kong accounted for 4 per cent of China's imports by value, and transshipments from China to third countries via Hong Kong for 6 per cent of China's exports. Hong Kong trading firms also performed an important brokerage role for China's direct trade, amounting to roughly 7 per cent of China's trade. In the absence of more recent data, the 1990 shares can be applied to 1993. The shares of China's exports consumed, re-exported, transshipped and intermediated by Hong Kong in 1993 then become 3 per cent, 51 per cent, 6 per cent and 7 per cent respectively, or 67 per cent in all. On the import side, the shares of China's imports produced, re-exported, transshipped and intermediated by Hong Kong in 1993 were 8 per cent, 34 per cent, 4 per cent and 7 per cent respectively, or 53 per cent in total. It is apparent from these figures that Hong Kong plays a crucial role in China's imports and exports.

It should be noted that China's exports of services to Hong Kong have increased rapidly in recent years. Chinese firms are active in construction projects in Hong Kong. A large number of mainland Chinese are working in Hong Kong, including manufacturing workers imported to relieve the labour shortage there and engineers working in China-owned factories. Hong Kong residents have also travelled to China for medical treatment, to take advantage of its lower price for health care.

Taiwan's investment in China

Despite the massive growth of Taiwan's investment in China in recent years, the total stock of contracted Taiwanese investment at the end of 1992 was only 12 per cent that of Hong Kong (Table 4.2). This indicates that there is considerable potential for further expansion of the Taiwanese share. Taiwan initially invested mainly in small-scale, labour-intensive operations producing light manufactures for export, such as textiles, shoes, umbrellas, travel accessories and electronics. These projects were concentrated in Fujian and Guangdong, but particularly in the Xiamen region of Fujian. Recently, however, Taiwan's investment has increased in size and sophistication to embrace a greater number of more technology-driven projects, such as chemicals, building materials, automobiles, and electronic products and components. Investment has also diversified from manufacturing into real estate, finance, tourism and agriculture. The location of investment has tended to spread inland from the coast.

This investment surge has raised fears of a hollowing out of Taiwanese industry while also posing perceived security threats. Since July 1990, the Taiwanese government has tried to dampen the China investment boom by improving the domestic investment environment and steering investment towards ASEAN. Both the carrot and the stick were used to prevent Formosa Plastics from implementing its gigantic project to build a naphtha cracking plant in Xiamen. Taiwan also authorised indirect investment in 3,319 products in September 1990, most of them labour-intensive items requiring a low degree of processing. Authorisation was not granted for investment in products that were still competitive in Taiwan, including naphtha, catalysts, knitwear, synthetic leather, sheet glass and glass fibres.

Taiwan's president visited the ASEAN countries in early 1994 in an effort to further improve the investment environment for Taiwanese investors. The government, it seems, is trying to guide rather than reverse the mainland investment boom. There are very real political differences dividing the mainland and Taiwan, and these will not disappear overnight. However, if Taiwan continues to liberalise its relations with the mainland, Taiwanese investment in China will probably rival that of Hong Kong in the long run.

China's trade with Taiwan

The explosive growth of Taiwan's trade with China in the form of re-exports via Hong Kong is well known and regularly reported. Hong Kong statistics on re-exports have often been used by researchers to gauge the magnitude of trade between Taiwan and China. What is not well known is that there is already substantial 'direct' trade between Taiwan and the mainland. This trade usually involves the switching of trade documents. Taiwanese exporters claim that their goods are destined for Hong Kong when the goods leave Taiwan. On arrival in Hong Kong, documents are switched to show that the goods are bound for China. As the goods are consigned to a buyer in China, they do not go through Hong Kong customs and no Hong Kong firm can claim legal possession of them. Such goods are regarded by the Hong Kong government as transshipments or 'cargo in transit'; they are not counted as part of Hong Kong's trade. We can call this kind of trade 'direct' trade: it involves two separate sets of trade documents and so appears to be indirect trade, but is more accurately defined as direct trade in that no third party buys the goods involved for resale. By switching trade documents, Taiwanese exporters save a minor amount in Hong Kong customs fees, which are set at 0.1 per cent of the value of the goods traded. 'Direct' trade also has the advantage of maintaining confidentiality as the statistics available on such trade are much less detailed than those for re-exports.

Transportation of 'direct' trade between Taiwan and China takes three forms: transshipments, transit shipments and illegal direct shipments. Transshipments involve the transfer of cargo from one vessel to another, usually in Hong Kong waters. As Taiwan does not permit regular shipping services between Taiwan and China, transshipments are the dominant mode of 'direct' trade. The Hong Kong government keeps statistics on the volume of transshipments by weight, but not by value.

Since October 1988, Taiwan has allowed chartered ships and airplanes flying the flags of third countries to travel between Taiwan and China, provided they stop in a third place on the way. This allows Taiwanese businesses to charter ships to carry cargo between Taiwan and China without changing vessels. The ships usually stop in Hong Kong, where goods are treated as 'cargo in transit'. Such transit shipments entail considerable savings in money as well as time, as cargo does not have to be transferred from one ship to another (Sung 1994, p. 13). The Hong Kong government does not maintain statistics on cargo in transit.

Press reports and interviews suggest that illegal direct shipments involving chartered ships flying the flags of third countries may not be uncommon. Though this practice obviously reduces transportation costs, it is risky; shipping records are public information, and the Taiwanese government can easily check whether or not a ship has passed through Hong Kong or a third port. There have been instances of ships being fined for making such shipments (Sung 1994, p. 14).

In all the above cases of 'direct' trade, on paper exports appear to be bound for Hong Kong. The value of Taiwan's 'direct' exports to China can be estimated, however, as the difference between Taiwan's exports to Hong Kong and Hong Kong's imports from Taiwan after adjusting for the cost of insurance and freight — that is, the difference between cif (cost, insurance and freight) and fob (free on board) prices. This represents an application of the trade partners statistical technique.

Table 4.6 estimates the value of Taiwan's 'direct' trade with China. From 1975 to 1987, before Taiwan's liberalisation of its policy on trade with China, Hong Kong's imports from Taiwan were 5 per cent larger than Taiwan's exports to Hong Kong. This probably represented the cost of insurance and freight, as 'direct' trade was almost non-existent until 1987. Since 1988, Taiwan's exports to Hong Kong have exceeded Hong Kong's imports from Taiwan by an increasingly large margin.

Table 4.7 shows Taiwan's 'direct' and indirect trade with China. In 1993, Taiwan's 'direct' exports to China amounted to US$6,973 million, compared with indirect exports via Hong Kong of US$6,596 million. Taiwan's 1993 exports to China via Hong Kong ('direct' plus indirect exports) were thus worth US$13,569 million, or 16.1 per cent of Taiwan's total exports. After adjusting for Hong Kong's re-export margin and the cost of insurance and freight, China's 1993 imports from Taiwan can be estimated at US$15,635 million, or 15 per cent of China's total imports.

Table 4.6   Taiwan's exports to Hong Kong and China, 1988–93 (US$ million)

	Taiwan's exports to Hong Kong				Taiwan's total exports to HK	'Direct' exports to China	China's imports from Taiwan
	Imports retained in HK	Imports re-exported to China	Imports re-exported elsewhere	Subtotal			
1988	3,209	1,964	171	5,344	5,580	236	–
	(57.5)	(35.2)	(3.1)	(95.8)	(100)	(4.2)	
1989	3,376	2,540	321	6,237	7,030	793	1,856
	(48.0)	(36.1)	(4.6)	(88.7)	(100)	(11.3)	
1990	3,832	2,875	338	7,045	8,570	1,525	2,254
	(44.7)	(33.5)	(3.9)	(82.2)	(100)	(17.8)	
1991	4,354	4,074	591	9,019	12,418	3,399	3,639
	(35.1)	(32.8)	(4.8)	(72.6)	(100)	(27.4)	
1992	4,607	5,509	606	10,722	15,427	4,705	5,881
	(29.9)	(35.7)	(3.9)	(69.5)	(100)	(30.5)	
1993	4,275	6,596	611	11,482	18,455	6,973	12,933
	(23.2)	(35.7)	(3.3)	(62.2)	(100)	(37.8)	

Note: Figures in brackets represent the percentage distribution of Taiwan's exports to Hong Kong. Data on Taiwan's exports to Hong Kong are obtained from *Monthly Bulletin of Statistics of the Republic of China*. The amount imported into Hong Kong is taken to be Hong Kong's imports from Taiwan (obtained from *Hong Kong Review of Overseas Trade*) less a 5 per cent margin to allow for the cost of freight and insurance. Taiwan's re-exports to China and elsewhere via Hong Kong are taken to be Hong Kong's re-exports of Taiwanese goods to China and elsewhere (obtained from *Hong Kong Review of Overseas Trade*) less a 15 per cent margin to allow for a re-export mark-up and the cost of insurance and freight. Taiwan's re-exports retained in Hong Kong are obtained as a residual, as are 'direct' exports to China. China's imports from Taiwan are obtained from *China Customs Statistics*.

Source: *Monthly Bulletin of Statistics of the Republic of China*, Directorate-General of Budget, Accounting and Statistics, Taiwan; *Hong Kong Review of Overseas Trade*, Hong Kong Census and Statistics Department, Hong Kong; *China Customs Statistics*, Economic Information Agency, Hong Kong.

Unlike exports to China, Taiwan's imports from the mainland are restricted to selected commodity categories. Other, prohibited, goods imported from China into Taiwan often bear fake country-of-origin certificates; a Thai certificate of origin can be purchased for a mere US$100 (Sung 1994, p. 19). This practice results in imports from China being recorded in Taiwanese statistics as imports from a third country such as Thailand. It is not possible, then, to estimate the extent of Taiwan's 'direct' imports from China by taking the difference between Taiwan's imports from Hong Kong and Hong Kong's exports to Taiwan.

Table 4.7   **Taiwan's 'direct' and indirect trade with China, 1986–93**

	Exports (US$ million)			Imports (US$ million)			Transshipments via Hong Kong (tonnes)	
	'Direct'	Indirect	Total	'Direct'	Indirect	Total	To China	From China
1986	23 (0.06)	705 (1.8)	728 (1.8)	4 (0.02)	151 (0.6)	155 (0.6)	1,392	800
1987	92 (0.17)	956 (1.8)	1,048 (1.0)	5 (0.01)	303 (0.87)	308 (0.88)	1,912	900
1988	236 (0.39)	1,964 (3.2)	2,200 (3.6)	14 (0.03)	502 (1.0)	516 (1.0)	8,096	2,595
1989	793 (1.2)	2,540 (3.8)	3,333 (5.0)	37 (0.07)	616 (1.2)	653 (1.2)	53,450	6,662
1990	1,525 (2.3)	2,875 (4.3)	4,400 (6.5)	70 (0.13)	804 (1.5)	874 (1.6)	81,195	12,447
1991	3,399 (4.5)	4,074 (5.3)	7,473 (9.8)	501 (0.80)	1,187 (1.9)	1,688 (2.7)	345,700	87,610
1992	4,705 (5.8)	5,509 (6.8)	10,214 (12.5)	1,219 (1.7)	1,184 (1.6)	2,403 (3.3)	872,292	211,026
1993	6,973 (8.3)	6,596 (7.8)	13,569 (16.1)	1,855 (2.4)	1,159 (1.5)	3,014 (3.9)	1,152,363	329,548

Note: Figures in brackets are percentages. Indirect exports are Hong Kong's re-exports to China of goods of Taiwanese origin less a 15 per cent margin to allow for a re-export mark-up and the cost of insurance and freight. Indirect imports are Hong Kong's re-exports to Taiwan of goods of Chinese origin plus a 5 per cent margin to allow for the cost of insurance and freight.

Source: *Monthly Bulletin of Statistics of the Republic of China*, Directorate-General of Budget, Accounting and Statistics, Taiwan; *Hong Kong Review of Overseas Trade*, Hong Kong Census and Statistics Department, Hong Kong; *China Customs Statistics*, Economic Information Agency, Hong Kong.

In Table 4.7, the value of Taiwan's 'direct' imports is calculated using the weight of Hong Kong's transshipments of Chinese goods to Taiwan and an estimate of the value per tonne of such transshipments across different commodity categories.[3] This results in an estimate for 1993 of US$1,855 million, an amount which exceeds the value of Hong Kong's re-exports of Chinese goods to Taiwan by a large margin. Hong Kong's re-exports of Chinese goods to Taiwan have stagnated since 1992, while transshipments of Chinese goods to Taiwan have soared (Table 4.7). Evidently, a substitution of 'direct' for indirect trade is under way.

Taiwan has a massive surplus in its commodity trade with China, partly because of its policy of importing only selected items from the mainland, but also because of China's inability to meet Taiwanese demand for certain goods. However, Taiwan has large deficits with China in tourism, gifts and remittances, and investment, evening up the balance of payments across the Taiwan Straits. Moreover, intraindustry trade is expected to develop rapidly with the surge of Taiwanese investment in China and further liberalisation of Taiwan's controls on Chinese imports.

As stated earlier, trade between Taiwan and China has grown rapidly to reach significant proportions. In 1992, China replaced Japan as Taiwan's second largest market after the United States. In 1993, the market shares of Taiwan's four most important export markets — the United States, China, Japan and Hong Kong — (excluding re-exports elsewhere) were 27.6 per cent, 16.1 per cent, 10.6 per cent and 5 per cent respectively. From 1979 to 1993, Taiwan's total exports to China increased 743 times, giving an average annual rate of growth of 60 per cent. As Taiwan's exports to the United States have declined in absolute terms since 1987, China may become Taiwan's largest market in a few years' time. In 1991, imports from Taiwan constituted 13 per cent of China's total imports, placing Taiwan ahead of Hong Kong and the United States and behind Japan as China's second largest supplier. If the present trend continues, Taiwan will soon become China's largest supplier.

Taiwan's imports from China are far smaller, partly because of Taiwan's restrictions on trade with China. In 1992, Taiwan's total imports from China via Hong Kong were worth US$2,403 million, or 3.3 per cent of Taiwan's total imports. After adjusting for Hong Kong's re-export margin and the cost of insurance and freight, China's exports to Taiwan in 1993 were US$2,100 million, or 2.5 per cent of China's total exports. In 1992, China was the fourth largest supplier of Taiwan after Japan (30.2 per cent), the United States (21.9 per cent) and Germany (5.4 per cent), and was just ahead of South Korea (3.2 per cent).

In 1993, Taiwan's imports from China grew by 25 per cent to reach US$3,014 million, or 3.9 per cent of Taiwan's imports. China's exports to Taiwan in that year were US$2,681 million, or 2.9 per cent of China's exports. Between 1983 and 1993, Taiwan's total imports from China via Hong Kong increased 30 times to yield an average annual growth rate of 40 per cent. Given this rate of growth, Taiwan's imports from China will soon be very significant.

Trade in services between China and Taiwan is largely restricted to tourism. After Hong Kong and Macau, Taiwan is the third largest source of tourism to China, accounting for 4 per cent of arrivals in 1993. Taiwan's share of tourist expenditure is likely to be several times higher than its share of arrivals because, on a per capita basis, Taiwanese visitors spend far more than shorter term visitors from Hong Kong and Macau. Most Taiwanese visiting China enter via Hong Kong. In recent years, Taiwan has been Hong Kong's main source of tourists; 1.75 million Taiwanese tourists visited Hong Kong in 1993, of whom 1.5 million went on to China (*Hong Kong Economic Journal*, 13 April 1994).

Trade and investment between Hong Kong and Taiwan

Until 1987, economic relations between Hong Kong and Taiwan were one-sided owing to Taiwan's protectionist stance and its stringent foreign exchange controls. Whereas in the mid 1970s Hong Kong was Taiwan's third largest market after the United States and Japan, accepting about 7 per cent of Taiwan's exports, significant barriers stood in the way of Hong Kong's exports to Taiwan. Although Hong Kong was the third largest investor in Taiwan, again after the United States and Japan, Taiwanese investment in Hong Kong was insignificant. By the end of 1989, Hong Kong's investment in Taiwan totalled US$1.2 billion, or 11 per cent of total inward investment in Taiwan, compared with US and Japanese investment of US$3 billion and US$2.9 billion respectively. By the end of 1991, Hong Kong's cumulative investment in Taiwan had reached US$1.6 billion (HKTDC 1992, p. 4).

In the late 1980s, however, economic ties between Hong Kong and Taiwan developed rapidly: Taiwan liberalised imports and relaxed its foreign exchange controls, the Taiwanese currency appreciated sharply, and Taiwan began to use Hong Kong as an intermediary in its interactions with China. Taiwan's share of Hong Kong's domestic exports jumped from 1 per cent in 1985 to 2.7 per cent (US$803 million) in 1993. Since 1986, Taiwan has been the seventh largest market for Hong Kong after the United States, China, Germany, the United Kingdom, Japan and Singapore.

As can be seen from Table 4.6, Hong Kong is an important final market (excluding Taiwanese goods re-exported via Hong Kong) for Taiwan. Taiwan's exports retained in Hong Kong were US$4,607 million in 1992, or 5.7 per cent of its total exports. Hong Kong was the fourth largest final market for Taiwan after the United States (28.9 per cent), China (12.3 per cent) and Japan (10.9 per cent). The share of Hong Kong as a final market for Taiwan declined slightly in the early 1990s due to the surge in Taiwan's exports to China. After adjusting for the cost of insurance and freight, Hong Kong's 1992 retained imports from Taiwan were US$4,837 million, or 9.7 per cent of total retained imports. Taiwan is the third largest supplier of Hong Kong's retained imports after Japan and the United States.

Taiwanese investment in Hong Kong has also soared. Cumulative investment from Taiwan had reached US$2 billion by the end of 1989, half of which was invested after 1987 (Zhou 1992, p. 167). Taiwan thus became the fifth largest investor in Hong Kong after China, Japan, the United States and the United Kingdom. By the end of 1991, cumulative investment from Taiwan was estimated at US$2.5–3 billion (HKTDC 1992, p. 4).

Integration of the labour market in Greater South China

China has few controls in place to prevent residents of Hong Kong and Taiwan working there. In the early 1990s, some 45,000–55,000 Hong Kong residents reported having worked in China (Census and Statistics Dept surveys). However, controls on visits from China are strict in both Taiwan and Hong Kong. This is especially true of Taiwan, though illegal migration to both countries does take place.

China and Hong Kong agreed to a quota restricting the number of migrants from China to no more than 75 per day in 1982. The quota was increased to 105 per day in 1993. The mainland Chinese relatives of Hong Kong residents thus have to wait in line, often for years, before they can migrate to Hong Kong. The Chinese spouses of Hong Kong residents typically wait 10 years. Though permanent migration is difficult, barriers to temporary stays have eased in recent years. Since 1989, when the Hong Kong government embarked on its first labour importation scheme, more and more Chinese workers have come to Hong Kong to work on temporary contracts. The third labour importation scheme, announced in January 1992, further doubled the quota to 25,000, practically all of which is taken up by workers from China.

Professionals from China now find it easier to become permanent residents of Hong Kong. Since 1990, Hong Kong employers have been permitted to employ mainland professionals who have stayed overseas for at least two years. In April 1994 the Hong Kong government announced a trial scheme to import 1,000 graduates from China.

It should be noted that there are few restrictions on mainlanders entering Hong Kong on official passports, and it is estimated that over 60,000 Chinese workers are employed in China-owned companies in Hong Kong. There is also a substantial but unknown number of illegal immigrants and short-term visitors from China participating illegally in Hong Kong's tight labour market. In a few years, tourism from China increased from a trickle to over 1.5 million visits in 1993, making China the second largest source of tourism to Hong Kong after Taiwan. Given present rates of growth, China will soon surpass Taiwan.

The Basic Law, or the future constitution of Hong Kong after its reversion to China, stipulates that direct relatives of Hong Kong residents have the right to enter Hong Kong. At present, there are around 75,000 direct relatives (children or spouses) of Hong Kong residents who have not yet migrated. This number will grow as intermarriage increases. By 1997, or even before then, the present strict controls on immigration from China will have to be relaxed.

The economic prospects of Greater South China

Economic forces point to a continuation of rapid economic integration within Greater South China. This hinges, however, on whether China can preserve law and order in the post-Deng era. The stability of Hong Kong, which is crucial to economic integration, is not assured. If China does manage to maintain stability in the post-Deng era, and if it does continue its pragmatic policy of reform, then it is safe to assume that Hong Kong will also enjoy stability and that Greater South China will continue to prosper. At present investors appear to be very bullish about the future of Hong Kong, discounting the breakdown in Sino–British negotiations over electoral reforms to Hong Kong's Legislative Council. Investment has sent prices on Hong Kong's real estate and stock markets to record heights. Emigration of Hong Kong's professionals has slowed, and there has been a marked increase in the number of migrants returning to Hong Kong.

Prospects for processing operations

With the hike in wages and land prices in Guangdong and with rising world protectionism, concern has been expressed that the outward-oriented, labour-intensive processing operations of southern China may have no future. This concern is premature. Though wages have increased in Guangdong, the yuan has depreciated, and wages have also risen in Hong Kong and Taiwan. The wage gap between Hong Kong and Guangdong has not shrunk (Liu et al. 1992, p. 77). Land prices have indeed risen in Shenzhen and other cities, but there are vast areas near Hong Kong where land is still cheap. Guangdong and Fujian have a population of nearly 100 million people, and the supply of out-of-province labour is more or less unlimited. Bottlenecks in supply occur because of the lack of roads, ports, power and infrastructure, not because there is a shortage of cheap labour or land.

Protectionism is certainly a problem. China's Most Favoured Nation (MFN) status in the United States is subject to renewal each year. China is running up against its quota for textiles and clothing exports, and the number of anti-dumping suits taken out against it has increased. However, the problem on the demand side is exaggerated. Take the case of the United States, for example, the largest market for China and Greater China (China, Taiwan and Hong Kong). Though China's exports to the United States have risen rapidly, Hong Kong's and Taiwan's exports to the United States have declined as a result of the relocation of industry to China. US exports to Greater China have also been increasing rapidly. The absolute size of the US trade deficit with Greater China has been roughly constant since 1987 (Ho 1993, ch. 17, p. 32), and its size relative to US exports has shrunk markedly.

Though China is facing constraints on its clothing exports, the possibility of quality upgrading should not be ignored. Thanks to improvements in quality, China's clothing exports registered healthy growth of 9.3 per cent in 1993 despite restrictions. Moreover, China has a large import market, giving it considerable clout in world trade. The growing opposition in the United States to revoking China's MFN status shows that even America now has to reckon with China's power in world trade.

The growth rate of Hong Kong's outward processing-related imports from China is a good indicator of the performance of outward processing operations in Greater South China. In 1990, 1991, 1992 and 1993, the rate was 28 per cent, 36 per cent, 29 per cent and 16 per cent respectively. Though growth has decelerated since 1992, it remains very high, showing that there is still appreciable potential for the further development of processing operations.

The opening of China's domestic market to foreign investment

Since Deng's tour of southern China in early 1992, China has relaxed its controls on joint ventures selling in the domestic market, leading to high expectations on the part of foreign investors. However, foreign firms interested in investing in China's domestic market will not be able to recoup their capital investment unless China makes the yuan more convertible. Though China is taking steps to facilitate convertibility, the yuan is vulnerable to rapid depreciation caused by inflationary pressure. China will find it difficult to liberalise its foreign exchange controls unless it succeeds in curbing inflation. The growth of foreign investment in China's domestic market will be limited by the pace of liberalisation of foreign exchange controls, and this in turn will be determined by the pace of reform of China's financial system, and of economic reform in general. Historical experience indicates that the reform of financial systems in communist or former communist countries takes time, and foreign investors should be cautioned against rosy expectations of being able to exploit a huge market of 1.2 billion people.

Allowing foreign-invested enterprises to sell in the domestic market could, indeed, be detrimental to China unless it liberalises its import controls to allow the direct importation of foreign goods. The flow of foreign capital into highly protected industries is likely to result in immiserising foreign investment; that is, China's economic welfare or GNP at international prices could fall with an increase in foreign investment. Protected industries usually lack comparative advantage. Allowing in-flows of foreign capital into a protected industry leads to a further expansion of that industry, and consequently to greater misallocation of resources.

Under the policy of 'exchanging markets for technology', China usually allows foreign investors to sell in the domestic market if the investor brings in valuable technology. Under permanent protection, this policy leads to the growth of protected industries lacking comparative advantage. Until recently, allowing foreign investors to sell domestically was the exception rather than the rule. Now that China is planning to give more foreign investors this right, import liberalisation has become an urgent priority.

Prospects for direct links between Taiwan and China

The prospects for trade between Taiwan and China are undoubtedly bright, as the two economies are both complementary and experiencing strong growth. Taiwan has made it clear that it will not sanction direct economic links with China unless Beijing renounces the use of force over the Taiwan Straits, an option which Beijing has so far been unwilling to give up. However, a breakthrough cannot be ruled out in the post-Deng era.

In view of Taiwan's proximity to China, the country's policy of prohibiting direct economic links with China involves significant increases in transportation and travel costs and time. It has been estimated that Hong Kong would lose US$1 billion if Taiwan did establish direct links with China in reduced demand for its transportation, trade, telecommunications and tourism services. Direct links would probably save Taiwan far more than this, and would open up many new economic opportunities.

However, the impact of the official opening of direct trade between the two economies might also not be as dramatic as expected because half of existing trade, as already described, is already 'direct'. Taiwan has increasingly softened the interpretation of its ban on trade with China, leading to a decrease in the cost of 'direct' trade and a substitution of 'direct' for indirect trade. On the other hand, China has continued to decentralise its trading system, leading to an increase in search costs and in reliance on Hong Kong's intermediation in particular.

In China's trade with its major partners (including the United States, Canada, Japan, Singapore, Germany, the United Kingdom, Australia, France and Italy), direct trade links have reduced the cost of trade. This effect has been more than offset by the impact of China's decentralisation. China thus relies increasingly on indirect trade via Hong Kong (Sung 1991b, pp. 141–3).

Trade between Taiwan and China provides an interesting case study of the impact of direct on indirect trade because of the significant advantages the former offers over the latter for Taiwan. Taiwan could make large savings in transportation costs through direct trade, and due to the cultural connections of the two countries its search costs would be comparatively low. Taiwanese firms also have large trading networks on the mainland. However, around half of Taiwan–China trade still takes the form of indirect trade via Hong Kong despite the availability of 'direct' trade. This again confirms the efficiency of Hong Kong as an intermediary. After the recent opening of 'direct' trade between South Korea and China, a substantial proportion of trade continued to go through Hong Kong (Sung 1994, p. 22). This could also prove to be the case if direct links were established between Taiwan and China.

Even if Taiwan decided to initiate direct links today, it should be noted that the negotiation of air and sea links is always a time-consuming process. Given the political mistrust on both sides, negotiations would probably be protracted. The impact of the opening of direct trade would, therefore, be very gradual.

Prospects for further integration

Due to the many differences in the political, legal and economic systems of China on the one hand and capitalist China (Hong Kong and Taiwan) on the other, economic integration is likely to be highly uneven. Between China and capitalist China, controls on the movement of goods are already relatively liberal compared with the stricter controls placed on capital and foreign exchange and the very strict controls on migration. Integration of the commodity market between China and capitalist China can be expected to proceed rapidly due to the relatively mild controls on the flow of goods. However, even in the case of the commodity market one needs to distinguish between export-processing and import-competing industries, The outward processing operations of capitalist China on the mainland have developed with great rapidity because products are exported, unhampered by China's foreign exchange regime. The growth of external investment in China's import-competing industries will necessarily be slower due to China's foreign exchange controls.

The integration of service industries between China and capitalist China will similarly be slow because most services cannot be exported. Moreover, services are performed on people and require personal contact. Capitalist China's controls on migration from China can be expected to impede the full integration of service industries as well as the integration of labour markets. The integration of financial markets will also be slow as China's foreign exchange controls on the capital account are likely to be quite strict even in the medium term.

Overall, the huge amount of cross-investment within the trio implies that the interests of southern China, Hong Kong and Taiwan are tied together. For instance, if the United States were to revoke China's MFN status, all three parties would lose heavily. Similarly, all three would gain from China's and Taiwan's entry into the GATT.

Though the economies of the trio are tightly linked, Greater South China is not an inward-looking trade bloc. As mentioned earlier, the United States and the European Union are still Hong Kong's largest markets, and Japan is easily the largest supplier of Hong Kong's retained imports. By any measure, the United States remains the major market for Taiwan, and Japan the major supplier. The same is true for China. The economic reality is that the United States is Taiwan's, China's and Hong Kong's largest market, while Japan is the largest supplier of capital goods and technology to all three. Greater South China thus looks outward for its capital goods, technology and markets.

Notes

1   Unfortunately, figures for other years and provinces are not available.

2   It should be noted that Hong Kong accounted for 98 per cent rather than 100 per cent of investment in processing operations in Guangdong. This implies that a minor part of Hong Kong's re-exports of goods from Guangdong's processing operations should be attributed to other foreign investors. However, a small proportion of the output of Hong Kong manufacturers in Guangdong is exported direct rather than through Hong Kong. The two errors are in the opposite direction and tend to offset each other.

3   For the pre-liberalisation era of 1983–87, the value of Taiwan's 'direct' imports (estimated by the trade partners statistical technique) was divided by the weight of Hong Kong's transshipments of Chinese goods to Taiwan. In the pre-liberalisation era, the use of fake certificates of origin was rare. The estimation appears to be quite robust; it yields similar results to those derived from another method of estimation (Sung 1994, p. 20).

References

Chia, Siow Yue 1993, 'Motivating Forces in Subregional Economic Zones', Pacific Forum/ CSIS Occasional Papers, Honolulu, December.

Ho, Yin-Ping 1993, 'China's Foreign Trade and the Reform of the Foreign Trade System', in Joseph Cheng and Maurice Brosseau (eds), *China Review 1993*, Hong Kong: Chinese University Press, ch. 17, pp. 1–41.

HKTDC (Hong Kong Trade Development Council) 1992, 'Hong Kong's Economic Relationship with Taiwan', Hong Kong, February.

Jao, Y.C. 1994, Financial Services, Paper prepared for the Forum on Hong Kong's Role in China's Development, City Polytechnic of Hong Kong and Central Policy Unit, Hong Kong Government, Hong Kong, 1 June.

Liu, P.W. et al. 1992, China's Economic Reform and Development Strategy of Pearl River Delta, Research report, Nanyang Commercial Bank, Hong Kong.

Scalapino, Robert A. 1992, 'The United States and Asia: Future Prospects', *Foreign Affairs*, Winter 1991/92, pp. 19–40.

Sung, Yun-Wing 1991a, 'Explaining China's Export Drive: The Only Success among Command Economies', Occasional Paper No. 5, Hong Kong: Hong Kong Institute of Asia–Pacific Studies, The Chinese University of Hong Kong, May.

_____ 1991b, *The China–Hong Kong Connection: The Key to China's Open Door Policy*, Cambridge: Cambridge University Press.

_____ 1992, 'Non-Institutional Economic Integration via Cultural Affinity: The Case of Mainland China, Taiwan and Hong Kong', Occasional Paper No. 13, Hong Kong: Hong Kong Institute of Asia–Pacific Studies, The Chinese University of Hong Kong, July.

_____ 1994, The Economics of Illegal Trade between Taiwan and Mainland China, Paper prepared for the International Pacific Rim Conference of the Western Economic Association, Hong Kong, 8–13 January.

Yeh, Milton 1994, Ask a Tiger for Its Hide? Taiwan's Approach to Economic Transaction across the Straits, Paper prepared for the Conference on Economic Interdependence and Challenges to the Nation State: The Emergence of National Economic Territories in the Asia–Pacific, Pacific Forum/CSIS, Hong Kong, 17–19 April.

Zhou, Ba Jun 1992, *Hong Kong: The Economic Transition Accompanying the Political Transition* [in Chinese], Hong Kong: Joint Publishing (HK) Co. Ltd.

5 Chinese capitalism in Thailand: embedded networks and industrial structure —————

Gary G. Hamilton and Tony Waters

Southeast Asia is in the midst of an economic transformation. Only two decades ago, the region showed few signs of the rapid growth that was even then beginning to take shape. Today that growth is unambiguous. Southeast Asian economies have recorded sustained growth rates rivalling those of any other country in the world, except perhaps China. Between 1980 and 1990, manufacturing grew at a rate of 8.8 per cent per annum in Malaysia, 8.9 per cent in Thailand, 6.6 per cent in Singapore and 12.5 per cent in Indonesia. In the 1990s, despite dramatic downturns in the core industrial economies of the United States, Europe and Japan, the pace of growth in Southeast Asia has not lessened; GNP in most ASEAN countries has grown at an annual rate of between 7.5 and 10 per cent. Even the Philippines has begun to show signs of awakening, with recent growth approaching 5 per cent.

As analysts have observed, the most important of the factors accounting for this rapid growth — namely the restructuring of the global economy and foreign direct investment — have external origins. A large number of multinational firms from the industrial economies have, for instance, moved a portion of their manufacturing facilities to Southeast Asia to take advantage of the region's cheap and relatively high-quality labour force. Japanese automobile makers and American semiconductor and disk drive producers are among those adopting this strategy of 'globalising the corporation'. Another strategy, pioneered by Western retailers, has been to design and merchandise products made on a subcontracted basis in Southeast Asia (as well as elsewhere) by local, independently owned firms. Textiles, footwear and some types of electronic products are commodities in this category; firms that employ this strategy include mass retailers (Wal-Mart and Target) and brand name merchandisers (The Gap and Nike). Yet another route by which companies arrive in Southeast Asia is to peddle their wares, services or expertise there. Companies from every industrialised region of the world are competing to construct the region's roads, subways, airports and telecommunications systems. Through joint ventures with local firms, distant manufacturers are selling the aeroplanes, cars, trains and cellular phones that go with the infrastructure. Fast food chains, firms offering financial services of every kind, shipping companies and fast freight forwarders have gone to Southeast Asia, hired local people to work in their branch offices, and contributed to the demand from which they hope to profit. Fast growth and high profits have created the expectation of more of the same, drawing even more foreign firms to the region.

Significant as these external factors are, merely listing them does not help us understand the transformation that is now under way in Southeast Asia. To be sure, the economic changes taking place there are not simply local phenomena, but rather aspects of a global transformation. At the same time, this global transformation has profound regional manifestations that are leading to a comprehensive reorganisation of Southeast Asian economies. In this chapter, I want to concentrate on these patterns of reorganisation. The key theme is that globalisation processes work to the particular advantage of Overseas Chinese entrepreneurs, who are able to call upon a mode of social organisation that allows them to seize or create transnational economic opportunities.

Industrial structure and economic organisation

If one looks out over the economic landscape of a capitalist society at any one point in time, one sees what economists call an 'industrial structure'. Industrial structures are the organisational makeup of economies and so should constitute an essential part of our understanding of how businesses operate in a given economic environment. The conceptual literature on industrial organisation, however, was developed at a time when globalisation was much less important than it is today; to a great extent it reflects economists' preoccupation with domestic market economies in the United States and Europe. Changes in the world economy have largely destroyed the boundaries of domestic economies and have made the former concepts of industrial structure appear anachronistic.

In the years leading up to the Vietnam War — roughly corresponding to the heyday of US capitalist hegemony — American corporations tended to be massive and intensively vertically integrated. Usually they faced little competition from firms organised differently, either in the domestic economy or in the international arena. Today, when the production of virtually any commodity, from aeroplanes to television sets, has become globalised (Dicken 1992; Gereffi and Korzeniewicz 1994; Gereffi and Hamilton 1992), many independent firms may have a role in the manufacture of a single product.

To take just one example, in any given location Compaq's market share for personal computers will be quite different from that of the manufacturer who makes the hard disk drives that go in the firm's PCs. The same will be true for the companies that make the semiconductor chips, motherboards, monitors and all other technical parts found in a Compaq personal computer. However, Compaq's market share, whether large or small, may have very little do to with Compaq as an owner of assets or as an employer of people — and the company that makes its monitors may, indeed, have most of its assets in a completely different industrial sector. Simply put, conventional measures of concentration do not synthesise the structure of economies with the accuracy that they did when major manufacturers were more vertically integrated than they are today.

Gereffi and Hamilton (1992) have proposed a way to conceptualise economic organisation more broadly so that configurations of ownership and production can be disentangled; each set can then be examined and explained separately and longitudinally.[1] Production and distribution of commodities is conceptualised as 'global commodity chains', and ownership and control of assets as 'embedded networks'.

Global commodity chains

Our analysis of global commodity chains focuses on the structure and dynamics of the global manufacturing system (Gereffi and Korzeniewicz 1994).[2] The framework adopts a very broad notion of production systems that connects the manufacturing stage of production both with raw material and component supply networks (backward linkages) and with related export, distribution and marketing networks (forward linkages). This framework allows us to specify more precisely, both in space and across time, the character of and changes in production systems.

One can think of commodity chains as having three main dimensions: an input–output structure (a set of production units of different sizes linked together); territoriality (spatial dispersion or concentration); and a governance structure (authority and power relationships) (Gereffi 1994, pp. 96–7). As Chandler (1977) has described for the United States, in the late 19th and early 20th centuries commodity chains were internalised within the organisational boundaries of vertically integrated corporations. In such cases, the governance structure was the 'visible hand' of corporate management. However, as commodity chains have become globalised in the last half of this century, each link in the chain has tended to become the task of a different and independent firm. The governance structure, though still essential to the coordination of transnational production systems, is no longer synonymous with a corporate hierarchy. Gereffi's (1994) research has shown that, although considerable variations in governance do exist, it is possible to distinguish clearly between two types of governance structures for networked global commodity chains. For the sake of simplicity, Gereffi calls these 'producer-driven' and 'buyer-driven' commodity chains.

Producer-driven, demand-creating commodity chains
Producer-driven commodity chains refer to those industries or industry segments in which large, usually transnational, corporations play key roles in coordinating global production systems (including backward and forward linkages). This type of chain is found most often in capital- and technology-intensive industries, such as the automobile, semiconductor, aircraft and electrical machinery industries. Although production is globalised, the actual number of production locations in the commodity chain varies. With labour-intensive production processes, global subcontracting of components

production is typical, and strategic alliances between international rivals are now commonplace. The critical characteristic of a producer-driven production system is the control exercised by the administrative headquarters of the transnational corporation over the entire production and distribution process.

Automobile production provides a good example of a producer-driven commodity chain.[3] Cusumano (1985) illustrated how Japanese car companies organise manufacturing into multilayered production systems that involve thousands of independent firms (including parents, subsidiaries and subcontractors). The Toyota group alone coordinates production of its automobiles by nearly 20,000 independent firms in Japan. In addition, it supervises nearly every aspect of domestic and global distribution, including the provision of credit services to the final consumer. Doner (1991) further demonstrated the complex forces that drive Japanese automobile firms to extend their local production networks by creating regional production schemes for the supply of auto parts in a half dozen nations in East and Southeast Asia — this in order to retain and perhaps increase their share of the global automobile market. In recent years, American automobile manufacturers have emulated Japanese practices by creating their own global subcontracting networks.

Buyer-driven, demand-responsive commodity chains

Buyer-driven commodity chains refer to those industries in which large retailers and trading companies play the central role in shaping decentralised production networks in a variety of exporting countries — often the rapidly developing countries of the former Third World. Buyer-driven chains are especially common in labour-intensive consumer goods industries, such as garments, footwear, toys and household electronics, and in a wide range of handcraft industries, such as furniture and jewellery. As with producer-driven chains, global subcontracting is common, with buyers or brand name merchandisers providing manufacturers with the design and quality specifications for products. Most manufacturing, however, is sourced from independently owned Third World factories under original equipment manufacturer (OEM) arrangements. Many consumer electronic products, such as computers and television sets, are OEM products sold under another brand name.

One of the main characteristics of firms that fit the buyer-driven model, including athletic footwear companies like Nike, Reebok and L.A. Gear, fashion-oriented clothing companies like Liz Claiborne, or even a growing number of US computer firms like Dell Computers, is that frequently they do not own any integrated production facilities. They are *manufacturers without factories*. 'These firms rely on complex tiered networks of subcontractors that perform almost all their specialised tasks' (Gereffi 1994, p. 99); they may farm out design, engineering, manufacturing, packaging, shipping and even accounts receivable to different agents around the world. The main job of the core company is to manage these relationships and make sure all the pieces of the business fit together.

Based on research to date, global manufacturing is gradually tending to shift from producer-driven to buyer-driven chains (Gereffi and Hamilton 1992). The key reason for this shift lies in the substantial advances made in the technology of mass marketing, which have allowed mass and niche retailers (Wal-Mart and The Gap, for example) to create significant barriers to entry in the area of merchandising. These advances, which include computerised inventory systems, professionalised buying methods and fast freight forwarding, have facilitated the development of highly differentiated products with lot orders matched to predicted sales, and have shortened product lifecycles. Product differentiation and shorter product lifecycles reduce the advantages of economy of scale (mass) production systems, favouring instead flexible specialisation strategies.

In summary, the organisation of global commodity chains stems from such economic factors as critical barriers to entry into an industry. In capital-intensive industries, such as automobile manufacturing, commodity chains tend to be producer driven. Buyer-driven commodity chains are more likely to be organised by mass merchandisers. Many commodity chains are neither producer nor buyer driven, but rather represent some combination of the two. In analysing the dynamics of these two types of commodity chains, it is essential to understand how the coordination of production and the control of assets, through ownership or other means, mutually influence the organisation of global commodity chains.

Embedded ownership and asset control networks

In the globalising world economy, the organisation of commodity chains and the ownership and control of assets are no longer conterminous, as they were in the vertically integrated, multidivisional corporations that Chandler and others described as being characteristic of American corporate structure (Chandler 1977, 1990; Chandler and Daems 1980). Instead, loosely defined networks of firms sharing some form of ownership or asset control have replaced the legally defined, clearly bounded corporation. These networks have varying degrees of economic integration, even though they are linked together through some sort of authoritative control structure (Hamilton and Feenstra 1995). With a degree of oversimplification, some types of ownership and asset control networks link firms in a hierarchical configuration that overlaps with commodity chains. Other types are far less hierarchical, linking firms horizontally across many sectors, with little apparent coordination of production and distribution. An examination of the economies of Japan, South Korea and Taiwan reveals the importance of vertical and horizontal control dimensions in the configurations of Asian business networks.

Vertically controlled networks
Although organised differently, the large interfirm networks of both Japan and South Korea are strongly hierarchical. They consist in both countries of firms linked through vertical controls designed to reinforce and maintain the integrity of networks over the long term. In South Korea, these interfirm networks, called *chaebol*, are owned by core families who exercise control through patrimonial means (Biggart 1990). Examples

include Hyundai, Daewoo and Lucky Goldstar. So large are some *chaebol* that the top 50 account for over 45 per cent of all manufacturing sales and nearly 20 per cent of the contribution of value-added to GNP (Orrù, Biggart and Hamilton 1991). In Japan, vertically arranged interfirm networks are called*keiretsu*. Examples include Toyota, Hitachi and Mitsubishi Heavy Industries. *Keiretsu*, which are composed sometimes of thousands of independent companies, form communities of firms controlled through an etiquette of intercorporate relations, sealed with majority shareholdings and long-term subcontracting ties (Gerlach 1992a; Orrù, Hamilton and Suzuki 1989). The largest *keiretsu* again dominate substantial portions of the total economy; the top 16 contribute 33 per cent of all manufacturing sales in Japan and 20 per cent of all employment in the manufacturing sector. Despite their differences, both Japan's *keiretsu* and South Korea's *chaebol* enable large firms systematically to control smaller firms in vast, vertically arranged networks.

The economic purposes of these vertical networks are readily apparent. They encompass many aspects of production. *Keiretsu* and *chaebol* form stable networks of firms for every major product they produce. Every conceivable part of the production sequence leading to the finished product is undertaken within the network, with each firm having a function in relation to the final outcome. Gerlach (1992b, pp. 33–4) demonstrated that the web of*keiretsu* affiliation 'has had the overall effect of loosening the boundaries of the firm in Japan as a means of creating flexible systems of information and resource flows'. This flexibility has in turn facilitated corporate entrepreneurship; it allows managers and owners to 'spin off' innovation into small, new firms that are free to utilise the resources of the overall network. According to Gerlach (1992b, pp. 35), these 'satellite groups and the broader networks that they constitute represent an "organisational technology" that is itself a form of innovation, and one that may be of comparable importance to understanding...the process and product technologies that they have spawned'.

The economic qualities of commodity chains show vertical networks to be producer driven in the sense that the main manufacturing firm tries to control the entire chain, from the input of intermediate goods and services to the final distribution and sale of the finished product. Vertically controlled networks are also demand creating: to maintain the long-term integrity of interfirm connections, they cannot simply respond to external demand, but rather must lead the market by actually creating demand for their new products. The economic efficiency and competitive advantage of such large vertical networks are located precisely in the stability and flexibility of interfirm relations; to survive in a highly competitive global economy, they must attempt to control the markets in which they are involved.

Horizontally controlled networks
In their degree of vertical integration and in their economic characteristics, Taiwan's interfirm networks differ markedly from those of Japan and Korea (Feenstra, Yang and Hamilton 1993; Hamilton and Feenstra 1995; Liu, Liu and Wu 1993; Hamilton 1991). Taiwan's networks tend to link people and firms horizontally rather than vertically.

Such vertical networks as do exist are found in relatively modest groups of small and medium sized firms controlled through family ties. Moreover, in contrast to the power exercised by families in South Korea's *chaebol*, the span of effective control achieved even in large family-owned conglomerates in Taiwan is narrow and fragmented. A large family-owned conglomerate may hold a single large firm or small group of firms controlling a very specialised niche market, but the remainder of the family's holdings would typically be diversified and segmented managerially into separate, unrelated businesses. Despite this narrowness of control and the fragmentation of group holdings, Taiwan has one of the world's most densely networked and highly productive economies. With a population of only 20 million people, it has accumulated one of the world's largest economic surpluses. Among world economies, it has one of the highest ratios of manufactured goods to total output, and the highest ratio of exported goods to total manufacturing.

Taiwan has achieved this position of industrial pre-eminence with an economic organisation founded on flexible, horizontally based, social relationships known as *guanxi* networks (Hamilton and Kao 1990; Numazaki 1991, 1993). The social foundations of *guanxi* networks rest in particular on kinship, school cohorts, and common regions of origin (King 1991; Yang 1989; Yao 1987). These social relationships provide the norms of trust needed to create interfirm networks that are able to respond to external demand. Research has shown that social networks of the *guanxi* type are easily converted into highly flexible economic organisations, which are in turn attractive to Western merchandisers seeking offshore manufacturing firms.

A number of researchers (Hamilton 1991; Redding 1990; Wong 1985) have suggested that the traits just described for Taiwan are, in fact, characteristic of the private sector in all Chinese-dominated economies, including Hong Kong, Singapore, parts of Southeast Asia and, increasingly, China. Although it is certain that Chinese economic practices have wide significance throughout both East and Southeast Asia, it is also the case that the social and historical context of these practices greatly influences their economic relevance. As I will show, historical and social circumstances shape the way the Chinese do business.

Chinese business networks in the Thai economy

How do global commodity chains and embedded ownership networks intersect in the organisation of Thailand's rapidly developing economy?[4] In answering this question, one immediately confronts two facts that emerge from Suehiro's (1989) excellent study of the Thai economy: the importance of networks of firms, and the dominance of Chinese ownership of these networks. Suehiro (1989, pp. 218–19) reported that most private firms and virtually all of the largest firms in the more advanced sectors of the Thai economy were 'members of "groups of companies" rather than large, independent firms'. Of Thailand's top 100 businesses — including Western and Japanese firms, as well as Thai business groups — domestic 'independent large-scale firms not belonging to any group accounted for only five firms, and their combined annual sales represented less than 2 per cent of the total sales of the 100 largest businesses. These findings, in turn, suggest the importance of "groups of companies" in the Thai industrial organisation' (Suehiro 1989, p. 219).

Suehiro's research also showed that ownership of these groups of companies was dominated by Thailand's Chinese minority. In his examination of more than 70 leading Thai business groups in the early 1980s, he found only three non-ethnic Chinese groups: the group of firms owned by the Crown Property Bureau, a group owned by the Military Bank, and the Siam Vidhaya group, owned by a Thai-Indian family. All the other business groups 'belonged to naturalised or local-born Chinese, all of whom held Thai citizenship' (Suehiro 1989, p. 9).

Suehiro defined these business groups in terms of ownership and asset control, that is, embedded networks in the sense discussed above. We need now to ask: 'What is the relationship between these embedded business group networks and the organisation of the economy in terms of commodity chains?'

Three periods of industrial formation

The answer to this question, while not simple, is nonetheless significant. Let me start by looking at companies traded on the Bangkok Stock Exchange. Listed companies can be divided into broad industrial sectors roughly equivalent to an economist's idea of industrial structure: *primary natural resource industries*, including mining, lumber and oil; *basic infrastructure industries*, including rail and highway transportation systems, electricity and heavy construction; *heavy industries*, which primarily produce intermediate inputs such as steel and chemical products; *final goods manufacturing*, producing finished products mainly for export sectors; and finally the *financial sector*, which includes banking, insurance and brokerage houses. An analysis of the ownership of companies in each of these sectors shows that the largest firms not only have distinctive forms of integration in the global economy, but also different sets of relationships linking embedded networks to economic organisation. The key finding is that industrial structures are not only economic, but also historical and sociological. Like the geological layering of the earth's crust, the sectoral layering of economies occurs at different times under the conditions of ownership and control that prevailed at the time. How industries, sectors and, ultimately, economies grow and change is significantly shaped by where they start.

Three distinct periods of industrial formation have been crucial in the building of Thailand's current industrial structure. The first period (1855–1932) started with the Bowring Treaty, which gave British merchants the same economic advantages as those possessed by local merchants (Hong 1984). From this point until the coup of 1932, the rulers of Thailand and their patrimonial household actively sought to develop sources of economic revenue to maintain their position and fend off the acquisitiveness of Western nations. The royal household initially established firms in the primary resource sector; later, after World War II, it used its continued control of these sectors to expand into heavy industries.

The second period (1932–73) began decisively with the coup d'état of 1932, in which junior military officials and civil servants forced the Thai king to accept comprehensive reforms creating a constitutional state. These reforms made the king something of a figurehead in an authoritarian state actually led by the military and bureaucratic arms of government. The authoritarian character of rule changed somewhat after the military coup of 1957, when the country's new leaders instituted a better informed domestic economic program that remained largely focused on import substitution. Military governments, aided by Chinese financiers, established important segments of the basic infrastructure and financial sectors during Thailand's second formative period. State dominance of the infrastructure sector and Chinese dominance of the financial sector continues even today.

The third period began in the 1970s; a convenient date is the 1973 formation of a civilian-led regime. This decade saw the pace of global economic development quicken considerably in Southeast Asia, partly as a result of the economic stimulus caused by the Vietnam War. Taking advantage of new opportunities, entrepreneurs transformed Thailand from a domestic-centred economy based primarily on import substitution policies into an export-oriented, trade-based location in a rapidly developing world economy. All the firms now important in the final manufacturing and food processing sectors came into prominence during this period. While Chinese businesspeople were the main entrepreneurs, their role was quite different from those of the Chinese financiers of the earlier postwar period.

During each of these three periods, capital formation occurred in different sectors and involved different groups of people. Subsequent development in these sectors depended on who controlled the assets and how these assets could be mobilised. I will discuss briefly the institutional foundations of each period and the primary sets of Sino-Thai relationships that contributed to the formation of key business groups. I will then trace the growth of three of the country's largest business groups: the Crown Property Bureau, the Bangkok Bank group and the Charoern Pokphand group. Each dates from a different period of capital formation and has a very different set of linkages to the current global economy.

The patrimonial state and the formation of crown enterprises

Thailand was the only country in Southeast Asia to escape being colonised by a Western country; it is today one of the few countries in the world to retain a traditional monarchy. This outcome can be traced to the second half of the 19th century, the period of greatest threat to Thai sovereignty from the West. At this time, the kings of Siam modernised their regimes, gave Western merchants access to the domestic economy and established an interlinked set of enterprises that monopolised core sectors of the economy. The royal house showed remarkable flexibility in retaining the patrimonial structure of its rule, rooted in loyalty and subservience, while simultaneously transforming the organisation and economic functions of the royal household. This flexibility explains the continuity of the royal household, as well as its current predominance in Thailand's capitalistic economy.

Before 1855, the king and his royal household generated a substantial portion of their total income from a trade-based tributary relationship with Imperial China (Hong 1984, pp. 9–37). The trading system became an essential source of revenue for the royal household, whose ability to tax land and people was severely undermined by the aristocracy's control of these resources. Unable to tax the agrarian economy directly, the royal household created reliable streams of revenue from royal monopolies and from taxes in kind on local products that were then exported to China. These products ranged from tropical lumber, tin ore and sugar to such luxury goods as bird's nests (for bird's nest soup) and ivory. To develop the tributary relationship with China, as well as to achieve distance and independence from the aristocracy, the Thai rulers cultivated a small Chinese minority as a privileged, but dependent, extension of the royal household. Using foreigners to enhance one's power is a political strategy commonly employed by patrimonial regimes (Eisenstadt 1963; Coser 1972; Hamilton 1978), and it was one that the Thai rulers used with considerable success. To the Chinese with whom they had the closest relationships they granted tax farming and trading monopoly licences.[5] Some Chinese became household officials with administrative duties and aristocratic titles. The economic endeavours of the royal house in the establishment of ports and river transportation — undertaken with the assistance of the Chinese — were primarily intended to facilitate the distribution of primary products, some collected through taxation in kind. The economy was embedded in patrimonial practices of patronage, dependency and monopoly.

The inward-directedness of this patrimonial kingdom ended in the mid 19th century, when it became evident that Western powers intended to conquer and colonise wherever possible in the name of free trade. Through abundant good fortune and clever calculation, the Thai kings were able to keep their throne by appearing to embrace the West. In the 1850s, tributary relations with China ended; in their place Western merchants established trading houses in Bangkok. The Western presence disrupted the tight-knit relationship at the top. Royal monopolies on overseas trade ceased. Although a few Chinese remained in royal service, primarily as tax farmers, Chinese merchants no longer exclusively served the royal household (Cushman 1991). Because of their connections in the countryside and some language ability acquired in missionary schools in Bangkok, the tax farming Chinese merchants were increasingly sought out by Western traders as compradors. Interest focused initially on trade in teak, rice and other primary products.

By the 1890s, the royal household's traditional sources of income, mainly tax farming, were in jeopardy (Hong 1984, pp. 111–33). Locked into a disadvantageous position, the king and his household officials searched for new ways to create wealth and preserve the political and economic privileges of the royal family. The Chakkri kings of Bangkok became increasingly intent on expanding their economic role so that they could participate in the emerging trade with the industrialising West. Like earlier kings, they relied on Chinese dependents to make the new strategy work. Using Chinese capital, expertise and labour, the royal household began to claim monopoly ownership, in the modern sense, over Thailand's infrastructure and primary resources. The Thai monarchy revitalised government trading monopolies, granting most of them to Chinese who could serve as brokers with such Western trading firms as Berli Jucker, Sime Darby and the East Asiatic Corporation, all of which continue to be prominent in the Thai economy.

At the end of the century, with patrimony still in full sway, the royal household and selected Chinese families established the first capitalist enterprises (Suehiro 1989). The core of these enterprises was the Privy Purse Bureau, which later became the Crown Property Bureau, the largest landowner and infrastructure conglomerate in Thailand today. Under the direct control of the king, the Privy Purse Bureau began to invest heavily in railways, tramways, shipping, mining, construction and banking, starting one or more firms for each endeavour (Suehiro 1989, p. 93). In each such venture, the royal household pooled its investment with money raised from Chinese who had previously been associated with it. Among the most important enterprises begun in this way were the Siam Commercial Bank and Siam Cement, founded respectively in 1906 and 1913. By the time of the 1932 coup d'état, the royal household had effective control over, and partial ownership of, most of the infrastructure then developed in Thailand.

Although tension and some animosity certainly existed between the Thai kings and the Thai Chinese, the royal household nonetheless relied on its links with selected Chinese families to make the switch from tributary trade and tax farming to managing modern enterprises. In the case of tributary trade, the Chinese had not only been an essential source of connections in China, they had also organised the Bangkok end of the trade and served as up-country tax farmers for most of the more important goods traded (Cushman 1991; Hong 1984). When the kings developed modern enterprises, the Chinese supplied both investment capital and managerial expertise. The Chinese, noted Hong (1984, p. 53), 'understood and accepted the power structure in the country, and sought to make a niche for themselves within that system. This they achieved by making their economic expertise available to those who could promote their well-being'. In the first period of capital formation, the king was the person best able to do this.

Capital mobilisation in the authoritarian state

In 1932, the Thai military toppled the patrimonial state and established a constitutional monarchy in a bloodless coup d'état. The outwardly reformist Thai military rulers removed the king from the exercise of day-to-day power and installed a bureaucracy-centred government led by a dominant political party, the People's Party. As was the case in many countries in the 1930s, the Thai regime was authoritarian, and the mood of the government nationalistic. For the next 40 years, the military and civil service elites, following accepted development theories of the day, further developed the financial and infrastructure sectors on which Thailand's economy is currently based.

Underlying this political shift were significant changes taking place throughout Southeast Asia. For the rapidly industrialising Western countries, the region had become a significant source of primary products, including metal ores such as tin, tropical lumber, tropical oils, tea and rice. Southeast Asia's booming trade-based economies were in the late 19th and early 20th centuries largely controlled by Western colonial powers and core Western merchant houses. A large part of the labour used to run these economies was, however, Chinese. A mass migration of Chinese from southern China had begun in the mid 19th century. Connected through various types of trading associations, regional clubs, secret societies and surname associations, Chinese merchants and petty traders quickly became prominent players in the new trade-based domestic economies of Southeast Asia.

Although Thailand was not colonised, a very similar economic process occurred there as elsewhere. Beginning in the late 19th century, a massive migration of people took place from the Chaoan region (then Teochiu) in southern China to Bangkok. Following lines of existing economic opportunity, these Chinese quickly established themselves in small, commercially oriented businesses, such as the sale of sundry goods, rice trading and milling, native banking and simple manufacturing (alcoholic beverages, soft drinks, bottling plants etc.). These small businesses were not dependent on royal concessions or other favours from the patrimonial state. The size and suddenness of the migration led to a substantial concentration of Chinese in Bangkok, where they soon comprised about half of Bangkok's total population. As described by Skinner (1958) so nicely, the Chinese community focused inwardly upon itself, setting up dialect-based groups, secret societies, and umbrella community associations such as the Chinese Chamber of Commerce. The relations of the new migrants with the Thai majority were strained from the first, and even King Rama VI in 1914 accused the Chinese of being the 'Jews of Asia' (cited in Landon 1941). After 1932, the nationalistic fervour of the military regime further awakened in the Thai people xenophobia about the Chinese minority.

The Chinese consequently had a fundamentally different relationship with the ruling classes after the 1932 revolution than they had hitherto enjoyed. Most of the economically privileged Chinese of the patrimonial state lost their patrons and positions in the second period. 'Indeed', as Suehiro observes, 'it is very rare when one finds the names of the descendants of the prominent tax farmer families in the major industries after the 1932 Revolution' (Suehiro 1989, p. 110). Most of the Chinese who rose to prominence during the nationalist period achieved success as owners of small businesses before becoming important in the Chinese community. These individuals used their standing in the community to become brokers between the Chinese minority and the Thai elites. They were representative of a new type of Sino-Thai relationship that arose as part of the government's attempt to isolate the 'Chinese problem'. Relations between the military and the Chinese were strained, and the channels of communication narrow. Interethnic arm-twisting replaced the patrimonial embrace of earlier times. The Chinese became a national minority who had to be cut off from external alliances and whose resources could be squeezed in the service of the state and of those who represented the state — that is, the military and civil service elites. Chinese intermarriage with members of the Thai elites was rare; as Skinner (1958) shows, alliances through marriage occurred primarily within the Chinese community, helping to build an ethnic solidarity that was unknown in the earlier period and that has largely disappeared today.

The Thai military rulers began to build a national economy. Along with their counterparts in most other countries in the 1930s, Thai leaders believed that local economies were in fact 'national', and that national economies needed to be more or less autonomous and self-sufficient. They further believed that, in order to build such an economy, development needed to be initiated by the state and the ruling party. Accordingly, through government and party channels, the military elite proceeded to claim those infrastructure- and resource-based areas of the economy not already the property of the Thai king, and to set up import substitution industries (Riggs 1967; Suehiro 1989, pp. 122–34). The government also established enterprises owned or controlled by the state to undertake electricity generation, petroleum processing, air transportation (including Thai Airways), telephone and telegraph transmission, and banking (with the exception of the bank already owned by the Crown Property Bureau, the Siam Commercial Bank). So critical were the areas developed during this era that, in 1986, 11 of Thailand's 19 largest companies were still owned by government ministries (Pan Siam Communications 1989).

To generate the financial resources needed to fund their projects, the military elite turned to the national groups having the most capital, particularly in the years after World War II. Foremost among these were the Chinese. The military formed alliances with those Chinese most capable of mobilising resources within their community — the richest and the best connected. Among these were the Lamsam family, which is influential even today. None was more important, however, than the Sophonpanich family, the founders and current owners of the Bangkok Bank.

Internationalisation and the Overseas Chinese connection

Thailand's industrial structure began to change in the late 1960s, largely in response to increased Western involvement in Southeast Asia brought about by the Vietnam War. Until then the focus had been on the domestic economy; activity in the international sphere had been confined mainly to exports of rice and lumber. The country's financial and industrial sectors were largely owned or sponsored by the state. The state-owned portion was split between the Crown Property Bureau and various government agencies controlled by the bureaucratic and military elites. A large part of the state-sponsored portion was in the hands of Chinese businesses. The elites provided these businesses with political support, receiving in return corporate positions and financial rewards.

This system of political patronage was undermined by a series of military coups after 1957 that kept the elites circulating at the top. Now with sizeable financial resources behind them, many Chinese entrepreneurs became less willing to court political favours. Moreover, a coup in 1973, which led to the establishment of a civilian-led regime, resulted in the seizure of the financial assets of many major military figures. This political change in turn initiated the process of disentangling capital formation from political privilege.

These uncertainties in the Thai political climate took place against a background of change in the Asian economy. In the 1960s and 1970s, Japan and then the Asian NIEs (South Korea, Taiwan, Hong Kong and Singapore) became aggressively export oriented. Investment by multinational corporations, both Japanese and Western, in Thailand began to change the structure of the Thai economy in the 1970s. By the end of the decade, Thailand had become a cheap labour platform for firms operating out of Japan, Hong Kong and Singapore. This trend accelerated in the 1980s, completing Thailand's transition from a politically bounded domestic economy to an export-oriented actor in the global economy.

The internationalisation of the Thai economy altered the country's industrial structure, as well as the ownership networks linking firms. The most significant change was the emergence of export-oriented industrial sectors, particularly in large-scale manufacturing and capitalist agriculture. Many firms in the manufacturing sector, including Siam Motors (automobile assembly), Saha Union (textiles) and Sahapathanapibul (consumer goods), owed their growth to the formation of joint ventures with Japanese or US producers, or to contract buying from Western merchandisers. These firms were often part of large industrial conglomerates that began systematically to exploit export opportunities in a wide variety of industries. The formation of these enterprises typically required large amounts of capital, as well as technical knowhow. The domestic financial sector, established in the previous era, provided a major portion of the initial investment required. Such institutions as the Bangkok Bank and the Thai Farmers Bank quickly became the banks of the new industrialists, and the banks themselves added industrial firms to their holdings. They did not, however, provide the entrepreneurial leadership for the internationalisation of the Thai economy. This was supplied instead by a new group of Chinese.

The newest Chinese business groups to emerge in Thailand have taken advantage of Thailand's large and growing pool of cheap skilled labour to establish a wide range of consumer-oriented manufactures. The families leading this industrial surge emigrated to Thailand in the 20th century; they are not part of the old Thai-Chinese community. These relative newcomers have maintained their contacts with Chinese communities in Hong Kong, Singapore, China and Taiwan. Any ties they may have had with the governing Thai elite and Thai royalty have tended to be weak and distant. Most of the new entrepreneurs started out as owners of small businesses that, over time, grew large. The initial capital for these enterprises may have come from joint ventures and bank loans, but their rapid expansion has been funded through alliances with internationally oriented capitalists, usually the Overseas Chinese. Good examples of such groups are the Charoern Pokphand agro-industrial conglomerate (described below) and the Sahapathanapibul group. Smaller groups include the automobile manufacturing enterprises of the Pornprapha family, Siam Motors; the textile conglomerate, Saha Union (a break-off enterprise from SPI); and steel-processing concerns founded on Japanese and Singaporean capital.

Globalisation as illustrated by three business groups

The legacy of Thailand's three periods of capital formation is found in the country's segmented industrial structure. The types of economic controls established at each historical juncture had different foundations, and these became the 'path-dependent' starting points for the establishment of some of Thailand's largest and economically most powerful business groups. Three examples — the Crown Property Bureau, the Bangkok Bank group and the Charoern Pokphand group — will serve to illustrate the path-dependent character of the interlinkages between global commodity chains and embedded networks. Each group was established in a different era and operates in distinct ways; each represents a different type of embedded network with different linkages to the global economy.

The Crown Property Bureau

The 1932 coup substantially changed the royal household's relationship with the state. From being virtually synonymous with government, it was marginalised by the military and bureaucratic elites. This distance was institutionalised in the formation of the Crown Property Bureau. Like the kings, the Bureau was neither strictly public nor strictly private, but existed ambiguously somewhere inbetween.[6] This ambiguity allowed closeness to political power without being tainted by it, and gave the Bureau leverage in government at important times. At the same time, the Bureau's distance from political turmoil permitted it to pursue business strategies independently of national politics. From an early date, the Crown Property Bureau hired professional managers and developed business strategies that would enhance its economic position relative to both the state and the private sector (Yoshihara 1988, p. 243).[7] The professionalisation of the Crown Property Bureau certainly enhanced the success of its firms, but did not result in a diffusion of control: all firms remained firmly under the direction of the royal household and, ultimately, the king. This centralisation of authority, coupled with the absolute legitimacy of the king, promoted the formation of vertically controlled networks, a business strategy actively pursued by the Crown Property Bureau.

The royal household has been able to maintain and even expand its control of some infrastructure sectors of the Thai economy. Today, the Crown Property Bureau is 'perhaps the wealthiest institution in Thailand' (*Far Eastern Economic Review*, 30 June 1988, p. 61) and is one of the foremost promoters of capitalism in Southeast Asia. An important part of its wealth comes from its long-term property holdings in Bangkok and surrounding areas and its financial operations. The main part, however, is derived from vertically integrated industries that supply intermediate products to fill downstream demand. The main industrial arm of the Crown Property Bureau is the Siam Cement group, which accounts for about 40 per cent of the group's total assets.

The core of Siam Cement's five internal subgroups (Yoshihara 1988, p. 243) is the construction materials group, which includes Siam Fibre-Cement, Concrete Products and Aggregate, Siam Iron and Steel, and Thai Ceramic. Firms in this subgroup were established in the 1950s and 1960s, when it was the government's policy to promote import substitution. With the steep increase in demand experienced since the 1970s, these core firms have expanded rapidly. In the mid 1980s, Siam Cement, running at full capacity, controlled over 65 per cent of the market for concrete, this despite the emergence of aggressive competitors.

Capitalising on opportunities that emerged in the 1970s, often through firm acquisitions and joint ventures, Siam Cement quickly diversified from its original emphasis on primary products to become Thailand's foremost producer of intermediate products. The four groups of firms established during this more recent period of growth were a machinery subgroup, consisting of Siam Nawaloha Foundry and Siam Kubota Diesel; a pulp and paper subgroup, headed by Siam Kraft Paper; a petrochemicals subgroup, including Thai Polyethylene, Pacific Plastics and Siam Tyre; and a marketing subgroup comprising the main trading companies of the entire group.

Strong vertical controls and vertical integration go hand in hand. The king provided the locus of control; the monopolisation of a portion of Thailand's natural resources at a crucial juncture in history provided the initial economic foundations for growth; and increasing demand for intermediate products in the Southeast Asian economic environment that contained few equally endowed competitors promoted a strategy of vertical integration. The Crown Property Bureau is the largest privately owned, vertically integrated heavy industry and natural resource based business group in Southeast Asia today.

The Bangkok Bank group

The Bangkok Bank group, like other banking groups formed between 1932 and 1958 (the Thai Farmer's Bank group controlled by the Lamsam family, for example), still bears the imprint of its founding. Part of the Sophonpanich group, the Bangkok Bank is the largest commercial bank in Southeast Asia. Apart from the royal household, Thailand's most influential, powerful, and wealthy business family is that founded by Chin Sophonpanich (1910–88).

Chin Sophonpanich was born to a Chinese father and a Thai mother in Thonburi near Bangkok. His father was a commercial clerk. He received his primary education in Shantou in southern China, returning to Bangkok at age 17. There he worked as a clerk, labourer and noodle seller before establishing his own business, a trading construction materials firm. Later he set up a hardware and canned goods store that engaged in trade with Hong Kong and Singapore. In 1944, using resources from a number of his own businesses and in cooperation with other business associates, Chin helped found and became a director of the Bangkok Bank (Hewison 1989). Immediately after World War II, Chin established several independent gold trading, currency exchange and insurance firms. These became the base for Chin's Asia Trust group, the assets of which he used to elevate his holdings in the Bangkok Bank. He became president of the bank in 1952. In the same year, Thailand's military government, which wished to tap the financial resources of the Chinese community, issued a directive requiring the Chinese to establish three associations, for gold trading, jewellery trading and banking. Chin became the head of the association of commercial bankers.

Using this position, Chin was able to work connections with several military officials to obtain substantial financial backing for the Bangkok Bank from the Ministry of Economic Affairs. In exchange, several generals were appointed to key positions on the bank's Board of Directors. The Ministry of Economic Affairs owned 60 per cent of total shares.

Chin's wealth and important positions gave him a central role in Bangkok's Chinese community in the early 1950s. Skinner (1958) ranked him as the sixth most influential figure in the Chinese community in 1952. In large part this was because of his position as banker, agent and spokesperson with the Chinese community for Police General Phao (Skinner 1958, p. 99). Like other Thai Chinese of his era, Chin took a Thai name, Sophonpanich, and obtained Thai citizenship. At the same time, however, he maintained his identity as an Overseas Chinese. In fact, so close was his attachment to his native region that he built a school (named after his father) in his home village in China. On one occasion, he disavowed his Thai citizenship on a trip to China in order to avoid the Thai military draft, but had it reinstated later (Skinner 1958, pp. 99–100). He was a fervent anticommunist and a strong supporter of the Kuomintang regime in Taiwan.

The period between 1957 and 1973 was a crucial period for the Bangkok Bank, as it was for other Thai banks. In 1957, the military faction that served as Chin's political patron was ousted from power, forcing Chin to flee. He lived in exile in Hong Kong for six years, leaving his son, Chatri, in charge of his Thai business affairs. While in Hong Kong, Chin made aggressive investments in Hong Kong financial markets and established an overseas arm of the Bangkok Bank. (This has recently become very important in the bank's attempt to internationalise its business.) Chin returned to Thailand in 1963, a time when the Thai economy was slowly starting to expand. The government had relaxed its anti-Chinese laws and had introduced laws allowing Chinese to obtain Thai citizenship more easily. Less subject to threats of arrest and deportation in the new political climate, Chin gradually began to increase his holding in the Bangkok Bank. By 1968, the Sophonpanich family held more shares then the government. The family holding was further augmented when Chin was able to gain control of the shares held by military leaders forced into exile in the coup of 1973. Suehiro's (1989, p. 247) analysis shows that the family controlled 32 per cent of the bank in 1982, compared with the government's 8.1 per cent. By placing a succession of powerful government figures on the Board of Directors, however, the government remained influential in bank affairs.

In the 1970s and 1980s the Bangkok Bank group rapidly expanded its sphere of influence. Although now greatly diversified, the group's major holdings remain in the financial sector and are still managed by Chin's sons.[8] Many of these firms have expanded in recent years to become international in scope. The group itself, though, reflects a time when Thailand's economy was more enclosed and tightly regulated. Like others formed in the same era, the Bangkok Bank group was the product of an alliance between the Chinese and the military based, according to Suehiro (1989), on mutual interest:

Chinese capitalists were able to obtain business security, official privileges, and in some cases government contracts in exchange for promises to the military groups of stock gratuities and director's posts in their firms. The military group, on the other hand, could utilise Chinese managerial skills, commercial acumen, capital funds, and established commercial networks in exchange for providing political patronage (Suehiro 1989, p. 170).

The family business groups that grew from these political foundations continue to benefit from, as well as to be channelled by, the restraints established at the outset. Although they have increasingly expanded into the international arena in recent years, they remain rooted in the Thai economy and in domestic business networks (Gray 1991).

The Charoern Pokphand group

In 1994, Charoern Pokphand, Thailand's biggest transactional business group, was one of the largest investors (or possibly the largest investor) in China. It was founded by two brothers, Chia Ek Chor and Chia Seow Nooy, the younger of whom (Seow Nooy) migrated from Shantou in Guangdong province to Bangkok as early as 1917.[9] Even so, the group's core firms did not begin to grow rapidly until the early 1970s. In the intervening years the two brothers ran a struggling seed business that specialised in the 1950s in supplying animal feed, especially for chickens. In the 1960s they came up with a formula for combining chicken breeding with feedmilling, which they implemented in cooperation with Arbor Acres, a firm in the Rockefeller group. This formula proved so successful that by 1969 the company had turnover of US$1–2 million.

From about 1970 the nature of the business began to change, as banks finally realised the potential for agriculture and food processing. One of the turning points came when the Bangkok Bank asked the firm to take over a bankrupt chicken farm. The brothers' strategy evolved to include loaning farmers money, helping them build infrastructure and teaching them how to raise chickens. Charoern Pokphand would supply farmers with poultry and feed, then buy back and market the grown chickens. The entire operation depended on successful marketing to large-scale buyers — such as grocery stores, restaurants and fast food franchises. From a ratio of one farmer to 10,000 chickens early on, in recent years the Charoern Pokphand group has had a ratio of one farmer to 50,000 chickens. In part, the group owed its initial growth to a policy of the Central Bank of Thailand that a certain percentage of banks' loan portfolios be in the agricultural sector. Because the Charoern Pokphand group was a relatively safe bet, government banks fulfilled this obligation by channelling money to the group, which would then loan it to the farmers.

What was safe for the banks and good for Thai farmers also proved very advantageous for the Charoern Pokphand group, which began to expand into other countries in the 1970s. Indonesia was its first production location, followed by Taiwan, China, Turkey, Portugal and the Philippines. In each country, the same formula was applied: the integration of feedmills, chicken breeding and contract farming, followed by poultry processing and marketing. As before, the marketing end of the commodity chain drove production.

By the 1980s, a number of firms were actively seeking joint ventures with the Charoern Pokphand group. In 1982–83, the group applied its formula for chicken to the raising of shrimp in central Thailand. In 1987, drawing on close connections in China, it set up a motorcycle joint venture and a beer brewing facility in Shanghai. The motorcycles were made under licence from Honda, and the beer under licence from Heineken. Also in 1987, the group obtained the Seven Eleven and Kentucky Fried Chicken franchises for Thailand and established the Makro retail store chain. In 1989 it entered the petrochemicals business through a joint venture with Solvay, the Belgium firm. In August 1992, it signed a contract to construct Thailand's telecommunications infrastructure. Worth US$3 billion, this is one of the world's largest privately owned public works projects. In 1994 it signed a joint venture agreement with Wal-Mart to establish super-retail stores throughout East and Southeast Asia.

Despite the diversity of the group's current business activities, all of its firms are run in a similar fashion. Each relies on networks of independent producers, independent investors, or both. Most of the group's manufacturing activities are based on joint ventures and subcontracting. In the late 1980s the Charoern Pokphand group reorganised its diversified global holdings into nine functional areas, all run from its headquarters in Bangkok. The group now relies heavily on professional managers. Although it stresses that it is not run as a family business, many relatives are employed in the group's firms, and all sons sit on the Board of Directors. Dhanin and Sument Chiaravanont, sons of the elder brother, make all the decisions.[10] The other sons own shares in the group, none of which are traded.

In contrast to the vertical integration of the Crown Property Bureau, the Charoern Pokphand group emphasises diversified holdings that rely on horizontal networks linking independent producers and investors into commodity chains that are responsive to consumer demand, that is, to the merchandising end of the chain. The group owes its rapid growth to deal making, a quintessential characteristic of the Overseas Chinese entrepreneur.

Conclusion

How, then, do global commodity chains and embedded ownership networks intersect in the organisation of the Thai economy? This chapter has provided some answers. Throughout all three periods studied, certain Chinese economic practices have been consistently important. These include family as the basis of enterprise organisation, patriarchal authority, partible inheritance, political alliances, and a high regard for the education of one's offspring. But these practices do not in themselves explain Chinese interfirm networks or the organisation of Chinese firms (Hamilton and Waters 1995).

We have seen that Chinese networks and Chinese-run firms are not uniform, but themselves constrained and channelled by the institutional environments in which the Chinese do business. As Skinner (1995) and others (Wickberg 1994; Hamilton 1977) have argued, the Chinese adapted differently to each of the Southeast Asian societies in which they settled. This conclusion is equally true for Thailand, and is seen in the enduring differences in the structure and business strategies of the Chinese business organisations that have characterised each formative period in Thailand's economic development. Established in part with Chinese capital and managed by Chinese, the Crown Property Bureau differs widely from all other major business groups in its size, centralisation and depth of vertical integration. Managed and now owned by a leading Chinese entrepreneurial family, the Bangkok Bank nonetheless retains its close identification with Thai elites and with the Thai domestic economy. To the Thai people, it is Thailand's bank, the bank of the royal household, and not 'Chinese' at all (Gray 1991). The bank has responded by developing a strategy of intensive localisation, in addition to pursuing its regional ambitions in Southeast Asia. The Chinese business groups of the third period, however, are linked directly in global commodity chains. The Charoern Pokphand group produces and markets chicken, beer and motorbikes globally, with the marketing end driving business. Not every Chinese business group of the third period is as diversified and independent as Charoern Pokphand, but all are linked extensively to global commodity chains through subcontracting and merchandising arrangements.

Judging from this analysis of the Chinese in Thailand, Chinese businesses can be said to take diverse forms depending on the environment in which they arise. The chapter has shown that Thailand's present industrial structure reflects and continues to be shaped by its historical origins. Different sectors of the economy have developed at different times, under very different institutional conditions. Although enterprises have changed with the times, they nonetheless carry their historical legacy with them — for instance, in the specific patterns of ownership and control that provide the baselines from which new decisions are made.

During the first major period of capital formation in modern Thailand, the royal household, as the patrimonial centre of the political system, claimed control over and developed substantial portions of the country's infrastructure. While Chinese networks were significant in the development and continuation of the Crown Property Bureau, they remained subservient to the authority of the king and to the king's control of important sectors of the economy. That control continues today. Profits from the Crown Property Bureau's enterprises have been ploughed back into the Thai economy to create an investment portfolio that 'holds stakes in about 40 companies, which span a wide spectrum of business activities, ranging from hotels and offshore mining to car assembly and office machines' (*Far Eastern Economic Review*, 30 June 1988, p. 61)

During the second major period of capital formation, the military government systematically developed additional portions of Thailand's infrastructure as well as import substitution industries. The firms it established rank high in sales and profits, and as they modernise and privatise they will operate outside the effective control of the Crown, as well as Chinese business groups. While military governments focused on developing the country's infrastructure, several Chinese families patronised by the elite created unassailable positions for themselves in the financial sector. Some of their accumulated capital was used to fund government projects. However, with the end of the military era at hand, large Chinese banking groups began to consolidate their ownership, diversify, and fund Thailand's export-oriented industrialisation. Each of the major banking groups now has a substantial stake in Thailand's industrial economy, through direct ownership and management of industries and, more importantly, through portfolio investments across industries.

In the most recent era of capital formation, a new group of entrepreneurs has emerged. Basing themselves on core non-financial business areas that have developed only since 1970, these entrepreneurs have been quick to take advantage of opportunities to establish linkages beyond the Thai economy. The new businesspeople, mainly Overseas Chinese, have joined a set of global entrepreneurs operating across national political boundaries. In recent years, Overseas Chinese networks have proved to be among the wealthiest foreign investors in the world, and the ones most aggressively bent on expansion (*Institutional Investor*, August 1991, pp. 29–43; Mackie 1992). For example, Thailand's largest multinational corporation, the Charoern Pokphand group, has companies whose shares are listed on stock exchanges in no less than eight countries.

In all three periods of capital formation, specific networks of Chinese and Thais were linked by mutual economic and political interests. In the first two periods Thailand's political economy dictated the nature of the interrelationship. The patrimonial structure of the first period turned the Chinese into a privileged, politically dependent ethnic group. The nationalistic and authoritarian structure of the second period made the Chinese community a subservient minority whose leaders became brokers with the political authorities. The network structure that developed in the third period, however, has changed Thailand's economic structure in decisive ways. Rather than being bound directly by political authority, Chinese entrepreneurs have internationalised their economic pursuits, integrated their interests in the global economy, and developed global networks capable of mobilising vast resources in a short span of time (*Institutional Investor*, August 1991, pp. 29–43; Mackie 1992). Wherever they do business, the Overseas Chinese are less bound now by domestic politics than they have been at any time in the past.

Notes

1   The main components of this conceptualisation were developed separately. Gereffi (1992) developed a typology of global commodity chains (described below) that makes clear distinctions between the economic factors influencing the formation of economic networks. Hamilton and Biggart (1988), Hamilton and Kao (1990) and Orrù, Biggart and Hamilton (1991) investigated ownership structure, or what they call 'embedded networks'. This collaborative research showed that all of the capitalist East Asian economies were densely networked in terms of ownership. Despite considerable uniformity in network configurations within each economy, however, there were considerable differences in configurations between economies. In trying to explain these differences in a comparative and historical fashion, the

authors argued that the exact configuration resulted from characteristics embedded in the society in question, such as kinship and inheritance practices and patterns of interpersonal relationships.

2　This section draws extensively on Gereffi and Hamilton (1992) and Gereffi (1994).

3　Another example was provided by Henderson (1989), who showed that the US semiconductor industry has maintained some control of the sector by establishing an East Asian division of labour.

4　This section draws on Hamilton and Waters (1995).

5　Chinese businessmen who were permitted to engage in these early enterprises had necessarily had a background in the administration of the patrimonial state — for example, through tax farming or the administration of peripheral provinces, labour corvees and opium concessions. The Chinese minority's special relationship with the Crown brought with it rights and privileges, for example, free movement within the kingdom, exemption from royal service (labour corvees), a monopoly on foreign trade, and payment of taxes in cash instead of kind.

6　Paisal Sricharatchanya cites one of the Bureau's directors as saying: 'Our charter appears to highlight the image of a public entity. But we also enjoy flexibility similar to (but not totally on a par with) a private enterprise' (*Far Eastern Economic Review*, 30 June 1988, p. 61).

7　It is worth noting that some Chinese and European capital and a great deal of Chinese commercial and managerial expertise went into the formation of the Crown Property Bureau. Unlike its links with military figures in the early 1950s, however, the Chinese community's connections with the royal household did not lead to the creation of independent, industrially oriented Chinese families. Once-prominent tax farming families such as the Khaws (Cushman 1991) lost their privileges and were largely absorbed into Thai society. A few Chinese families closely connected with the royal family in the 1920s — members of the Sarasin family, for example (Suehiro 1989) — served as managers of Siam Cement and other firms. Later, however, these families were associated more with the political than the industrial development of Thailand.

8　Chin groomed his sons carefully to take over the family businesses. His second son, Chatri (b. 1934), inherited his father's position at the Bangkok Bank and is today one of Thailand's most prominent businesspeople. Unlike other major Thai business figures, though, he was educated in Shantou in southern China and in Hong Kong. (His younger brothers and sister were educated in a combination of elite Thai schools, Australian elementary schools, and British and American universities.) In 1986, three of Chin's sons held positions on the Bangkok Bank's Board of Directors. A fourth, Chai, was director of Bangkok First Investment and Trust, and a fifth, Cherdchu, was a major figure in Bangkok First Investment and Trust, as well as a director of Asia Insurance (Hong Kong).

9　The history of the Charoern Pokphand group is based on interviews with several of Chia Seow Nooy's sons.

10　Around 1965, the family took Thai names to avoid the prejudice they experienced from Thai officials. Chiaravanont is a Thai version of the family's Chinese name.

References

Biggart, Nicole Woolsey 1990, 'Institutionalised Patrimonialism in Korean Business', *Comparative Social Research*, 12, pp. 113–33.

Chandler, Alfred D. Jr 1977, *The Visible Hand: The Managerial Revolution in American Business*, Cambridge, MA: Harvard University.

_____ 1990, *Scale and Scope: The Dynamics of Industrial Capitalism*, Cambridge, MA: Harvard University.

Chandler, Alfred D. Jr and Herman Daems (eds) 1980, *Managerial Hierarchies: Comparative Perspective on the Rise of the Modern Industrial Enterprise*, Cambridge, MA: Harvard University Press.

Coser, Lewis 1972, 'The Alien as a Servant of Power: Court Jews and Christian Renegades', *American Journal of Sociology*, 37, pp. 574–80.

Cushman, Jennifer 1991, *Family and State: The Formation of a Sino-Thai Tin-Mining Dynasty, 1797–1932*, Oxford: Oxford University Press.

Cusumano, Michael A. 1985, *The Japanese Automobile Industry: Technology and Management at Nissan and Toyota*, Cambridge, MA: Harvard University Press.

Dicken, Peter 1992, *Global Shift: The Internationalisation of Economic Activity*, New York: Guilford Press.

Doner, Richard F. 1991, *Driving a Bargain: Automobile Industrialisation and Japanese Firms in Southeast Asia*, Berkeley, CA: University of California Press.

Eisenstadt, S.N. 1963, *The Political Systems of Empires*, New York: Free Press.

Feenstra, Robert C., Tzu-han Yang and Gary G. Hamilton 1993, 'Market Structure and International Trade: Business Groups in East Asia', National Bureau of Economic Research Working Paper Series, No. 4536, Davis, CA: University of California.

Gereffi, Gary 1994, 'The Role of Big Buyers in Global Commodity Chains: How U.S. Retail Networks Affect Overseas Production Patterns', in Gary Gereffi and Miguel Korzeniewicz (eds), *Commodity Chains and Global Capitalism*, Westport, CT: Greenwood Press, pp. 95–122.

Gereffi, Gary and Gary G. Hamilton 1992, Modes of Incorporation in an Industrial World: The Social Economy of Global Capitalism, Unpublished paper presented at the Annual Meeting of the American Sociological Association, Pittsburgh, Pennsylvania, August.

Gereffi, Gary and Miguel Korzeniewicz 1994, *Commodity Chains and Global Capitalism*, Westport, CT: Praeger.

Gerlach, Michael 1992a, *Alliance Capitalism: The Strategic Organization of Japanese Business*, Berkeley, CA: University of California Press.

_____ 1992b, Economic Organization and Innovation in Japan, Unpublished paper.

Girling, John 1981, *Thailand, Society and Politics*, Ithaca, NY: Cornell University Press.

Gray, Christine E. 1991, 'Hegemonic Images: Language and Silence in the Royal Thai Polity', *Man* (new series), 26, pp. 43–65.

Hamilton, Gary G. 1978, 'Pariah Capitalism: A Paradox of Power and Dependence', *Ethnic Groups: An International Periodical of Ethnic Studies*, 2, Spring, pp. 1–15.

_____ 1977, 'Ethnicity and Regionalism: Some Factors Influencing Chinese Identities in Southeast Asia', *Ethnicity*, 4, pp. 337–51.

_____ (ed.) 1991, *Business Networks and Economic Development in East and Southeast Asia*, Hong Kong: Centre of Asian Studies, University of Hong Kong.

Hamilton, Gary G. and Nicole Woolsey Biggart 1988, 'Market, Culture, and Authority: A Comparative Analysis of Mangement and Organization in the Far East', *American Journal of Sociology*, 94 (Supplement), pp. S52–94.

Hamilton, Gary G. and Robert Feenstra 1995, 'Varieties of Hierarchies and Their Market Structures', *Industrial and Corporate Change*, 4(1) (forthcoming).

Hamilton, Gary G. and Cheng-shu Kao 1990, 'The Institutional Foundations of Chinese Business: The Family Firm in Taiwan', *Comparative Social Research*, 12, pp. 95–112.

Hamilton, Gary G. with Tony Waters (1995), 'Chinese Capitalism in Thailand', in Anthony Reid and Daniel Chirot (eds), *Entrepreneurial Minorities in the Modern Transformation of Europe and Southeast Asia* (forthcoming).

Henderson, Jeffery 1989, *The Globalisation of High Technology Production: Society, Space and Semiconductors in the Restructuring of the Modern World*, New York: Routledge.

Hewison, Kevin 1989, *Bankers and Bureaucrats: Capital and the Role of the State in Thailand*, Monograph Series 34, New Haven, CO: Yale Centre for International and Area Studies.

Hong, Lysa 1984, *Thailand in the Nineteenth Century: Evolution of the Economy and Society*, Singapore: Institute of Southeast Asian Studies.

Jorgensen, Jan J., Taieb Hafsi and Moses N. Kiggundu 1986, 'Towards a Market Imperfections Theory of Organisational Structure in Developing Countries', *Journal of Management Studies*, 24(4), pp. 419–42.

King, Ambrose Yeo-chi 1991, '*Kuan-Hsi* and Network Building: A Sociological Interpretation', *Daedalus*, 120(2), pp. 63–84.

Landon, Kenneth Perry 1941, *The Chinese in Thailand*, New York: Russell and Russell.

Leff, Nathaniel 1977, 'Capital Markets in the Less Developed Countries: The Group Principle', in Ronald I. McKinnon (ed.), *Money and Finance in Economic Growth and Development: Essays in Honor of Edward S. Shaw*, New York: Dekker, pp. 97–122.

_____ 1978, 'Industrial Organisation and Entrepreneurship in the Developing Countries: The Economic Groups', *Economic Development and Cultural Change*, 26(4), pp. 661–75.

Liu, Paul C., Ying-Chuan Liu and Hui-Lin Wu 1993, 'The Manufacturing Enterprise and Management in Taiwan', Discussion Paper No. 9304, Institute of Economics, Academia Sinica, Taipei.

Mackie, Jamie 1992, 'Changing Patterns of Chinese Big Business in Southeast Asia', in Ruth McVey (ed.), *Southeast Asian Capitalists*, Ithaca, NY: Cornell University Southeast Asia Program.

Numazaki, Ichiro 1991, 'The Role of Personal Networks in the Making of Taiwan's *Guanxiqiye* [Related Enterprises]', in Gary Hamilton (ed.), *Business Networks and Economic Development in East and Southeast Asia*, Hong Kong: Centre of Asian Studies, University of Hong Kong.

_____ 1993, 'The *Tainanbang*: The Rise and Growth of a Banana-Bunch-Shaped Business Group in Taiwan', *The Developing Economies*, 31(4), pp. 485–510.

Orrù, Marco, Nicole Biggart and Gary G. Hamilton 1991, 'Organizational Isomorphism in East Asia: Broadening the New Institutionalism', in Walter W. Powell and Paul J. DiMaggio (eds), *The New Institutionalism in Organizational Analysis*, Chicago, IL: University of Chicago Press, pp. 361–89.

Orrù, Marco, Gary G. Hamilton and Mariko Suzuki 1989, 'Patterns of Inter-Firm Control in Japanese Business', *Organization Studies*, 10(4), pp. 549–74.

Pan Siam Communications Co. Ltd 1989, *Million Baht Business Information*, Bangkok.

Redding, S.C. 1990, *The Spirit of Chinese Capitalism*, Berlin: Walter de Gruyter.

Riggs, Fred 1967, *Thailand, The Modernization of a Bureaucratic Polity*, Honolulu: East-West Centre Press.

Scherer, R.M. and David Ross 1990, *Industrial Market Structure and Economic Performance*, Third edition, Boston, MA: Houghton Mifflin Company.

Skinner, G. William 1958, *Leadership and Community in the Chinese Community of Thailand*, Ithaca, NY: Cornell University Press.

_____ 1995, 'Creolized Chinese Societies in Southeast Asia', in Anthony Reid (ed.), *Strangers, Sojourners, and Settlers: Southeast Asia and the Chinese* (forthcoming).

Suehiro, Akira 1989, *Capital Accumulation in Thailand, 1855–1985*, Tokyo: Centre for East Asian Cultural Studies.

Wickberg, Edgar 1994, 'The Chinese as Overseas Migrants', in Judith Brown and Rosemary Foot (eds), *Migration, The Asian Experience*, London: Macmillan.

Wong, Siu-lin 1985, 'The Chinese Family Firm: A Model', *British Journal of Sociology*, 36, pp. 58–72.

Yang, Mayfair Mei-hui 1989, 'The Gift Economy and State Power in China', *Comparative Studies in Society and History*, 31(1), January, pp. 40–1.

Yao, Souchou 1987, 'The Fetish of Relationships: Chinese Business Transactions in Singapore', *Sojourn*, 2, pp. 89–111.

Yoshihara, Kunio 1988, *The Rise of Ersatz Capitalism in South-East Asia*, Oxford: Oxford University Press.

6 On the causes of low levels of FDI in Japan

Ryuhei Wakasugi

In the 1980s and early 1990s, foreign direct investment (FDI) in the United States, Europe, Asia and other regions increased sharply. OECD data indicate that foreign investment by OECD countries has risen four to five times in the past decade (OECD 1993),[1] far more than the increase during that period in the volume of international trade. In contrast to the rising penetration by foreign firms of other countries, FDI in the Japanese market remains remarkably low. This has often been the subject of criticism at bilateral trade negotiations — at the US–Japan talks on Structural Impediments Initiatives (SII) in 1989–90, for example. European countries have also raised the issue, citing it as evidence of a closed Japanese market. In response to such complaints, the Japanese government committed itself to action to liberalise procedures for FDI in Japan in addition to offering financial incentives to foreign firms to encourage them to invest in Japan. It also issued a formal policy statement to the effect that it welcomed direct investment in Japan.

From discouraging all forms of FDI from abroad in the earlier postwar period, the Japanese government has gradually altered its policy direction so that it now actively encourages foreign firms to enter the Japanese market. Recent policy does not, however, seem to be derived from a careful consideration of the facts. I propose to examine here the causes of the low level of entry of foreign firms, patterns of foreign investment in Japan and the policy implications of an expansion of FDI.

Some facts about FDI

Statistics on FDI in Japan are of two sorts: data on long-term capital inflows contained in *Balance of Payments Statistics* published by the Bank of Japan; and data on recent FDI notifications recorded in *Statistics of FDI Notifications* issued annually by the

The author gratefully acknowledges the comments of Richard Caves, Hugh Patrick, Denis Simon, Ippei Yamazawa and other participants at the 21st PAFTAD Conference in Hong Kong.

Ministry of Finance. Figure 6.1 shows the value of FDI over the past two decades according to each of these sources.

In general, the notifications data give a higher value for FDI than balance of payments data; this is unsurprising given that the former show the gross value of all FDI notifications and the latter only the net inflow of foreign capital. Data on notifications do not tell us whether firms registering an interest in FDI actually carry out their plans, nor do they indicate the extent of withdrawal of foreign firms from the Japanese market. (The significant widening of the gap between notifications and capital inflows in the late 1980s seen in Figure 6.1 can in fact be attributed to the

Figure 6.1   **FDI in Japan: net inflow of foreign capital and FDI notifications, 1970–92 (US$ million)**

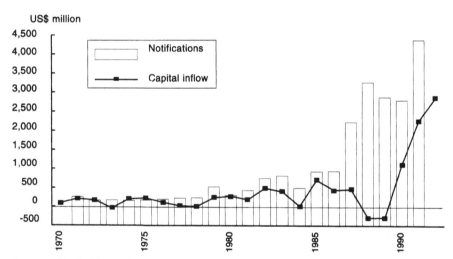

Source: Bank of Japan, *Balance of Payments Statistics*, Tokyo, various issues; Ministry of Finance, *Statistics of FDI Notifications*, Tokyo, various issues.

successive withdrawal of foreign firms.) The data on notifications are, however, informative about the number of foreign firms intending to enter the Japanese market and the value of FDI by industry, data not available in *Balance of Payments Statistics*. The data indicate that there was a gradual increase in FDI notifications until 1980 and a rapid rise in most subsequent years.

Figure 6.2 shows FDI in the manufacturing and other sectors from 1971 to 1991. The average annual growth rate of FDI throughout the 1980s was 42.6 per cent for manufacturing industry, 42.6 per cent for wholesale and retail industry, and 55.9 per

Figure 6.2 **FDI in Japan by sector, 1971–91 (US$ million)**

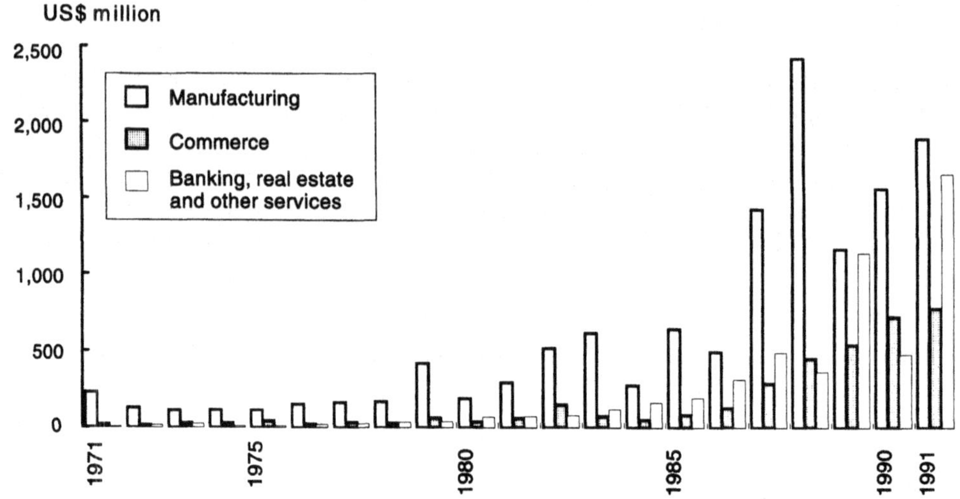

Source: Bank of Japan, *Balance of Payments Statistics,* Tokyo, various issues; Ministry of Finance, *Statistics of FDI Notifications,* Tokyo, various issues.

cent for other non-manufacturing industry (compared with 9.4 per cent, 18.4 per cent and 46 per cent respectively in the 1970s).

In the second half of the 1980s, FDI rose not only in Japan but in the United States and Europe as well. As shown in Figure 6.3, FDI as a share of GNP increased more rapidly in the United States, the United Kingdom and France than it did in Japan. Compared with international levels, FDI in Japan remains low. The ratio of FDI inflow to GNP in Japan is 0.1–0.2 per cent: one-tenth the ratio in the United States, the United Kingdom and France, and about the same as in Germany. There is also a large disparity between Japan and other countries in the ratio of outward to inward FDI stocks, as described by Mason in chapter 7.

Causes of low levels of FDI in Japan

Legacy of past regulations

FDI was restricted for many years under the Foreign Exchange and Foreign Trade Control Law established in 1949 and the Foreign Capital Control Law enacted in 1950. Throughout the 1950s, FDI was permitted only in the rare instances in which it might benefit the industry concerned. With its acceptance in 1963 of Article 8 of the

Figure 6.3   International comparison of FDI inflows, 1982–91 (per cent of GNP)

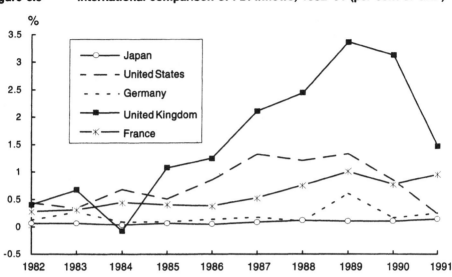

Source: OECD, *International Direct Investment Statistics Yearbook,* Paris, 1993.

IMF Agreement and its admission to the OECD in 1964, Japan was forced to relax its stance on FDI: investment was henceforth to be prohibited only in industries identified as being in need of protection. In this way, the government was able to maintain its policy of promoting selected infant industries. In order to fulfil its obligations under the OECD Code for Liberalisation of Foreign Capital Transactions, the Japanese government announced further concessions on the movement of foreign capital five times between 1967 and 1973. On each occasion, it not only presented affected industries with the proposed schedule of liberalisation in advance of the announce-ment, it also softened the blow by offering them low interest loans and preferential tax treatment. Regulations remained in place to protect infant industries throughout this period.

Liberalisation was carried out in such a way that many obstacles continued to lie in the path of foreign firms hoping to invest in Japan. They were thus effectively denied access to the Japanese market at the optimal time: while they still maintained a technological and managerial advantage over their Japanese counterparts. By the time foreign firms were able to gain access to the Japanese market, domestic firms were no longer at a disadvantage in these respects. Many of the most prominent foreign affiliates currently operating in Japan — including a number of petroleum firms, IBM and Texas Instruments — first entered the market shortly after World War II. The situation for FDI in Japan would be very different today if regulations had not kept foreign firms out of the market for several decades. This legacy even now has a negative effect on levels of FDI in Japan.

Current regulations and business practices

FDI was liberalised substantially in 1980 when the Foreign Capital Control Law was abolished and some of its contents absorbed under the Foreign Exchange and Foreign Trade Control Law. In the new regulations, the principle of access to Japanese markets through FDI was finally accepted (although in fact regulations were already being applied less strictly from as early as the late 1970s). The rise in FDI that followed the relaxation of controls in 1980 can be seen in Figure 6.1.

It should not be forgotten that FDI in Japan was and still is restricted by many other kinds of government regulations. The code for the transportation and telecommunications industries, for example, contains a discriminatory article on foreign ownership. The banking, insurance and distribution industries have to comply with detailed regulations on their business operations in the domestic market which, although not directly discriminatory, make it difficult and expensive for foreign firms to enter these markets.

Of course, regulation of specific industries is not peculiar to Japan; the United States and European countries also control business activity in key industries in this way. Some businesspeople may exaggerate the effects of regulations, using them as an excuse for their own failure to succeed in Japan. Interestingly, a number of successful foreign firms are reported to favour some Japanese regulation.

Factors other than regulations have played a part in determining Japan's levels of FDI. The petroleum industry, for example, has a high proportion of foreign ownership. Apart from the fact that major foreign oil companies invested in Japan long before the implementation of government regulations, vertical integration also ensures that only they can supply crude oil to Japan.

There are several ways to invest in a foreign country. One attractive alternative to greenfield investment is to merge with or acquire an existing firm. Mergers and acquisitions are an effective short cut for firms seeking to enter an unfamiliar market in that they enable the investor to take advantage of existing systems of employment, procurement of intermediate goods, marketing and sales, and financing. A large proportion of Japanese FDI abroad in the 1980s took the form of mergers and acquisitions.

The share of mergers and acquisitions in total FDI in the Japanese market is far smaller than it is in the United States and Europe. Even among large Japanese firms, however, mergers and acquisitions are rare. The explanation for this is found not in regulations but in peculiarities of the Japanese management system. Japanese firms tolerate little shareholder interference in the running of a company. They actively seek to cultivate a stable group of shareholders who are supportive of management and unlikely to sell their interest in the firm to a third party. In the SII talks between the

United States and Japan, the US government argued that restrictions on takeover bids under Japan's Security Transactions Law were a major impediment to mergers and acquisitions. In 1990 the Japanese government amended the law so as to make Japanese and US procedures for takeover bids almost the same. Despite this, the number of mergers and acquisitions has not increased, for the reasons cited above. Takeover bids for two companies, Sankyo Seiki and Miyairi Valve, were unsuccessful, not for institutional reasons but because they were actively opposed by managers and employees. The well-known case of a takeover bid for Koito Company by Boon Pikens failed for the same reason: Koito's managers objected to the idea of a new shareholder interfering with management. The difficulty of merging with or acquiring Japanese firms can be said to constitute a non-institutional barrier to the participation of foreign firms in the Japanese market.

Changes in market conditions

The attractiveness of investing in Japan is determined by relative changes in market conditions (such as exchange and wage rates) between Japan and other countries. The effect on FDI in Japan of market conditions is discussed here using the following simple model. A foreign firm carrying out FDI is assumed to be able to exploit its technological and managerial advantage to command a monopolistic position in the Japanese market. Of course, the foreign firm may prefer to export its goods produced in the home country to Japan. The firm thus faces a choice between exporting and local production through FDI. Which alternative it chooses will depend on where the maximum profit is to be made. For simplicity, we assume that there is only one commodity and one firm without competitors in the market.[2]

To produce a commodity in the home market and export it to Japan, the foreign firm must procure labour, capital and other production factors in the home country market, apply specific production technology, and pay transportation costs and any import duties. The maximum profit the foreign firm can make in the Japanese market is therefore determined by the price elasticity of demand (it is assumed here that the foreign firm faces a given demand elasticity), production factor prices, transportation costs, and the cost generated by any trade-restrictive measures. The maximum profit the same foreign firm can make by operating in Japan is determined by the price elasticity of demand and production factor prices in the Japanese market, assuming that the same production technology is used as in the home market and that all production factors are procured in each market. Although the foreign firm can save on transportation costs and import duties by producing in Japan, because of its unfamiliarity with the local market it may incur additional charges for such things as information collection, advertising, and rental of buildings and factories.

Whether it exports to Japan or produces locally, the firm's profit will be determined by market parameters (exchange rates, production factor prices, transportation costs, degree of trade restrictions, additional costs of local production etc.). Its decision will, therefore, ultimately be determined by changes in those parameters.

The following conclusions about the behaviour of foreign firms can be derived from study of changes in the market parameters.

1   If the home currency depreciates, the firm will shift operations from FDI to exporting.

2   If factor prices in the home market rise, the firm will shift from exporting to FDI. Conversely, if factor prices in Japan rise, the firm will shift from FDI to exporting.

3   If tariffs rise or import quotas become more restrictive in Japan, the firm will shift from exporting to FDI.

4   If the additional costs of FDI increase, the firm will shift from FDI to exporting.

5   If managerial resources accumulate at a given fixed cost, the firm will shift from exporting to FDI.

The above results satisfy the sign of the ratio of local production (Lp) to exporting (Ex) with regard to change in each variable (e, w_d, w_f, t, FC_f), as follows:

$$\overset{(-)\ \ (+)\ \ (-)\ \ (+)\ \ (-)}{\frac{Lp}{Ex} = F(e, w_d, w_f, t,\ FC_f)}$$

where: e =   exchange rate (expressed in terms of the home currency);

w_d =   price of input factors in the home country;

w_f =   price of input factors in Japan;

t =   a parameter expressing the difference in product price between Japan and the foreign market due to trade restrictions; and

FC_f=   additional costs incurred through operating in Japan.

Table 6.1 shows movements in exchange rates, wage rates and rental costs in the United States and Japan from 1975 to 1991. The following conclusions can be reached by applying these to the model.

1   A strong appreciation of the Japanese yen against the US dollar had a negative effect on the FDI of US firms in Japan.

2   Rising wages in Japan in the latter half of the 1980s had a negative effect on FDI, although wages had been rising at a faster rate in the United States than in Japan in the early 1980s.

3   The difference in rental costs between the United States and Japan had a negative effect on FDI in the second half of the 1980s.

118

Table 6.1   **Changes in market parameters in the United States and Japan, 1975–91 (per cent)**

	Exchange rate	Wage rate			Rent		
	(¥/US$)	Japan	US	Difference	Japan	US	Difference
1975–91	3.88	5.41	5.65	-0.24	4.83	5.07	-0.24
1976–80	5.47	8.00	8.57	-0.57	7.99	8.12	-0.13
1981–85	-0.64	4.03	5.61	-1.59	3.94	4.87	-0.93
1986–90	7.64	3.76	2.57	1.19	3.76	3.18	0.58

Source: IMF, *International Financial Statistics*, various issues; US Dept of Labor, *Monthly Labor Review*, various issues.

The cost of finance does not seem to have been a crucial factor in FDI, probably because international firms can borrow money in whatever country provides the most favourable conditions.

In the mid 1980s to early 1990s, FDI abroad by Japanese firms increased sharply. In this period Japanese firms shifted their production bases overseas — to the United States, Europe and Asia — at a faster pace than at any other time. This movement, viewed as the 'de-industrialisation' or hollowing out of the Japanese economy, has caused serious concern. The drastic changes in economic conditions that brought about this alteration in the business behaviour of Japanese firms have also made FDI in Japan a less attractive proposition.

Determinants of the pattern of FDI

Technological advantage

It is well known that comparative advantage is determined, among other things, by differences in technological level, and that gains in international trade are realised even when there is no difference in factor endowment between two countries. This theoretical argument can be adapted to the case of FDI. Under given market conditions, technological skills and managerial knowhow will determine comparative advantage in FDI among industries. The competitive edge a foreign firm holds in managerial resources and technological skills over its Japanese competitors is crucial to its decision to undertake FDI. If it is superior in these respects, it will have a greater incentive to enter the market.

There are no great differences in labour/capital endowment of production factors among developed countries. Japan's large share of the world market for consumer durables, such as electrical machinery, electronics and automobiles, is due mainly to

Japanese firms' technological advantage in these areas. Superior technology has enabled some foreign firms — IBM, Texas Instruments and DEC Corp., for example — to operate in the Japanese market.

The pharmaceuticals industry has an exceptionally high penetration ratio of foreign firms. Pfizer, Hoechst, Ciba-Geigy and BASF are just a few of the foreign pharmaceuticals firms firmly entrenched in the Japanese market. Success in this industry is linked to the ability to develop and produce new drugs. Parent firms have traditionally transferred the benefits of their superior R&D capacity to foreign affiliates in Japan, a trend seen in the large royalties paid by these affiliates to parent firms and the quantity of intermediate products procured from them. Transfer of R&D from abroad is rarely hampered by institutional barriers. The advantage held by foreign pharmaceuticals companies in R&D — a far more important resource in the case of this industry than manufacturing technology — has accelerated FDI by this industry in Japan.

We look now at how differences in technology levels have affected the pattern of FDI in Japan. In order to discuss this issue quantitatively, we examine first the composition of FDI in Japan by industry and royalties paid by Japanese firms on foreign technology. It is expected that the larger the share of royalties paid by an industry, the larger its share of FDI will be. The indices are defined as follows:

$$S_{iT} = \frac{T_{ix}}{\sum_j T_{jx}} \qquad SALESH_i = \frac{SALES_i}{\sum_j SALES_j}$$

where T_{ix} is royalties on foreign technology in the ith industry; S_{iT} is the ith industry's share of royalty payments to total royalties; $SALES_i$ is total sales of foreign firms in the ith industry in Japan; and $SALESH_i$ is the share of sales of the ith industry.

As Figure 6.4 shows, in 1985–90 the electrical machinery, chemicals and pharmaceuticals industries recorded a large share of both royalty payments and local sales by foreign firms. A high correlation between royalty payments and local sales is confirmed by Spearman's rank correlation coefficient of 0.769 for each industry pair, calculated by taking the relative ranking of two observations. This is statistically significant at the 1 per cent level. Kendall's rank correlation coefficient is 0.790. Both are shown in Table 6.2.

Next, we examine whether technological advantage helps foreign firms penetrate the Japanese market. Technological advantage is defined as:

$$TA_i = \frac{T_{ix} - T_{im}}{T_{ix} + T_{im}}$$

where T_{ix} is royalties paid by Japanese firms on the technology of foreign firms in the ith industry, and T_{im} is royalties received from foreign firms for Japanese technology in the same industry. A high value for TA_i, that is, a large difference between royalties

Table 6.2   Spearman's and Kendall's rank correlation coefficients

	S_{iT}, $SALESH_i$	TA_i, $RATIO_i$	
		(1)*	(2)
Spearman's ρ	0.769	0.648	0.436
Kendall's τ	0.790	0.689	0.618
Number of industries	15	10	11

Note: *   Excludes chemicals industry.

Source: Wakasugi's estimates.

Figure 6.4   Sales of foreign firms as a share of Japanese sales, and royalites paid by Japanese firms on foreign technology, by industry (per cent)

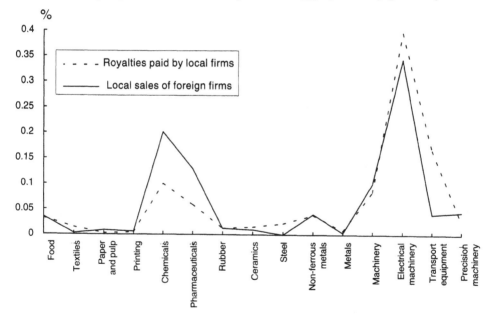

Notes: Based on average value of sales and royalties in 1985–90 of each industry expressed as a percentage. The petrochemicals industry, but not the petroleum industry, is included in chemicals.

Source: Management and Coordination Agency, *Report of the Survey of Research and Development,* Tokyo, various issues; MITI, *Survey of Business Activities of Foreign Firms,* Tokyo, various issues.

paid (technology imports) and royalties received (technology exports) indicates that foreign firms have a greater technological advantage over Japanese firms. The degree of penetration by foreign firms of the Japanese market is defined as follows:

$$RATIO_i = \frac{SALES_i}{DM\ SALES_i}$$

where $DMSALES_i$ is the total domestic sales of Japanese firms. As Figure 6.5 indicates, industries in which foreign firms have a high technological advantage over Japanese firms also record a high penetration ratio.

Spearman's rank correlation coefficient for technological advantage in 1985–90 is 0.648 for 10 industries (Table 6.2). This is significant at the 5 per cent level. If the chemicals industry, which has an unusually high penetration ratio, is included, the

Figure 6.5   Technological advantage and share of local production of foreign firms

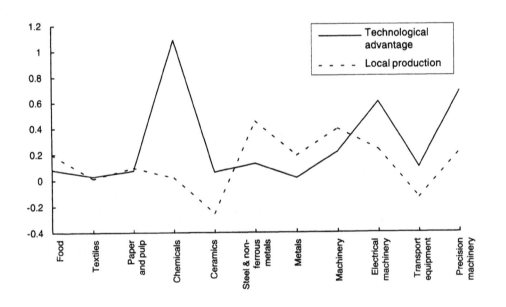

Notes: Local production is value of sales of foreign firms in Japan as a percentage of total Japanese sales. Based on data for 1985–90.

Source: Wakasugi's estimates.

122

correlation coefficient becomes 0.436. Kendall's rank correlation coefficient is 0.689 for 10 industries and 0.618 for 11 industries.

The statistical evidence supports the hypothesis that technological advantage has an impact on the industry composition of FDI and raises the penetration ratio of foreign firms. It has, then, helped determine the pattern of foreign investment in Japan.

Transfer of firm-specific technology

Transfer of managerial resources is carried out in a number of ways — through the movement of human resources, procurement of intermediate products, and technology transactions — and has been the subject of much empirical work. The following study is an application of earlier research into FDI in Japan.[3]

We assume that a foreign firm produces goods and services in Japan using capital and labour, and a stock of specific managerial resources. Because of the difficulty of acquiring firm-specific managerial resources in the local market in the short term, it is logical to assume that the parent firm supplies its foreign affiliate with managerial resources for a considerable time after the initiation of FDI. If the managerial resources supplied by the parent firm are superior to those of local firms, the foreign affiliate will have a competitive edge. Because it will then be able to supply goods and services at a lower cost than its Japanese competitors, it will gain a large share of the market. It can therefore be assumed that the ratio of local sales by foreign firms to sales by domestic firms will reflect firms' relative stocks of managerial resources.

Our hypothesis is that the market share of foreign firms in the Japanese market is affected positively by the following variables: technological knowledge, procurement of intermediate products, movement of human resources such as managerial staff and engineers, and corporate brand name. In addition to these, the R&D expenditure of foreign firms in Japan is taken into account. The equation for estimation is as follows:

$$\log S + a_0 + a_1 \log X_1 + a_2 \log X_2 + a_3 \log X_3 + a_4 \log X_4 + a_5 \log X_5$$

where: S = market share of foreign firms in Japan (the ratio of foreign firms' sales to total Japanese sales in the industry);

X_1 = ratio of royalties paid to parent firm to sales;

X_2 = ratio of imports from parent firm to total purchases of intermediate products;

X_3 = ratio of managers from parent firm to total number of managers;

X_4 = ratio of exports to total sales; and

X_5 = ratio of R&D expenditure to total sales.

The export ratio is used as a proxy for the corporate brand name of the parent firm. (Brand name is considered to be a strategic factor in the success of a foreign firm's exports in an overseas market).

The empirical testing was limited by the availability of data. However, a data set was constructed on a cross-section and time-series basis using information provided by MITI for 11 industries — food, textiles, pulp and paper, chemicals, ceramics, metal products, general machinery, electrical machinery, transportation equipment, precision machinery, and other industries (Table 6.3).

Table 6.3   **Regression coefficients of explanatory variables**

	(1)	(2)
S	-2.0172***	-1.7638**
	(-2.1659)	(-1.9503)
X_1	0.3816*	0.4587***
	(1.6467)	(2.2224)
X_2	0.3216*	0.3159**
	(1.5544)	(1.8970)
X_3	0.5807**	0.4964*
	(1.8454)	(1.6951)
X_4	0.0584	
	(0.3287)	
X_5	-0.1883	
	(-0.7682)	
R^2	0.1766	0.1937

Notes: Case (1) contains the explanatory variables X_4 and X_5; case (2) does not.
S = market share of foreign firms in Japan; X_1 = ratio of royalties paid to parent firm to sales; X_2 = ratio of imports from parent firm to total purchases of intermediate products; X_3 = ratio of managers from parent firm to total number of managers; X_4 = ratio of exports to total sales; and X_5 = ratio of R&D expenditure to total sales. Estimates in the table show the elasticity of the foreign firm's market share to each of these variables.
Numbers in brackets are t-statistics.
*, ** and *** indicate a significance level of 10, 5 and 2.5 per cent respectively.

Source: Wakasugi's estimates.

The results of the regression can be interpreted as follows.

1   Industries with a high ratio of royalties, implying a high dependence on the technological knowledge of the parent firm, record high penetration of the Japanese market.

2   Industries with a high ratio of imports from the parent firm record high penetration of the Japanese market. (A high procurement rate is implicitly understood to indicate the transfer of managerial resources contained in intermediate products from the parent firm.)

3   Industries with a high ratio of managerial staff from the parent firm record a significantly high penetration of the Japanese market.

4   Other variables do not affect the entry of foreign firms.

Demand and profitability

The ratio of FDI inflows to imports of manufactured goods over the last 10 years provides no statistical evidence of substitution between imports and FDI.[4] If the good produced in a foreign country and imported to Japan were not a perfect substitute for the good produced by a foreign affiliate in Japan, and if a change in Japanese income altered the demand pattern, then the ratio of FDI to imports may have stayed at the same level in spite of unfavourable economic conditions for FDI in Japan.

Demand has two components: demand for the good itself, and demand for the service incorporated in the good. It is quite possible that the service portion of demand for a good cannot be supplied by foreign firms through international trade, but only by local firms. Demand for an imported automobile, for example, will be influenced by the ability of the maker to supply service and parts.[5]

With the increase in income over the past decade, the preference of Japanese consumers has shifted from demand for commodities towards demand for services (MCA, various issues). Because an increase in demand for services encourages foreign firms to change their strategy from exporting to local production, this change can be expected to have had a positive effect on FDI in Japan. In spite of such disincentives as exchange rate changes and rising factor prices, FDI has not been replaced by imports owing to the relatively large increase in demand for services and the consequent shift by foreign firms to local production.

MITI's *Survey of Business Activities of Foreign Firms* identifies the major motivations for firms to invest in Japan as being the growth potential of the Japanese market and the strategic importance of this market for business expansion into Asia. The sharp increase in FDI observed in the latter half of the 1980s can thus be interpreted as reflecting rising interest in the potential for growth of the Japanese and Asian markets and foreign firms' positive evaluation of the Japanese market. Of course, as discussed earlier, firms were also responding to the easing of government regulations.

Profitability is another aspect considered carefully by foreign firms thinking of entering the Japanese market. Although most firms anticipate making higher profits than they would in the home market, the profit rates recorded by Japanese manufacturing industry are low by international standards. Foreign affiliates operating in Japan's manufacturing sector have tended to record higher profit rates than do Japanese firms (Figure 6.6), mainly because of their competitiveness in the market. However, if foreign firms enter and remain in the Japanese market only when they can expect to enjoy a monopolistic position and secure high profits, their business opportunities will be limited. Mason identifies differences in corporate strategy as

Figure 6.6   **Profit rates of Japanese and foreign firms in Japan's manufacturing sector, 1985–90 (per cent)**

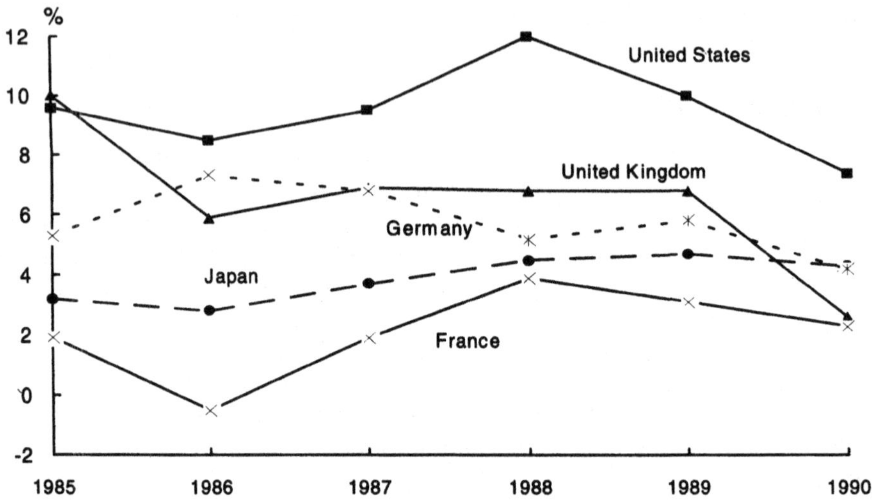

Source: MITI, *Survey of Business Activities of Foreign Firms,* Tokyo, various issues.

being another factor in the higher profit rates of foreign firms (ch. 7). It has been pointed out, for example, that foreign firms — and US firms in particular — tend to stress short-term profitability over long-term business prospects.

Policy implications

The low levels of FDI in Japan compared with those in other OECD countries have been criticised by the United States and European countries as symbolising the insular nature of the Japanese market. In response to such criticisms, the Japanese government recently announced several policies to stimulate inflows of FDI. The major thrust was to provide foreign firms with preferential tax treatment (carrying over of deficit accounts, favourable depreciation rates, exemption from special land holding tax), support services such as the supply of business information, and low interest loans from the Japan Development Bank.

Although it is not yet possible to evaluate the impact of these new policies on FDI, it is unlikely to be great. Both the government and the private sector have hesitated to provide the kind of policy support that would give foreign companies an advantage over domestic firms. The value of low interest loans issued by the Japan Development Bank has not yet reached US$1 billion, indicating that the subsidies announced with such fanfare by the Japanese government were in fact quite small.

Securing a supply of superior goods and services from foreign firms through FDI would stimulate competition and efficient resource allocation in the Japanese market. The removal of obstacles to investment and the creation of equivalent market conditions for Japanese and foreign firms can only increase the welfare of the Japanese economy, and so should be encouraged. Rather than attempting to attract investment by providing policy incentives, the government should look at reforming basic institutional impediments to FDI in such areas as government regulations, business practices, market conditions and managerial resources in sectors where FDI is likely to grow fastest.

FDI policies need to address the underlying issues. Although FDI is no longer strictly regulated, the cumulative effect of past regulations and existing restrictions on business activity has been to keep levels of FDI low. These restrictions add to the costs of foreign firms lacking familiarity with the Japanese market, and thus constitute an entry barrier — even when they are applied in a non-discriminatory way. Expenditure on information collection and marketing is sunk as a fixed cost. Restrictive business practices among Japanese firms also raise the entry cost for foreign firms. What is now required is the removal of existing government regulations that disadvantage newcomers (both foreign and Japanese) and of anticompetitive business practices. Current policy focusing on subsidies and assistance to foreign firms can only give rise to new forms of market distortion.

Conclusion

The study has shown that the current low levels of inward FDI are the result mainly of economic factors. In the late 1980s, a significant appreciation of the yen, rising wages and high rental costs discouraged FDI in Japan, but strongly accelerated the pace of FDI abroad by Japanese firms. The industry composition of FDI in Japan reflects the considerable technological advantage enjoyed by foreign affiliates. Evidence of advantage in a number of managerial resources is also found in the high market share of foreign firms. It would seem, then, that FDI in Japan is subject to market forces, even though the level of activity is low.

Merger and acquisition practices, government regulations on business activity, and anticompetitive business practices still stand in the way of foreign firms attempting to enter the Japanese market. The Japanese government and business need to act to remove these obstacles, thus making the local market genuinely more accessible to both foreign and domestic firms. Policies such as subsidies and support for foreign firms are of cosmetic use only, and should not be given priority.

Notes

1   OECD (1993) provides comprehensive statistics on the FDI inflows and outflows of member countries.

2   See Wakasugi (1994) for details of this model.

3   Studies of the role of advantage in managerial resources include Horst (1972), Ray (1977), Baldwin (1979), Grubaugh (1987) and Drake and Caves (1992).

4   The ratio of FDI inflows to imports of manufactured goods has remained constant at around 1.5 per cent from 1982 to 1991.

5   Wakasugi (1991) argued that the success of European automobile companies in Japan has been a result of their ability to supply good service to Japanese customers.

References

Baldwin, R.E. 1979, 'Determinants of Trade and Foreign Investment: Further Evidence', *Review of Economics and Statistics*, 61(1), pp. 40–8.

Drake, Tracey A. and Richard E. Caves 1992, 'Changing Determinants of Japanese Foreign Investment in the United States', *Journal of the Japanese and International Economies*, 6, September, pp. 228–46.

Grubaugh, S.G. 1987, 'Determinants of Foreign Direct Investment', *Review of Economics and Statistics*, 69(1), pp. 149–52.

Helpman, E. and P. Krugman 1985, *Market Structure and Foreign Trade*, Cambridge, MA: MIT Press.

Horst, T. 1972, 'Firm and Industry Determinants of the Decision to Invest Abroad: An Empirical Study', *Review of Economics and Statistics*, 54(3), pp. 258–66.

Krugman, P. 1979, 'A Model of Innovation, Technology Transfer and the World Distribution of Income', *Journal of Political Economy*, 87(2), pp. 253–66.

Lucas, R.B. 1993, 'On the Determinants of Direct Foreign Investment: Evidence from East and Southeast Asia', *World Development*, 21(3), pp. 391–406.

MCA (Management and Coordination Agency), various issues, *Survey of Household Expenditure*, Tokyo.

OECD (Organisation for Economic Cooperation and Development) 1993, *International Direct Investment Statistics Yearbook: 1993*, Paris: OECD.

Ray, E.J. 1977, 'Foreign Direct Investment in Manufacturing', *Journal of Political Economy*, 85(2), pp. 283–97.

Wakasugi, R. 1991, 'Distribution of Imported Goods and Transaction among Firms', in Y. Miwa and K. Nishimura (eds), *Distribution System of Japan*, Tokyo: University of Tokyo Press.

_____ 1994, 'Why Is FDI in Japan So Small?: An Examination of the Entry of Foreign Firms', Yokohama National University Discussion Papers, Series 94–4, Yokohama.

7 Japan's low levels of inward direct investment: causes, consequences and remedies ———

Mark Mason

The paucity of foreign direct investment (FDI) in Japan has emerged as a major international economic and political issue in the 1990s. Few dispute the potential benefits of such investment. For the foreign firm, FDI can often facilitate greater access to Japanese markets than is possible through exports or licensing alone, and improve its capacity to monitor domestic competitors and otherwise profit from a local presence. Recent findings suggest that at least certain kinds of FDI in Japan may increase substantially the foreign economy's overall level of exports to Japan. And for the Japanese economy, direct investment from abroad can encourage the rapid transfer of superior foreign techniques and stimulate greater competition in a wide variety of domestic industries.

Despite these and other potential benefits, relative levels of FDI in Japan remain exceptionally low. The United States has managed to invest far greater amounts in much smaller economies than it has in the Japanese economy. When adjusted for the size of its economy, Japan has received relatively less FDI from *all* foreign sources than has virtually any other major industrialised nation. The recent surge of Japanese FDI abroad has only served to accentuate the meagre foreign presence in Japan.

This lack of FDI in Japan raises critical questions for scholars and practitioners alike. Why has so little FDI penetrated the Japanese economy? Do home country conditions provide the critical explanation, or do factors associated with the host country furnish the primary reason? What have been some of the principal effects of this subdued foreign presence? And what can be done to facilitate greater FDI flows to Japan? To address these and related questions, this chapter will examine in particular the record of US FDI in Japan.

The author gratefully acknowledges the comments of Hugh Patrick, Denis Simon and other participants at the 21st Pacific Trade and Development Conference, and the research assistance of Ferenc Kovacs and Sanjay Ramesh.

Foreign direct investment in Japan: an overview

Virtually every important statistical measure suggests that Japan, as a host to FDI, is an outlier among the major industrialised nations. Consider, for example, overall measures of US direct investment abroad. On a stock basis, at the end of 1992 total US direct investment in Japan ranked well below similar US investment in smaller economies such as the United Kingdom, Canada, Germany and even Switzerland (Figure 7.1).[1] Although historical experience in part explains the limited US FDI position in Japan, this position has changed little even in more recent years (Figure

Figure 7.1   US FDI position abroad: main hosts as of 1992 (US$ billion)

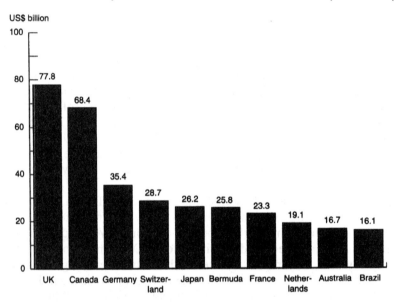

Source: US Department of Commerce, *Survey of Current Business*, 73(7), July 1993, p. 100.

7.2).[2] The modest amounts of US FDI in Japan, together with the recent surge of Japanese direct investment in the United States, have produced an enormous bilateral imbalance in FDI (Figure 7.3).

Host country indicators suggest that the United States is not the only economy with a limited FDI presence in Japan; on the contrary, it is far and away the largest single direct investor in Japan (Figure 7.4). Perhaps still more telling, accumulated FDI in Japan from all foreign sources as a percentage of GDP remains far below similar percentages in major industrialised nations such as the United Kingdom, the United States and Germany (Figure 7.5).

130

Figure 7.2   US FDI position in Japan and other G-5 countries, 1980–92 (US$ billion)

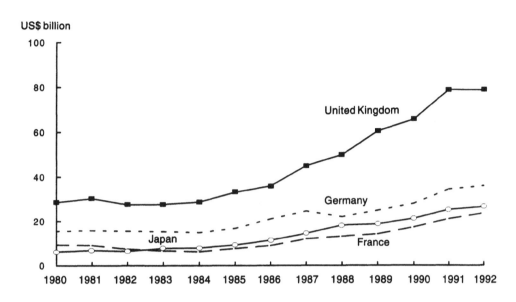

Source: US Department of Commerce, *Survey of Current Business*, various issues.

This limited foreign presence in Japan, together with the massive increase in Japanese FDI abroad, has produced enormous disparities in the ratios of outward to inward FDI stocks between Japan and other large market economies. At the end of 1991, for example, the value of accumulated stocks of British FDI abroad as compared to the value of accumulated FDI stocks in Britain stood at rough parity, the ratio for the United States at about 1:1, and the ratio for Germany at approximately 1:4. By contrast, in the same year Japanese stocks of FDI abroad exceeded FDI stocks in Japan by a ratio of more than 15:1.[3]

Individual (and often highly publicised) examples of successful foreign companies in Japan notwithstanding, these macroeconomic measures are generally reflected in microeconomic indicators as well. Many recent accounts of FDI in Japan emphasise the successful investment experiences of a small number of foreign companies (Abegglen et al. 1985, ch. 9; Morgan and Morgan 1991; MITI 1994 and other MITI publications). Frequently cited American success stories include the Japanese operations of Coca-Cola, Texas Instruments and IBM. This success literature on FDI in Japan also singles out for special mention numerous European-based companies, such as Nestlé, Rank Xerox and Bayer, whose Japanese affiliates have achieved impressive performance levels. Indeed, many such firms have achieved high market shares,

Figure 7.3 **US FDI position in Japan versus Japanese FDI position in the United States, 1980–92 (US$ billion)**

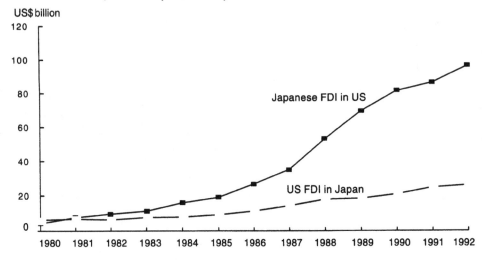

Source: US Department of Commerce, *Survey of Current Business*, various issues.

Figure 7.4 **Principal source countries of FDI stocks in Japan as of 1992 (per cent of total stocks)**

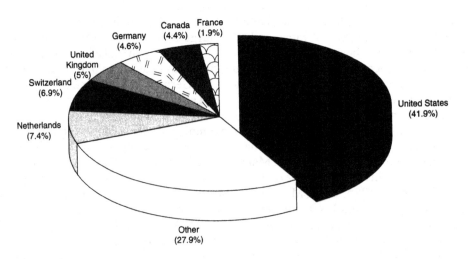

Source: Unpublished data provided by Ministry of Finance, Tokyo.

132

Figure 7.5   **FDI position in the United States, United Kingdom, (West) Germany and Japan, 1983–91 (per cent of GDP)**

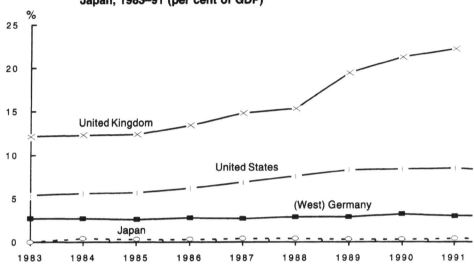

Source: Bank of Japan, *International Economic Statistics Annual*, various issues; Economic Planning Agency, *National Economic Statistics Annual*, various issues; US Department of Commerce, *Survey of Current Business*, various issues.

incomes and profit levels. Table 7.1 provides a list of the 25 most successful foreign-affiliated companies in Japan, as measured by 1992 reported income.

Despite these and a relatively small number of other such successes, microeconomic data suggest that the foreign presence in most sectors of the Japanese economy in fact remains extremely minor. The manufacturing sector, which accounts for a majority of all FDI in Japan, stands as a case in point (see Figure 7.6 for a breakdown of FDI by industry). According to data compiled by the Japanese Ministry of International Trade and Industry (MITI), in 1991 foreign-affiliated manufacturers based in all overseas locations represented just 2.2 per cent of the total capitalisation, 2.5 per cent of the total sales, and 1.2 per cent of the total employees of manufacturing firms in Japan (MITI 1993, p. 38). The US Department of Commerce (January 1994, pp. 38, 53), by contrast, reports that in 1990 foreign-affiliated manufacturing companies in America accounted for no less than 14.5 per cent of the total sales of all manufacturing firms in the United States and 10.6 per cent of the total employees of such firms.

The data on FDI in individual Japanese sectors is even more compelling. In 1988, the capitalisation of foreign-affiliated companies amounted to well below 1 per cent of the capitalisation of all firms in Japan in the following industries: paper and pulp (0.6 per cent), transportation machinery (0.6 per cent), coal (0.4 per cent), food (0.4 per cent), metallurgy (0.1 per cent), printing and publishing (0.09 per cent), lumber

Table 7.1   Top 25 foreign-affiliated companies in Japan by reported income, 1992

Rank	Company name	Parent firm	Nationality
1	Coca-Cola (Japan)	Coca-Cola Export	US
2	Showa Shell Oil	Shell Petroleum, others	UK, others
3	Matsushita Electronics	Philips	Netherlands
4	Tonen	Esso Eastern, others	US
5	Amway Japan	Amway International	US
6	Salomon Bros Asia	Salomon Bros	US
7	Nestlé	Nestlé	Switzerland
8	American Family Life Insurance	American Family Life Insurance	US
9	Fuji Xerox	Rank Xerox	UK
10	General Petroleum	Esso Eastern	US
11	Esso Oil	Esso Eastern	US
12	Bayer Pharmaceutical	Bayer	Germany
13	Banyu Pharmaceutical	MSD International, Merck, others	UK, others
14	Mitsubishi Petrochemical	Shell Petroleum	UK, others
15	Mobil Oil	Mobil Petroleum	US
16	IBM Japan	IBM World Trade	US
17	Sumitomo 3M	Minnesota Mining Manufacturing	US
18	Toppan Moore	Moore Corporation	Canada
19	NCR Japan	NCR	US
20	Ariko Japan	–	–
21	Mazda	Ford Motor	US
22	Japan Petroleum Refining	Caltex Petroleum	US
23	Unisys Japan	Unisys	US
24	MacDonald's Japan	MacDonald's Corp.	US
25	Louis Vuitton Japan	Louis Vuitton Malletier	France

Source: Adapted from 'Gaishikei Kigyo Rankingu' [Ranking of Foreign Capital-Affiliated Companies], *Toyo Keizai*, 29 May 1993, p. 758.

and lumber products (0.07 per cent), textiles (0.03 per cent) and steel (0 per cent). In fact, even in electrical machinery and chemicals — two of the largest recipient FDI sectors in Japan — the capitalisation of foreign-affiliated firms accounted for just 2.9 per cent and 5 per cent respectively. Only FDI in the petroleum sector recorded a sizeable share of total capitalisation (22.9 per cent) in 1988 (JDB 1991, p. 45).

In sum, at either the macroeconomic or microeconomic level, and from either the home or host country perspective, among major industrialised nations Japan has received an exceptionally small amount of direct investment from abroad. Japan's outlier status raises important questions for government policy makers and business managers, as well as academic analysts.

Causes

Home country factors

Why is there so little US FDI in Japan? Home country factors offer a partial explanation, and include the strategic errors of certain American firms. As far back as the early postwar period, at least two major American multinationals chose not to take advantage of opportunities to establish major manufacturing operations in Japan. Foreseeing neither the spectacular postwar rise of the Japanese automobile industry nor the development of a large Japanese car market, towards the close of the Allied Occupation both Ford and General Motors decided not to make the effort to resume prewar operations in that market, even when seemingly offered the chance to do so (Mason 1992a, ch. 3). Otis Elevator and Carrier Corporation are other commonly cited examples of such failure of effort, based in part on American business underestimation, at least in the early postwar years, of potential Japanese economic growth (see, for example, Abegglen and Stalk 1985, ch. 9).

In addition to lack of effort, critics have blamed some American companies for other strategic errors. The decision by American telecommunications giant ITT to sell off its one-third equity stake in NEC from the late 1950s has been offered as an important example of US business impatience in seeking modest short-term profit instead of greater potential long-term gain (Abegglen and Stalk 1985, p. 220). And Eastman Kodak's decades-long strategy of relying on wholly Japanese-owned

Figure 7.6   FDI stocks in Japan by sector, 1992 (per cent of total stocks)

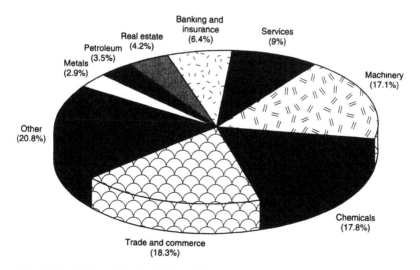

Source: Unpublished data provided by Ministry of Finance, Tokyo.

135

companies for local distribution of its products has been cited as an illustration of, among other things, one major American firm's failure to understand the importance of achieving greater control over distribution channels in the Japanese market (Abegglen and Stalk 1985; interviews with Kodak management). These three strategic errors — lack of effort, lack of patience and lack of understanding — have been cited time and again by those who emphasise the role of American business mismanagement in explaining the low levels of US direct investment in Japan.

The shifting fortunes of various sectors of American industry also help explain the modest US FDI presence in Japan. Persistent difficulties encountered by American consumer electronics companies at least as early as the 1970s may have limited their enthusiasm for major new FDI commitments in countries with strong, entrenched competitors such as Japan. And the relative decline in international competitiveness of the major American auto producers in the late 1980s may have discouraged them from pursuing more aggressively investment opportunities in that market.

In addition to such microeconomic factors, surely larger macroeconomic forces in the American economy at times also contributed to the paltry amounts of US FDI in Japan. Throughout much of the postwar period, the rapid growth of the US economy apparently encouraged some American firms to focus their resources on developing domestic markets. As well, low US rates of saving, particularly in recent years, may conceivably have influenced outflows of US FDI to Japan and other countries.[4]

At the same time, there is a great deal of evidence to suggest that host country factors are also critical in explaining the unusually small amounts of US FDI in Japan. American multinationals, for example, have managed to invest relatively far greater sums in virtually all other developed (and even some developing) market economies. In addition, almost every other nation has failed to directly invest in Japan even a substantial fraction of the US amount. And at least one major study of American multinationals in Japan suggests that the behaviour and interests of domestic firms, among other local considerations, have often played a crucial role in determining the outcomes of investment attempts by foreign companies (Mason 1992a).

Host country factors

One group of such host country impediments to inward FDI stems from Japanese government policy. As is well known, Japan's public authorities operated a regulatory system which severely limited inflows of FDI for more than three decades after World War II (Mason 1992a, pp. 152–61). Based largely on the 1949 Foreign Exchange and Foreign Trade Control Law and the 1950 Foreign Investment Law, this system subjected virtually every potential foreign direct investment to a rigorous, complex and lengthy screening procedure. Few foreign applicants ultimately succeeded in gaining the requisite permissions, and those which did generally possessed peculiar marketing, technology or other assets that were not domestically available to Japanese entrepreneurs.[5]

Indeed, the three American 'success stories' most commonly cited to demonstrate the supposed accessibility of the postwar Japanese market through FDI — Coca-Cola,

IBM and Texas Instruments — illustrate vividly the enormous difficulties which confronted even fortunate American companies such as these. Consider, for example, Coca-Cola. Although Coke managed to establish limited bottling facilities in Japan at the beginning of the Occupation period, it was permitted to distribute and sell its soft drink only to non-Japanese consumers connected with the Occupation or for other reasons then resident in Japan. Indeed, despite Coke's substantial expenditure of time, effort and other resources, the Japanese government prevented it from selling its drink to Japanese nationals for fully 15 years after the company's initial entry and investment in Japan. Only after repeated, failed attempts by domestic competitors to produce an adequate substitute, together with an eventual alliance between Coke and key Japanese rival Kirin, did the government finally, in 1960, allow the American firm to market its product to Japanese consumers.[6]

The postwar entry experience of IBM similarly highlights the very substantial obstacles the Japanese authorities placed in the way of even the most powerful and determined American direct investors. Although IBM managed to resume after World War II the limited operations it had first begun in Japan before the war, the Japanese government would neither allow the American company to produce its computing machines locally nor to repatriate profits or principal from these operations. Indeed, like Coke, IBM gained official approval to manufacture in Japan only after the American firm agreed, also in 1960, to license its most critical computer patents to each of its major Japanese rivals and to meet other conditions as well (Mason 1992a, pp. 114–30, 187–91).

The entry of Texas Instruments (TI) followed much the same pattern. Here again a highly competitive and fiercely determined American company was consistently denied access to the postwar Japanese market through FDI despite strenuous efforts to do so. After frustrating attempts beginning in the 1950s to sell substantial quantities of its electronics products in Japan through exports from the United States, in early 1964 the firm applied to MITI for permission to set up a wholly TI-owned Japanese manufacturing plant. Despite an intense campaign waged by TI through public and private agencies to obtain such permission, for several years the ministry simply refused to issue the requisite licences. Only after sustained pressure from both the company and the US government, together with a formal pledge that TI would license its Kilby patents on the integrated circuit to the principal Japanese electronics manufacturers, did MITI finally (in 1968) agree to permit the entry of the American firm on a restricted basis (Mason 1992a, pp. 174–87).

Many other American multinationals confronted still greater official resistance to their proposed investments. For example, throughout the 1950s the Japanese authorities flatly refused to allow Singer Sewing Machine to manufacture locally — even on a joint venture basis (Mason 1992a, p. 194). And when the 'Big Three' American auto makers tried to invest in manufacturing facilities in Japan beginning in the late 1960s, the local authorities first obstructed their attempts and later agreed to permit only minority American ownership of second-tier domestic auto firms (Mason 1992, pp. 231–40).

In contrast to these longstanding policies, in more recent years the Japanese government has modified its approach to inward FDI significantly. Following completion of a phased, 13-year process of 'capital liberalisation', in 1980 the government officially abolished the three-decade-old Foreign Investment Law and significantly modified the Foreign Exchange and Foreign Trade Control Law (Mason 1992a; Encarnation and Mason 1990). Indeed, beginning in the mid 1980s certain agencies of the Japanese government actively sought to *encourage* inward FDI through a variety of incentives and other means. These initiatives now include modestly subsidised, low-interest loans provided through the Japan Development Bank and other official lending agencies, informational seminars and related activities conducted by local prefectural governments as well as national public agencies, and even free counselling offered on a temporary basis by the recently created, government-backed Foreign Investment in Japan Development Corporation.[7]

Despite these and other changes, government policies continue to inhibit fresh inflows of direct investment from abroad. Japan still restricts FDI in a number of sectors through national legislation and international codes. Japanese laws formally limit FDI in, for example, the air transportation, banking and securities, broadcasting, insurance, marine transportation and telecommunications industries. In addition, like most other countries Japan maintains the right to prohibit FDI which could threaten national security or related interests. Japan also has entered as reservations under the OECD Code of Liberalisation of Capital Movements FDI in agriculture, forestry and fisheries, mining, oil, and leather and leather products (Mason 1992b, pp. 106–7). Although it is true that most formal restrictions on FDI in the Japanese manufacturing sector have now been removed, Japan is no longer an attractive site for foreign producers in many industries due to rising local costs and other factors.

Numerous other government policies and practices impede inward FDI. Import constraints such as special duties, product testing procedures, price controls and insurance reimbursement schemes not only hamper the operations of existing foreign companies in Japan but also limit the attractiveness of the Japanese market for future foreign direct investors. Also significant are restricted access to bidding on various government procurement contracts and limited protection of intellectual property, both of which can discourage potential FDI. Lack of transparency and administrative guidance are other features of the Japanese political economy that often place foreign companies at a competitive disadvantage vis-à-vis established local firms.[8]

The efforts of the American firm Cargill to establish a cattle feed plant in Kyushu in the 1980s illustrate some of the barriers confronting foreign direct investors even in 'liberalised' Japan. One of the world's largest and most experienced grain traders, Cargill enjoys enormous scale economies and other competitive advantages in its fields of activity. In the mid 1980s, this firm identified a major opportunity to export and sell cattle feed to Japanese farmers. Farmers were purchasing their feed from an informal cartel of Japanese trading companies and agricultural cooperatives at prices well above prevailing international levels, and Cargill calculated that it could reduce those prices substantially yet still obtain sizeable profits. The American company therefore conducted a search to identify a suitable location for its prospective feed importing, storage and distribution facilities, and in 1985 found that a new, government-controlled industrial park in Shibushi, on the southern island of Kyushu, offered one of the very few viable locations.

Although the process of capital liberalisation had been completed in 1980, Cargill soon discovered that Japanese authorities still placed major obstacles in the way of its direct investment plans. When Cargill approached the prefectural government that administered the Shibushi site about leasing a parcel of land there, it was told that it would first have to receive various licences from the national government. Cargill then approached the authorities in Tokyo, to be told that discretion in fact resided with the prefecture. At about the same time, Cargill discovered that members of the informal grain cartel — arguing that Cargill's entry would challenge the position of entrenched but less competitive domestic firms and thereby cause unwanted economic dislocation — were intensively lobbying both the national and prefectural governments, as well as potential farmer-consumers and the general public, to keep Cargill out. In a process that was in many respects reminiscent of the difficulties encountered by other American firms during the preliberalisation period, Cargill finally managed to obtain permission to lease a site at Shibushi only after long delays, the direct intervention of the US government, and acceptance by Cargill of various operating conditions which would limit its future ability to expand its position in Japan.[9]

Also illustrative of Japanese government regulations which continue to hinder US FDI is the experience of Toys 'R' Us — one of the most recently publicised American success stories. Already a highly successful toy distributor with numerous locations in the United States, Europe, Asia and elsewhere, in the late 1980s the firm sought to establish a chain of retail toy stores in Japan. Toys 'R' Us understood that Japanese consumers were forced to pay unusually high prices for toys due in large part to a complex, multitiered distribution system whose numerous retailers were in general small in scale and relatively inefficient. By setting up larger retail outlets and effecting other efficiencies, the American firm calculated that it could profitably supply a wide variety of toys in Japan at a fraction of prevailing Japanese toy prices.

Yet here again, a highly competitive American company would discover that government regulations could still impede FDI significantly, even after capital liberalisation. When Toys 'R' Us sought to pursue its Japanese strategy by establishing an initial store in the Nagoya area, it discovered that, for an indefinite period of time, MITI could effectively block the effort by invoking provisions of the Large-Scale Retail Store Law. This legislation empowered the ministry to deny potential retailers permission to set up stores if the size of the proposed operation exceeded a modest 5,400 square feet of floor space. In judging whether to grant such permission, MITI in general deferred to the wishes of smaller retailers already operating in the locale. Like the agricultural and trading interests which had opposed Cargill's investment in Shibushi, the less efficient, higher priced small toy retailers in Nagoya fought to keep out Toys 'R' Us. Only the direct intervention of the US Trade Representative — together with widespread publicity about the case in the United States and Japan —

eventually convinced MITI in 1990 to change its position and limit to 18 months the application procedure under the Large-Scale Retail Store Law. Having met this initial challenge, Toys 'R' Us then confronted a major new obstacle. Domestic toy makers, fearful that the American company would lower their profits by following its standard worldwide practice of selling toys at levels below suggested retail prices, joined forces and pledged not to sell their toys to the potential American entrant. In the end, only a direct threat by Toys 'R' Us to stop distributing abroad products manufactured by powerful industry opposition member Nintendo finally split the domestic industry coalition and enabled the American company to establish its first Japanese retail establishment in December 1991 (Mason 1992b, pp. 108–9).[10]

In addition to Japanese government policies, local business practices also continue to inhibit inward FDI flows. Limited access to various private industry associations, for example, can deny foreign companies access to important channels of information and opportunities to build critical relationships in their sectors. Complex distribution systems can render more costly and time-consuming the task of delivering goods and services to final consumers. Japanese human resource management strategies, including the lifetime employment system, often contribute to the problems foreign firms encounter when they attempt to hire sufficient numbers of experienced, qualified local personnel. These and other business practices are gradually changing, and often pose considerable problems for Japanese newcomers as well, but the difficulties they pose for American investors remain substantial nonetheless.

Perhaps the most serious impediment to the entry of foreign companies arising from Japanese business practices stems from the structure and behaviour of *keiretsu* and similar business groups. Preferential buyer–supplier and other economic relationships between members of these groups can limit the ability of foreign companies to transact business with such firms. These domestic alliances can also make more difficult foreign competition against one or more Japanese firms allied within such a network.[11]

Even more problematic are the impediments such domestic groups pose to foreign companies seeking to invest in Japan through acquisitions of existing enterprises. Historically, of course, American multinationals have found great advantage in undertaking acquisitions in order to expand abroad rapidly and effectively. Indeed, many US firms have found that acquisitions are a particularly effective means to enter complex overseas markets such as those in Japan, where longstanding relationships often prove critical to business success. Unusual systems of corporate governance, relatively small amounts of publicly traded stocks of individual Japanese firms, limited disclosure requirements of listed companies and a general Japanese dislike for hostile takeovers — whether Japanese or foreign — have rendered acquisitions unusually difficult, even since the removal of formal government controls on foreign acquisitions in 1980. In addition, the high levels of intercorporate shareholdings between allied members of *keiretsu* business groups (greatly increased during the 1960s explicitly to prevent foreign takeovers after completion of the government's capital liberalisation program) have contributed to the problems encountered by potential foreign acquirers in Japan (see, in particular, Lawrence 1993). Figure 7.7

Figure 7.7   Japanese mergers and acquisitions, 1981–92 (no. of cases)

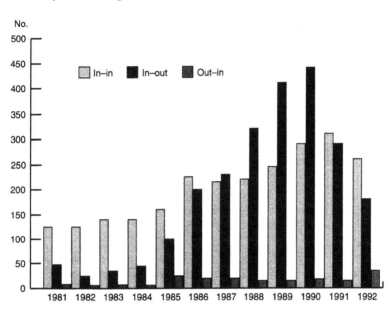

Source: Unpublished data provided by Yamaichi Securities, Tokyo.

illustrates the low levels of foreign mergers and acquisitions in Japan (out–in), compared to the far more substantial levels carried out by Japanese companies both at home (in–in) and abroad (in–out).

Many of these challenges faced by foreign firms are exemplified by the experience of American pharmaceuticals firm Merck & Co., which scored a highly publicised success by acquiring a controlling interest in a Japanese drug maker in the years following capital deregulation. Having made a substantial investment in the development of a new series of pharmaceutical products, in the early 1980s Merck was eager to sell these products in the huge and potentially lucrative Japanese drug market. Although it initially explored the possibility of exporting its products to Japan, licensing its techniques locally or even creating a joint venture with a domestic firm, the US company eventually judged that acquisition of a controlling interest in an existing Japanese pharmaceuticals firm provided the most promising means of exploiting the potential of its new products in that market.

Yet Merck had to confront enormous challenges to its FDI strategy even after it had managed to identify a promising Japanese acquisition candidate. Intercorporate shareholdings and other relationships between many individual Japanese drug firms and their associated business groups greatly limited from the outset the number of viable acquisition candidates. In addition, a number of local drug firms not intimately

141

bound up within *keiretsu* or similar business groups simply did not wish to be acquired. Ultimately Merck selected instead the relatively independent, family-owned Banyu Pharmaceutical, an ailing drug company that wished to gain access to new drug products and with which Merck already had a trustworthy, long-term business relationship (Mason 1992b, pp. 109–12).

Even the eventual identification of this ideal candidate did not solve all of Merck's acquisition difficulties. For one thing, Banyu's management warned Merck that its acquisition by a foreign company might demoralise Banyu employees and perhaps even lead to serious resignations or defections to competing drug firms.[12] In addition, both firms worried that this planned *friendly* takeover by an American firm could seriously harm Banyu's reputation in the eyes of Japanese industry and the public more generally. In 1983 Merck finally did manage to acquire 50.02 per cent of Banyu — the largest foreign acquisition in history of a controlling interest in a Japanese company listed on the First Section of the Tokyo Stock Exchange — yet Merck's eventual success illustrates as much the obstacles to such acquisitions in Japan as it does the opportunities for other foreign companies to pursue similar investment strategies in the future.[13]

Finally, recent changes in the Japanese macroeconomic environment also help explain the low levels of inward FDI. Perhaps most importantly, the rising value of the yen has greatly increased the costs American and other foreign firms must bear in order to invest directly in Japan. Since the 1985 Plaza Accord, the value of the yen has risen from about ¥240 to roughly ¥100 per US dollar. This major revaluation has raised considerably the costs to foreign investors of acquiring or leasing offices and other business premises, employing local personnel, sourcing domestic products and obtaining advertising and other business support services.[14] Indeed, the steady rise in the value of the yen has so elevated labour costs in some sectors of Japanese industry that many American and other foreign investors cannot now justify establishing local manufacturing operations.[15]

Added to the deterrent effects of yen revaluation has been a generally discouraging Japanese business environment created by the nation's current economic recession. Although certain sectors of the economy have avoided the worst consequences of the recession, substantial business difficulties in many industries, stagnation of consumer spending and other factors have all retarded local demand for goods and services which foreign investors might supply. This recession helps to explain the vast amounts of American investment capital now 'going around' Japan en route to better perceived opportunities in China, Southeast Asia and elsewhere.[16]

Consequences

Low levels of US FDI in Japan have had a number of negative consequences for Japanese and American interests alike. Limited American direct investment has deprived the Japanese economy of the rapid transfer to Japan of new technologies, knowhow and various firm-specific assets possessed by potential American investors.

The introduction of such assets, combined with the resulting increase in domestic competition, would in all likelihood raise the efficiency of less competitive sectors of Japanese industry such as large-scale retailing and financial services. This in turn could significantly enhance Japanese consumer welfare.[17]

The lack of greater direct investment by US-based firms has also harmed American interests. It has, for instance, prevented many individual American companies from gaining better access to Japanese markets attainable through direct investment. Low levels of US FDI in Japanese wholesaling and distribution, to cite two obvious examples, have impeded the ability of American firms in a wide variety of industries to sell their products more effectively to Japanese consumers. The paucity of US FDI in Japan also may prevent at least some American companies from competing more effectively against Japanese firms which charge inflated prices at home (and thereby earn unusually high profits) because they operate in locally imperfect markets. The invulnerability of such 'profit sanctuaries' can in turn enable Japanese firms to cross-subsidise their foreign operations and thereby gain price and other advantages over American companies in markets outside Japan.[18] The meagre US FDI presence in Japan may also limit the ability of some American firms to monitor effectively the actions of Japanese competitors operating in home markets, and may even hinder potential US access to other Asian markets (see, for example, Abegglen 1994, especially pp. 44–6).

There is some evidence to suggest that US FDI in Japan tends to stimulate US exports to that market, and that the paucity of US FDI in Japan may therefore significantly limit such exports.[19] US Department of Commerce data indicate that those American affiliates which do manage to operate in Japan generally consume high levels of exports from the United States.[20] Indeed, preliminary 1991 data indicate that American affiliates in Japan consumed more than 20 per cent of all US merchandise exports to Japan during that year (US Department of Commerce 1993).[21]

Moreover, *majority* American-owned affiliates in Japan tend to import far greater levels of US goods and services as a percentage of their total sales than do such American affiliates operating in virtually all other countries (Table 7.2). In 1991, for example, imports from the United States accounted for less than 5 per cent of the total sales of majority American-owned affiliates operating in all industries in France, Germany and the United Kingdom. Indeed, with the exception of neighbouring Canada and Mexico, it has been estimated that in 1991 imports from the United States by majority American-owned affiliates throughout the world accounted for a mere 5.7 per cent of the total sales of these firms (US Department of Commerce 1993).

By contrast, imports of US goods and services by majority American-owned affiliates in all sectors in Japan amounted in 1991 to an unusually high 11.6 per cent of total sales. That ratio stood at a remarkable 10.4 per cent across the entire manufacturing sector, and no less than 25.8 per cent in the wholesale sector (Table 7.3). In other words, in 1991 each dollar of sales by the average majority American-owned affiliate in Japan generated almost 12 cents worth of exports from the United States, compared with just over 4 cents generated by its UK counterpart.

Table 7.2   US exports to majority American-owned affiliates as a percentage of affiliates' total sales, preliminary 1991 estimates

Country/region	All industries	Manufacturing
Japan	11.6	10.4
France	4.8	4.5
Germany	4.6	4.6
United Kingdom	4.1	5.2
World (excluding Canada and Mexico)	5.7	6.2

Note: If geographically proximate Canada and Mexico are included in 'world', the figure for 'all industries' becomes 8.8 per cent and that for 'manufacturing' 12.2 per cent.

Source: US Department of Commerce, 1993.

It seems, though, that the degree of US ownership of affiliates in Japan plays a critical role in their import propensity from the United States (Encarnation 1992, p. 31, pp. 82–3). Thus although, as stated above, imports from the United States in 1991 accounted for some 11.6 per cent of total sales by majority American-owned affiliates in Japan, in the same year imports from the United States amounted to just 1.6 per cent of total sales by equal partnership or minority American-owned affiliates in Japan (US Department of Commerce 1993). By contrast, in 1991 imports from the United States accounted for 2.1 per cent of total sales by equal partnership or minority American-owned affiliates throughout the world. If US FDI in Japan does indeed tend to stimulate US exports to that market, then these data suggest that increased US investment in *majority American-owned affiliates* in Japan might well stimulate far greater levels of US exports to Japan than investment in affiliates with lesser degrees of American ownership.[22]

Remedies

What can be done to facilitate greater US FDI in Japan? Part of the answer surely depends on US initiatives. American firms should devote adequate resources to monitoring and evaluating potential Japanese investment opportunities in cases where they do not already do so, and demonstrate the necessary effort and patience to follow through on promising opportunities. FDI in Japanese wholesale and distribution operations, as has already been suggested, might well prove attractive to certain categories of American manufacturers. Other American firms may find that continued Japanese deregulation and other changes in the host environment will open up additional possibilities. And although the rising value of the yen has made FDI in Japan

Table 7.3   **US exports to majority American-owned affiliates in Japan as a percentage of affiliates' total sales, preliminary 1991 estimates**

	US exports (US$ million)	Affiliate sales (US$ million)	Ratio (%)
Petroleum	32	12,577	0.3
Manufacturing	2,719	26,132	10.4
Food	26	2,362	1.1
Chemicals	325	4,442	7.3
Primary and fabricated metals	42	430	9.8
Machinery	(D)	(D)	(D)
Electronics	613	3,831	16.0
Transport equipment	19	180	10.6
Other	(D)	(D)	(D)
Wholesale trade	5,257	20,369	25.8
Finance	0	7,941	–
Services	(D)	1,712	(D)
Other	(D)	819	(D)
All industries	8,037	69,550	11.6

Note: 'D' denotes data suppressed in order to conceal the identity of individual companies where sample size of specific categories is small.

Source: US Department of Commerce, 1993.

more expensive in recent years, US business must also evaluate correctly the trade-offs between the increased risk of the greater (dollar-denominated) costs of the initial investment and the increased potential rewards when proceeds from these investments are converted back into dollars.

The American government can act to improve significantly the environment for US direct investment in Japan. First, US authorities should intensify their efforts to establish an international legal framework for FDI similar to that spelled out for trade in the GATT. Although the GATT was concluded in 1947, no similar accord has been established for FDI almost half a century later. Various draft treaties, codes and declarations of principles at the regional and global levels have been proposed in recent years, yet no comprehensive international agreement has been reached.[23] Increased American support for such initiatives would surely hasten the adoption of a suitable international framework and consequently encourage greater business confidence in direct investment abroad.[24]

Second, in negotiations with their Japanese counterparts, American officials should assign FDI issues the higher priority they clearly deserve. It is true that the July

1993 bilateral framework accord does include such investment questions in its economic harmonisation basket, but US negotiators have so far chosen to emphasise other economic issues in the framework discussions.[25] The real possibility of important linkages between FDI and trade described above (and elsewhere) should in themselves encourage the United States to reconsider the importance it attaches to FDI as a means to gain improved access to Japanese markets.

Third, the Clinton Administration should consider converting the Office of the US Trade Representative into the Office of the US Trade *and Investment* Representative. Such a measure would not only signal America's new-found determination to confront vigorously barriers to US direct investment in Japan and elsewhere, but also enable the Administration to coordinate more effectively policies affecting the increasingly interrelated fields of trade and investment.[26]

At the same time, many of the critical remedies depend upon changed Japanese business practices and government policies. By eliminating or modifying a number of its practices, the Japanese private sector could significantly improve the environment for inward direct investment. Revised membership rules in various private industry associations to enable foreign companies to obtain full membership would certainly prove helpful in a number of sectors. Vigorous efforts by firms in *keiretsu* and similar Japanese business groups to boost their interactions with foreign companies where economically justifiable could provide far more opportunities for non-Japanese firms. Greater private sector support for new public FDI initiatives could facilitate the crafting, adoption and implementation of such initiatives.[27]

Changes in Japanese government policies and practices could also improve the environment for US and other FDI. The Japanese government, as has been suggested, has already acted in a number of ways to increase the opportunities for foreign investors. Future public action should build on these initiatives as well as expanding into new domains.

First, standard economic arguments suggest that the Japanese government should continue to pursue deregulation of its domestic economy. To further this goal, the authorities could, for example, expand the resources and powers of specialised public bodies charged with encouraging or maintaining free and open domestic markets. The important tasks assigned to the Office of the Trade and Investment Ombudsman are hampered by limited resources and overdependence on the very government agencies whose regulations it is often called upon to evaluate (*JEI Report*, 35A, 24 September 1993). Indeed, despite much progress, more than one-quarter of the cases the Office reviewed through late 1993 were concluded without any change in the government regulations which gave rise to the initial complaint.[28] Although the Office has recently been strengthened, greater autonomy and authority, together with a larger, permanent, full-time staff of knowledgeable and independent officials, would improve its effectiveness still further.[29] Similar action could improve the performance of other specialised public organisations such as the Fair Trade Commission — thereby advancing the government's stated aim of identifying and addressing persistent regulatory impediments to increased foreign competition in Japan.[30]

In addition, individual government agencies should persist in the identification and dismantling of specific regulatory barriers to greater FDI in those sectors under their control. The Ministry of Finance, for instance, could pursue deregulation of controls limiting access by foreign companies to various sectors of the Japanese financial services industry, such as insurance and pension fund management. Removing requirements in these and related sectors that firms obtain ministry approval for each new financial instrument also could spur greater innovation and competition.

The government should also further its efforts to open up public procurement to foreign firms considering direct investment in Japan. Already, the Ministry of Construction, among other public agencies, has improved opportunities for foreign firms to participate in a variety of public works projects. Further liberalisation of government procurement could be undertaken in construction and several other fields, including agriculture and telecommunications.

In addition to economic arguments for greater government deregulation, important *political* considerations suggest that Japanese officials should act in additional ways to facilitate greater US and other FDI in Japan. Although standard economic theory may not suggest that the huge imbalance between US FDI stocks in Japan and Japanese FDI stocks in the United States is undesirable, the very existence of that imbalance contributes mightily to the foreign perception that Japanese markets remain relatively closed (see, for example, *The New York Times*, 7 July 1993, p. D1). Proactive Japanese policies which go beyond deregulation could address these foreign concerns and thereby serve to modify political difficulties for Japan created by these concerns. In addition, an increased presence of foreign firms in Japan might also create stronger political interest groups in foreign countries promoting improved economic and other relations with Japan.

Proactive policies could include increased tax breaks, loan subsidies and guarantees, and similar financial assistance for foreign direct investors. Financial incentives similar to those granted in the 1980s by some US state governments to encourage FDI in America (or by the British government to encourage FDI in the United Kingdom) could serve as useful guidelines for the range and levels of assistance that public agencies in Japan might offer. Although the ultimate effects of such incentives on the FDI decisions of foreign multinationals are debatable, these incentives would at least provide clear *political* signals abroad that the Japanese government is working seriously to improve the FDI environment in Japan.

Second, the Ministry of Justice and other relevant public agencies could build upon earlier initiatives to expand the rights of shareholders in Japanese corporations. Such initiatives might include expanded powers for large minority shareholders as well as increased public disclosure requirements for listed corporations. These measures could significantly increase opportunities for foreign investors to gain a greater voice in the governance of those Japanese corporations whose stocks they do manage to acquire, and thereby render FDI more attractive in some instances.[31]

Finally, the government might well consider initiating a domestic campaign of moral suasion to demonstrate that direct investment from abroad can contribute to the strength and prosperity of the Japanese economy. From the great 'Buy Japanese' campaigns of the prewar era to the energy conservation campaigns of the postwar period, the government has often managed to influence private economic behaviour to great effect. Such a campaign in the 1990s — which might be modelled on Japanese government efforts in the 1980s to convince Americans that inward FDI carried significant benefits for the United States — might produce the kind of fundamental shift in Japanese attitudes that would encourage still greater change in the environment for FDI in Japan.

Notes

1   Unless otherwise indicated, the following stock data are calculated on a historical cost basis.

2   On a flow basis, in 1988 and 1989 the United States was a net FDI *disinvestor* in Japan. Major Japanese purchases of stocks in existing US affiliates in part explain this net disinvestment. Indeed, on this basis, all foreign countries together were net FDI disinvestors in Japan during these two years (OECD 1993, p. 139). Although US FDI in Japan has increased somewhat since 1980 (Figure 7.2), the comparative increase during this same period in US FDI in, for example, the United Kingdom (which was undertaken in large part to boost US access to the greater European market) has been much larger.

3   OECD data based on balance of payments measurements, as reported in OECD (1993, p. 17).

4   These low rates of savings would, however, surely have had far less (if any substantial) impact on large, established American multinationals with easy access to international capital markets.

5   Previous negotiations between the US and Japan did oblige the Japanese government from 1956 to permit American firms to directly invest without approval under the Foreign Exchange and Foreign Trade Control Law or the Foreign Investment Law. However, these 'yen-based' companies were not permitted to repatriate either profits or principal from such ventures, and the Japanese authorities in any case abolished the system in 1963 in anticipation of foreign exchange deregulation (Mason 1992a, pp. 192–4).

6   Even in 1960, however, the Japanese government obliged Coca-Cola to abide by various restrictions on price, marketing methods and other matters (Mason 1992a, p. 173).

7   Established in June 1993, this is a private corporation which receives substantial assistance both from the Japanese government and business interests.

8   For a typology of such restrictive government policies, see, for example, Lincoln (1990, ch. 2).

9   This discussion draws on internal Cargill documents, interviews with Cargill management and various articles in the Japanese media.

10 Toys 'R' Us now operates a number of stores in Japan.

11 Though perceived as a trade and investment impediment by some American companies, one survey suggested that at times such *keiretsu* groups can in fact have a positive impact on US firms' trade and investment in Japan (ACCJ 1991, p. 53, 55). Contrast the findings of this report, however, with those of previous ACCJ reports, such as ACCJ (1987).

12 In the event, a series of carefully orchestrated moves by Merck and Banyu, together with difficulties then being experienced throughout the Japanese drug industry, prevented major losses of personnel.

13 For additional examples of recent merger and acquisition difficulties encountered by foreign firms in Japan, see Wakasugi in this volume (ch. 6).

14 On these costs, see, for example, US House of Representatives (1993). On the other hand, the current economic recession has somewhat modified these effects through the recent declines in Japanese land and stock prices.

15 Estimates of 1993 hourly labour costs in manufacturing, for example, now place Japan above the United States and virtually all other major industrialised nations except western Germany (data from Morgan Stanley, as cited in *The Economist*, 2 April 1994, p. 69). These and other factors have had a considerable impact on the composition of FDI in Japan: whereas most accumulated FDI in Japan in 1992 was still in manufacturing, the majority of FDI inflows to Japan in 1989, 1991 and 1992 went to the non-manufacturing sector.

16 It is estimated that net US FDI capital outflows to Singapore alone far exceeded similar US outflows to Japan in both 1991 and 1992 (*Survey of Current Business*, July 1993, p. 122).

17 Some analysts point out, however, that FDI restrictions that force foreign companies to license to Japanese firms rather than invest in Japan in some cases could increase Japanese welfare by shifting rents from foreign to Japanese firms (see, for example, Lawrence 1993, p. 106).

18 Just such fears motivated Motorola's management to redouble its efforts to invest in Japan during the late 1970s and Kodak to boost its Japanese presence in the 1980s, according to Motorola and Kodak management. The rise of labour and other manufacturing costs due to the appreciation of the yen and the fall of various import barriers have presumably eroded many of these profit sanctuaries in recent years.

19 The direction and, indeed, the very existence of causality between US FDI in Japan and US exports to Japan requires further research. A pioneering analysis of the linkages between trade and FDI, particularly as they relate to US–Japan economic relations, is Encarnation (1992).

20 However, the propensity of American affiliates in Japan to import goods and services from the United States and elsewhere varies significantly. In addition to the degree of American ownership, the corporate strategy of individual firms and other factors play a key role. As a matter of company policy, for example, Coca-Cola (Japan) intentionally limits its imports from the United States as well as from all other external sources. Texas Instruments Japan, on the other hand, freely imports a very high percentage of intermediate products from America and elsewhere, according to interviews with Coca-Cola (Japan) and Texas Instruments Japan management.

21 The author is indebted to Raymond Mataloni of the US Department of Commerce's Bureau of Economic Analysis for assistance in locating and analysing the following trade-related FDI data for US affiliates located in Japan and elsewhere.

22 For a recent analysis of trade and FDI in the United States, see the US Department of Commerce's *Survey of Current Business* (October 1993, pp. 52–65).

23 At a global level, the joint World Bank/IMF Development Committee recently drafted a Legal Framework for the Treatment of Foreign Investment. In addition, a number of regional FDI initiatives have emerged in recent years, including a proposed non-binding code of investment principles for the Asia Pacific region.

24 In so doing, the United States could join with the European Round Table, a group of European business leaders which recently called explicitly for just such a framework (*The Economist*, 18 September 1993, p. 75).

25 US emphasis on impediments in service sectors such as financial services and telecommunications should at least indirectly facilitate FDI because overseas operations in these sectors often entail a sizeable foreign investment in office space, business equipment and other items.

26 Robert Reich (1991, p. 87) recently proposed the creation of a separate United States Investment Representative. Growing understanding of the important linkages between trade and FDI provided by Encarnation (1992) and others, however, suggests that a single government agency with combined responsibility for both areas of economic activity merits serious consideration.

27 Recent reports by the powerful Japanese industry association Keidanren (Federation of Economic Organisations) have offered other constructive proposals for Japanese private sector action that might improve the environment for FDI in Japan (see, for example, Keidanren 1992).

28 Specifically, formal complaints about FDI and trade issues failed to bring about any change in government regulations in 132 out of a total of 470 cases (roughly 28 per cent) brought to conclusion with the involvement of the Office of the Trade and Investment Ombudsman as of late 1993 (Economic Planning Agency 1993, p. 12).

29 The Office was strengthened in February 1994 following a Japanese Cabinet decision to revise its operations. The two key changes were: to raise the rank of officials in the Office of Market Access from vice-ministerial to ministerial level; and to empower the Market Access Ombudsman Council (formerly the Office of the Trade and Investment Ombudsman Advisory Council) to make voluntary recommendations even when not explicitly asked by the Office of Market Access to do so (Economic Planning Agency 1994).

30 Despite its recent strengthening, the Free Trade Commission reportedly has not been vigorous in pursuing a number of complaints by foreign companies through the Anti-Monopoly Law (see, for instance, *JEI Report*, 12 March 1993, pp. 3–5).

31 The Japanese government has entertained a number of proposals to modify certain parts of the Japanese Commercial Code, but enactment of such modifications has been complicated in part by the current long-term project to revise the code (interviews with Japanese and US government officials).

References

Abegglen, James C. 1994, *Sea Change: Pacific Asia as the New World Industrial Center*, New York: The Free Press.

Abegglen, James C. and George Stalk, Jr 1985, *Kaisha: The Japanese Corporation*, New York: Basic Books.

ACCJ (American Chamber of Commerce in Japan) 1987, *Direct Foreign Investment in Japan: The Challenge for Foreign Firms*, Tokyo: ACCJ.

_____ 1991, *Trade and Investment in Japan: The Current Environment*, Tokyo: ACCJ.

Economic Planning Agency 1995, *Shijo Kaiho Mondai Kujo Shori Suishin Honbu: Kujo Shori Kisseki Soran* [Office of the Trade and Investment Ombudsman: Overview of Results Concerning Processed Complaints], Tokyo, November.

_____ 1994, Reinforcement of the Office of the Trade and Investment Ombudsman, Tokyo, mimeo, February.

Encarnation, Dennis J. 1992, *Rivals Beyond Trade: America versus Japan in Global Competition*, Ithaca, NY: Cornell University Press.

Encarnation, Dennis J. and Mark Mason 1990, 'Neither MITI nor America: The Political Economy of Capital Liberalization in Japan', *International Organization*, 44(1), pp. 25–54.

JDB (Japan Development Bank) 1991, 'Tainichi Chokusetsu Toshi no Bunseki' [An Analysis of FDI in Japan], Research Report No. 151, July.

Keidanren 1992, *Waga Kuni Toshi Kankyo no Seibi to Tainichi Chokusetsu Toshi no Sokushin* [Aspects of the Japanese Investment Environment and the Promotion of Foreign Direct Investment in Japan], Tokyo: Keidanren.

Lawrence, Robert Z. 1993, 'Japan's Low Levels of Inward Investment: The Role of Inhibitions on Acquisitions', in Kenneth A. Froot (ed.), *Foreign Direct Investment*, Chicago, IL: University of Chicago Press.

Lincoln, Edward 1990, *Japan's Unequal Trade*, Washington DC: Brookings Institution.

Mason, Mark 1992a, *American Multinationals and Japan: The Political Economy of Japanese Capital Controls, 1899–1980*, Cambridge, MA: Harvard University Press.

_____ 1992b, 'United States Direct Investment in Japan: Trends and Prospects', *California Management Review*, 35(1), pp. 98–115.

MITI (Ministry of International Trade and Industry) 1993, *Gaishikei Kigyo no Doko* [Trends of Foreign-Affiliated Enterprises], 26, Tokyo.

_____ 1994, Invitation to the Japanese Market: Keys for Successful Business in Japan, Tokyo, mimeo, January.

Morgan, James C. and J. Jeffrey Morgan 1991, *Cracking the Japanese Market: Strategies for Success in the New Global Economy*, New York: The Free Press.

OECD (Organisation for Economic Cooperation and Development) 1993, *International Direct Investment Statistics Yearbook: 1993*, Paris: OECD.

Reich, Robert 1991, 'Who is Them?' *Harvard Business Review*, 69(2), March–April, pp. 77–89.

US Department of Commerce 1993, *US Direct Investment Abroad: Operations of US Parent Companies and Their Foreign Affiliates (Preliminary 1991 Estimates)*, Washington DC: Government Publishing Office, July.

_____ (various issues), *Survey of Current Business*, Washington DC: Government Publishing Office.

US House of Representatives, *Beyond Revisionism: Toward a New US–Japan Policy for the Post-Cold War Era*, Washington DC: House Wednesday Group.

8 Multinational corporations and technology transfer in Penang and Guadalajara

Juan J. Palacios

The potential for foreign direct investment (FDI) to induce international technology transfer in the Pacific Rim in the 1990s is a topic of continuing interest. This chapter considers the case of the electronics industry, focusing on the experience of two regions on opposite sides of the Pacific: Penang in Malaysia, and Guadalajara in Mexico. Both have been dubbed Silicon Valleys because of their resemblance to the original high-technology conglomerate that developed in California. Moreover, both Malaysia and Mexico are typical examples of host countries to FDI in the Pacific and, under NAFTA's provisions, are likely to become either partners or rivals as they strive to secure access to the huge US market.

This chapter examines the extent to which technology has been transferred in each setting from multinational firms to the local milieu, and the channels through which the process has taken place. FDI is seen as a major instrument for the corporate expansion of multinational firms. Patterns of FDI have changed since the 1980s as these firms have adapted to the new global era of 'systemofacture' (Kaplinski 1985).

Multinational enterprises (MNEs) have both costs and benefits for host countries. In the past decade, researchers have tended to stress their potential to contribute to structural transformation and the development of a domestic technological capacity in developing countries. The single most important contribution the multinational firm makes is said to be technology transfer; MNEs are the main source of technological innovation, a key factor in economic growth and competitiveness. However, in general multinational firms are reluctant to share their cutting-edge technologies, even through joint ventures. These technologies are, after all, a precious asset: they provide corporations with technological rents in oligopolistic international technology markets. The argument here is that developing countries should build a critical indigenous capacity for the generation of new technologies. This would enable governments and companies to select the technologies most suited to their problems and resources, and would enhance their bargaining power to negotiate the acquisition of new technologies.

Multinational corporations and technology transfer

For decades MNEs were called the agents *par excellence* of Western capitalism and, at the same time, the promoters of the de-industrialisation of mature capitalist economies in the West. Since the 1980s, however, critique of these radical perspectives has led to a wider knowledge of the role of the MNE in global processes.

Researchers have shown that MNEs are not committed to inducing artificial industrialisation in developing countries as opposed to the kind of industrialisation domestic firms would promote in their absence (Evans 1981, cited in UNCTC 1988). Critical geographers such as Corbridge (1986) have in turn argued that whereas MNEs do promote growth without development in poor countries with weak governments (like some African states), leading to the creation of a dual economic structure, in the Asian NIEs (Singapore, South Korea, Taiwan and Hong Kong) and other countries they have contributed to high rates of growth of GNP, exports and wages. Corbridge thus makes a strong case for a more disaggregated approach to assessing the role MNEs play in developing countries.

In countries or regions lacking the conditions or resources necessary to ignite the process of industrialisation, foreign enterprises are often able to make a positive contribution. As MNEs transfer production operations from developed countries (usually through subsidiaries or subcontracting arrangements), the productive structure of such countries and regions changes — from dependence on exports of primary goods to increased reliance on exports of manufactures. Another major contribution the MNE can make because of its position as a key technological innovator is the transfer of technology. By transferring technology MNEs can enhance the technical level of host countries, thereby leading to an increase in productivity and higher rates of growth.

The ability to generate and improve technologies determines competitiveness and even survival in today's stagnant world economy; innovation is the key to reducing production costs and thus maintaining an edge in international markets. The pace of technological change is increasing, R&D costs are rising, and so the gap between developing and developed countries continues to grow even wider. The ability to assimilate foreign technologies or to develop an independent technological capacity has thus become crucial to the growth and competitiveness of developing countries (UNCTC 1988). National and local governments play an important role in attracting FDI and promoting ventures in their country or region, as Rajah (1988) and Chalmers (1991) have shown for Malaysia and Singapore respectively.

Types and mechanisms of technology transfer

Technology transfer is generally believed to be a unidirectional, sequential process whereby technical information flows from R&D centres and laboratories to manufacturing plants and, on the international plane, from innovating to recipient countries. The problem with this approach is the difficulty of defining where one stage ends and the next begins, even when the various activities are carried out in completely different locations. The process is not, in fact, simply a series of steps proceeding in one direction, but rather a circular and continuous line of tasks and operations involving the application of scientific knowledge to productive activities. Wang (1991, p. 21) put it correctly when he defined technology transfer as 'the ongoing efforts to maximise the exchange of information in the dynamic process from the initial idea formulation through prototype and product stages to final successful technological diffusion, with numerous feedback loops from later to earlier stages and continuous multi-level person-to-person relationships'.

The nature of the information transferred thus differs from one stage to the next, taking different forms as the process unfolds. The three main forms of technology transfer are direct productive investment, supply of machinery and equipment, and provision of unpackaged technology. Although usually associated with industrial activities, technology transfer can also take place in service areas such as tourism, real estate and banking.

There are four basic types of technology according to the productive task involved: product, process, quality control and management technology. Each may take the form of hardware (machinery and equipment), software (formulas and process description) or services (management and marketing knowhow, and process and product design) (UNCTC 1988). Transfers may take the form either of transactions between MNEs and domestic firms in host countries or equity participation arrangements. The latter include direct investment in subsidiaries and the establishment of joint ventures, and these are the most important forms of FDI; the former are more diversified and include licensing, franchising, international subcontracting, management contracts, marketing and advertising contracts, technical service contracts and turnkey contracts. These mechanisms define the uses MNEs can make of the technologies they generate: external (in joint or non-equity ventures) and internal (in wholly owned subsidiaries) (UNCTC 1988).

Once these aspects have been settled, the transfer of technology proceeds through a number of channels. In the case of international transfers through FDI, major channels include the training and skills development of employees (in-house programs and the provision of scholarships and financial support for local educational programs, for example); stimulation of local capacity for innovation (by carrying out R&D operations in subsidiaries or by contracting local R&D centres or engineering firms); and technology diffusion (by developing local suppliers through the encouragement of spin-offs and local ancillary industries, and the exposure of local firms to new technologies).

Appropriate technology and host country productivity

A much debated topic within the broader discussion of international technology transfer is whether the technologies transferred by MNEs to host countries are appropriate. It has traditionally been assumed that, because they tend to be capital intensive, such technologies are wholly inappropriate. Stewart (1976) pointed out in the mid 1970s that the products made by MNEs in low-income countries are often alien to domestic tastes, needs, culture and incomes.

More recent accounts have shown that other factors, such as availability of skilled labour, industry type, product type and the production stage transferred, determine capital intensity to a greater extent than ownership per se (UNCTC 1988, p. 183). These studies do not address the issue of the appropriateness of what is produced, however. What is clear is that promoting capital investment, both domestic and foreign, in host countries is a more effective and viable way of fostering job creation than trying to limit the technological options of MNEs. While not significant in the short term, in the long run the adoption and application of modern technologies could become an important factor in the growth of productivity and employment, given that job creation increasingly depends on competitiveness, and that competitiveness in turn increasingly depends on technological advancement.

Penang: the Silicon Valley of the East

The rise of the electronics industry in Malaysia

Over the past two decades the electronics industry has become thoroughly globalised. The Asia Pacific region has emerged as a major centre for this dynamic industry. Malaysia and the Philippines have been major producers of semiconductors for many years. In 1980, semiconductors accounted for 90 per cent of the output of the electronics industry in Malaysia and for 65 per cent in the Philippines (Chen 1990, p. 52).

Malaysia's impressive lead in the global electronics industry was made possible by two waves of FDI, the first in 1972–74 in direct response to government promotion of the industry, and the second in 1979–81 due mainly to a massive relocation of labour-intensive MNE operations from Singapore. During the 1970s, the share of electronic products in Malaysia's total manufacturing exports rocketed from 1.8 to 50 per cent (Chowdury 1988, cited in Chalmers 1991). In 1978 Malaysia accounted for over one-fifth (21 per cent) of all semiconductors imported into the United States (Rajah 1988, p. 33). By 1980, Malaysia had become the world's main supplier of semiconductors, exporting US$1,066 million worth of semiconductors to OECD countries compared with Singapore's US$821 million, the Philippines' US$482 million, South Korea's US$385 million and Taiwan's US$359 million (Chen 1990, p. 58).

Whether in terms of production, exports or employment, the electronics industry is Malaysia's primary manufacturing activity. The industry's output accounted for 25 per cent of GDP in 1990, 30 per cent in 1991 and 35 per cent in 1992 (Ismail 1994; PDC 1993a, p. 11). Electronics exports increased from RM6,568 million (US$2,495 million) in 1986 to RM34,712 million (US$13,190 million) in 1992, with the largest jump occurring in industrial electronics: RM146 million (US$55 million) to RM10,341 million (US$3,930 million) (Ismail 1994, p. 31). Although production of components, mainly semiconductors, continues to dominate the industry, the share of this subsector declined from a peak of 90 per cent in 1980 to 82 per cent in 1986 and 58 per cent in 1990 (Table 8.1).

Table 8.1   Structure of Malaysia's electronics industry, 1986 and 1990 (per cent)

	1986	1990
Electronic components	81.5	57.6
Consumer electronics	12.3	23.2
Industrial electronics	6.2	19.2
Total	100.0	100.0

Source: Ismail, 1994.

Federal government policies have played a key role in the birth and development of Malaysia's electronics industry. The industry has been guided by a comprehensive and coherent development planning mechanism instituted by the Malaysian government over the past two decades. This has comprised medium-term plans of five years, prepared under the broader view of longer term schemes called Outline Perspective Plans. The first Outline Perspective Plan concluded in 1990, and the second runs from 1990 to 2000. Malaysia's sixth five-year plan covers the period 1991–95. The fifth and sixth five-year plans have specifically addressed how to advance science and technology, considered crucial to the attainment of national development goals (Rahman and Smith 1991). Both the Outline Perspective Plan and the sixth five-year plan were formulated within the context of an even longer term plan called Vision 2020, whose aim is to make Malaysia a fully industrialised society by 2020.

The birth of the electronics industry in Penang

Penang's electronics industry was initiated by the state government of Dr Lim Chong Eu, who took office in 1969. Dr Lim commissioned Nathan & Associates, a US consulting firm, to prepare a master plan for the development of the state. The Nathan Report, which later became part of the Penang Master Plan, recommended a thorough restructuring of Penang's economy on a solid industrial base. To implement the directions of the plan, the Lim government created the Penang Development Corporation (PDC) in November 1969 with federal government support.[1] The new agency set out to promote the state's industrial development through the construction of industrial estates called free industrial zones. The strategy was to concentrate on the establishment of labour-intensive, export-oriented industries with the potential to set the industrialisation process in motion.

The electronics industry was selected because of its dynamic growth record and broad technological potential. The PDC sought to attract foreign firms, to free industrial zones in particular, by providing generous incentives and superior industrial infrastructure. The agency was also charged with the responsibility of setting up the first indigenous plant, which was expected to be the detonator of industrial growth in

157

the state. Using Silicon Valley as its model and inspiration, the PDC established the first electronics factory, Penang Electronics, in Penang in 1970. In January 1972, the first free industrial zone opened at Bayan Lepas on the east side of Penang Island. This major initiative, coupled with the establishment of Penang Electronics, quickly attracted other new industrial ventures to the area. MNEs soon began to flock to Penang (Table 8.2).

By the mid 1980s Penang was the world's largest exporter of microchips (Rajah 1988, p. 32). Propelled by the commitment of the PDC and the establishment of MNE subsidiaries in Penang, in the 1970s and 1980s the electronics industry came to constitute the mainstay of Penang's industrialisation. For this reason, this small Malaysian state is today often called the Silicon Valley of the East.

Most of the initiatives taken both by the PDC and the state government have been conceived within the organisational framework of short-term and medium-term plans, as is the case at national level. In its most recent plan, the 10-year Penang Strategic Development Plan launched in 1992, the state government sets out programs for development in four key sectors: manufacturing, trade and services, tourism and agriculture. Major objectives of all Penang's development plans have been to enhance the participation in industrial activity of *bumiputeras* — indigenous Malaysians and Malay companies — and to promote indigenous manufacturing capability through the development of local small and medium sized industries.

Penang's locational advantages

Areas designated by the PDC as industrial estates may be either free industrial zones proper or industrial parks. The zones are designed to promote the establishment of export-oriented industries, whether local or foreign-owned, by reducing customs controls to a minimum and eliminating duty both on imported inputs and equipment and on exports of finished products. Eligible industries are those exporting 100 per cent of their output, although in exceptional circumstances companies exporting at

Table 8.2   **Growth of factories in Penang's industrial estates, 1980–93**

	All industries		Electrical/electronics	
	No. of plants	No. of employees	No. of plants	No. of employees
1980	216	56,012	23	24,638
1992	629	146,382	129	77,577
1993[a]	637	156,861	142	89,402

Note: a   As of 30 June.

Source: PDC, 1993a; unpublished PDC materials.

least 80 per cent of their output may also be approved. Factories whose raw materials and components are mainly imported are also eligible for free industrial zone location (PDC 1993b). Industrial parks are manufacturing complexes. While open to all types of industry, they are best suited to ancillary and support industries, which may be either locally owned or set up as joint ventures. At present there are two free industrial zones (Bayan Lepas and Prai) and five industrial parks (Mak Mandin, Bayan Lepas, Prai, Bukit Tengah and Seberang Jaya) in Penang. Twelve free industrial zones have been established nationwide. Prai has Penang's largest concentration of plants, as shown in Table 8.3.

Table 8.3   **Distribution of factories in Penang's industrial estates, 1993[a]**

	No. of factories	Share (%)
Industrial parks		
Mak Mandin	91	14.3
Bayan Lepas	82	12.9
Prai	288	45.2
Bukit Tengah	35	5.5
Seberang Jaya	20	3.1
Subtotal	516	81.0
Free industrial zones		
Bayan Lepas	83	13.0
Prai	38	6.0
Subtotal	121	19.0
Total	637	100.0

Note: a   As of 30 June.

Source: Unpublished PDC documents.

Firms not located in a free industrial zone may be given the status of 'licensed manufacturing warehouse'. These benefit from the same facilities and special treatment given firms in free industrial zones — and must meet the same eligibility requirements. Through the creation of licensed manufacturing warehouses, the Malaysian government hopes to encourage the geographical dispersal of export-oriented industries. Licensed manufacturing warehouses are becoming a major alternative instrument for industrial promotion and, according to some PDC officials, may soon overtake free industrial zones in popularity.

Penang's industrial estates offer the following significant locational advantages: a convenient location on either Penang Island or the mainland; superior industrial infrastructure; good roads and highways; proximity to air and sea facilities; well-developed ancillary and support industries and related business services; and proximity to both established population centres and new townships. In addition, companies operating in free industrial zones and industrial parks, as well as those opting for warehouse status, can enjoy a wide array of investment incentives extended by the federal government to new industrial ventures. These incentives, contained in provisions of the 1986 Promotion of Investments Act and the 1967 Income Tax Act, include tax exemptions for companies granted pioneer status; investment and reinvestment tax allowances; soft credit and venture capital for export financing; industrial building allowances; tax deductions for R&D, technical training and industrial adjustment; and concessionary tax schemes for firms establishing their corporate headquarters in Malaysia (PDC 1993b). In addition, potential investors can take advantage of a flexible equity participation policy that allows full foreign ownership — that is, no equity conditions — for projects that export over 80 per cent of their output.

Fiscal incentives provide for tax holidays of up to 10 years, enabling MNEs to transfer substantial profits through intrafirm pricing manipulation. Like cheap labour, this has turned out to be a powerful motivation for MNEs to relocate their manufacturing operations to Malaysia and other tax havens (Rajah 1988). Still, the most compelling advantages for MNEs to operate in Penang, and in Malaysia, have been the access they gain to a large pool of disciplined, easy-to-train, English-speaking workers, especially women; wages about 10 times lower than those in the United States or Japan; flexible legislation that allows three shifts per day and night work; prolonged political stability; and a relatively efficient government bureaucracy with minimal corruption (Rajah 1988).

The structure of Penang's electronics industry

Penang comprises two territories, Penang Island and Wellesley Province, of 293 and 738 square kilometres respectively. In 1990 the state's population was 1.15 million inhabitants, of whom 34 per cent were Malay, 53 per cent Chinese, 12 per cent Indian and 1 per cent other nationalities.

In June 1993, the electrical/electronics industry employed 89,402 people, or 57 per cent of all workers in Penang's industrial areas. Most of these were involved in production (Table 8.4). As already noted, wages are low compared with those in developed economies. In December 1992, the average monthly salary of managerial and middle management staff was RM5,100 (US$1,940) and RM2,050 (US$780) respectively, while that of engineers and technicians was RM2,150 (US$820) and RM690 (US$262) respectively. Wages of production operators were even lower: RM450 (US$170) per month for skilled workers, and only RM360 (US$140) per month for unskilled workers (PDC 1993a, p. 7).

Table 8.4   Employment structure of electrical/electronics industry in Penang's industrial estates, 1993[a]

	No. of employees	Share (%)
Professional and management	5,427	6.1
Supervisory and technical	11,300	12.6
Clerical and sales	3,817	4.3
General workers	2,852	3.2
Factory workers	66,006	73.8
Skilled	37,710	
Unskilled	28,296	
Total	89,402	100.0

Note: a   As of 30 June.

Source: PDC, 1993a, p. 6.

Most of the companies that make up the electronics industry in Penang (60 per cent) are located in free industrial zones, and the remainder in other PDC industrial estates (Table 8.5). The large concentration of electronics plants in Bayan Lepas Free Industrial Zone may be explained by the fact that this industrial complex is situated

Table 8.5   Location of electronics factories in Penang's industrial areas, 1992

	No. of factories	Share (%)
Industrial parks		
Mak Mandin	2	1.9
Bayan Lepas	5	4.7
Prai	23	21.7
Bukit Tengah	6	5.7
Seberang Jaya	9	8.5
Subtotal	45	42.4
Free industrial zones		
Bayan Lepas	46	43.4
Prai	15	14.1
Subtotal	61	57.5
Total	106	100.0

Source: PDC, 1992, pp. 1–7.

adjacent to Bayan Lepas Airport on Penang Island. It is just a few miles from Georgetown, Penang's capital, where large pools of labour can be found, and is close to the University Sains Malaysia, the Penang Skills Development Centre, and other training institutions and technical colleges.

Penang's electronics industry mainly carries out assembly and testing operations, though other higher end productive processes are expanding rapidly, especially in the factories of MNE subsidiaries. In mid 1992, 89 of Penang's 110 electronics companies were either fully or partially foreign owned, most of them by FDI ventures from Taiwan (29 firms), Japan (21 firms) and the United States (19 firms) (*Penang Development News*, Special Edition, 1992, p. 16)

The industry's product mix is dominated by integrated circuits (ICs) and printed circuit boards (PCBs) (Table 8.6). This does not mean, however, that Penang's electronics industry is restricted to semiconductor production, as some analysts have suggested (Rajah 1988, for example). The product mix is in fact highly diversified and extends across consumer and industrial electronics as well as electronic components, thus reflecting the general trend reported by Ismail (1994) for Malaysia's electronics industry as a whole. Manufacture and assembly of audio and video equipment and of telecommunications equipment and components ranks second to IC and PCB production and can be expected to grow rapidly in the future. Penang is thus well placed for the development of these other two subsectors of the electronics industry. As Sharp Corporation's Senior Executive Vice-President for International Business stated recently, 'all things considered, ASEAN is the most suitable region in the world for large-scale production bases for consumer electronics' (Wada 1994, p. 6).

Another important development is the appearance of higher end operations in semiconductor production, such as IC and wafer final testing. In 1992 over a dozen companies operating in zones and parks had the capacity to carry out these operations (Table 8.6). This represents a departure from the trend reported by Chen (1990) for Hong Kong and Singapore to become the testing centres of the international semiconductor industry. Production of high-technology products, such as optoelectronic components, LED displays and liquid crystal displays, also broadens the scope for technology transfer to take place from MNE subsidiaries to local firms, and through them to the local economy.

Nevertheless, assembly remains the dominant operation in most of the electronics industry's three subsectors. Technological upgrading and industrial deepening will, therefore, continue to be a high priority in Penang's development efforts. There is also a need for MNE subsidiaries to encourage greater vertical integration and the production of higher end electronic products.

The experience of the pioneering MNEs
As discussed earlier, the establishment of Penang Electronics and the first free industrial zone in Bayan Lepas was intended to kick-start the development of an electronics industry in Penang, and by extension the state's industrialisation process.

Table 8.6   Major electronics products manufactured in Penang, 1992 (no. of producers)

Product/process	No. of producers
IC assembly and testing	13
PCB assembly, burning and lamination	12
Capacitors and varistors	10
Car radios, stereos, speakers, antennas	7
Telecommunications, power and optic fibre cables, magnetic wires	7
Telephone sets and answering machines	6
Disk drives and components	6
Power transformers, power supplies, voltage regulators	6
Carbon resistors	6
Assembly of radios, TV sets and cassette recorders	5
Audio equipment	5
Loudspeakers	4
Computers and parts	3
Rectifiers	3
Wafer fabrication and testing	3
LED displays, optoelectronic components and electrophotographic printheads	3
Thin-film head assembly	3
PCB display panels and moulds	2
PABX systems	2
Fax machine assembly	2

Note: Total number of producers is not given as some companies manufacture more than one product.

Source: Compiled from data in PDC, 1992, pp. 1–7.

Soon after the government-led venture began operations, MNEs began to flock into Penang. In 1971 and 1972, seven subsidiaries — Clarion, National Semiconductor, Siemens Litronix, Robert Bosch, Intel, Advanced Micro Devices and Hewlett Packard — established plants in Penang, mainly in the Bayan Lepas Free Industrial Zone. All seven continue to be major producers in the region. Other leading subsidiaries presently operating or soon to operate in Penang's industrial areas are Acer, Motorola, Canon, Digital, Hitachi, Seagate, Phillips, Sanyo and Sony.

Clarion (M)
This subsidiary of Japan's Clarion Corporation began operations in September 1971 at Bayan Lepas with about 30 employees. Originally producing 8-track cartridge players, by the late 1970s it was making car audio systems based on the latest product

and process technologies. Clarion (M) now produces over 50,000 high-quality car radios and car stereo systems annually for such leading auto makers as Ford, Volvo, Mazda and Land Rover. In recognition of the high quality of its products, in 1991 this factory became the first off-shore subsidiary to receive the Ford Motor 'Q1' Award from Ford Motor Company (Australia).

From the outset, Clarion (M) has stressed in-house training as a major channel for transfer of the parent company's technologies. Senior technical personnel sent to Japan under the company's 'train a trainer' scheme have returned to Penang to transmit their newly acquired knowledge to local employees. Technical upgrading has also been facilitated by the frequent introduction of advanced technology from Japan, backed up by Japanese organisational and industrial methods and philosophy. Clarion (M) plans to establish a modern engineering department in Penang by the mid 1990s to facilitate further transfer of advanced technology from the parent company.

National Semiconductor

This subsidiary of the US-based multinational started operations with 120 employees in December 1971, less than three months after Clarion (M), and also at Bayan Lepas. Two years later the plant was already producing one million Penang-made ICs annually, and by 1986 National Semiconductor was among Malaysia's top 10 exporters and employers. In 1990 production passed 100 million units a month, with total investment reaching US$850 million.

Present operations include wafer fabrication and testing; manufacture of ICs (advanced bipolar circuits, CMOS logic circuits, advanced interfaces and peripherals); full testing of the plant's own products as well as some produced by other National Semiconductor subsidiaries; and development of testing software by local technicians. Technology transfer is facilitated by the use of the latest production technology and by permanent, in-house, on-the-job training programs.

Siemens Litronix Malaysia

This plant started out as Litronix Malaysia in April 1972. In 1976 it became the first MNE subsidiary in Penang to be fully managed by Malaysians. From originally making light-emitting diodes, by the mid 1970s the plant was manufacturing LED displays, LED games, watches and calculators. In 1979 it moved into optoelectronics, producing LED lamp optocouplers, intelligent displays and custom-designed optoelectronic devices, as well as carrying out wafer testing. Litronix Malaysia became a wholly owned venture of the German multinational, Siemens AG, in 1981.

Technology transfer has been pursued largely through the introduction of advanced automation techniques and processes, notably automatic die bonding, wire bonding, device testing and punching. A major initiative in this direction was the establishment in 1990 of an IC wafer testing facility at the Penang factory. Through these developments, semiconductor production has advanced from first to third generation technology.

Robert Bosch Malaysia

A subsidiary of Germany's Robert Bosch AG, Robert Bosch Malaysia began operating in Bayan Lepas Free Industrial Zone in April 1972. Its domestic sister company is called Malaysian-German Automotive Equipment. From originally manufacturing exposure meters for silent movie cameras, in 1973 Robert Bosch Malaysia began to assemble 8 mm movie cameras and to produce car indicators. In 1989 it was awarded a government contract to manufacture a wide range of Bosch and Blaupunkt products for Malaysia's national car, the Proton Saga. Today it is the largest producer of Blaupunkt products, accounting for nearly one-third of this MNE's world production volume.

Robert Bosch Malaysia has been an active promoter of technological upgrading and transfer. In April 1973, just one year after starting operations, it became the first MNE subsidiary in Penang to set up a design department. Managed by a German engineer, the department started out with four local engineers and two local technicians. In 1978 Robert Bosch Malaysia produced the first wholly locally designed sound movie camera and took over production of this product line from parent company plants. By 1992 the design department had grown to a solid team of 30 engineers, 13 technicians, one clerical staff member and one German manager.

Marking a radical change in direction, in 1983 the plant began to manufacture manually tuned car stereos, the first locally designed products of this kind. Digital car stereos, also designed by the subsidiary's own R&D team, followed in 1987. In 1992 Robert Bosch Malaysia took over from German parent plants the manufacture of a complete range of loudspeakers, and started production of state-of-the-art CD stereo systems for cars.

Robert Bosch Malaysia set up the Bosch Research and Design Centre in 1992, a US$5 million investment. This was the company's first R&D centre, and it was staffed mainly by *bumiputeras*. The new centre has had several technological achievements, putting it on a par with the Bosch R&D centre in Germany. Malaysian engineers today design and develop sophisticated car audio systems and other high-quality auto equipment that rival those of the parent firm's plants in Germany.

Intel Malaysia

Intel Malaysia began operations in August 1972 in Bayan Lepas Free Industrial Zone with a workforce of about 100 employees. This subsidiary of the giant US chip maker originally produced the 1103 1 kilobit DRAM chip; by 1973 it was manufacturing more than one million ICs annually. Today, Intel's Penang factory is the main producer of 80386 and 80486 microprocessors.

Like Robert Bosch, Intel Malaysia has been active in promoting the transfer of technological knowhow. In 1978 it established the region's first testing plant, Intel Technology. Intel thus became the first semiconductor plant in Penang to have a testing facility directly linked to assembly. Intel Technology soon advanced from the testing of DRAMs and EPROMs to testing microcontrollers and microprocessors. Intel also established Southeast Asia's first 8-bit and 16-bit microcontroller design centre. Full responsibility for engineering will soon be given to the local technical team operating this centre.

In 1985 Intel Malaysia, which had been given responsibility for liaising directly with customers on product quality and design, set up a fully equipped laboratory for product design and development on its premises. In an effort to systematise and enhance its in-house training practices, the subsidiary also founded Intel U, a human resource training and development centre located in the Intel Malaysia complex.

Advanced Micro Devices Export

Advanced Micro Devices Export (AMD) began assembly of ICs in September 1972, only three years after the establishment of the US parent company, Advanced Micro Devices Corp. Its workforce then numbered 150. After the merger of the US parent with Monolithic Memories, Inc., in 1987 two plants were added to the initial factory in the Bayan Lepas Free Industrial Zone (one was an IC testing facility that now operates as Advanced Micro Devices Sdn Bhd). This move made the Penang subsidiary the largest assembler of AMD products worldwide. Up to 90 per cent of the parent company's products are tested at the Bayan Lepas facilities, from where they are shipped direct to customers in Europe, Asia and the United States. AMD now produces microprocessors, memory and programmable logic device circuits for telecommunications equipment, office automation equipment and network applications.

AMD has encouraged the transfer of technology through in-house training programs, along with a corporate policy of employing mostly local labour. Indeed, with about 5,000 employees, mostly Malaysian, the firm is one of Penang's largest employers. In addition the company has adopted a performance-based promotion and remuneration scheme. These practices and programs are reinforced by the systematic introduction of the latest production technologies from the parent company, such as the 100 hermetic assembly and the 2000 plastic assembly methods.

Hewlett Packard (Pg)

This was the last of the pioneering subsidiaries to establish a plant in Penang, again in the Bayan Lepas Free Industrial Zone. Hewlett Packard (Pg) opened in October 1972 with about 60 employees. It was founded on an initial investment of US$1.3 million. From manufacturing core computer memory, in 1974 the factory added three new product lines: LED displays and indicators, microwave diodes and die preparation. In 1987 a further line was introduced, electrophotographic printheads. By 1992, the Penang subsidiary was a leading manufacturer of high-quality optoelectronic and microwave components.

Hewlett Packard (Pg) has achieved a high level of quality in its products and excellent productive performance. It won the Best Quality Management Award of the National Productivity Centre in 1989; the HP Golden Eagle Award for Error-Free and

On-Time Accounting in 1989, 1990 and 1991; and the Best Quality Control Circle Award at the Singapore International Exposition of Quality Control Circles in 1990 and 1991. In 1992 the subsidiary employed more than 3,000 people and its invested capital had grown to over US$50 billion.

Hewlett Packard (Pg) has taken several important steps towards the effective transfer of advanced technology to the local milieu. In 1975 it created an engineering department devoted to product design and improvement. This was transformed in 1991 into a fully fledged R&D centre. The company's engineers now design and build, entirely within the Bayan Lepas factory, automated machinery to replace manual processes, equipment which would formerly have been purchased from other Hewlett Packard plants or even from other firms. Hewlett Packard (Pg) was also a founder of the Penang Skills Development Centre, donating US$200,000 worth of equipment for use in its computer laboratory.

Collective initiatives for technological transfer and upgrading

In addition to the individual efforts already reviewed above, MNEs operating in Penang and the state government (primarily through the PDC) have taken collective action to promote technological upgrading and human resource technical development in the region.

Penang Skills Development Centre

The Penang Skills Development Centre, established in 1989, was the joint initiative of 51 companies operating in Penang. The project had the support and assistance of the PDC and the participation of the University Sains Malaysia and other local educational institutions. All seven subsidiaries reviewed above were major contributors. The centre's basic objective is to upgrade and update the skills and technical knowledge of local workers and technicians in order to fill the growing needs of participating companies. Trainers and specialists come from local subsidiaries, their parent companies and R&D centres.

Penang International Education and Technology Centre

This centre was established as a joint venture between the PDC and IJM Corporation Bhd under the name Worldwide Ventures, Sdn Bhd. Inaugurated in August 1992, the centre offers educational programs in technical disciplines at both the undergraduate and postgraduate levels in conjunction with international universities. The goal is to provide Penang with highly skilled technicians and engineers.

Penang Technoplex

Proposed by the PDC, this is the most ambitious initiative yet for promoting technology transfer in Penang. The plan involves constructing a science and technology park on a 60-hectare site in the Bayan Lepas Industrial Park, adjacent to Bayan

Lepas Free Industrial Zone. The project was proposed in response to the state government's call for locally based companies to automate their plants and move into higher end production methods and processes.

The Technoplex has two general objectives: to stimulate existing R&D activities by providing the necessary facilities and technical infrastructure; and to attract new, technology-based, high-technology industries. In order to fulfil these objectives, the PDC, with the support of the state government and the private sector, plans to install three specialised training centres at the Technoplex: the Plastics Technology Training Centre, the Wood-Based Furniture Design and Training Centre, and the Automation Applications Centre. All three are meant to complement the role of the Penang Skills Development Centre.

The above collective initiatives are backed at federal level by the Cabinet Committee on Science and Technology created in 1990; the Council for the Coordination and Transfer of Industrial Technology established in 1986 within the Ministry of Science, Technology and the Environment; and the National Council for Scientific Research and Development formed in 1975. These organisations are responsible for carrying out the national science and technology policy pursued by the Malaysian government since 1986. The central goal of this policy is the promotion of science and technology as an instrument for economic development and the realisation of national scientific and technological self-reliance (Rahman and Smith 1991).

Technology transfer through local supporting industries

The rapid growth of MNE subsidiaries in Penang has given rise to a variety of local supporting industries in the state. These are largely run by *bumiputeras* who have managed to take advantage of the niche markets opened by local MNE production. According to directories compiled by the PDC, there are 71 local supporting enterprises operating in three major industrial sectors: metal-working and machinery, plastics, and packaging. The largest concentration (37 enterprises) is found in the first sector, followed by packaging (18) and plastics (16). Most metal-working ventures (92 per cent) are wholly owned by *bumiputeras*; the corresponding figures for packaging and plastics are 78 per cent and 75 per cent respectively.

The development of ancillary industries has been accompanied by a significant transfer of technology and knowhow from the MNEs operating in Penang. Two examples of fully locally owned and successful supporting companies illustrate how this process has taken place.

Eng Hardware Engineering

This company started out in 1974 as a backyard family business making DC converters for hawkers of Air Itam. In a visionary move, the small company began to invest its profits in precision tool and die equipment with the aim of becoming a supplier to the MNEs located in Penang. It achieved this goal in the late 1970s. This gave Eng Hardware Engineering access to two channels of technology transfer: exposure to the products and services required by MNE subsidiaries; and collaboration with top-notch MNE engineers and technicians. The company used these channels to improve the quality of the services it offered.

Eng Hardware Engineering later diversified into production system automation and metal stamping services, and began investing in new product lines such as tungsten carbide tooling and disk drive peripherals and components. In 1988 it created a new venture, Eng Teknologi, to provide services to high-technology MNE engineering areas. At present, Eng Hardware Engineering is one of the world's top five manufacturers of E-blocks, a key component for computer hard disk drives requiring precision manufacturing.

Loh Kim Teow group

This group began in the 1950s as a small foundry producing window grilles, fences, metal doors and minor replacement parts for vehicles and ship engines. In 1960 the factory began to manufacture piling equipment, mobile cranes and cement mixers for the construction industry, which was at the time experiencing an upswing. With the opening of the Bayan Lepas Free Industrial Zone, the company established a third production facility called Loh Kim Teow Engineering, devoted to the manufacture of high-precision tools and parts needed by MNEs. In 1984 the group relocated its operations to a new industrial site in the Bayan Lepas Free Industrial Zone.

A new department created in 1988 within Loh Kim Teow Engineering for the design and manufacture of automation equipment soon evolved into a separate corporate branch, Semiconductor Equipment Manufacturers. This has become a leading *bumiputera* centre for the design and manufacture of high-end automation equipment and software for the semiconductor industry.

A fifth branch of the group, called Plastics Technology, produces plastic components, equipment frames, electronic parts and sophisticated plastic frames and moulds. These latter are exported, mainly to Europe. The corporate and technological development of the Loh Kim Teow group has been based on continual upgrading of the technical skills of its workforce through extensive in-house training programs.

In general, the development of the electronics industry in Penang was initiated and continues to be driven by the subsidiaries of large MNEs that have found it profitable to relocate their operations to Malaysia. The process has been highly dynamic; the number of companies in Penang's industrial areas has grown rapidly and continues to grow. Although the presence of multinationals stimulated the development of local supporting industries, a new trend is emerging in the consumer electronics industry for MNEs to bring in captive suppliers (Ismail 1994). This could become a serious threat both to the creation of new local supporting industries and to their role as a major channel for technology transfer.

Penang's success has to a great extent been made possible by the sound and aggressive initiatives of the state government, foremost among which was the establishment of the PDC. This shows that government policies and support are crucial for the development of a thriving electronics industry and any other FDI-based economic activity. Although assembly continues to dominate Penang's electronics industry, there is a clear trend towards the upgrading of technology and production knowhow as higher end operations are performed by a growing number of MNE subsidiaries. This in turn indicates that the international division of labour that took shape in the 1970s and 1980s in the Asia Pacific, as characterised by Chen (1990), is beginning to change.

Guadalajara: Mexico's Silicon Valley

The Mexican electronics industry: an overview

In the late 1970s Mexico was the only Latin American country to figure among the top exporters of semiconductors to the United States, after the Asian NIEs and Malaysia. Of total US semiconductor imports of US$3,110 million in 1977, imports from Malaysia were worth US$658 million, while imports from Singapore, South Korea, Taiwan and Hong Kong respectively were worth US$591 million, US$510 million, US$214 million and US$193 million. Mexico was sixth at US$178 million (Rajah 1988, p. 33).

The Mexican electronics industry experienced rapid growth during the 1980s. Total capital invested increased from US$30 million in 1983 to US$80 million in 1987; the gross value of production grew from US$108 million in 1983 to US$649 million in 1991; and exports expanded from US$65 million in 1980 to US$573 million in 1990. In 1990 the electronics industry had 147 firms and a total of 10,500 employees (Mattar and Schatan 1993, p. 114). The industry is largely made up of MNE subsidiaries, and is therefore highly dependent on foreign imports, mainly of ICs, PCBs, power sources, diodes, disk drives, transistors and testing equipment. Assembly is the dominant operation, with the main local inputs being labour, metal parts, condensers, screwdrivers, resistors and packaging materials.

The confidence of MNEs in Mexico's electronics industry is indicated by their willingness to expand the operations of their Mexican subsidiaries. IBM invested an additional US$62 million in Mexico in 1993 (*Lloyd Economic Report*, February 1993, p. 2), despite retrenching 50,000 employees worldwide and incurring losses of over US$8,000 million in that year (*Siglo XXI*, 28 July 1993). Although it has shut down four manufacturing plants worldwide in the last few years, computer giant DEC Corp. expanded its production facilities in Chihuahua. The new plant manufactures all of the PCBs for DEC's new Alpha-AxP processor, using the latest surface mount technology ('La Computación, en Transición', *Expansión*, March 1993).

Mexican firms depend on multinationals, especially US multinationals, for the transfer of technical knowledge and knowhow, usually through joint ventures. Little transfer of the latest cutting-edge technology has taken place, however, because of an alleged lack of capacity on the part of Mexican firms to absorb it (Mattar and Schatan

1993). It is therefore unclear whether Mexico will be able to develop a fully fledged electronics industry, or will simply continue to assemble imported inputs.

The Mexican government has attempted since the 1970s to regulate and promote the development and technological upgrading of the electronics industry through a series of legislative and policy initiatives. In 1973 it passed a law regulating technology transfer and the use of patents and trademarks. In 1981 a presidential decree instituting a program for the promotion of the electronics industry was gazetted; its aim was to counter technological dependence and the growth of imports, and to foster vertical integration and exports. In 1990, a fiscal incentive program was established to promote the modernisation of the computer industry. Because of its dynamic growth and broad technological potential, this industry was selected as a key instrument for the future development of the Mexican economy.

Mexican policy on technology transfer may change in line with new legislation on FDI passed by Congress at the end of 1993. Changes made so far in response to NAFTA provisions do not seem to be significant. Chapter 17 of NAFTA stipulates that members give citizens and firms of the United States, Canada and Mexico the same treatment as that accorded their own nationals with respect to the protection of intellectual property rights. The only direct references to technology transfer are contained in Article 1709 on patents and Article 1710 on semiconductor IC drawing schemes (SECOFI 1993). It can be expected, though, that as NAFTA is implemented over the next 15 years, new legislation and policies on technology transfer between Mexico and its northern neighbours will emerge that are consistent with the more liberalised trade and investment climate NAFTA is supposed to bring about.

Guadalajara as export platform

Located in the central west, about 300 kilometres from the Pacific Coast, Guadalajara is Mexico's second largest city and the capital of the state of Jalisco.[2] Although it officially has a population of 1.65 million people (1990 National Census) and a land area of 188 square kilometres, over the last two decades Guadalajara and its related economic activities have extended over neighbouring municipalities and towns to form a metropolitan region of about 720 square kilometres with nearly four million inhabitants.[3] This vast area encompasses the El Salto Industrial Corridor and the Guadalajara Industrial Park, the focus of much of the region's industrial growth.

Since the mid 1980s the Guadalajara region has become an attractive site for the establishment of in-bond assembly plants — referred to in Mexico as *maquiladoras* — as firms have relocated from cities along the Mexico–US border towards the interior (Palacios 1990). Because of the *maquiladoras*' export orientation, Guadalajara emerged in the late 1980s as a thriving export platform. Table 8.7 shows that in 1990 Jalisco had the highest concentration (10 per cent) of major exporting companies after Nuevo León and the Federal District (Mexico's most industrialised states) and the northern border states (where most *maquiladoras* are still located). The state's most dynamic export sector for the last decade has been the electronics industry. According

Table 8.7   Location of major exporting companies by state, 1990 (no., per cent)

State	No. of companies	Share (%)
Nuevo León	86	17.2
Federal District	66	13.2
Jalisco	49[a]	9.8
Border states[b]	75	15.0
Other states	224	44.8
Total	500	100.0

Notes:　a　44 of these are located in the Guadalajara region.
　　　　　b　Comprises Baja California, Coahuila, Chihuahua, Sonora and Tamaulipas.

Source:　Ministry of Trade and Industrial Promotion, *Directory of Major Exporting Companies*, Mexico, 1990.

to the Jalisco office of the Foreign Trade National Council, in 1993 the electronics industry was easily the state's single most important exporter. It accounted for nearly half (47 per cent) of the state's total exports of US$2,183 million in that year, followed by the film and camera and auto parts industries with only 7 and 3 per cent respectively.

All the companies that make up the state's electronics industry are located in the Guadalajara region. According to the Jalisco office of the Electronics and Communications Industry Chamber, three-quarters of these firms are subsidiaries of such leading MNEs as IBM, Motorola, Hewlett Packard, NEC and AT&T. These subsidiaries dominate the industry with the scale of their operations: according to the Foreign Trade National Council, in 1993 IBM's overseas sales (of US$558 million) alone accounted for as much as 25 per cent of Jalisco's total exports. Because of the prevalence of MNE subsidiaries and related industries and services in the region, since the late 1980s Guadalajara has been referred to as the Mexican Silicon Valley, both in international and domestic business circles (see, for example, *Business Week*, 3 April 1989, p. 3; *Expansión*, September 1989, cover article).

The development of the electronics industry in Guadalajara

The origins of the electronics industry in Guadalajara can be traced back to the late 1960s when the first two MNE subsidiaries established operations in the region. Motorola de Mexico and Industrias Mexicanas Burroughs began operations in 1968, the former assembling semiconductors, radios and microphones, and the latter producing electronic cable, power supplies and harnesses. Both subsidiaries took advantage of the Temporary Importation for Export program, through which parts, components and equipment could be imported and the finished product exported duty free. This program was introduced to encourage the development in Mexico of export-oriented industry. Siemens, the German MNE, had already set up a factory at La Tijera, a semirural locality about five kilometres south of Guadalajara, by taking over a locally owned enterprise. The Siemens plant began manufacturing electrical motors, contactors and low-tension switches in 1962, with almost all inputs and materials being sourced locally.

In 1965, the Mexican government had instituted the *maquiladora* program to promote the establishment of in-bond plants on a 20-kilometre strip along the Mexico–US border. The program was designed to take advantage of provisions 806.30 and 807.00 of the US tariff system. As a result, the northern border strip became virtually a huge export-processing (or free industrial) zone, where in-bond plants could operate without paying duties. In 1972, the *maquiladora* program was extended to the rest of Mexico, thus widening the choice of duty free locations for FDI ventures. Motorola and Burroughs (which later became Unisys when the parent company merged with Sperry) soon applied for *maquiladora* status in Guadalajara to enjoy the facilities provided under this regime.

These pioneering MNEs were attracted to Guadalajara both by duty exemption schemes and, more importantly, by the various advantages offered by the region (Palacios 1988). Labour-related advantages included a large labour pool; ready availability of skilled workers and technicians; a stable labour force with an established work ethic; low turnover; and docile local unions. Locality-related advantages included fairly well-developed industrial infrastructure; efficient communications and industrial services; a diversified industrial apparatus; five major universities and several technical schools in the vicinity; an adequate water supply; and a wide variety of recreational and cultural amenities.

During the 1970s two more major MNE set up subsidiaries in Guadalajara. In 1974 General Instrument (which later became C.P. Clare Mexicana) established a plant in Tlaquepaque under the *maquiladora* program to assemble relays and electrical surge suppressors. In 1975 IBM built its first Mexican manufacturing plant in the El Salto Industrial Corridor to produce typewriters for the export and domestic markets. This was its chief product until 1987, when IBM de México opened a new, wholly IBM-owned plant at its El Salto premises to manufacture microcomputers for export. The authorisation of this plant constituted a major shift in Mexican policy towards FDI, from a strongly nationalist stance to a more liberal and open approach (Whiting 1992).

Consolidation

During the 1980s a second wave of FDI took place, largely stimulated by the favourable environment produced in the region by the presence of the pioneering electronics companies. New ventures included wholly owned subsidiaries, joint ventures, local start-ups and, for the first time, spin-offs.[4] In other words, over the past decade the development of the electronics industry in Guadalajara has begun to resemble the cascade-like process of firm creation that has been occurring in Silicon Valley in California for almost three decades.

In 1982 Hewlett Packard established its first Mexican manufacturing plant in Zapopan under the provisions of the 1981 Program for the Promotion of the Electronics Industry, to produce minicomputers. Two years later the company set up its first PC manufacturing plant in Latin America from where it launched its new touchscreen technology. Its R&D department, with about 15 local engineers, has won international recognition for the design of computer memory, as well as components and circuits for minicomputers.

In 1986 Wang established a plant in the El Salto Industrial Corridor, and Tandem Computers a factory for assembling PCs in the Alamo Industrial Zone. Wang, which manufactured power supplies and workstations at its plant in addition to assembling PCs and minicomputers, was forced to close down its factory in late 1992 in the face of stiff competition from the Asian NIEs. In the same year Kodak, as Industria Fotográfica Interamericana, expanded its Guadalajara operations to begin manufacture of floppy disks for PCs, harnesses and PCBs for photocopiers, and medical equipment. In January 1993 the company was awarded ISO-9000 status, an indispensable quality requirement for exporting to Europe.

Three more subsidiaries set up operations in Guadalajara in the mid 1980s: Cherokee Electrónica started out in 1985 as a joint venture between the United States and Mexico assembling power supplies; Tulon de México, a wholly US-owned venture, was established to make circuit board drills, also in 1985; and Shizuki Electronics, another wholly US-owned subsidiary, set up operations in a new industrial area south of Guadalajara (by the city's Peripheral Loop) in 1986.

The initial goal of IBM's new manufacturing plant in El Salto was to make 600,000 PCs in its first five years; later, new products, such as magnetic disks, were introduced. The project included a wide range of related initiatives aimed at integrating the new plant into the local milieu: an international distribution centre; a Spanish-language software development centre; a computer manufacturing centre for original equipment manufacturers (OEMs); an international purchasing program to assist local firms in developing products for IBM plants worldwide; partnership programs with local universities and technical schools; a scholarship program for Mexican scientists to study at IBM plants and laboratories; a program to train and develop local suppliers; and a Mexican semiconductor technology centre. These initiatives have significantly enhanced technology transfer and the local integration of the IBM computer plant, which is now the largest of its kind in Latin America. In 1993, IBM invested an additional US$15 million to expand its El Salto plant's capacity and produce PS/Value, PS/1 and Notebook microcomputers.

Attracted by the sizeable industrial conglomerate that had formed in Guadalajara, by the large agglomeration economies that this concentration had generated and by the locational advantages of the region, in 1990 NEC and AT&T took advantage of the *maquiladora* scheme to join the cluster. These two giants of the telecommunications and information technology industries joined an incipient local telephone industry made up of a group of MNE subsidiaries already producing conventional telephone sets in Guadalajara: Wang, Telectra (a German venture) and Mitel (a subsidiary of the well-known French-Canadian corporation).

NEC set up its premises in the El Salto Industrial Corridor. This joint venture with minority equity Mexican participation mainly produces microprocessor-based cellular telephone sets. AT&T established operations in the South Peripheral Loop industrial area based on a US$20 million investment. Its workforce of 1,500 employees, mostly Mexican, is expected to increase to 15,500 when the plant is in full operation. Using the latest technology, the plant produces telephone answering machines in a fully computerised industrial complex. The AT&T factory is investing another US$2,400 million in an R&D facility to be backed by the renowned Bell–AT&T Laboratories.

The establishment in recent years of new foreign and joint ventures in Guadalajara indicates that MNE-led growth of the electronics industry will continue to be a dynamic process. Two examples are Panamericana de Tecnología (with 49 per cent US equity) and Circuit Assembly de México (with 99 per cent US equity), which have joined what Wilson and Palacios (1988) have termed Guadalajara's high-tech industrial cluster.

Spin-offs / start-ups

As in the case of Penang, the presence of large MNEs in the Guadalajara region has induced, directly and indirectly, the creation of ancillary enterprises and other ventures within the local electronics industry. These include captive suppliers, local start-ups, full spin-offs and other enterprises.

In 1970 Electrónica Zonda, a locally owned start-up, began production of TV sets and home audio stereo systems; in 1989 it closed its plant and began to import these products from Southeast Asia. Electrónica Zonda was part of the Suma Group, comprising Tijuana-based Laptec and Sonymex, and Logix, a local start-up that began making one of the most popular PCs in the Mexican market under its own brand name in 1987. Microton, a local start-up that appeared in 1979, produced its own PCs until 1986. The company then became Info-Espacio, a new firm assembling buffers and providing PC repair and maintenance services. In 1981 Wind, a local Apple-like garage shop, began assembling PCs designed by the company but using imported components and parts. Wind also carried out burning and testing, packaging and marketing operations. This local venture had considerable potential, but collapsed in less than a decade after the untimely death of its founder. In 1982 Kitron was started as a local garage shop to manufacture digital control instruments; by 1990 the company had a small design department with about 10 engineers.

During the mid to late 1980s, a number of spin-offs and one more local start-up were established in the Guadalajara metropolitan region. Sistemas Delphi was founded in 1983 by a former General Instrument plant manager who formed a joint venture with Telmex, Mexico's national telephone company. This firm makes PC keyboards and PCBs for Telmex and occasionally for local MNEs such as Hewlett Packard and IBM. Encitel was created in the same year under the Temporary Importation for Export program as a subsidiary of Siemens de México, but with 100 per cent Mexican capital; it focused on PCB assembly. In 1985 Electrónica Pantera was established by a former Burroughs general manager in a joint venture with a local partner; the firm makes cable and harnesses for local computer companies. Poder Digital, a local start-up, began operations in the same year, assembling power supplies for computers and electronic equipment.

In 1986 Burroughs de México formed a joint venture with Mexican investors called Compubur. This had two divisions: Multilayer Printed Circuits, located in the Guadalajara Industrial Park, and Microsystems, at Burroughs's factory in the Guadalajara industrial zone. The former assembled multilayer PCBs, while the latter inserted PCB components using through-hole techniques. Both divisions supplied their products to Burroughs — later Unisys — as well as to other computer companies in the region. This venture was dissolved at the end of 1993, a year after the Unisys plant in Guadalajara closed down. In February 1994 a new company with the same name was established by Mexican investors from Mexico City. At present it assembles PC parts and components only, at the former Guadalajara Industrial Park facilities.

Winners of a quality contest conducted by IBM to find local suppliers of sophisticated PCBs, Adelantos de Tecnología (ADTEC) began operations in late 1987 at the entrance to the El Salto Industrial Corridor. The company was set up under the Temporary Importation for Export scheme as a joint venture between US giant Space Craft, Inc. (49 per cent) and Mexico's Chihuahua-based Elamex group (51 per cent). Although the Elamex group considered locating its new plant in Ciudad Juarez, IBM required that it be located in Guadalajara. ADTEC was the first PCB maker in Mexico to use surface mount technology. It made PCBs, first for IBM PCs, and soon after for other computer makers in the region such as Hewlett Packard, Tandem and Unisys. ADTEC even had overseas clients, including SMC, Olivetti and Control Data.

Another local venture created during the 1980s was Molex, a wholly owned Mexican company that set up a plant in 1989 in the Guadalajara Industrial Park. Molex produced interconnectors for use in PCBs, catering to IBM and other PC makers in the region.

The most recent wave of local start-ups took place in the early 1990s with the establishment of new ventures such as Electron, Scale Computers and Advanced Electronics. Electron manufactures PCs, printers and peripherals, while Advanced Electronics produces high-technology PCBs. Located in Ciudad Granja in Zapopan municipality, Scale Computers also manufactures PCs. It is a wholly Guadalajara-owned company, signalling that the future growth of the electronics industry in the region may increasingly be propelled by local ventures. The closing of the Unisys and Wang factories in recent years also points in this direction.

In sum, the electronics industry in Guadalajara has been dominated by the assembly of PCs and PC components, though efforts have been made to incorporate higher end production stages. Local computer start-ups, for example, have taken over such operations as product design and improvement, testing and burning, and marketing. The local Motorola factory, in addition to assembling transistors, diodes and other semiconductors, has recently moved into wafer fabrication. This constitutes a significant upward movement on the part of this MNE, which has also actively promoted technological upgrading through such schemes as the Technical Excellence Program, initiated in 1991. The program aims to encourage the firm's local engineers to develop new technologies to improve productivity and quality standards at the Guadalajara plant. This should enhance the plant's ability to compete with semiconductor makers (including other Motorola plants) worldwide, but especially those located in Southeast Asia.

The product mix of the electronics industry is dominated by PCs, minicomputers, computer peripherals, PCBs, ICs, power supplies, relays and surge suppressors, cellular telephone sets and answering machines, digital control instruments, and cable and harnesses. Specific differences notwithstanding, this productive structure is similar to that observed in Penang.

Collective initiatives for technology transfer and upgrading

As already indicated, a number of MNE subsidiaries and local electronics companies have carried out R&D activities of some kind in Guadalajara. Hewlett Packard, AT&T and IBM stand out among the former group, while the latter group includes Kitron, Logix, Electron, Scale Computers, Microton and Wind. In addition to the in-house efforts of such firms, a number of joint initiatives to foster technology transfer in the region have been undertaken by MNE subsidiaries and local institutions.

Semiconductor Technology Centre
In collaboration with the Centre for Advanced Studies and Research of Mexico's National Politechnic Institute, IBM de México established the Guadalajara Advanced Electronics Unit in 1988 on a site donated by the Jalisco state government. The unit includes a metrology centre, a communications laboratory and, notably, a Semiconductor Technology Centre staffed by Mexican scientists and engineers. The centre has the technical support of IBM and is working on the development of local semiconductor technologies. It has established links with other MNE subsidiaries, such as Hewlett Packard, Motorola, Mitel and Kodak, although collaboration with locally owned companies has been rather poor.

Tecnopolis
The University of Guadalajara, Jalisco's public university, finalised plans for this ambitious project in early 1994. The Tecnopolis is to be a fully fledged science and technology park. Its goal is to promote the development of technology-based and high-technology industries by providing incubator facilities for up to 35 enterprises at different stages of development. Assistance includes technical help from university researchers, professors and students and access to Internet, the university's internal

communications network. The ultimate objective is to assist the ventures to use leading-edge technologies to carry out production processes. Under an agreement reached in April 1994 between the university and the Guadalajara Metal-Mechanic Industry Chamber, the latter has reserved a five-hectare site for the development of new enterprises in the metals industry. The Tecnopolis will be located in the university-owned Los Belenes Industrial Park in Zapopan and will require a long-term investment estimated at up to US$25 million.

Collaboration with local universities

Two years ago, Hewlett Packard signed an agreement with the University of Guadalajara to develop a program to strengthen links between the university and industry. Under the program, students and professors were encouraged to design software and hardware in exchange for computing equipment and technical assistance. Similarly, in the late 1980s IBM, Hewlett Packard, Unisys-Compubur, Mitel and Motorola, in a joint initiative with the Autonomous University of Guadalajara (a local private institution) and Stanford University, established a Master's program in electronic engineering with special focus on information technology and semiconductors. The goal was to produce skilled engineers to meet the shortage in the local labour market. In the program's first few years, 80 per cent of students in the program were employees of participating MNE subsidiaries (Castel 1993, p. 18)

Exchange of information

As part of its program to foster local technological development, in November 1993 Motorola's subsidiary in Guadalajara organised the first Regional Symposium on Electronics Manufacturing. The idea was to have an open exchange among all those involved in the region's electronics industry on technological advances they had made in the field. The symposium reflected Motorola's belief that the best chance for Mexico's electronics industry to gain a competitive advantage over its Asia Pacific counterparts lay in the development of local technologies.

Government-sponsored initiatives

The National Council for Science and Technology has recently reached broad agreement with four local universities — the Aremajac Valley University, Occidental Higher Studies Institute, University of Guadalajara and Monterrey Institute of Higher Studies (Guadalajara campus) — and the state's leading private business organisations to promote the technological upgrading of Jalisco's industrial activities. These projects are to be funded by a US$3.5 million grant. The agreement covers an environmental management program for foundries, the automation of Jalisco's electronics industry, the completion of the Jalisco 2000 study and the organisation of a symposium, similar to Motorola's, called Tecnología '94. Support for these initiatives also comes from the Industrial Production Technology Program and the Technology

Parks Development Program, both operated by Nacional Financiera, Mexico's main development bank.

Such initiatives notwithstanding, it should be pointed out that Mexico lacks both a comprehensive policy on technology to set national priorities and strategies and a national industrial policy. Technological and industrial development has been left to market forces and comparative advantage, in line with the neo-liberal thinking of the present federal administration.

In short, the electronics industry in Guadalajara owes its development to the establishment of subsidiaries by leading MNEs. Their presence in the region has triggered the growth of local and foreign ancillary industries, local start-ups and spin-offs. Thus although Guadalajara's experience is similar to that of Silicon Valley in some respects, local ventures have in general played a subordinate role, derived from Mexico's position as a host, rather than home, country for FDI.

Although assembly operations predominate, recent trends in Guadalajara's electronics industry indicate a shift towards higher end operations. This is mainly seen in semiconductor production, but also in the extension of PC assembly to design and testing stages. These trends have been strengthened by the significant advances in R&D made by major MNE subsidiaries in the region. The environment for the transfer and sharing of technology has improved as the number of companies — mainly MNEs — and academic institutions committed to R&D has grown and pressure from foreign competition has mounted. Another major factor facilitating transfer is the multinationals' growing need for engineers, which has led them to enhance their in-house training schemes and human resource development programs.

Technology transfer from MNEs has in fact taken place through a variety of channels, including the creation of spin-offs, local start-ups and local supporting industries; in-house and on-the-job-training of employees; transfer of R&D activities to subsidiaries; establishment of local R&D centres with technical support from MNEs; local supplier training and development; scholarship programs for local engineers and technicians to study at MNE plants and laboratories; joint technical programs with local universities; and technology sharing initiatives between MNEs and local institutions.

Nevertheless, in general the technological level of local electronics companies remains low. Consequently, technological dependence continues to be high: cutting-edge technologies, state-of-the-art equipment and advanced managerial knowhow are still imported into MNE plants in Guadalajara. Indigenous companies should perhaps focus on product and process innovation with the objective of finding specific niches that offer reasonable competitiveness and opportunities for growth. One necessary step is for local enterprises to establish links with local universities and R&D centres, notably the Semiconductor Technology Centre. This in turn requires a commitment on the part of these institutions, as well as state and federal governments, to foster the growth of local enterprises. Initiatives like the Tecnopolis project, the programs of the

National Science and Technology Council and the Motorola symposium are all effective means of achieving this end.

Penang and Guadalajara compared

The establishment of MNE subsidiaries was the catalyst for the development of an electronics industry in Guadalajara and in Penang. In both cases this process took place over 20 years. MNEs have spearheaded the growth of ancillary industries and local start-ups in both regions. What differentiates the two experiences, however, is the appearance in Guadalajara of MNE-originating spin-offs, a distinctive feature of the original Silicon Valley phenomenon in California not seen in Penang. Again, whereas in the Malaysian case the industrialisation process was initiated mainly by deliberate government action, in the Mexican instance the process started more or less by chance. In both instances, MNEs were attracted by regional advantages, including government incentives for FDI, political stability, benign labour legislation and docile labour unions. In general, the availability of cheap labour has become a less important factor in corporate decisions on location. This is because, with technological upgrading, MNEs are experiencing an increasing need for skilled professionals. Transfer of technology is more likely to occur in these circumstances, as the experience of both Guadalajara and Penang shows.

Rajah's (1988) observations about the likely permanence of MNEs in Penang have so far proved to be correct: to date virtually no subsidiary has moved back to its home country as a result of automation or the adoption of flexible production techniques, as predicted by Kaplinski (1985), or because of changes in international markets. This has also largely been true for Guadalajara, with some major exceptions (the Unisys and Wang plant closures) that reveal the high dependence of MNE subsidiary operations on the strategic decisions adopted by the parent firm in response to changes in global markets.

Penang is both a typical example of an MNE enclave based on export-processing zones and a case study of high-tech regional development. Its experience confirms the view expressed by the World Bank's Industry Development Division (World Bank 1992) that export-processing zones, or free industrial zones as they are called in Penang, are an effective way of attracting FDI to countries in the early development stages (a time when these countries are unable to institute nationwide duty exemption and drawback systems). Penang's success shows that, in order for this strategy to succeed, the following conditions must obtain in the country in question: favourable business and living conditions, low labour costs, social and political stability, efficient transport and communications systems, direct control of operational and promotional aspects by the free industrial zones, and incorporation of zones into an overall development strategy at the national level (World Bank 1992, p. 21). Virtually all of these conditions were met in Penang.

In the Mexican case, the Temporary Importation for Export and *maquiladora* programs gave FDI ventures a status similar to that of Malaysia's licensed manufacturing warehouses, encouraging a wider geographical dispersion of firms. In its concentration of large MNEs with duty free status, Guadalajara resembles one of Penang's free industrial zones. Given its large area, however, this Mexican metropolis can also be regarded as what Scott (1987) has termed a localised territorial complex. This is close to the concept of high-technology, export-oriented, industrial clusters advanced by Wilson and Palacios (1988) to describe Guadalajara's experience. If we accept Scott's (1987) characterisation, Guadalajara may be in the process of becoming a successful proto-industrial complex similar to those that have emerged in major cities of the Asia Pacific, such as Hong Kong, Seoul, Manila, Singapore and Taipei (Scott 1987).

Technology transfer has taken place in both Penang and Guadalajara through essentially the same channels: the creation of start-ups and spin-offs; the transfer of R&D tasks to subsidiaries; the establishment of local R&D centres; in-house and on-the-job training in the use of advanced technologies; and sponsorship of local development and upgrading programs. Although, according to World Bank (1992 p. 20), in dynamic industries like electronics 'there is a general agreement that the direct transfer of product and process technology from [export processing zones] has been very small', this has not been the case in Penang. This achievement reflects a significant trend characterised recently by Dr Soonhoon Bae, president of Daewoo Electronics, as 'market-driven' technology transfer (Bae 1994). Market-driven technology transfer reflects the new trend in the electronics industry for plants to be located closer to final markets. MNEs are seeking to cut costs by extending vertical integration in host countries to include product development and other R&D operations. Another compelling reason for the transfer of R&D to subsidiaries is the far lower wages of skilled technicians and engineers in host countries, as exemplified by the case of Penang.

Guadalajara's experience in turn shows that technology transfer can occur when local companies acquire sufficient capacity to absorb new technologies and when local entrepreneurs stand ready to start new ventures designed to meet the needs of MNE subsidiaries. This is true of Penang, too, despite the lack of spin-offs. In essence, though, the development of the electronics industry in Penang rests on a broad social consensus about the state's development goals and a firm commitment to the technological and industrial upgrading of its economic activities. This coordinating framework of state and national development strategies is nourished by the prosperity Malaysia now enjoys. This conducive environment, largely lacking in the Mexican case, has enhanced the capacity of Penang's economy to absorb technology.

The case for the development of an indigenous capacity

The behaviour of MNEs is changing in the present era of systemofacture as the international division of labour, of which MNEs are the chief architects, assumes new patterns (Hoffman and Kaplinski 1988). Rising R&D costs are forcing MNEs to maintain their existing corporate structures or to disperse costs over a larger corporate structure. As multinationals seek to locate production closer to end markets, R&D activities are being transferred to off-shore subsidiaries. Market competition is also driving MNEs to transfer technology more extensively in order to reduce their R&D costs: the salary levels of technicians and even of highly skilled engineers are far lower in host than in home countries.

The extent and the content of technology transfer depend on which production stages are located off-shore. This in turn is determined by the strategies and decisions that MNEs take at the corporate level in response to major technological break-throughs and the changes in the international division of labour these new technologies bring about. Such breakthroughs will continue to be generated in developed countries, where conditions are right for basic generic research. The gap between developing host countries and developed home countries thus continues to widen as the pace of technological innovation increases. Because proprietary technology continues to be controlled by developed countries, international technology markets are becoming more oligopolistic (World Bank 1992, p. 1); as long as developing countries are merely importers of technology, monopolistic technological rents will obtain (Katz 1986). As summarised by the president of Taiwan Semiconductor Manufacturing, 'the guy who creates the system drives the business all the way down to the components' (*Businessweek*, 7 December 1992, p. 129).

The 'flying geese' metaphor seems to prevail in the global electronics industry. This process was described by Chen (1990) for the Asia Pacific region as follows: Japan leads initial development of the industry; the Asian NIEs carry out assembly, later passing this task on to the ASEAN-4 (Indonesia, Malaysia, the Philippines and Thailand); FDI from the NIEs pours into the ASEAN-4 and China; the Asian NIEs engage in wafer fabrication and design; and Japan maintains its lead in cutting-edge production technology.

What are fledgling host countries to do? A common-sense response would be that they should make the most of the existing hierarchical structure by developing a basic indigenous capacity for technological innovation. Hyung-Sup Choi of Korea's Research Institute of Industrial Science and Technology has warned that developing nations should avoid engaging in the 'noble, but certainly financially unrewarding exercise of reinventing the wheel' (Choi 1991, p. 2). Nelson (1990, p. 39) holds a similar view, believing that '"stand alone" technological self-sufficiency is rare, even in the advanced countries'. The experience of countries like Brazil shows that Choi's and Nelson's observations may be valid in countries where nationalistic, self-reliant technological strategies are taken to autarchic extremes. Brazil attempted for seven years — from 1975 to 1992 — to foster the development of an indigenous computer industry by creating a 'market reserve' for Brazilian companies. This included closing national markets to foreign products and prohibiting MNEs from making computers in Brazil. Although the strategy produced impressive results in its first few years, later domestic firms began to make obsolete computers at prices much higher than those prevailing on international markets.

It is also unwise to go to the other extreme — adopting policies that preclude domestic effort on the basis that developing countries should not waste their scarce resources on the development of technologies that can just as easily be imported from abroad. This seems to be the trend in Latin America, including Mexico. Singer (1976) pointed out in the mid 1970s that there are two basic reasons for developing countries to make a critical effort to generate an indigenous technological capacity: that the technology developing countries need simply may not exist; and that an indigenous technological capacity enables the developing country to know what technologies are available, which technologies are most appropriate for it, where technologies can be obtained, the most suitable form of the technology, and the terms on which the purchase should be carried out. An implicit objective would be to give developing countries the bargaining power to negotiate on more equal terms for the acquisition of new technologies.

Singer's views have been echoed in the 1990s by Engardio and Gross (*Businessweek*, 7 December 1992), who observed that, after being engaged in assembly operations for two decades, Asian NIEs will have to move into real innovation in order to create a solid technological base to sustain their expanding industrial apparatus. The NIEs are on the right track: rather than trying to leapfrog developed countries, they are absorbing new technologies that can be applied quickly to the production of niche products; rather than competing with developed countries head on, they are opting to join forces through strategic alliances. Their strategy is based on directing government support to basic research in promising industries; placing priority on applied research to fill selected market outlets; and forming close alliances with MNEs via joint ventures (*Businessweek*, 7 December 1992).

One type of venture with considerable potential for technology transfer is the 'design–manufacture' alliance. Exemplified by ventures in the late 1980s between VLSI Technology and Hitachi, LSI Logic and Toshiba, and IBM and Intel, design–manufacture alliances are cost-cutting initiatives in which one partner provides design software and the other supplies process technology (Mody 1989). They usually take place in the mature phase of product development, in which profits begin to decline and cost reductions become critical. A more widely available and cheaper source of technology is the 'open standards' generated by leading companies in the form of packages of non-proprietary technologies. For example, in the 1980s IBM teamed up with Intel and Microsoft to create the IBM PC and challenge Apple, then the world's leading maker of microcomputers (Mody 1989).

The experience of Penang and Guadalajara shows that it is possible for developing countries to generate an indigenous technological capacity. Even though developing countries cannot alter the international division of labour or hope to compete directly with MNEs, this does not mean that they need to adopt a passive role. Instead, they should concentrate on developing a critical capacity for knowing what they need, within the framework of policies and strategies to guide technological development according to national goals and aspirations.

Notes

1 Discussion of the origins, development and salient features of Penang's electronics industry is based mainly on information obtained from the PDC in March 1994, interviews with PDC officials and a visit to Penang's free industrial zones. Materials used include annual reports, brochures, unpublished data and various issues of *Penang Development News*, a periodical published by the PDC.

2 Unless otherwise stated, this and subsequent sections are based on and update my previous studies of the electronics industry in Guadalajara (Palacios 1990, 1992). These earlier studies report results of research carried out in the Guadalajara region between 1988 and 1991, including interviews with the plant and marketing managers of about 15 companies and the heads of relevant local industry chambers.

3 This area includes the entire municipalities of Guadalajara, Tlaquepaque, Tonalá and El Salto, as well as part of Zapopan

4 Spin-offs are new companies set up by former employees of firms in a given locality, in this case MNEs operating in Guadalajara prior to 1980. Start-ups are new ventures formed by local entrepreneurs with no previous connections with existing MNEs.

References

Bae, Soonhoon 1994, Consumer Electronics in the Pacific, Paper presented at the 10th International General Meeting, PECC, Concurrent Session on Consumer Electronics, Kuala Lumpur, March 23.

Castel, Odile 1993, La Formación de un Distrito Industrial de la Electrónica en Guadalajara, Paper presented to the seminar El Patrón de Industrialización, Transferencia Tecnológica y Relaciones Laborales en México, El Colegio de la Frontera Norte, Monterrey, June 15–17.

Chalmers, Ian 1991, 'International and Regional Integration: The Political Economy of the Electronics Industry in ASEAN', *ASEAN Economic Bulletin*, 8(2), pp. 194–209.

Chen, Edward K.Y. 1990, 'The Electronics Industry', in Hadi Soesastro and Mari Pangestu (eds), *Technological Challenge in the Asia–Pacific Economy*, Sydney: Allen and Unwin, in association with the PECC Secretariat and The Australian National University.

Choi, Hyung Su 1991, 'International Technical Cooperation in the Socioeconomic Development of Developing Countries', in Karen Minden (ed.), *Pacific Cooperation in Science and Technology*, Hawaii: The East West Center, in cooperation with the PECC Science and Technology Task Force.

Corbridge, Stuart 1986, *Capitalist World Development: A Critique of Radical Development Geography*, London: Macmillan.

Hoffman, Kurt and Raphael Kaplinski 1988, *Driving Force: The Global Restructuring of Technology, Labor, and Investment in the Automobile and Components Industries*, Boulder, CO: Westview Press.

Ismail, Muhd Salleh 1994, Restructuring of the Consumer Electronics Industry in the Pacific and Its Implications for Local Companies: Malaysia's Experience, Paper presented at the 10th International General Meeting of PECC, Concurrent Session on Consumer Electronics, Kuala Lumpur, March 23.

Kaplinski, Raphael 1985, 'Electronics-Based Automation Technologies and the Onset of Systemofacture: Implications for Third World Industrialisation', *World Development*, 13(3), pp. 423–40.

Katz, Jorge M. 1986, *Importación de Tecnología, Aprendizaje e Industrialización Incipiente*, Mexico: Fondo de Cultura Económica.

Mattar, Jorge and Claudia Schatan 1993, 'El Comercio Intraindustrial e Intrafirma México-Estados Unidos: Autopartes, Electrónica y Petroquímicos', *Comercio Exterior*, 43(2), pp. 103–24.

Mody, Ashoka 1989, 'Staying in the Loop: International Alliances for Sharing Technology', World Bank Discussion Papers, 61, Washington DC: World Bank.

Nelson, Richard R. 1990, 'Acquiring Technology', in Hadi Soesastro and Mari Pangestu (eds), *Technological Challenge in the Asia–Pacific Economy*, Sydney: Allen and Unwin.

Palacios, Juan José 1990, 'Maquiladoras, Reorganización Productiva y Desarrollo Regional: El Caso de Guadalajara', in Bernardo González-Aréchiga and José Carlos Ramírez (eds), *Subcontratación y Empresas Transnacionales. Apertura y Reestructuración en la Maquiladora*, Mexico: El Colegio de la Frontera Norte and the Friedrich Ebert Foundation.

——————— 1992, 'Guadalajara: Valle del Silicio Mexicano?', *Tiempos de Ciencia*, 27, April–June, pp. 7–17.

PDC (Penang Development Corporation) 1992, *Factories: Penang, Malaysia*, Bayan Lepas: PDC.

——————— 1993a, *Statistics: Penang, Malaysia*, Bayan Lepas: PDC.

——————— 1993b, *Policies & Incentives: Penang, Malaysia*, Bayan Lepas: PDC.

Rahman, Omar Abdul and Michaela Y. Smith 1991, 'Science and Technology Planning: With Special Reference to the Malaysian Experience', in Karen Minden (ed.), *Pacific Cooperation in Science and Technology*, Hawaii: The East–West Center, in cooperation with the PECC Science and Technology Task Force.

Rajah, Rasiah 1988, 'The Semiconductor Industry in Penang: Implications for the New International Division of Labour Theories', *Journal of Contemporary Asia*, 18(1), pp. 25–46.

Scott, A. J. 1987, 'The Semiconductor Industry in South East Asia: Organization, Location and the International Division of Labour', *Regional Studies*, 21(2), pp. 143–60.

SECOFI 1993, *Tratado de Libre Comercio de América del Norte*, Mexico: Ministry of Trade and Industrial Promotion.

Singer, Hans W. 1976, 'Science and Technology for Poor Countries', in Gerald M. Meier (ed.), *Leading Issues in Economic Development*, New York: Oxford University Press.

Stewart, Frances 1976, 'Inappropriate Products and Inappropriate Technology', in Gerald M. Meier (ed.), *Leading Issues in Economic Development*, New York: Oxford University Press.

UNCTC (United Nations Centre on Transnational Corporations) 1988, *Transnational Corporations in World Development: Trends and Prospects*, New York: United Nations.

Wada, Yutaka 1994, Address on Corporate Strategies and the Localization of Consumer Electronics Industries in the Asia Pacific Region, Paper presented at the 10th International General Meeting, PECC, Concurrent Session on Consumer Electronics, Kuala Lumpur, March 23.

Wang, Yunshi 1991, 'New Mechanisms in Technology Transfer: Experience of Shenzhen Science and Industry Park', in Chi-ning Liu (ed.), *Science and Technology Parks: Proceedings of the Shanghai Workshop*, Shanghai: Scientific and Technical Publishers, in collaboration with PECC.

Whiting, van R., Jr 1992, *The Political Economy of Foreign Investment in Mexico. Nationalism, Liberalism, and Constraints of Choice*, Baltimore, MD: The Johns Hopkins University Press.

Wilson, Patricia A. and Juan J. Palacios 1988, The Development of the *Maquiladora* Industry and Local Economic Linkages in the Interior: The Case of Guadalajara, Unpublished report on research carried out under the US Commission on International Migration and Cooperative Development.

World Bank 1992, 'Export Processing Zones', Policy and Research Series, 20, Washington DC: World Bank.

9   A study of the operations of Japanese firms in Asia: the electrical machinery industry —

Motoshige Itoh and Jun Shibata

The sales, production, marketing and R&D activities of many Japanese firms extend far beyond national borders. Compared with American and European firms, a higher proportion of the activities of Japanese firms are concentrated in Asia. Although this is in part explained by geographical proximity, special characteristics of Japanese firms are another important factor.

Much Japanese activity in Asia is based on labour-intensive technology. Labour, of course, is readily available and cheap in many Asian countries. A comparison of the overseas operations of Japan's electrical machinery and automobile industries, two of the country's major export industries, reveals a concentration of the former in Asia and of the latter in North America and Europe. The transportation costs for automobiles are high, and auto makers naturally wish to reduce these costs by locating their plants close to end markets. In contrast, because many of its parts production and assembly processes are labour intensive, the electrical machinery industry can make consider-able savings by operating in Asia. In fact, it is even possible to identify differences in the foreign operations of two of the industry's subsectors: whereas firms in the home electrical appliances industry tend to be concentrated in Asia, firms in the industry-use electrical machinery industry are more likely to be located in industrialised countries.[1]

Here, we focus on the activities of the Japanese electrical machinery industry in Asia. A major characteristic of the industry is that production can be divided into a number of stages, with a large number of firms thus being able to participate in the production process. In this respect, the division of labour in the industry is similar to that described by Adam Smith in *The Wealth of Nations* for pin production. In the case of the electrical machinery industry, this division of labour generates an interesting organisational structure, characterised by such features as subcontracting, long-term transactional relationships, original equipment manufacturer (OEM) agreements, and regional concentration of firms.[2]

In the popular perception, all production stages in Japan's electrical machinery industry are carried out within the country, with the industry deriving its strength from this local concentration. Although this image is no longer correct, it does provide a good starting point for discussion. We believe that the industry's division of labour and organisational structure before it began to invest actively abroad have had a significant impact on its present international division of labour and overseas business strategies, affecting the location of plants and patterns of intrafirm trade. An examination of these issues may help us to predict the future of the industry in Japan.

In this chapter we investigate the activities of the Japanese electrical machinery industry in Asia. We examine when and where firms started their operations, the distribution pattern of factories, and how this pattern has affected regional trade (often intrafirm trade) of electrical products.

General trends in foreign direct investment

Japan's foreign direct investment (FDI) increased rapidly in the latter half of the 1980s; on a balance of payments basis, direct investment was about seven times greater in 1989 than in 1985 (MITI 1994). This expansion was due in part to the appreciation of the yen, which rose from ¥240 to the US dollar in 1985 to ¥100 to the dollar in 1994. These were also boom years for the corporate sector, which invested extensively both in Japan and abroad during the second half of the 1980s.

Although the share of Japan's FDI in Asia still lags behind its direct investment in North America and Europe, it has gradually been increasing. In fact, in spite of a fall in Japan's total FDI since 1990, reflecting weak economic conditions, the amount of Japanese direct investment in Asia has remained largely unchanged, or has even increased in some years. As a share of its total FDI, Japan's direct investment in Asia has in fact risen substantially in the 1990s. Figure 9.1, which compares FDI flows to Asia from Japan, the United States and the European Union, confirms the importance of Japanese direct investment in Asia.[3] Although FDI by the United States and Europe increased in 1987–91, the rise in Japanese direct investment was far greater.

Cumulative Japanese investment in Asia rose sharply in the late 1980s and early 1990s. The share of the electrical machinery industry in total Japanese FDI increased in most Asian countries, exceeding 15 per cent in Thailand and Malaysia since 1985 and surging in China in the 1990s (MITI 1994).

Table 9.1 shows the distribution and number of employees of foreign affiliates of the Japanese electrical machinery industry in Asia. According to the table, of 924 Japanese affiliates in the electrical machinery industry worldwide, 545 (59 per cent) were in Asia. Malaysia had the highest proportion (24 per cent), followed by Taiwan (17 per cent), Singapore (13 per cent) and Thailand (12 per cent). These four countries together accounted for 66 per cent of Japanese affiliates in Asia.

A high proportion of the industry's labour force is also located in Asia: 70 per cent, or 397,701 employees (Table 9.1). A comparison of this share (70 per cent) with that of affiliates (59 per cent) confirms that the operations of the industry are indeed generally more labour intensive in Asia than in other parts of the world. Malaysia accounts for a high 30 per cent of the labour force in Asia. Matsushita, which is active

Figure 9.1   **Direct investment in Asia by Japan, the United States and the European Union, 1987–91 (US$ billion)**

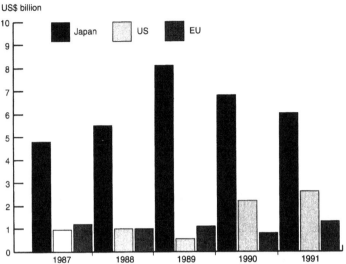

Note: Direct investment is calculated on a balance of payments basis.

Source: OECD, *International Direct Investment Statistics Yearbook*, Paris, 1993.

Table 9.1   **Distribution of foreign affiliates of the Japanese electrical machinery industry in Asia, 1993 (no., per cent)**

Host country	Number of firms	%	Number of employees	%
Korea	61	11	31,831	8
Taiwan	90	17	48,631	12
Hong Kong	24	4	32,534	8
Singapore	71	13	38,290	10
Thailand	68	12	49,704	12
Malaysia	132	24	118,222	30
Philippines	19	3	24,485	6
Indonesia	21	4	11,139	3
China	59	11	42,865	11
Total				
Asia	545	100	397,701	100
World (except Japan)	924		570,167	
Asia/World		59		70

Note: World is total number of foreign affiliates in Japan's electrical machinery industry.

Source: NDKK, 1994.

189

in Malaysia, alone employs over 20,000 workers. This represents a steep rise from the 4,500 employed by Matsushita in 1985. The table also shows that although Singapore has more affiliates than Thailand, affiliates in the latter country employ more people. This indicates that affiliates in Thailand are larger in scale and more labour intensive than their Singaporean counterparts.

The single most important factor in the rapid increase in FDI in Asia, in particular by the electrical machinery industry, has been spiralling wage costs in Japan. Japan's per capita GDP of about US$10,000 in 1985 had risen to around US$30,000 in 1993: a threefold increase in only eight years. Most of this was due to the rapid appreciation of the yen against most currencies, and, hence, higher unit labour costs in Japan relative to those in other countries.

Division of labour

The structure of an industry's division of labour will influence the pattern of its international operations.[4] Here, we provide a brief overview of the division of labour in the electrical machinery industry, contrasting it with the case of the automobile industry.

Figure 9.2 describes the assembly process for automobiles and VCRs. The assembly process for cars is familiar. The central plant not only assembles the vehicle, but also manufactures heavy components such as the engine and the body.[5] Most other parts are supplied by subcontractors. The subcontracting system has a multilayer structure. The first layer consists of suppliers of large parts, who are also engaged in subassembly. The second layer consists of smaller firms producing smaller parts. Firms carrying out assembly depend heavily on suppliers both for the production of parts and for product design. This practice of suppliers participating in the design of parts is common in Japan. The Just-in-Time system, through which product assembly and parts delivery are coordinated, is also widely used in the Japanese automobile industry. In Japan, the share of value-added contributed by assembly firms in the total value of the final product stands at around 30 per cent. This is lower than the corresponding figure for American automobile firms, although there are differences even among US firms (Cusumano 1985).

The production process for VCRs is similar to that for automobiles in that it depends heavily on suppliers. However, in the case of VCRs and other products made by the electrical machinery industry, the main components — in this instance, drums, video heads and small motors — are both manufactured and assembled by the parent firm. This point is important when analysing the international operations of the industry, since it allows manufacturers to delegate the entire production process, from parts manufacture to assembly, to an affiliate, or assembly or parts production only.

Two important characteristics of the electrical machinery industry are that transportation costs relative to the value of the main components and final product are low, and that the cost of setting up factories (relative to the automobile industry, for example) is low. It is thus easier for electrical machinery manufacturers to choose

Figure 9.2   Assembly process for automobiles and VCRs

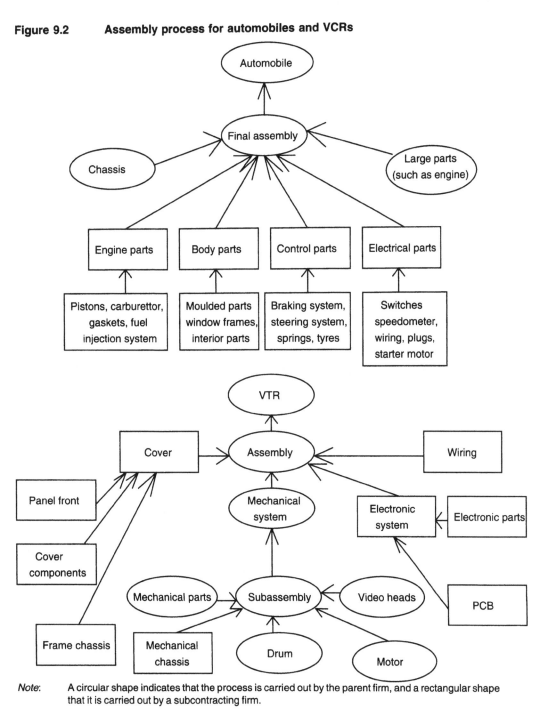

Note: A circular shape indicates that the process is carried out by the parent firm, and a rectangular shape that it is carried out by a subcontracting firm.

different locations for parts production, assembly and the marketing of products. As we will see later, differences between the electrical machinery and automobile industries are reflected in trade and investment patterns.

We examine now the division of labour in the electrical machinery industry using the case study of colour TVs manufactured by a representative firm in Nagano prefecture in Japan. Production of colour TVs typically involves subcontracting in three areas (electrical/electronic parts assembly, pressing processes, and plastic moulding) and at least 130 main suppliers.[6]

Electrical/electronic parts are of two types. Crucial components, such as picture tubes and semiconductors, are made either by the assembly firm itself or by specialised manufacturers. Such parts require sophisticated technology and a large capital investment. Their manufacture is characterised by economies of scale in production and high development costs, making it essential for manufacturers to be able to sell a large quantity. They are thus a major factor in the success of the product and hence of the assembly firm. The second type is general purpose parts, including condensers, switches, speakers, printed circuit boards (PCBs) and resistors. These products are manufactured by medium sized firms, which usually supply their products to two or more assembly plants. In this sense the subcontracting relationship is not a strict one. Of around 200 firms in Japan making resistors, for example, only 40 manufacture them under their own name.

The structure of the division of labour is surprisingly complex in the case of colour TVs. Take PCBs, for example. Our firm manufacturing TVs in Nagano prefecture (which we will call N Electronics) subcontracts the manufacture of PCBs to a first-tier subcontractor (Firm N), which also coordinates subassembly. Firm N again subcontracts to second-tier subcontractors, who may subcontract work to even smaller firms. Altogether, about 30 firms and 600 workers are involved in the production of PCBs for N Electronics.

The PCBs are semifinished in the factory of Firm N and shipped to second-tier suppliers for subassembly. Some of the assembled parts are then returned to Firm N for use in colour TVs or computer monitors, with the remainder being sent to another of Firm N's factories. S Electronics, a highly automated parts supplier contracted by Firm N to manufacture PCBs, also subcontracts some work to a small factory specialising in manual mounting processes.

It is evident from this discussion that N Electronics is heavily dependent on subcontractors — for over 60 per cent of production, in fact.[7] These subcontractors in turn rely on a low-paid, largely female workforce. The competitiveness of Firm N in the production of PCBs is derived from the low wage base. Relative to the cost of labour in other Asian countries, however, the wages paid by Firm N in Japan are high. With a complex division of labour of the type just described, it is clearly advantageous for plants to be concentrated in a particular region. Outweighing this, however, is the lure of low labour costs, which have enticed manufacturers to shift production overseas. The case of Matsushita (discussed below) is of particular interest in that this firm has managed to organise a complex division of labour of the type just described, but in Malaysia rather than in Japan.

Two other important developments have taken place in Japan's electrical machinery industry in recent years. One is that there has been a gradual increase in the share of parts imported into Japan (Figure 9.3), although it should be noted that in absolute terms the share remains low. Because many of the parts used in the home electrical appliances industry are manufactured by labour-intensive methods, there is great scope for further sourcing of parts in Asia. As Figure 9.3 shows, the industry itself predicts that the proportion of imported parts will continue to rise.[8] Interestingly, the share of parts exported to Japan by the local affiliates of Japanese firms is quite small. This suggests that a large proportion of imported parts is supplied by independent Asian firms, and not through intrafirm trade.

The second development worth mentioning is that the internal production ratio of the home electrical appliances industry has been rising (Figure 9.4). This reflects the increasing importance of sophisticated components such as integrated circuits (ICs).

Figure 9.3   **Share of imported parts in output of Japan's home electrical appliances industry, 1985–2000 (per cent)**

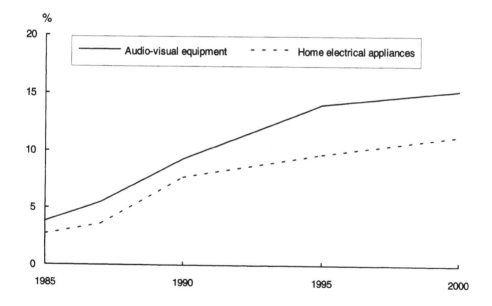

Note: Data for 1995 and 2000 are projections.

Source: Sangyo Kenkyujo, 1990.

Figure 9.4   **Share of internal production of parts in home electrical appliances industry, 1985–2000 (per cent)**

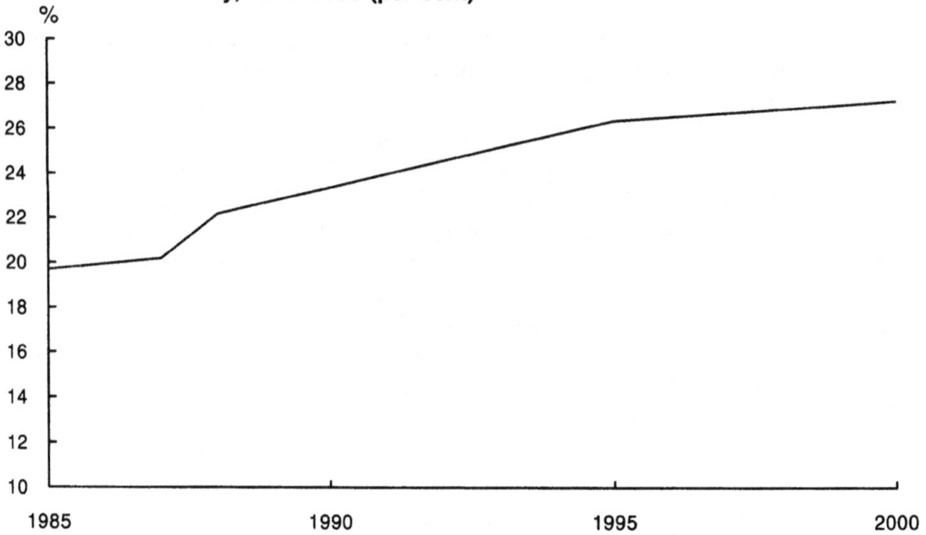

Note: Data for 1995 and 2000 are projections.

Source: Sangyo Kenkyujo, 1990.

Changes in the foreign operations of Japanese firms: three case studies

The foreign operations of Japanese firms in the electrical machinery industry have changed considerably. Examining the developments that have taken place for representative firms will provide a better picture of overall changes in the corporate strategies of Japanese firms operating abroad. Here we discuss three such firms: Matsushita, Sanyo and Sony.[9]

Matsushita

Matsushita's foreign production as a share of its total world production was 14 per cent in 1993. Although Matsushita initiated direct investment in Asia as early as 1961, the pace of investment accelerated only in the latter half of the 1980s. This was, of course, in part due to the rapid appreciation of the yen. In the early 1960s Matsushita established factories in Thailand and Taiwan to manufacture such products as batteries; in 1967 it established a factory in the Philippines to make and market home electrical appliances. Matsushita's operations in Thailand and Taiwan were motivated by low labour costs, and its operations in the Philippines by local demand. It is interesting to note that initially the production of dry batteries played an important role in the firm's foreign operations. This was because of the technical simplicity of this product and the low start-up costs required.

Production of electrical/electronic parts and assembly of appliances began in the early 1970s. Products requiring a high level of skill and precision were manufactured in Singapore, while those requiring lower skill levels (such as switches) were produced in Malaysia. Notably, Matsushita was the first Japanese manufacturer to establish an area management company — in Singapore in 1974. In the latter half of the decade Matsushita set up a marketing company in Malaysia, thus expanding its activities there from parts production and assembly to domestic sales. Two other developments during this period deserve our attention: the establishment of an international procurement office (IPO) in Singapore to promote the procurement of parts in Asia, and of a production skills training centre, also in Singapore.

In 1982 Matsushita set up an affiliate in Hong Kong to source suppliers in the region, indicating that the company was already in a position to utilise supporting firms. In the latter half of the 1980s it greatly expanded its operations in Malaysia; 11 of 18 new affiliates established by Matsushita between 1986 and 1991 were situated there. The production of electrical devices in China started in 1987.

Two major trends can be identified for the 1990s. The first of these has been the shift to Malaysia of air conditioner production, including assembly, parts production and some R&D activities. The second has been the growth of investment in China; 10 of 14 affiliates established since 1992 are located in China. These firms are engaged in assembly and sales activities.

Sanyo

Sanyo's foreign production as a share of its total world production was 25 per cent in 1993. The first Japanese manufacturer to operate extensively in Asia, in the 1960s Sanyo had already established production and sales facilities serving the local market in such countries as Taiwan, Malaysia and Thailand. It had also established assembly plants in Hong Kong and Singapore.

In the first half of the 1970s Sanyo set up local offices in Hong Kong and Korea to market electrical devices. Sanyo was more active in the sale and production of these products in this period than either Matsushita or Sony. In the latter half of the decade Sanyo began to produce and market electrical/electronic parts in Taiwan, and to manufacture VCRs in Korea. These developments suggest that Sanyo's parts supply system was already fairly well organised.

Sanyo set up its first Chinese subsidiaries in the first half of the 1980s, before either Matsushita (1987) or Sony (1993). These affiliates were responsible for the production of such parts as micro motors, the assembly of tape recorders, and the assembly and sale of air conditioners and calculators. In 1984 Sanyo established a plastic moulding plant in Singapore. Even today, neither Matsushita nor Sony has a materials manufacturing plant in Asia. Sanyo's higher share of foreign production than these firms may be due to its overseas factories' high rates of internal production. In the latter half of the decade Sanyo set up plants to make electrical devices in China and electrical/electronic parts in Indonesia. A Singaporean affiliate was established to market electrical devices, and a Korean affiliate to manufacture and sell audio equipment.

In 1992, Sanyo set up an affiliate in Malaysia to develop, manufacture and market car stereo equipment. This project was a joint venture with Mazda and Ford, which both operate automobile assembly plants in Malaysia. Our information suggests that this is one of only two R&D facilities established by Japanese firms in Asia.[10]

Sony

Sony's foreign production as a share of its total world production was 20 per cent in 1993. The pattern of Sony's foreign operations has differed quite markedly from that of either Matsushita or Sanyo. Sony's active involvement in Asia dates only from the latter half of the 1980s. Another area of difference is that Sony has very few factories carrying out both assembly and electrical/electronic parts production on the same premises.

In the second half of the 1980s Sony's Asian production facilities were concentrated in Malaysia, Singapore and Thailand. In the 1990s, it has set up assembly plants in Indonesia and China.

On the whole, Sony has been less active in Asia than the other two firms studied here. Sony's significant share of foreign production reflects its high concentration of plants in North America and Europe. In this sense Sony's strategy can be said to have been more market than cost oriented.

Overseas production and patterns of trade

The patterns discussed above reflect larger changes in international trade. It has been widely reported that Japan is now a net importer of colour TVs;[11] the number of imported sets jumped from about 2 million in 1992 to 3.7 million in 1993 (*Nihon Keizai Shimbun*, 23 February 1994). This sharp rise in imports is explained by the FDI activities of Japanese TV manufacturers in the 1980s and 1990s.[12] Table 9.2 shows trends in Japan's exports to and imports from Malaysia of electrical machinery. It can be seen that both have expanded rapidly in the past decade.

It can be expected that the pattern of Japan's imports will be reflected in the location of sales. Figure 9.5 compares the markets for parts and final products manufactured by Japanese affiliates of the electrical machinery and automobile industries in Asia. More than 90 per cent of automobiles manufactured in Asian factories in 1993 were sold in the host country, compared with only 45 per cent of electrical machinery. This gap between the two industries was apparent in 1984 and has widened since then. Quite large changes can be observed in the location of sales of electrical/electronic products manufactured by affiliates in Asia. Whereas the shares of host and 'other' countries

Table 9.2   **Japan's exports to and imports from Malaysia of electrical machinery, 1985 and 1993 (US$ thousand)**

	1985	1993
Exports		
Electrical power control equipment	82,503	601,599
Audio-visual equipment	129,499	685,268
Monitors	14,479	22,207
Radio receivers	27,464	9,331
Parts	32,334	601,945
Domestic electrical equipment	26,675	25,536
Refrigerators	6,007	1,82
Washing machines	8,513	6,820
Parts	na	7,264
Semiconductors and integrated circuits	69,958	1,507,324
Total	561,744	3,679,827
Imports		
Electrical power control equipment	585	154,749
Audio-visual equipment	12	405,023
Monitors	na	119,407
Radio receivers	na	133,363
Parts	na	58,301
Domestic electrical equipment	4	25,945
Refrigerators	na	10
Washing machines	na	3,146
Parts	na	3,458
Semiconductors and integrated circuits	42,764	216,667
Total	55,446	1,022,131

Source: JETRO, Trade Statistics Database, Tokyo.

decreased between 1985 and 1992, the shares of Japan and other Asian countries increased markedly. This is consistent with the steep increase noted earlier in Japan's imports of colour TVs. It would appear, then, that FDI by Japanese firms is a driving force behind the changing structure of Japanese imports. Note, too, that the appreciation of the yen since 1985 has increased the relative size of the Japanese market; the rise from ¥250 to ¥105 yen to the US dollar between 1985 and 1993 more than doubled its dollar value (and that is before we consider the growth of the market in yen terms).

The share of affiliates' exports to other Asian countries (excluding Japan), of both final electrical products and electrical/electronic parts, has increased substantially. This suggests that the foreign operations of the Japanese electrical machinery industry

Figure 9.5 **Location of sales of automobiles and electrical machinery, 1984 and 1993; location of supply of automobile and electrical/electronic parts, 1984 and 1992 (per cent)**

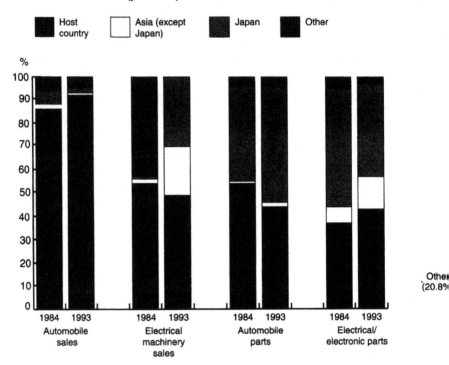

Source: MITI, *Kaigai Kigyo Katsudo Kihon Chosa* [Foreign Operations of Japanese Firms], Tokyo, 1994.

in Asia have promoted intraregional trade, a trend not observed for automobiles or auto parts.

As mentioned earlier, automobiles and electrical machinery require very different manufacturing and marketing strategies. In the case of automobiles, production needs to be located near the end market because of high transportation and set-up costs. These costs are far less relevant in the case of electrical machinery, although the level of technology and labour intensity required to manufacture products varies widely within the industry. The transportation costs of refrigerators and washing machines, for example, are far greater than those of colour TVs and VCRs. The cost of transporting small parts, such as ICs, is very low indeed relative to the value of the product. Despite these variations in cost, in general firms in the electrical machinery industry have greater freedom in choosing where to locate their overseas plants.

Table 9.3 illustrates some export patterns for electrical/electronic parts made in the Malaysian and Singaporean plants of Japanese affiliates. The sample data were distributed according to the percentage of sales to Japan and to third countries. It is interesting to note first that the majority of affiliates sold less than 25 per cent of their products to Japan; most of their output was probably sold to firms in other parts of Asia. The Japanese market was thus not crucial for these firms. Nearly three-quarters (74 per cent) of affiliates in Singapore exported at least 25 per cent of their products to third countries (the corresponding figure for Malaysia was 66 per cent), indicating that there is considerable trade in electrical/electronic parts among Asian countries. The location pattern for factories also suggests that some division of labour takes place among host countries in the production of parts. This is an important aspect of the electrical machinery industry.

We look next at the pattern of Japan's exports. As Figure 9.6 shows, the share of parts in Japan's total exports of machinery is far higher for Asian countries than for either North America or Europe. This difference stems from the high proportion of electrical/electronic parts in total exports. Whereas the share of such parts is below 15 per cent in North America and Europe, it is over 30 per cent in both the Asian NIEs and the ASEAN-4 countries. Japanese FDI in Asia has promoted this trading pattern.

Table 9.3   Export pattern for parts made in Malaysia and Singapore (no., per cent)

Percentage of parts exported to Japan	0–25		25–50		50–75		75–100		Total	
	No.	%	No.	%	No.	%	No.	%	No.	%
Malaysia										
0–25	16	25	11	17	8	13	16	25	51	80
25–50	1	2	3	5	3	5	0	0	7	11
50–75	1	2	1	2	0	0	0	0	2	3
75–100	4	6	0	0	0	0	0	0	4	6
Total	22	34	15	23	11	17	16	25	64	100
Singapore										
0–25	7	19	18	50	3	8	3	8	31	86
25–50	0	0	2	6	0	0	0	0	2	6
50–75	1	3	1	3	0	0	0	0	2	6
75–100	1	3	0	0	0	0	0	0	1	3
Total	9	25	21	58	3	8	3	8	36	100

Source: NDKK, 1994.

Figure 9.6   **Share of parts in Japan's total machinery exports by region, 1993 (per cent)**

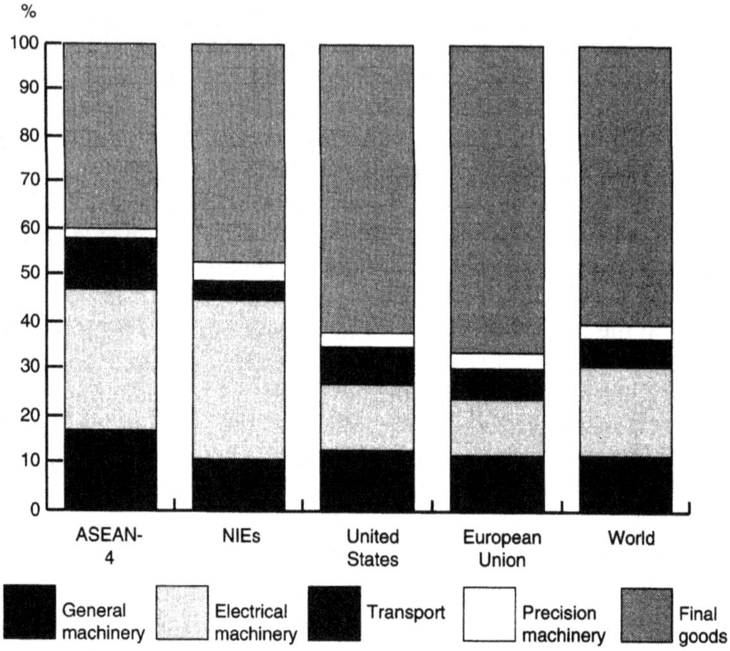

Source: MITI, 1994.

Concluding remarks

Japan's electrical machinery manufacturers have been investing actively in Asia since the latter half of the 1980s. This process has been facilitated by special characteristics of the industry, including products with many parts and diverse technological requirements, and generally low transportation costs.

Whereas the location of automobile production is heavily dependent on the size of the local market, the location of electrical machinery production depends more on the availability of cheap factors of production and scale economies, and on market size. With economies of scale, some manufacturing facilities (Matsushita's colour TV and air conditioner factories in Malaysia, for example) have become very large indeed, and are able to export their products both to Japan and to third countries.

Japan's active FDI in Asia has affected the pattern of trade between Japan and the rest of Asia. Japan's exports to Asia of electrical/electronic parts occupy a large share of the country's total electrical machinery exports. It is probable that many of these parts are exported to Asian factories for use in products that are then exported back to Japan. This trend has changed the pattern of Japan's imports from Asia; imports of electrical machinery are increasing rapidly.

The Asian region has a wide spread of income levels and, hence, labour costs. The locational choice of Japanese firms is affected by this diversity among countries in the region. The wide range of products made by the electrical machinery industry allows some flexibility in the strategic choice of location; even Japanese firms making similar goods will sometimes choose quite different locations for their overseas plants.

Notes

1   In 1991, Malaysia, with 36 firms, ranked first in terms of the number of Japanese affiliates making home electrical appliances. It was followed by the United States (31 firms) and Taiwan (23 firms). In the case of the industry-use electrical machinery industry, the United States ranked first (45 firms), followed by the United Kingdom (18 firms) and Taiwan (16 firms) (NDKK 1994).

2   Theoretical consideration has recently been given to the relationship between trade and regional concentration of industries (Krugman 1991).

3   In this paper Asia is defined as comprising Hong Kong, Korea, Singapore, Taiwan, Indonesia, Malaysia, the Philippines, Thailand and China. The Asian NIEs are Hong Kong, Korea, Singapore and Taiwan; and the ASEAN-4 countries are Indonesia, Malaysia, the Philippines and Thailand.

4   The division of labour is considered to play an important role in the expansion of international trade, generating both efficient production based on comparative advantage and scale economies. Refer to Ethier (1982) for a discussion of this latter point.

5   A large company like Toyota delegates assembly to other companies. At present seven plants assemble passenger cars for Toyota (*Nihon Keizai Shimbun*, 22 May 1994).

6   The following analysis is based on KSKKK (1986, 1992). According to KSKKK (1986), a 'typical' TV manufacturer (an actual firm manufacturing TVs in Nagano prefecture) uses 17 pressing companies, two grinding companies, two face treatment and coating process companies, 13 plastic processing companies, one lens maker, three metal (*kanagata*) firms, 23 electrical/electronic parts and assembly firms, and 69 other miscellaneous firms.

7   Firm N has about 400 employees (including those engaged in the manufacture of personal computers). This rises to about 640 if we include employees of subcontracting firms carrying out subassembly for Firm N. If we add to this the number of employees in subcontracting firms for N Electronics (about 250), the total number of employees in subcontracting firms carrying out subassembly becomes about 900.

8   The share is increasing faster for some sectors than for others. The dependence of personal computer manufacturers on imported parts, for example, has increased rapidly in the last few years.

9   The following discussion of the operations of Matsushita, Sanyo and Sony is based on Toyokeizai (1994).

10 The other is Matsushita's air conditioning R&D facility, also in Malaysia.

11 More than 95 per cent of TV imports came from Asia: 44.8 per cent from the Asian NIEs, 43.2 per cent from ASEAN-4 countries and 8.4 per cent from China. In value terms, Japan's exports of TVs (worth about ¥178.3 billion) far exceeded its imports (worth about ¥69.2 billion).

12 It should be noted, however, that a proportion of imported colour TVs sets are Korean products supplied under OEM agreements.

References

Cusumano, M.A. 1985, *The Japanese Automobile Industry*, Cambridge, MA: Harvard University Press.

Ethier, W.J. 1982, 'National and International Returns to Scale in the Modern Theory of International Trade', *American Economic Review*, 72, pp. 389–405.

Krugman, P. 1991, 'Increasing Returns and Economic Geography', *Journal of Political Economy*, 99, pp. 483–99.

KSKKK (Kikai Shinko Kyokai Keizai Kenkyujo) [Economic Research Institute, Japan Society for the Promotion of the Machinery Industry] 1986, *Denshi Denki Kikai ni okeru Seisantaisei no Henka to Shitauke Chushokigyo no Taiou ni kansuru Chosa* [A Study on the Structural Change of Production Systems and the Response of Subcontractors in the Electrical/Electronics Industry], Tokyo: KSKKK.

_____ 1992, *Kikai Sangyo no Torihikikankou ni kansuru Kokusai Hikaku Kenkyu* [An International Comparison of Trade Practices in the Machinery Industry], Tokyo: KSKKK.

MITI (Ministry of International Trade and Industry) 1994, *White Paper on International Trade and Industry*, Tokyo: MITI.

NDKK (Nihon Denshi Kikai Kogyokai) [Japan Industry Association of Electronics] 1994, *Kaigai Hojin Risuto* [List of Overseas Corporations], Tokyo: NDKK.

Sangyo Kenkyujo [Japan Industrial Policy Research Institute] 1990, *Kaden Seihin no Kyokyu Kozo no Choki Tenbo ni kansuru Chosa Kenkyu* [A Study of the Long-Term Prospects of Supply for Home Electrical Appliances], Tokyo.

Toyokeizai 1994, *Kaigai Shinshuto Kigyo Soran* [Directory of Overseas Corporations], Tokyo.

10 Technological change, foreign investment and the new strategic thrust of Japanese firms in the Asia Pacific

Denis Fred Simon and Yongwook Jun

Profound changes are taking place in the nature of international business, in terms both of the forces that drive transborder transactions and the strategic orientation of the firms that engage in these transactions. According to the UN-based Centre on Transnational Corporations, foreign investment flows have been growing faster than trade flows in recent years (UNCTC 1993): companies are increasingly recognising the need to establish a local presence as a way of entering overseas markets or gaining access to critical production or R&D assets that lie abroad. In contrast to the 1960s and 1970s, the present period is distinguished by the emergence of new forms of international expansion, most clearly manifested in the proliferation of strategic alliances and other new forms of cross-border collaboration. In addition, there has been a growing emphasis on the formation of global and regional networks as the preferred form of competitive organisation.

Globalisation and regionalisation have been two of the main factors in the transformation taking place in the way firms behave with respect to their foreign operations. Globalisation has led firms to rethink their perspectives on such issues as the nature of competition in their respective industries, new ways to compete and the evolving role of overseas planners. The world has now become the playing field for most of the Global 1,000 (as defined by *Businessweek*); not only must global firms have a presence in the markets of the triad economies (the United States, Western Europe and Japan), they must also be in a position to plug into local factor markets at appropriate times as a means to sustain or enhance their competitive edge. Whereas in the past the decision to go overseas was usually a defensive one (based on the need to protect export markets), the move to establish a factory, research laboratory or distribution centre abroad now tends to be an integral part of the firm's overall business strategy. As Porter (1990) has suggested, to compete in today's global business environment a firm must understand that what it does in one market, or what its competitors do in that market, may have an important impact on its competitive position and potential in other markets.

Regionalisation, on the other hand, has assumed a slightly different meaning for many of these same firms. While some observers of the formation of the European Union or NAFTA would like to claim that regionalisation is a necessary precursor to the true onset of globalisation — in the sense of the 'borderless world' as defined by Ohmae (1990) and others — the reality may be just the opposite. If we extrapolate from the case of the European Union, it is clear that regionalisation can be anything but global in intent. Globalisation has largely been engendered by the *micro level actions of firms* behaving according to their competitive instincts in a world increasingly dominated by the forces of liberalisation, deregulation and privatisation. Regionalisation, on the other hand, has been driven by *macro level forces such as government actions* — taken, in most cases, to diminish any negative impact that a more open, borderless world economy might have on the competitiveness of local companies. Regionalisation, such as that which has occurred in the European Union and NAFTA, has tended to be a politically induced process that requires companies, local and foreign, operating within a particular domain in many cases to suppress their global strategic intent so that they can accommodate more localised imperatives.[1] Still, however, the point remains: that these larger macro level forces — while more limiting and parochial than globalists like Ohmae would suggest — do act as a stimulus for firms to build a regionally defined presence across the triad, sometimes even leading to the creation of a regionally segmented mode of organisation and operation.

While it is the dynamic forces of globalisation and regionalisation acting in a dialectical manner that form the umbrella under which international business activities now take place (Simon 1995a), it has been the impact of technological change that has enabled the firm to act both globally and locally. Technological change has not simply altered the way in which the firm conducts its overseas business activities, it has also made possible the creation of a new architecture for carrying out and overseeing the diverse set of operations that takes place around the globe. This new architecture is manifested in the 'network firm' — a firm that may be both regionally and globally dispersed, but that has developed new governance and operational structures that facilitate the smoother movement of resources, information and technology across multiple environments (Figure 10.1). The growing movement towards the building of networks, either on a regional or transregional basis, has largely been made possible by the revolution that has taken place in microelectronics and in information technology, broadly defined. As a result, the overall process and strategic thrust of foreign investment have been altered in a fundamental fashion. This is particularly evident if we focus on the actions of the world's larger corporations, most of whom have begun to envision new ways to leverage overseas investment and related activities as a means to enhance their ability to compete globally.

The purpose of this chapter is to examine the impact of technological change on the process of foreign investment in the Asia Pacific region. The main focus will be on the changing behaviour of Japanese companies in the region, many of whom have moved away from the hub–spoke structures and Tokyo-oriented operating mentality that have

Figure 10.1   FDI and the emergence of networks

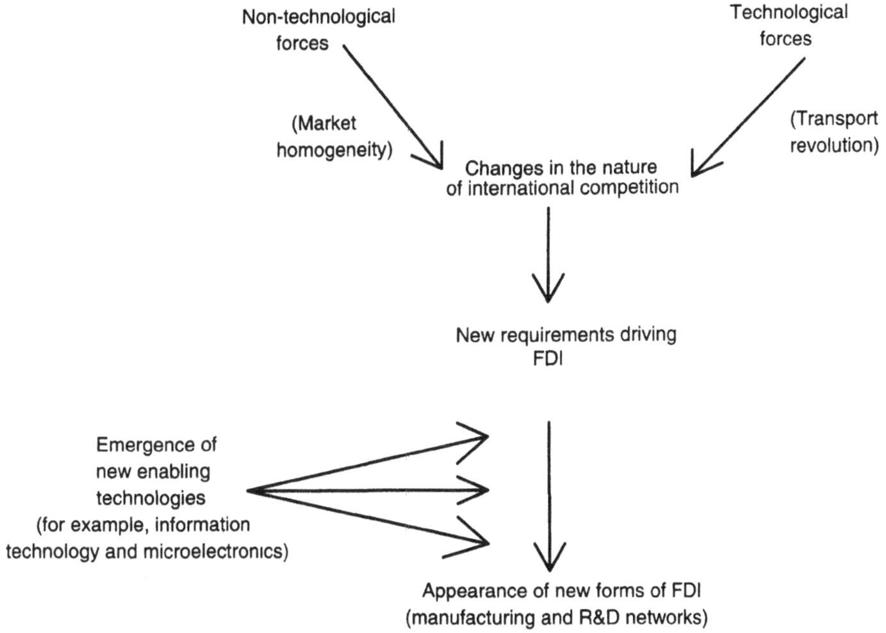

Non-technological
forces

Technological
forces

(Market
homogeneity)

Changes in the nature
of international competition

(Transport
revolution)

New requirements driving
FDI

Emergence of
new enabling
technologies
(for example, information
technology and microelectronics)

Appearance of new forms of FDI
(manufacturing and R&D networks)

Source: Simon, 1995b.

long dominated their behaviour. While a number of 'push factors' account for the recent expansion of Japanese foreign direct investment (FDI) in the western Pacific Rim — among them domestic economic restructuring and the appreciation of the yen — new and critical 'pull factors' (such as the upgrading of the technological base within the Asian NIEs and ASEAN economies) have also been at work. These new factors have contributed to the process of change taking place within Japanese firms, leading to the appearance of several different modes of overseas expansion. One such arrangement is non-equity avenues that rely on coordination rather than control as the primary managerial orientation. The chapter draws on the experiences of NEC, Hitachi, Fujitsu and Matsushita to highlight the ways in which technology has altered the strategic thrust of Japanese firms in the Asia Pacific region. It concludes with an assessment of the policy implications for the economies of the Pacific Rim.

The impact of technological change on FDI

As authors from Schumpeter to Porter have understood, technological change[2] has the potential to alter, in a fundamental fashion, the nature and thrust of competition.[3] As the nature of competition has changed, so have the perspectives of companies on their overseas expansion and operations. Analysts of international business activity have long been interested in the reasons underlying decisions on the location of overseas production, though few have focused on the question of technology change in particular. Economic geographers have helped us appreciate that locational shifts in manufacturing are inspired by technical as well as economic and organisational factors. Technological change, especially in the transportation and communication industries, has obviously reduced some of the constraints on overseas expansion via investment or licensing.

The main body of thought that actually addresses the relationship between technological change and investment location decision is the product lifecycle theory, developed by Vernon and Wells (1976) and others. Most technologies experience a three-stage process of evolution (Vernon 1966). The first stage involves the initial introduction of the technology into the market via a new product. The originating company is able to achieve a monopolistic position in the market as long as the technology remains solely within its control. During the second stage, the technology usually undergoes a process of standardisation as it diffuses into the hands of other firms; competition becomes focused on reducing costs as firms struggle with each other for market share. During the third stage, the technology goes through a process of further maturation, that is, greater standardisation. The drive to reduce costs becomes even more intense, leading some firms to relocate their production overseas and export products back to the innovating country. Since this is a dynamic process sustained by the continuous flow of new innovations, product lifecycle theory has been a useful way of explaining the critical role of technological change over time in the relocation of production abroad.

Today, however, the basic essence of the product lifecycle theory has been called into question by four main forces. To begin with, the income gap between countries, especially major industrialised countries, has narrowed. Accordingly, there is no longer a hierarchical sequence with respect to investment location. Second, the length of the lifecycle has shortened considerably, largely because of the growing emphasis on technology as the basis for competition. A good example of this can be seen in the rapid transition of the Intel-based 286 microprocessor used in personal computers to the 386, 486 and Pentium chips. Third, the process of technology commercialisation — and hence the time from product conceptualisation to actual introduction into the market — has been compressed substantially. The pressure to bring new products to market grows daily more intense, making access to high-calibre technological resources a critical necessity. The previous focus on low-cost labour has become subordinated to a new focus on product re-engineering to allow for the use of fewer components and more efficient throughput in manufacturing (*Business International*, 23 January 1989, p. 22). Those firms that are the technological leaders and that are first to get their products onto the market set the rules of the game, establish the critical standards and thus define the overall terms of competition. Finally, the investment costs of creating new technologies and producing new products have been rising steadily. This has made it increasingly difficult for any one firm to handle all costs itself. In the field of semiconductor development and manufacturing, for example, the cost of building a new, state-of-the-art facility is rapidly approaching the US$1 billion mark (*Electronic Business Asia*, July 1993, pp. 32–47).

Taken together, these four forces have led to technologies being introduced overseas at an earlier point in the lifecycle as firms search for new partners to share the costs and diversify the risks of investment, as well as to add value. The once sequential nature of movement of technology overseas has been replaced by the simultaneous exploitation of technology in multiple domains. Manufacturing as well as R&D have become truly global in scope ('A Survey of Manufacturing Technology', *The Economist*, 5 March 1994). In addition, as van Liemt (1992) stressed in a recent report published by the International Labour Organisation, the increased rapidity and frequency of changes in demand has put a new premium on production close to the market. In many instances, the locational hierarchies that were once prominent in such industries as consumer electronics have started to give way. The movement of technology overseas has, in terms both of production location and R&D site, moved in the direction of what Teece (1987) has termed 'the search for complementary assets'. Whereas in the past the product lifecycle focused on the one-way movement of technology from the originating country to the new low-wage production location, the impact of globalisation has been to shift the focus toward a bilateral process whereby all the participating parties bring something of value to the table. Firms that engage in overseas operations on either the R&D or production side may therefore be less inclined to rely primarily on traditional entry modes, such as licensing or equity-based investment, and opt instead for what Oman (1984) has termed 'new forms of foreign investment'.

Technological developments in two other areas — microelectronics and information technology — have also played a key role in transforming the strategy of firms with respect to their foreign location decisions. On the production side, the microelectronics revolution has helped to accelerate the transition away from Fordist models of production towards a production paradigm based on the concept of flexible specialisation.[4] The Fordist model of mass production involves the manufacture of standardised products in high volumes using special purpose machinery and predominantly unskilled labour (Stopper and Scott 1992). In contrast, the paradigm of flexible specialisation involves the manufacture of a wide and changing array of customised products using flexible, general purpose machinery and skilled, adaptable workers (Stopper and Scott 1993). Because of the new types of reprogrammability that have been introduced into the manufacturing process — what the Japanese have called mechatronics — an entirely new set of economic forces has become predominant, leading to new ideas about production volume, mix and tooling ('The Future Surveyed', *The Economist*, 11 September 1993, pp. 70–2).

To start with, there has been a reduction in the minimum efficient size of production lots and production units, providing greater room for customisation of output. The costs usually associated with customised production have diminished greatly as a result of increased emphasis on economies of scope. The flexibility that comes with microelectronics-induced reprogrammability has led to a shift in attitude towards specialisation; firms are no longer looking simply to internalise (through vertical integration) many of the sourcing, assembly and standard production activities covered by the value chain. According to Antonelli (1988), the effects of microelectronics on production functions tend to be basically centrifugal, reducing the role of technical economies of scale by lowering the minimum efficient size of production units (Figure 10.2). This has already led to the emergence of 'microfactories': smaller units of production that can thrive because technological change has redefined the economics of scale.

The stress on flexible specialisation has led to reduced emphasis on costs and greater emphasis on quality.[5] This change has been fostered by the shift in global competition away from variable and towards fixed cost competition. Because of the global integration of factor and capital markets, firms must place more weight on product differentiation and customer responsiveness (via high-quality products and reliable service and maintenance). There is also growing evidence to show that labour accounts for a decreasing percentage of overall costs for most products — the

Figure 10.2   Impact of the microelectronics revolution

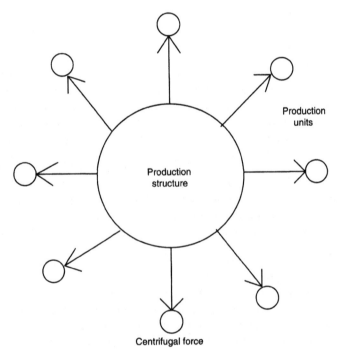

Production units

Production structure

Centrifugal force

automobile being a prime example. Within such a system, non-price competitive factors take on greater significance than price-related factors; this is not to say that costs are not important, but only that the successful firm must be mindful of the full range of competitive factors.[6] As Dunning (1988) has indicated, successful multinational firms are those that can manage a broad range of value-added activities across a diverse set of geographical boundaries, capitalising on the distinct advantages offered in each domain. Overseas site selection then becomes geared much more to accessing higher value-added resources than to simply taking advantage of the availability of cheap labour or of traditional types of tax holiday.

This need to address the challenges of managing a larger number of smaller, more specialised units on a global or regional scale highlights the second type of technological change that has led to a revision of the foreign investment process, namely the information technology revolution. Just as the microelectronics revolution has caused a profound change in the economics and structure of production, the information revolution has led to a revision of the organisation of production and R&D. Information technology has enabled internationally oriented corporations to meet their worldwide communication requirements. Even more importantly, the expanded use of information technologies within the multinational corporation has allowed it to implement many of the organisational changes necessitated by the changing requirements of global competition. In particular, it has now become possible to enlarge the scope of sourcing and procurement from a domestic to a regional or global basis. Antonelli (1994) suggests that the effects of information technology on corporate governance have been centripetal; corporations are now better able to assert their influence over and monitor a larger, more diverse range of production entities (Figure 10.3). This accords well with the current trend in manufacturing towards greater reliance on a large number of small specialised entities. From an international business perspective, this means that the multinational corporation now possesses the tools to orchestrate an entirely new production architecture that places more weight on *coordination* than *control*. In fact, control through ownership has become less important now that transaction costs can be reduced substantially by using information technology. This gives the firm greater discretion over the type of relationship it wishes to develop with a particular supplier, assembler or distributor. It also allows multinational corporations to be more footloose, and less entrapped by the consequences of an equity investment.

From an organisational perspective, then, the information technology revolution has helped to give birth to an entirely new type of structure: the network firm. As Naisbitt (1994) has argued, the network firm represents a new model of global/regional expansion; multinational corporations will increasingly operate like networks of small local companies. Forsgren and Johanson (1992, p. 5) go further to suggest that 'the competitive situation of the firm is a matter of the networks they operate in or may operate in...there is a great difference between being an insider and an outsider...'. They go on to argue that 'the ability to manage and coordinate these relationships is one of the intangible [competitive] assets of the firm' (p. 5). Given the

Figure 10.3   Impact of the information technology revolution

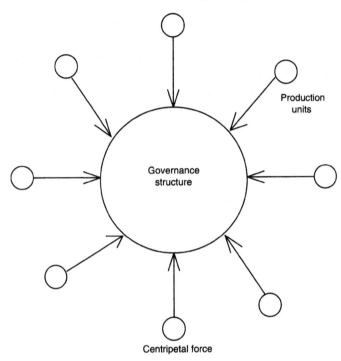

reduced cost of both market and non-market coordination, firms now have the capability to combine what Imai (1988) has suggested is a blend of the global factory and the company town. From an international business perspective, business networks have become the new means for effectively handling and monitoring *activity interdependencies* among the operational tasks performed by the firm across national boundaries. Hakansson (1989) suggests that an industrial network consists of companies linked together by the fact that they either produce or use complementary or competitive products. Imai and Baba (1991), though more directly concerned with innovation-related processes, offer a broader definition also useful for the purposes of this paper.

> A network can, in terms of theory, be viewed as an interpenetrated form of market and organisation. Empirically, it is an organisation with a structure marked by loose linkages and...with both weak and strong ties between constituent members. The network enables corporations to identify emergent opportunities for linking flexible specialisation across boundaries of firms, and for triggering continuous interactive innovation (Imai and Baba 1991, pp. 391–2).

A great deal of the literature on networks originated in Scandinavia as part of the study of marketing. The network concept was later expanded and refined by Hakansson (1989), Axelsson and Easton (1992), Biemans (1992), Forsgren and Johanson (1992) and others.[7] The main point of many of these authors is that operationally networks are vehicles for transcending traditional markets and hierarchies in business; they all concur that business exchange transactions can best be conceptualised and studied within the context of network structures, whether these structures be functionally based (for example, marketing or manufacturing), culturally linked or whatever. As firms make the transition from a vertical orientation, decentralising away from the hub–spoke model often associated with multinational structures, networks have started to become the preferred mode of organisation.

Generally speaking, all networks are composed of four main elements. First, there are the *actors*. These may be private sector firms, government organisations or universities. Size is usually not a critical issue given the move towards flexible specialisation. Second, there are the *activities* that occur within the confines of the network. These may include: a broad range of manufacturing tasks, such as subassembly and assembly operations as well as the production of parts and components; design and re-engineering tasks; applied R&D; and the exchange of personnel, especially skilled technicians and engineers. Third, there are the *resources* that form the focal point of the exchanges conducted within the network. These may include the local array of technological assets and the technologies or knowhow provided by the coordinating organisation to each of the network members. Finally, there are the *bonding mechanisms* that hold together the various elements within the network. Depending on the context, these may include formal licensing arrangements, equity agreements, strategic alliances, supplier or original equipment manufacturer (OEM) contracts, and subcontracting agreements. Each network operates according to a set of formal and informal exchange rules that define the expectations and obligations of members. The key point, however, is that with the technologies in place to provide the capability for coordinating a diverse set of activities and relationships independent of geographical location, new forms of corporate organisation and overseas expansion are now possible, and these are even more attractive than traditional modes of foreign investment.

Technical change on the demand side: the impact on investment

Technical change can be a major barrier to entry for new players attempting to establish a competitive position in a particular industry or market segment. At the same time, however, it is also the case that such barriers to entry are rarely static; the expanded and rapid diffusion of technology worldwide through increased foreign investment and international trade has made it difficult for any company or country to rely too extensively on what usually turns out to be a thin and often fleeting technological edge to sustain its position in the marketplace. The growing technological prowess of the economies in the Asia Pacific region illustrates just how rapidly technical barriers to entry that were once formidable can be overcome through a combination of state-led and private sector initiatives. In essence, a new technological trajectory has begun to emerge in the Pacific Rim — one that appears to be significantly different from the 'flying geese' model that was once the predominant paradigm used to explain growth patterns on a national and regional level (*Forbes*, 23 November 1992, p. 108). As one commentary in *Businessweek* (7 December 1992, p. 126) has suggested, the Asian economies: 'are embracing a new definition of catch-up. Rather than try to leap frog the advanced economies, the secret is to absorb new technologies that can be quickly applied to niches in the marketplace. And, rather than go head to head, the idea is to join forces as strategic partners'. In contrast to the hierarchies that were prevalent in the past, there is now a greater degree of collaboration and interaction based on non-hierarchical forms of cooperation as Asia's steadily improving technological assets become increasingly important in the context of regional and global competition.

Soaring labour and production costs and a growing sense that the international technology market is becoming more constrained have spurred Pacific Rim economies to upgrade technology.[8] With the growing emphasis in world markets on technology-based competition, policy makers and corporate executives in Asia have recognised that their economic future lies in an ability to develop knowledge- and information-intensive industries.[9] In other words, the days of industrialisation based on ready availability of cheap labour seem destined to end soon for most countries, even China. There is little doubt that many economies in the region have both the talent and the financial and technological resources to engage in the type of economic transformation that is called for by the changing dynamics of global competition (Bergsten and Noland 1993). Manufacturers have learned how to meet global standards and quality requirements through their experience as OEM suppliers to some of the world's leading multinational corporations; these same factories are now branching out on their own into higher value-added segments of the market (*Free China Review*, March 1994, pp. 42–50). According to the US National Science Foundation (1993), since 1980 R&D spending has grown at annual rates ranging from 15.8 per cent in Taiwan to 23 per cent in South Korea. Singapore, which spent 1 per cent of its GDP on R&D in 1991, plans to double its level of investment by 1995 under a US$1.2 billion national technology plan. And, according to the magazine *Science* ('Science in Asia' [Special Issue], 15 October 1993), the Asian NIEs (Taiwan, South Korea, Hong Kong and Singapore) currently spend about two-thirds as much as Japan and over half as much as the United States each year on their scientists and engineers. This reflects the strong commitment of NIEs to upgrading the technological orientation of their economies.

In the evolving context of global competition, a series of new roles has emerged for Asia Pacific economies, especially NIEs, but increasingly including the ASEAN-4 (Malaysia, Thailand, Indonesia and the Philippines) and China (Simon 1994). These roles include high value-added manufacturing, small batch production of, for example, application-specific integrated circuits (ASICs), specialised engineering for initiating rapid design changes, high-technology production of both software and hardware, and low-cost, high-quality R&D (*Electronic Business Asia*, December

1991, pp. 42–52). Korean and Japanese companies are now vying for a share of the global semiconductor market, and Taiwan has become a leading producer of information technology products, including personal computers, motherboards, computer monitors and related peripheral devices. (It has been estimated that close to 70 per cent of the motherboards used in personal computers around the world come from Taiwan [*Free China Review*, August 1992]). By linking up with suitable partners in the NIEs and ASEAN, foreign firms have the potential to bridge more effectively the gap between R&D and manufacturing, as well as to forge closer links with their customers.

The evolving role of Japanese firms in the Pacific Rim

The role of Japan as a driver of economic dynamism in the Pacific Rim has continued to increase in importance since World War II, despite continued memories in the region of Japanese militarism during the war. The Japanese government has made a determined effort to overcome the image of the 'ugly Japanese' that is still fairly pervasive in Northeast and Southeast Asia (Bartu 1992). Today, Japan is the largest source of foreign investment and aid in the Asia Pacific region. In 1992 and 1993, despite a decline in Japanese FDI in almost every other region of the world, direct investment by Japanese firms in Asia — especially China and Indonesia — actually increased (Table 10.1).[10] Two-way trade with Japan has also started to rise as political pressure and economic imperatives have made it necessary for Japanese companies to rely more on imports from the ASEAN-4 and the Asian NIEs (referred to by some in Tokyo as the 'Japan NIEs'). In fact (and not unexpectedly), in 1986–92 exports to Japan of Japanese firms operating in the Asia Pacific region were higher than those of Japanese firms operating in North America and Europe. Some observers have taken the expanded Japanese presence in the region as indicating a possible return to the concept of a 'sphere of coprosperity' in Asia. In reality, though, the present situation is driven largely by the Japanese private sector and is a response, for the most part, to global patterns of economic and technological competition in such industries as microelectronics, telecommunications and machine tools (Encarnation 1992).

Japanese firms attach importance to the Pacific Rim in four identifiable ways. First, they see the region as an expanding market. According to an article in the *Japan Times* (2 September 1991, p. 6): 'Japan's direct investment in Southeast Asia is increasingly driven by the objective of establishing strategic control of the mega-markets of the next decade. By the year 2001, there will be some 600 million customers along the diagonal from Tokyo to Jakarta, and that excludes all but the two southern provinces of China'. The Asian economies have continued to grow at fairly constant rates since the mid 1980s, weathering many of the world's more serious economic downturns better than most Western industrialised nations. During this period, the growth rates of Pacific Rim economies have been above average: over 6 per cent in most cases. Growing industrial and consumer demand, fuelled by rising per capita incomes, have made it impossible for Japanese firms to ignore or pay lip service to developments in the region.

Table 10.1   Location of Japanese FDI, 1988–92 (US$ million)

	1988	1989	1990	1991	1992	Cumulative (to 31 March 1993)
North America	22,328	33,902	27,192	18,823	14,572	169,580
Europe	9,116	14,808	14,294	9,371	7,061	75,697
Asia	5,569	8,238	7,054	5,936	6,425	59,880
Indonesia	586	631	1,105	1,193	1,676	14,409
Hong Kong	1,662	1,898	1,785	925	735	11,510
Singapore	747	1,902	840	613	670	7,837
Thailand	859	1,276	1,154	807	657	5,887
Malaysia	387	673	725	880	704	4,815
South Korea	483	606	284	260	225	4,623
China	296	438	349	579	1,070	4,472
Philippines	134	202	258	203	160	1,943
Latin America	6,428	5,238	3,628	3,337	2,726	46,547
Oceania	2,669	4,618	4,166	3,278	2,408	23,783
Africa	653	671	551	748	238	6,813
Middle East	259	66	27	90	709	4,231
Total	47,022	67,540	56,911	41,584	34,138	386,580
Manufacturing	13,805	16,284	15,486	12,311	10,057	103,981
Non-manufacturing	32,634	50,517	40,620	28,809	23,720	275,666

Source: Ministry of Finance, Tokyo, 1993.

As each economy in the region upgrades its infrastructure and production base, it finds itself becoming increasingly tied to the Japanese economy.[11] One Korean expert in the Electronics Industry Association of Korea has gone so far as to suggest that for every dollar of revenue generated by increased Korean exports to the United States, there is a concomitant increase in Korean imports of machinery and equipment from Japan (pers. comm.). In Thailand, Japanese computer numerically controlled (CNC) machine tool manufacturers control 70.3 per cent of the domestic market; their customers include a large number of Japanese firms operating inside Thailand as well as a number of local enterprises (*National Trade Data Reports*, 16 February 1994, p. 3).

A related trend is the growing presence of Japanese equipment and machinery manufacturers in the region. Many of these have established a production base in East or Southeast Asia so as to be able to supply advanced equipment to Japanese corporate customers who have begun to expand their overall operations in the Pacific Rim. Yamazaki Mazak, for example, set up Singapore's most advanced machine tool components manufacturing plant using state-of-the-art, computer-integrated, manufacturing and flexible manufacturing system technology.[12] The plant is almost fully automated. Its main customers are other Japanese firms operating in ASEAN countries, many of whom are deploying equipment and technology just as if not more advanced than that being used in their factories back in Japan.

Second, Japanese firms continue to regard many Asian economies (Indonesia and Malaysia, for example) as important manufacturing bases where they can still source low-cost components and utilise an existing pool of relatively inexpensive labour. In many ways, Japanese investment in the 1990s builds on the foundation laid by Japanese investment in the 1980s (*Nikkei Weekly*, 11 April 1994, p. 7). An appreciable number of Japanese firms have also started to move into manufacturing with higher value-added. In large part this has been in response to the growing technological prowess of Asian economies, most of whom have invested substantial sums of money to create a modern, smoothly functioning, technologically advanced economic system. Canon, one of the world's largest producers of cameras and photocopiers, decided to move a significant portion of its very sophisticated 35 mm camera production activities to Taiwan (*Japan Economic Journal*, 26 January 1991, p. 16).[13] Mitsubishi likewise is talking about sourcing semiconductors for its Japanese customers from Taiwan's increasingly sophisticated microelectronics industry through contractual arrangements with the Taiwan Semiconductor Manufacturing Corporation.

A large number of Japanese companies have decided to set up international procurement offices in the region as well. The preferred target has been Singapore because of its strong telecommunications, transportation and transshipment infrastructure. Using advanced information technology systems to track parts and components as well as to receive and transmit data about availability, delivery and so forth, many Japanese companies have been able to build their regional networks into a global supply chain.

Third, Japanese firms have increasingly come to view their counterparts in Asian economies as actual or potential strategic partners.[14] The development of a high-technology capability among the Asian NIEs and China has altered the traditional division of labour in the Pacific Rim; as suggested earlier, the technological trajectory of the region has taken on a new shape as firms move away from the hierarchical structure of the past to place more stress on complementary relationships among the various actors in the region. Here again, Japanese corporate behaviour has been motivated by the enhanced capability of the Asian economies. The decision by Hitachi, a leading producer of semiconductors, to transfer advanced production knowhow to Korea's Lucky Goldstar — beginning with 1 MB, then proceeding to 4 MB and most recently 16 MB DRAM technology — is representative of this type of behaviour. Through this agreement, Hitachi aimed to build a strategic relationship with its Korean partner that would allow it to refocus its resources on the next generation of semiconductor chips while ensuring its existing customers had a secure supply of reliable memory chips. While costly in terms of upfront payments and royalties, the agreement enabled Goldstar to move beyond emphasis on consumer electronics and enhanced its ability to compete with Samsung, its chief domestic rival. Hitachi's decision also occurred in the context of continuing dissension between the Japanese and Korean governments over the pace and depth of technology transfer from Japan to South Korea.

Finally, Japanese firms have expanded their movement into the Asia Pacific region to tap into its steadily improving R&D and engineering resources, particularly in the area of software development; it could be said that Japan's technology strategy is becoming regionalised as well as globalised. Just as many Japanese companies have established R&D centres in the United States, a select number of firms is now moving to harness Asia's steadily improving skills in science and technology. Responding to concerns about a projected shortage of approximately 500,000–700,000 software engineers in Japan by the end of the century, many Japanese computer companies have sought out qualified individuals in universities and research institutes in China, for example, as a means to reinforce their ranks. The talents of many of these people are grossly underutilised within the Chinese science and technology establishment. As one Japanese human resources manager has remarked of China, 'the country is really a goldmine of brilliant human resources' (*Japan Times Weekly*, 25–31 March 1991, p. 17). Leading firms like Oreton, NEC, Fujitsu and Hitachi, to mention just a few, have established good working relations with institutes under the Chinese Academy of Sciences and with renowned Chinese universities such as Shanghai Jiaotong University and Fudan University.

Significantly, these R&D-oriented relationships have started to extend beyond software engineering into new areas such as consumer electronics, semiconductors and air conditioning. The Japanese identify the main purpose of these new facilities as the performance of 'D&D': design and development. Toshiba, for example, has moved total responsibility for the design of its VCRs from Japan to Singapore through the establishment of a local subsidiary (*Business Times*, 18 May 1994, p. 8). Among Japanese manufacturers, though, Matsushita has probably put together the most well-articulated strategy for the Asia Pacific region. As of 1992, close to 60 per cent of this company's non-Japanese manufacturing was conducted in the Asia Pacific region (*The Economist*, 24 April 1993, p. 33). Matsushita's operations in Malaysia serve to illustrate the point. Matsushita has 16 manufacturing and sales companies in Malaysia which, according to 1992 data, generate approximately 4 per cent of Malaysia's annual GDP. Matsushita has established an advanced R&D centre for home air conditioning technology outside Kuala Lumpur as part of its goal to make Malaysia a major regional and international air conditioning production site. Already, Matsushita Malaysia supplies about 10–15 per cent of world demand, serving the US, Chinese and Japanese markets (*Asian Wall Street Journal Weekly*, 24 May 1993, p. 2). Company officials have suggested that in five years or so, the Kuala Lumpur research centre may become the focal point of development and refinement of air conditioner models for the entire company.[15] Matsushita has also set up an engineering redesign centre for colour televisions in Malaysia. Already, significant progress has been made in cutting the overall manufacturing costs of 17" and 19" colour televisions.

This was achieved by reducing the total number of parts used in each set and resulted in savings of 10–15 per cent per unit.[16] Eventually, as traditional television technology is superseded by high-definition or digital television technology in Japan, Malaysia (along with China) may become Matsushita's main R&D and production site for serving those markets where significant demand for the traditional product still exists.[17]

The increased interest by Japanese firms in Asia is also a response to the intense competition that exists in Japan's domestic market. Spurred on by the need to obtain some form of business advantage over their rivals at home, Japanese firms have sought an edge in cost, time and product design through expanded collaboration in Asia. Of course, Japanese firms are also aware of growing competition from within the Pacific Rim as well as from US and European firms. Still, there has tended to be an almost 'follow-the-leader' pattern, or what the Japanese call *yoko narabe* ('me-too-ism'), to the corporate behaviour of Japanese firms (*Electronic Business Asia*, April 1994, pp. 40–7). This can been seen in the investment and licensing practices of Japanese firms in product lines such as VCRs and microwave ovens (Table 10.2). Each company in a particular industry watches, and sometimes follows, the actions of its counterparts, often leading to similar overseas investment activity, though with different partners and at times in different locations.

Emerging Japanese networks in Asia

As suggested earlier, the current transition away from unilateral patterns of technology transfer and towards bilateral patterns of technology sharing represents a profound change in the global market for technology. While continuing to expand the scope and quantity of their strategic alliances with American and European firms, Japanese firms are, with caution as well as optimism, forming similar alliances with

Table 10.2   Japanese firms manufacturing VCRs in the Pacific Rim

Company	Country	Start-up date	Annual ouput (units)
JVC	Malaysia	May 1989	800,000
Hitachi	Malaysia	June 1989	600,000
Toshiba	Singapore	Feb 1990	1,000,000
Sharp	Malaysia	June 1990	250,000
Mitsubishi	Malaysia	Sept 1990	200,000
Funai	Malaysia	Late 1990	na
Sony	Malaysia	Oct 1992	360,000

Source: *Japan Economic Journal*, 2 June 1990, p. 16.

some Pacific Rim companies. The case of the Hitachi–Goldstar agreement cited above is just one example of the expansion of Japanese strategic alliances in Asia. In early 1993, Toshiba and Samsung — major competitors in the world DRAM market — agreed to collaborate on the development of a new type of semiconductor chip called flash memory.[18] Similar arrangements have been forged between NEC and Samsung and between Fujitsu and Hyundai, both in the field of microelectronics.[19] Japan's exports of technology were worth 339.4 billion yen in 1990, with about 47 per cent of this going to the Asia Pacific region. Ironically in view of Korea's assertion that Japan withholds its technology, Korea, at 14 per cent, was the largest recipient of Japanese technology. Increasingly, Japanese firms are recognising that technology transfer is the key to gaining access to regional markets as well as to taking advantage of Asia's technological resources.[20] As one policy maker in Singapore remarked in 1992, 'the new currency of exchange in Asia is now technology and markets'.

In essence, what appears to be emerging in the Pacific Rim is a series of Japanese-engineered, well-orchestrated and well-articulated production and R&D networks (Figure 10.4) designed to tap into the labour skills and advanced production assets of the region (*Nikkei Weekly*, 17 May 1993). This finding appears compatible with a more general conclusion reached in UNCTC 1993. According to an earlier version of this report (UNCTC 1991), there is evidence that Japanese transnational corporations are building regionally integrated, independently sustainable networks of overseas investments centred on a triad member. The creation of these networks seems to reflect a fundamental change in focus — what the noted Japanese management specialist Imai (1988) has termed 'a shift in focus from transactions costs to transactions benefits'. Japanese firms now seem far more willing to go outside their traditional subcontracting and sourcing relationships and to put down deeper roots in the local economies of the region.[21] This has led to an opening up of many existing networks to qualified local firms throughout the Pacific Rim, especially in Malaysia, Thailand and Singapore (*Asian Business*, April 1994, p. 21).

In constructing networks, Japanese firms look for partners who can contribute high value-added (Tokunaga 1992). Sony, for example, has alliances with 130 Taiwanese electronics companies, many of whom manufacture sophisticated components for use in Sony VCRs (*Electronics Weekly*, 3 April 1991, p. 2). In many cases, partners are bound not by common ownership or equity arrangements but rather, as already suggested, by various types of contractual and non-contractual arrangements that provide both partners with flexibility and autonomy. The shift away from traditional equity arrangements makes it difficult to measure the extent of Japanese presence in the region using investment and trade data alone.[22] The suggestion being made here is that, irrespective of what the data might say, the influence of Japanese companies in the Asia Pacific region is expanding through new forms of overseas engagement (*Business Tokyo*, July 1992, pp. 10–15).

NEC's operations in Hong Kong provide an excellent example of one of these new types of arrangement (Figure 10.5). NEC's Hong Kong office is responsible for overseeing the production of three products: dot matrix printers, personal computers

Figure 10.4   NEC: networks, alliances and D&D in the Pacific Rim

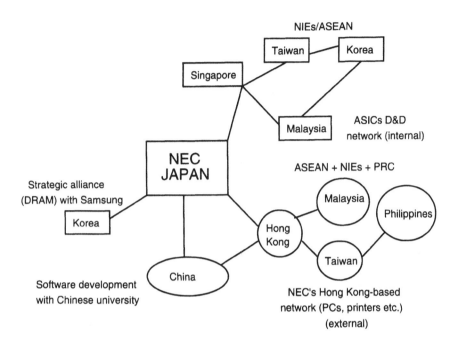

Source: Simon, 1995b.

and hard disk drives. Rather than itself owning and managing several manufacturing plants, NEC has a staff of 26 production engineers based in Hong Kong who travel around the region coordinating production of these products via networks of local firms. Together these firms form the manufacturing arm of NEC Technologies Hong Kong. As one NEC executive has said, 'in Hong Kong, NEC is a company without a factory'. Manufacture of main components and all stages of assembly of dot matrix printers are carried out in six to eight factories in southern China; responsibility for design is increasingly in the hands of the Hong Kong office. Personal computers are assembled using components procured primarily in Hong Kong and South China as well as other parts of Southeast Asia (Thailand and Malaysia). Production of hard disk drives is coordinated by a number of factories in the Philippines. The team of roving production specialists makes sure that sufficient attention is paid in all factories to such aspects as quality control and product reliability. The coordination needed to make this type of manufacturing architecture work is facilitated by an advanced information technology infrastructure that enables communication between the

Figure 10.5   NEC's PC business network

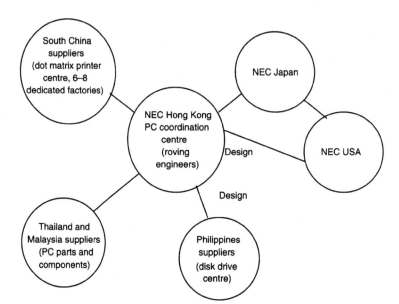

various players in the network and the team of Hong Kong-based engineers. Links are also maintained with NEC Technologies in Massachusetts since this plant is a major user of parts sourced in Hong Kong. Eventually, products carrying the NEC brand name are shipped to world markets — the United States, the European Union, the Middle East and Asia — without ever actually having passed through an NEC-owned manufacturing facility.

Similar networks have been created for the design and manufacture of ASICs. Companies such as Fujitsu, NEC and Toshiba have set up local D&D centres in the Asia Pacific region to customise chips to meet the requirements of local end users. Their networks rely on advanced information technology infrastructure and comprehensive libraries in Japan containing a vast assortment of semiconductor designs. NEC engineers in Taiwan, for example, can acquire relevant information from the main NEC technical design library to design ASICs that meet the specific requirements of customers. NEC initially set up its Taiwan design centre in 1988 with 15 engineers. It has since expanded the activities of the centre to include design of gate array semiconductors and chips for its high-speed workstations (*Business Taiwan*, 18 December 1991, p. 2). Several other Japanese firms, including Sharp and Hitachi, have also selected Taiwan as a base for integrated circuit design. The cost of operating such a network is minimal because each centre requires only a small dedicated staff and several powerful computer workstations. The benefits, however, are substantial, and include closer links between ASIC suppliers, designers and end users.

Even China is being drawn into this new and exciting revised division of labour through the rapidly growing presence in the country of Japanese firms. According to a report on Japanese foreign investment issued by Japan's ExIm Bank in March 1994 (*Japan Overseas Investment, 1993*), China has become the main target of present and future overseas expansion for Japanese corporations operating in Asia. Japanese investment in China, which has grown fairly rapidly since 1991, is concentrated in the northeast, especially in the city of Dalian. Toshiba is one Japanese company manufacturing consumer electronics and related products in Dalian. Several of Toshiba's supplier firms have also set up in the city, as well as in Hangzhou near the Yangtze River delta. Toshiba has linked the activities of these and a growing number of domestic Chinese firms with its operations in Thailand as part of an expanding regionally based production network.

Prospects and conclusions

Simon conducted extensive interviews with leading executives in Japan's top companies in 1991–93. These provided support for the view that technological change is indeed altering the scope and nature of Japan's emerging business relations with the Asian NIEs, China and the ASEAN-4 (Simon 1995b), especially in the area of technology cooperation. Ohmae (1993) talks about Japan's rise as a 'regionally oriented nation-state', implying that this may be a precursor to the birth of a truly globalised Japanese economy. Ohmae, however, may be missing an important point in his discussion of trends in Japan. Clearly the Japanese are identifying regional sources of competitive advantage. It may no longer be useful to think of Japan's technological assets as being confined to the Japanese islands. In essence, Japan has gone beyond even Porter's (1990) concept of the competitive advantage of nations — Japanese firms in aggregate have begun to create regional sources of national competitive strength and capability through their expanding access to and ability to harness the technological assets of Asian economies (Porter 1990).

This new strategic thrust will have important consequences for regional and global competition in the coming years. Japanese firms, both large and small, are strengthening their ties with economies in the region and are successfully plugging into the 'emerging pockets of excellence' in Asia. In an age when the fragmentation of the world economy into trading blocs threatens to become a reality, Japanese and Asian firms appear increasingly poised to respond in kind should the European Union or NAFTA adopt a strongly protectionist stance. It has been estimated that between 1993 and 1996, over 50 per cent of Japanese foreign investment will go to Asia. Even if the actual figure is lower, the fact remains that Japan will continue to exert a tremendous influence on the direction and pace of economic and technological change in the region. Rather than a *trading* bloc, however, we may be witnessing the emergence of a new type of regional *technology* bloc: the coming together of Asia's technological resources in a vast array of highly focused networks, coordinated mainly by Japanese firms. Some Asian economies are hesitant to encourage closer involvement with Japanese companies for a number of reasons, the main one being a desire to avoid excessive technological dependence on Japan. Japan will have to walk softly and adopt a low posture if it is to avoid stirring up the negative images of the past.

The trend towards reliance on network structures has important policy implications for the economies of the Asia Pacific region. First, existing policies in many of these countries on FDI would seem to require substantial revision. Countries that wish to have a place in the emerging network architecture will need to enact policies that promote the greater openness and flexibility required by these networks. Second, as cost factors become subordinated to the need for high-level skills and advanced infrastructure, Asia Pacific economies will have to upgrade their domestic human resource base and expand their investment in telecommunications and transportation. As discussed earlier, the search by leading multinational firms for attractive partners will increasingly focus on the availability of complementary assets that can be harnessed to achieve greater overall competitiveness. Economies lacking these assets will not be well positioned to tap into network structures. Third, for Asia Pacific economies, joining the global information revolution is no longer a luxury but a necessity. Information technology is the glue that holds together communication and coordination within networks. Economies that are unable to build and use the information channels created by the integration of computers and telecommunications technology will also be marginalised. Finally, the shift towards dependence on networks as the primary mode of production and R&D organisation raises critical questions about technology transfer. It remains to be seen whether networks will facilitate technology transfer or inhibit the access to technology of those firms considered to be outsiders. It is clear, however, that the route to ensuring a substantial role in these network structures is to have in place a significant range of technological capabilities in manufacturing and R&D. Increased investment in science and technology will, therefore, also be needed if Asia Pacific countries are to keep pace with the changes taking place in the global technology system.

The growth of networks raises a set of new and important issues for policy makers in the Asia Pacific region as well as in other parts of the world. In contrast to the 1960s and 1970s, when the movement of capital and technology abroad by large multinationals was seen as threatening sovereignty and distorting development, countries are today vying with each other to develop more intimate relations with foreign companies. This is not to say that these issues are dead; as network structures become more common, critical questions about national economic and technological independence are sure to be asked. Networks do pose sovereignty related questions for many economies because the multinational corporations orchestrating them are more mobile and less constrained than in the past.

Nonetheless, in a globalising world economy, the key actors — private and public — in the Asia Pacific region must come to terms with the fact that new rules are emerging to define the nature of economic and technological intercourse. While there is definitely room for national leverage, this can only be achieved by creating the sources of competitiveness required by the changing technological environment.

Notes

1   One of the major questions regarding regional integration in the Asia Pacific region is whether or not a political consensus can ever be built to formalise some of the regional initiatives being taken under the aegis of such organisations as APEC, PECC and PBEC. So far, regionalisation in the Pacific Rim has been more market driven, which may help to explain why many people are sceptical about further institutionalisation occurring in this part of the globe.

2   The notion of technological change used in this paper is drawn from Moore (1983). According to Moore (1983, p. 5), 'technological change is defined as the provision of new information or knowledge that is used effectively in industrial operations and has measurable effects on costs, product qualities, level of output or sales, and other auxiliary operations of the firm'.

3   Semiconductor manufacturing, for example, uses a range of technologies largely developed within the past 30 years to build products undreamed of before that time; semiconductors are the basis of computing, but also would be impossible without it ('A Survey of Manufacturing Technology', *The Economist*, 5 March 1994).

4   The following discussion of Fordist production models and the concept of flexible specialisation is drawn largely from Storper and Scott (1992).

5   See the comments regarding flexible manufacturing made by Fumio Kodama in *Japan Economic Journal* (25 May 1991, p. 8).

6   One of the essential features of lean manufacturing has been to show that volume is not the only way to make money; firms can be profitable by eliminating unnecessary processes, cutting time to market and focusing on the needs of individual customers (*Computer World*, 28 February 1994, pp. 93–4).

7   For an overview of the literature see Nohria and Eccles (1992) and Ferdows (1989) in addition to the authors cited here.

8   For a discussion of the imperatives driving technological upgrading in Taiwan, see Kuo Nan-hung (1992).

9   See Japanese economist Toshio Watanabe's comments about Taiwan's need to boost its investment in higher value-added manufacturing (*Japan Economic Journal*, 18 May 1991, p. 8).

10   Japanese new investment in the United States dropped from US$3.85 billion (122 projects) in 1991 to US$1.92 billion (78 projects) in 1992 (*Asian Wall Street Journal Weekly*, 1 February 1993, p. 26).

11   In 1993, Japanese exports to Asia were US$134.6 billion, while imports from Asia were only US$81 billion. The Japanese trade surplus with Asia exceeded its trade surplus with the United States.

12   According to an article in the *Straits Times* (6 May 1992, p. 36), the Yamazaki Mazak plant was Singapore's first state-of-the-art manufacturing facility to rely on

computer-integrated manufacturing technology. The plant is highly automated; although it has a staff of just 17, it is capable of generating output equivalent to that of 288 workers operating in a conventional manufacturing plant.

13 A portion of Canon's offshore camera production is also carried out in China.

14 According to *Business Times* (18 May 1994, p. 8), in the early 1990s many Japanese firms were engaged in a process of rethinking their strategic posture towards the Asia Pacific region.

15 As part of its technology transfer program, Matsushita hopes to expand significantly the number of local engineers working at the R&D facility. The ratio of local to Japanese staff is to grow from 59:16 in 1992 to 110:35 by 1997.

16 When the centre opened in 1989, all product designs originated in Japan. Matsushita's goal is to totally indigenise TV design capability by the mid 1990s.

17 In April 1994, Matsushita decided to convert some of the production capacity of its Malaysian plant to computer monitors. Demand for computer monitors in the mid 1990s is estimated at about 35 million units worldwide and the demand for colour TVs at about 90 million units (*Business Times*, 16 April 1994).

18 Toshiba agreed to license its knowhow to Samsung in return for financial and manufacturing support for the project (*Far Eastern Economic Review*, 7 January 1993, p. 57).

19 The NEC–Samsung agreement involves the construction of a facility to develop and produce a 256 MB DRAM chip. Samsung now has three critical relationships with Japanese firms (NEC, Oki and Toshiba) to upgrade its semiconductor capabilities. The Fujitsu–Hyundai accord involves production of 16 MB and 64 MB DRAM chips (*Nikkei Weekly*, 7 March 1994, p. 8).

20 For a discussion of technology transfer in the context of Japan's relations with Taiwan, see *Free China Review* (August 1991, pp. 54–9).

21 This is consistent with trends observed in Japan. According to *The Economist* (10 October 1993, pp. 71–4), Japanese firms are loosening their ties with subcontractors, dumping inefficient parts makers, cutting costs and reducing the number of models offered for any one category of product.

22 It is important to remember when assessing Japanese influence in the region that cross-border investment data do not necessarily include *re*investment within countries in the upgrading of facilities, plant expansion etc. A great deal of economic activity involving Japanese companies in Asia is hidden if we focus merely on cross-border flows of capital. For a discussion of the Malaysian case, see *Business Times* (28 June 1993).

References

Antonelli, Cristiano (ed.) 1988, *New Information Technology and Industrial Change: The Italian Case*, Boston, MA: Kluwer.

Axelsson, Bjorn and Geoffrey Easton 1992, *Industrial Networks: A New View of Reality*, London: Routledge.

Bartu, Friedemann 1992, *The Ugly Japanese: Nippon's Economic Empire in Asia*, Singapore: Longman.

Bergsten, C. Fred and Marcus Noland (eds) 1993, *Pacific Dynamism and the International Economic System*, Washington DC: Institute of International Economics.

Biemans, Wim 1992, *Managing Innovation within Networks*, London: Routledge.

Dunning, John 1988, *Explaining International Production*, Boston, MA: Unwin Hyman.

Encarnation, Dennis 1992, *Rivals Beyond Trade: America versus Japan in Global Competition*, Ithaca, NY: Cornell University Press.

Ferdows, Kasra (ed.) 1989, *Managing International Manufacturing*, Amsterdam: North-Holland.

Forsgren, Mats and Jan Johanson (eds) 1992, *Managing Networks in International Business*, Amsterdam: Gordon and Breach.

Hakansson, Hakan 1989, *Corporate Technological Behaviour: Cooperation and Networks*, London: Routledge.

Imai, Ken'ichi 1988, 'Technological Change in the Information Industry and Implications for the Pacific Rim', Discussion Paper No. 130, Institute of Business Research, Hitotsubashi University, July.

Imai, Ken'ichi and Y. Baba 1991, 'Systemic Innovation and Cross-Border Networks: Transcending Markets and Hierarchies to Create a New Techno-Economic System', in OECD (ed.), *Technology and Productivity: Challenges for Economic Policy*, Paris: OECD, pp. 389–403.

Kuo Nan-hung 1992, 'Accelerating the Development of Practical Science and Technology', *Industry of Free China*, August, pp. 31–50.

Liemt, Gijsbert van (ed.) 1992, *Industry on the Move*, Geneva: International Labour Organisation.

Moore, Frederick 1983, 'Technological Change and Industrial Development: Issues and Opportunities', World Bank Staff Working Paper No. 613, New York: World Bank.

Naisbitt, John 1994, *Global Paradox*, New York: William Morrow.

Nohria, Nitin and Robert Eccles (eds) 1992, *Networks and Organizations: Structure, Form and Action*, Cambridge, MA: Harvard Business Press.

Ohmae, Kenichi 1990, *The Borderless World*, Homewood, IL: Dow Jones-Irwin.

_____ 1993, 'The Regional Nation-State', *Foreign Affairs*, Spring.

Oman, Charles 1984, *New Forms of International Investment in Developing Countries*, Paris: OECD.

Porter, Michael 1990, *The Competitive Advantage of Nations*, New York: The Free Press.

Simon, Denis Fred (ed.) 1994, *The Emerging Technological Trajectory of the Pacific Basin Economies*, Armonk: ME Sharpe.

_____ (ed.) 1995a, *Corporate Strategies towards the Pacific Rim*, London: Routledge (forthcoming).

_____ 1995b, *The Technology Strategy of Japanese Firms towards the Pacific Rim*, Cambridge: Cambridge University Press (forthcoming).

Storper, Michael and Allen Scott (eds) 1992, *Pathways to Industrialisation and Regional Development*, London: Routledge.

Teece, David (ed.) 1987, *The Competitive Challenge: Strategies for Industrial Innovation and Renewal*, Cambridge, MA: Ballinger.

Tokunaga, Shojiro (ed.) 1992, *Japan's Foreign Investment and Asian Economic Interdependence*, Tokyo: University of Tokyo Press.

UNCTC (United Nations Centre on Transnational Corporations) 1991, *World Investment Report 1991*, New York: United Nations.

US National Science Foundation 1993, *Human Resources for Science and Technology: The Asian Region*, Washington DC: US National Science Foundation.

_____ 1993, *World Investment Report 1993*, New York: United Nations.

Vernon, Raymond 1966, 'International Investment and International Trade in the Product Cycle', *Quarterly Journal of Economics*, May.

Vernon, Raymond and Louis T. Wells 1976, *Economic Environment of International Business*, Englewood Cliffs, NJ: Prentice-Hall.

11 The international procurement and sales behaviour of multinational enterprises ────

Chia Siow Yue

Developing East Asia has been experiencing a surge in foreign direct investment (FDI).[1] Traditional investors from the West have been joined by investors from East Asia itself, with favoured destinations now including the ASEAN economies, China and Vietnam as well as the Asian NIEs. Since the mid 1980s, domestic cost–push factors and major exchange rate realignments have fuelled outward investment by Japan and the Asian NIEs. Neighbouring East Asian economies have been favoured for their geographical proximity and abundant natural and labour resources, their rapidly growing incomes and markets, and their sharply improved investment climates following major economic policy reforms and the adoption of more liberal foreign investment and trade regimes.

While earlier waves of FDI were largely directed at natural resource development and import substitution industries, flows to developing East Asia over the past decade have been directed increasingly at the creation of export-oriented industries. This has led to rapid growth in the region's manufactured exports and to a surge in intraregional trade. Host countries have sourced a large part of their capital goods and intermediate inputs in Japan, exporting most of their final manufactures to markets in North America and Western Europe. A triangular trade pattern has thus emerged between Japan, developing East Asia, and North America and Western Europe. Apart from improving the export capability of host economies, the foreign multinational enterprises (MNEs) operating in Asia have developed linkages with local supporting industries, providing an important mechanism for the transfer of technology to local small and medium sized enterprises. This chapter examines the international procurement and sales behaviour of MNEs, with the focus on East Asia.

International procurement and sales behaviour

The FDI–trade nexus

Direct investment abroad and foreign trade are increasingly interlinked through the activities of the multinational corporation, and often take the form of intrafirm trade.

MNEs, through their majority equity ownership, are able to exercise considerable control over subsidiaries' decisions on the sourcing of capital equipment and intermediate inputs, and on the marketing of production. UNCTAD (1993) reported that in 1989 some 80 per cent of US exports and imports were undertaken by MNEs (the US parent companies of MNEs, the overseas affiliates of US MNEs and the affiliates of foreign MNEs in the United States). One-third of these exports and over two-fifths of imports took the form of intrafirm trade.

Direct investment has an impact on trade at both the macroeconomic and firm levels. It can be either trade creating or trade suppressing,[2] depending on national trade and industry strategies, sectoral orientation, corporate strategies and the lifecycle of the FDI project. In East Asian developing economies FDI tends to be more trade creating because of the growing emphasis on export-oriented manufacturing. Although traditional FDI in the natural resources sector targeted the export market, the relative importance of MNEs in resource industries has declined in recent decades. Host countries have restricted foreign ownership in land and natural resources, devised non-equity forms of foreign participation, and switched to industrialisation as the preferred means of economic development. In the 1960s, advocates of import substitution argued against FDI in natural resources with its growth-inhibiting trade in favour of manufacturing production for the domestic market, which had a high degree of domestic linkages. Import substitution failed to live up to the expectations of its advocates, and a growing number of empirical studies in the late 1960s and 1970s highlighted the inefficiencies of this strategy. Since the late 1970s, FDI in manufacturing for the export market has grown rapidly in East Asia. Manufactured exports have risen sharply, facilitated by the increasingly export-oriented nature of FDI and the improved export competitiveness of host countries arising from the transfer of technological and managerial skills by MNEs. The importance of transnational corporations in host country exports is seen in the rising share of total manufactured exports generated by foreign MNEs and in the changing composition of exports. At the microeconomic level, the trade effects of FDI vary with the lifecycle of the project, from initial dependence on imports of capital goods and intermediate inputs from the home country and elsewhere, to a subsequent decline in demand for imported intermediate inputs as local suppliers emerge, leading finally to exports of output to the home country and/or third countries.

Export-oriented FDI provides host countries with access to the international procurement and sales networks of MNEs through foreign subsidiaries, which use the global trading and distribution channels established by parent firms to procure capital goods and intermediate inputs and to export their production. For the home country, the impact on trade of outward FDI is more uncertain: initial demand for capital goods expands the home country's exports, while subsequent production sold in the host country may replace home country exports; sales to the home country may replace or complement home country production, giving the home country access to cheaper parts and components, and making its exports more competitive; and third country sales may or may not replace or compete with home country exports.

Direct investment in East Asia is also enabling home countries to enhance their global competitiveness. With FDI, competition among countries has extended beyond national production to encompass offshore production and sales as well. For some major investing countries, sales generated through offshore production now exceed sales from exports manufactured at home. International sourcing of labour-intensive intermediate and final products in developing East Asia has grown rapidly. Since the late 1960s, US and Japanese MNEs have established a growing number of production facilities, first in the Asian NIEs and later in ASEAN countries, to make use of local raw materials and low-wage labour to produce more competitively priced, labour-intensive components for export back to the home country. The emergence of a regional division of labour, with production facilities for parts and components and final products located across different countries, has resulted in more efficient resource utilisation, lower production costs, and greater intraregional trade. In the semiconductor industry, for example, integrated circuits may be manufactured in Japan, packed in Malaysia, tested in Singapore and assembled in Hong Kong before being exported to a consumer electronics firm in the United States (UNCTAD 1993).

Direct investment has meant that trade among countries increasingly takes the form of intrafirm trade between MNE parents and their foreign subsidiaries, rather than arm's length transactions between unaffiliated suppliers and buyers. Majority owner-ship enables the MNE to maintain managerial control of affiliates located in various regions and helps to reduce the high costs that characterise arm's length transactions. In intrafirm trade, initial trade flows from the parent to the foreign subsidiary are typically followed by reverse trade, in which the subsidiary begins to export goods and services back to the parent as well as to other related affiliates.

The importance of FDI in exports of manufactures in East Asia grew throughout the 1980s. By the mid to late 1980s, foreign affiliates generated a significant proportion of the exports of many host countries, in the manufacturing sector in particular, notwithstanding the significant growth of exports by local firms (Table 11.1). In Malaysia and the Philippines, foreign affiliates have accounted for more than 50 per cent of manufactured exports over the past decade.

Perhaps nowhere is the role of FDI in a country's manufactured exports more evident than in the case of Singapore. Table 11.2 shows the importance of foreign firms in general, and of wholly foreign-owned firms in particular, in the Singaporean economy. In 1991, wholly foreign-owned firms and joint ventures together accounted for an overwhelming 91.5 per cent of direct exports — the former for 73.6 per cent and the latter for another 17.9 per cent. US firms had a 40.3 per cent share of total exports, followed by Japanese and EU firms. Wholly locally owned firms generated only 8.5 per cent of the manufacturing sector's exports. The large share of MNEs in Singa-pore's exports of manufactures reflects not only their dominance in the manufacturing sector but also their high export orientation. While the manufacturing sector as a whole had an export/total sales ratio averaging 61.5 per cent, foreign firms with at least 50 per cent foreign equity had a ratio of 69.5 per cent, and wholly foreign-owned firms a ratio of 72.7 per cent. This high export propensity reflects Singapore's role as a

Table 11.1   **Share of foreign affiliates in total exports of East Asian host countries (per cent)**

| Host country | Primary sector | Secondary sector | | | | Tertiary sector |
		Electrical/ electronic products	Chemical products	Motor vehicles	Total	
Hong Kong (1984)	–	–	–	–	16.5	–
South Korea (1978)	–	–	–	–	24.6	–
Taiwan (1986)	18.5	43.6	30.8	–	18.5	3.6
Singapore (1988)	–	–	–	–	86.0	–
Malaysia (1986)	32.6	–	–	–	51.2	15.9
Philippines (1983)	–	–	–	–	51.5	–
Thailand (1980)	–	–	–	–	37.3	–

Note: Year in brackets refers to year of data.

Source: UNTCMD, 1992, Table Annex 9.

regional centre and export platform. Intrafirm sales are important for many foreign MNEs, with exports being directed to the home country as well as to other affiliates in the Asian region. By nationality, Swedish firms had the highest export propensity of 91.5 per cent, followed by American firms with 83.2 per cent and Japanese firms with 62.9 per cent. EU firms had an average export propensity of only 59.3 per cent, with sharp differences between EU countries. Wholly locally owned firms had an export/total sales ratio of only 32.6 per cent, reflecting the greater difficulty they have in penetrating export markets without the advantage of the MNEs' global marketing networks, and also their position as suppliers of parts and components to foreign MNE affiliates in Singapore. It should be noted, however, that the export propensity of local firms is no lower than that of their counterparts in many East Asian countries. Evidence at industry level shows a strong positive correlation between the extent of foreign ownership in an industry and its export propensity.

Table 11.3 shows the export propensity of foreign affiliates in selected East Asian host countries. Except for Thailand in 1984, foreign affiliates have tended to be more export oriented than local firms. In South Korea, where Japanese FDI dominates, the export/sales ratio of foreign firms stood at around 35 per cent during the late 1970s, to advance to almost 50 per cent by the mid 1980s. In Taiwan, where Japanese direct investment has again played a major role, the export/sales ratio of foreign affiliates stood at 59 per cent in manufacturing, 68 per cent in electronics and 96 per cent in garments. In Thailand, 1984 data show that local firms were more export oriented than foreign affiliates, particularly in the electronics industry. In the ASEAN-4 economies, foreign multinationals, especially those of Japan and the United States, were heavily

Table 11.2 Export ratios[a] of foreign and local manufacturing firms in Singapore, 1991 (per cent)

	Gross output	Value-added	Employ-ment	Direct exports	Exports/ total sales (%)
Total firms	100.0	100.0	100.0	100.0	61.5
Wholly foreign owned	62.1	64.0	48.6	73.6	72.7
More than half foreign owned	13.1	8.2	9.5	11.6	54.1
Less than half foreign owned	8.7	10.3	11.4	6.3	32.6
Wholly locally owned	16.1	17.4	30.5	8.5	32.6
By major source of capital (50% equity cut-off)					
Singapore	24.7	27.1	41.9	14.9	37.1
Foreign	75.3	72.9	58.1	85.1	69.5
United States	29.8	40.5	22.6	40.3	83.2
Japan	20.3	18.5	19.9	20.7	62.9
European Union	17.5	18.2	9.3	16.7	58.5
United Kingdom	4.1	8.6	2.1	5.0	72.6
Netherlands	9.2	6.6	2.3	6.3	41.9
Germany	1.4	2.1	1.9	2.0	89.1
France	1.4	1.1	1.7	1.6	69.9
Other European	1.4	2.4	1.7	1.6	69.3
Other	6.4	3.9	4.5	5.8	56.2

Note: a   Exports/total sales.

Source: Singapore, *Report on the Census of Industrial Production 1991*.

involved in exporting. JETRO (1993b) reported recently that some 85 per cent of Japanese affiliates in Thailand and nearly 60 per cent of Japanese affiliates in Malaysia exported 80 per cent or more of their production. As Japanese manufacturers shift their export bases to Asian locations in the drive to maintain their international competitiveness, the operations of Japanese corporations in Asian countries are becoming increasingly export oriented.

Apart from contributing to the volume of exports, FDI has led to progressive shifts in the export composition of host developing countries towards more technologically advanced products. From an initial emphasis on labour-intensive products and processes, production and exports are moving rapidly up the technological ladder. Developing East Asia accounts for a growing share of US subsidiaries' exports in the electrical and electronic equipment, non-electrical machinery, chemicals and transport equipment industries. In some of these industries, production is often vertically integrated across countries.

Table 11.3   **Export ratios[a] of foreign affiliates in selected East Asian host countries (per cent)**

Host country	Year	Coverage	Local firms	Foreign affiliates	Japanese affiliates	US affiliates
South Korea	1974–78	All sectors	–	35.0	–	–
		Manufacturing	23.5	35.1	49.0	21.0
Taiwan	1974–80[b]	All sectors	–	58.1	–	–
		Manufacturing	33.9	58.9	58.2	63.4
		Textiles	33.5	82.5	81.9	75.6
		Garments etc.	93.2	95.7	96.6	84.1
		Chemicals	9.8	47.4	40.6	27.3
		Machinery	25.8	32.1	69.2	26.3
		Electronics	48.1	68.0	53.0	94.9
	1980–85	All sectors	–	52.5	–	–
		Manufacturing	–	53.3	–	–
		Textiles	–	68.0	–	–
		Garments etc.	–	93.6	–	–
		Chemicals	–	33.1	–	–
		Machinery	–	29.3	–	–
		Electronics	–	74.3	–	–
Singapore	1977–80	Manufacturing	35.4	74.9	68.7	79.8
	1981–85	Manufacturing	43.3	71.9	64.6	70.7
Thailand	1979	Manufacturing	20.9	31.5	17.6	41.7
		Food/beverages	52.5	53.7	–	–
		Textiles/apparel	15.9	41.8	–	–
		Basic metals	3.4	9.8	–	–
		Electronics	0.5	16.8	–	–
	1984	Manufacturing	39.0	33.0	21.0	35.0
		Food/beverages	55.1	56.4	–	–
		Textiles/apparel	47.3	49.4	–	–
		Basic metals	6.7	2.8	–	–
		Electronics	63.1	28.6	–	–

Notes: a   Exports/total sales.
　　　　　b   1976 for local firms, 1979–80 for Japanese firms, 1974–78 for US firms.

Source: UNESCAP, 1993.

FDI also has an impact on host country imports. The extent of an affiliate's imports varies during the lifecycle of the investment project. Imports tend to be more important in the initial phase, when the foreign affiliate needs to import machinery and equipment and when unfamiliarity with host country suppliers limits local sourcing of inputs. As operations mature, the affiliate is likely to switch to greater use of local goods and services. However, it may still favour foreign sourcing if bulk purchasing is available from the parent firm, or if it wishes to have greater control over the quality and reliability of supply. During the 1980s, imports of capital goods by US affiliates accounted for about 5 per cent of the total machinery and equipment imported by developing countries in the Asia Pacific region (UNTCMD 1992). Imports of machinery and equipment, parts and components, and financial, transportation and telecommunications services have helped host economies to overcome bottlenecks in domestic supply and to improve their technological competitiveness.

Imports of capital and intermediate goods are undertaken not only by foreign manufacturing affiliates but also by foreign marketing affiliates. UNTCMD (1993) refers to US statistics which show that about 17 per cent of total merchandise imports by the overseas affiliates of US firms in 1989 were by marketing affiliates located in developing countries, and that 86 per cent of such imports from both developed and developing countries comprised intermediate and capital goods.

A significant proportion of the imports of foreign affiliates located in developing East Asia are from the home country. Intrafirm exports by parents to affiliates accounted for almost one-third of both the total and manufactured exports of US and Japanese parent firms. US parent firms generally tend to import more from their affiliates in developing East Asia than they export to them. However, parent firms' exports to ASEAN-4 nations have on average been large, comprising, for example, about 40 per cent of total US electronics exports to these countries. The share of intrafirm exports in total exports is especially large in the case of Malaysia. Intrafirm exports by MNE parents accounted for less than 15 per cent of Japan's manufactured exports, a surprisingly low proportion considering that Japanese affiliates in ASEAN-4 countries are known to rely heavily on parent firm sourcing of intermediate and capital goods. One possible explanation is that the data pertain only to trade with majority-owned subsidiaries, thus excluding the substantial trade with minority-owned joint ventures (UNESCAP 1993).

Offshore production versus exporting

MNEs from the United States, Japan and Western Europe invest in majority-owned subsidiaries abroad to produce goods and services that they would otherwise export from the home base. Pressure for offshore production has intensified as foreign governments have restricted or threatened to restrict imports, foreign buyers have demanded closer relations with their suppliers, and companies have sought the locational advantages offered by foreign countries. Sales by these overseas affiliates may be to host country markets, the home country markets of parent firms, or nearby third country markets.

US survey data dating back to 1957 show that in the late 1950s the production and sales activities of US manufacturing subsidiaries abroad (concentrated in developed countries) were worth twice as much as US manufactured exports. By 1966, the value of US offshore production was three times that of US manufactured exports, a ratio that remained largely unchanged in 1988. US offshore production in the developing economies has consistently been worth less than US manufactured exports. Japan's ratio of offshore production to home exports has risen rapidly, but remains below that of the United States. In 1977, the production and sales activities of Japanese manufacturing subsidiaries abroad were worth only one-quarter as much as Japan's manufactured exports. This share had risen to one-half by 1988, reflecting the sharp rise that had occurred in the country's outward FDI.

Japan's outward direct investment has surged since 1985 in response to worsening labour shortages and rising production costs in Japan, trade conflicts with the United States and Western Europe, and the yen appreciation following the Plaza Accord of September 1985. The Japanese corporate response to domestic and foreign pressure has taken several forms (JETRO 1993a). First, companies have rationalised domestic production and shifted towards more sophisticated products with higher value-added. Second, to maintain their cost competitiveness Japanese firms have relocated lower end processes and products, including the manufacture of parts and components, to offshore production locations in East Asia. This has led to rising overseas parts procurement ratios and imports of lower end, standardised products from offshore plants. Japanese parts manufacturers are continuing to relocate and enlarge their production bases in lower cost East Asian economies. In countries with more advanced facilities and greater technological expertise, such as Singapore and Malaysia, local procurement has expanded to include a wide range of parts and components following improvements in the quality and production capabilities of supporting industries. The increase in offshore production, procurement and marketing activities is leading to a closer integration of East Asian economies. The third strategy pursued by Japanese firms has been to invest massively in the United States and Europe in an attempt to secure markets and overcome protectionist barriers. During 1986–91, Japanese corporations invested US$3,300 billion at home in new plant and equipment, while outward FDI reached US$269 billion. This surge in outward FDI brought the share of offshore to total Japanese production from 3 per cent in 1985 to 5.7 per cent in 1989. Intrafirm trade also rose, both between Japanese parents and overseas production affiliates, and among overseas affiliates.

The yen rise in 1993–94 is triggering another round of Japanese corporate adjustment, most evident in the electronics industry. Japanese manufacturers are shifting production of more sophisticated electronic products to the Asian NIEs, providing them with the technology to become original equipment manufacturer (OEM) suppliers. Production of standardised products, meanwhile, is being moved to the relatively more advanced ASEAN economies of Malaysia and Thailand, while production of labour-intensive products with lower value-added is being transferred to countries with abundant low-cost labour, such as Indonesia and China. Parts production has also been relocated, from Japan to Singapore and then to the other ASEAN countries. Whereas the ASEAN region is emerging as the export production base of Japanese corporations, Japan's rapidly growing investments in China are geared more towards gaining access to that country's huge domestic market.

The production shift has led to greater sourcing of machinery and equipment in Japan, accompanied by an increase in imports into Japan and accelerated local procurement of parts. Japanese companies are importing more lower end electronic products, such as small colour TV sets, air conditioners and refrigerators, from East Asian developing countries. In an effort to cut costs and in response to improved supply conditions in host countries, Japanese manufacturers are also importing more parts produced overseas, mostly from Japanese affiliates. Local procurement of components and parts has risen significantly as sourcing in Japan has declined. One study (*Nomura Asia Focus*, December 1993–January 1994) noted that VCR manufacturers in Malaysia now procure about 70 per cent of parts in Malaysia and Singapore, while the local procurement ratio for manufacturers of audio products has risen to around 80 per cent. In each case about 50 per cent of parts is supplied by Singapore and the balance by Malaysia; the proportion of parts imported directly from Japan has fallen to less than 10 per cent. For some categories of products, the local content ratio has already reached 90–100 per cent. Manufacturers of colour TV sets in Thailand now import only certain types of semiconductors from Japan, procuring most other parts within the region (including Malaysia and Singapore). Japanese affiliates are also now producing key electronic components in Thailand.

A questionnaire distributed to Japanese firms on the effects of the 1993 yen appreciation (JETRO 1993b) found more Japanese corporations promoting imports through offshore procurement of parts and semifinished goods, as well as through imports of products manufactured by overseas affiliates (Table 11.4). In support of this strategy, a majority of the firms surveyed pointed to the cost advantage of such imports, the improved quality of imported goods, and the need to diversify sourcing to assure supplies.

Intrafirm trade

Although intrafirm trade is rising, the larger part of international transactions continues to be arm's length trade between unrelated parties. Intrafirm trade replaces market transactions with internal transactions conducted within the multinational corporation. While intrafirm trade results from FDI, not all FDI generates intrafirm trade. The growing proportion of trade now taking place between parents and affiliates and among affiliates has important implications for both corporations and countries. For corporate parents, intrafirm trade ensures greater control over both upstream supplies and downstream markets and involves lower transaction costs than arm's length transactions between unaffiliated buyers and sellers. For countries, intrafirm trade can exert a strong influence on overall trade patterns and mitigate the impact of exchange rate and trade policies.

Limited information is available on the behavioural differences of intrafirm and arm's length trade. According to Benvignati (1990), the results of regression analysis

Table 11.4   Measures taken by Japanese firms to cope with yen appreciation

Response	Exporting firms' measures				Most effective measures			
	1988 yen rise		Recent yen rise		1988 yen rise		Recent yen rise	
	No.	%	No.	%	No.	%	No.	%
Total no. of responses	636	100.0	714	100.0	181	100.0	268	100.0
Shift some exports to domestic sales	127	20.0	101	14.1	15	8.3	15	5.6
Develop new markets	204	32.1	250	35.0	8	4.4	27	10.0
Transfer increased costs to US$-denominated export prices	197	31.0	214	30.0	20	11.0	21	77.8
Avoid exchange risks through increased yen-denominated export contracts	201	31.6	140	19.6	25	13.8	15	5.6
Reduce exports by increasing % of overseas production	81	12.7	119	16.7	12	6.6	22	8.2
Establish new overseas affiliates	88	13.8	77	10.8	13	7.2	21	7.8
Increase overseas sourcing of components/semifinished products	118	18.6	200	30.8	7	3.9	38	14.2
Shift to higher value-added, higher quality products	291	45.8	349	48.9	29	16.0	63	23.5
Increase imports from overseas manufacturing affiliates	58	9.1	136	19.0	5	2.8	13	4.9
Reduce costs through rationalisation	437	68.7	468	65.5	61	33.7	76	28.4
Diversify business	60	9.4	106	14.8	3	1.7	7	2.6
Other	5	0.8	40	5.6	-	-	1	0.4

Note: Based on survey carried out by JETRO on manufacturers' responses to the appreciation of the yen. Percentages do not sum to 100 as multiple answer responses were allowed.

Source: JETRO, 1993b.

provided only weak support for internalisation theory, which assumes that the behaviour of intrafirm trade is different from that of arm's length trade. Based on the theory of vertical integration, Lall (1978) investigated the reasons MNEs undertake intrafirm exports, while Helleiner and Lavergne (1979) examined the case for intrafirm imports. A regression study by Siddharthan and Kumar (1990), based on 1982 benchmark survey data for the United States, found that R&D intensity was the most important determinant of both intrafirm exports and imports; the study also found that the proportion of sales and administrative expenditures was positively and significantly correlated with the ratio of intrafirm exports, and that US antipollution laws may have stimulated intrafirm imports of pollution-intensive products.

An OECD study identified two of the factors contributing to intrafirm trade as market imperfections and high transaction costs, which create incentives for the internalisation of goods embodying firm-specific knowledge and expertise (OECD 1993). The study showed that intrafirm trade was more prevalent among internationally oriented manufacturing industries characterised by a high degree of R&D, technical and marketing expertise. Such MNEs preferred to rely on affiliates for the sale of finished products in foreign markets for reasons including the desire to control distribution channels, the need to provide specialised after-sales service and to maintain and upgrade products, and the importance of direct representation and close communication with customers in foreign markets.

A multinational corporation may also prefer to utilise its internal structure for the transaction of intermediate products that are highly firm-specific, that require close monitoring of quality and the timing of delivery, or that lend themselves to the exploitation of scale economies at various stages of production. Using Siddharthan and Kumar's methodology, OECD examined intrafirm exports and imports using data from the US 1989 benchmark survey of manufacturing industries. The regression results revealed a positive relationship between intrafirm exports and a firm's R&D intensity, skill intensity and international orientation (sales of foreign affiliates divided by sales of the US parent), and a negative relationship with pollution abatement costs. Intrafirm imports were positively related with R&D intensity, physical capital intensity and selling expenses intensity; in contrast to the Siddharthan and Kumar study, intrafirm imports were negatively related with pollution intensity.

The decision of MNEs to internalise market transactions may also be influenced by home and host government policies, including tax, tariff, competition, exchange rate and investment policies. US tariff provisions 807.00 and 806.30, for example, have contributed to the growth of offshore processing and intrafirm transactions. Empirical studies to determine the extent to which government policies affect decisions on intrafirm trade are, however, scarce. Grubert and Mutti (1991), who examined the impact of host government policies on the behaviour of US multinationals, found that tax and tariff policies had a substantial impact on the global operations of MNEs: the lower the tax rates of the host country, the greater the quantity of exports shipped by US parents to their foreign affiliates. This finding indicated that there was an incentive for MNEs to use transfer pricing practices.

OECD (1993) identified a number of implications of intrafirm trade for trade policy. First, the trade liberalisation movements of recent decades, which have enabled MNEs to rationalise their global and regional production and marketing networks, appear to have stimulated intrafirm trade. Second, to the extent that intrafirm trade involves the diffusion of embodied technology and standards, it may lead to pressure for harmonisation of standards and regulations. Third, transfer pricing in intrafirm trade may create distortions in the valuation of international trade, and particularly in customs valuation for the imposition of tariffs and other border measures. Fourth, any negative reactions to the effects of intrafirm trade in host countries may lead to demands for more restrictive foreign investment policies. On the tax front, while intrafirm trade may facilitate the dissemination of real transaction prices between parent firms and affiliates, the increasing firm-specificity of products also makes it difficult for tax authorities to determine the real value of goods. Finally, depending on the circumstances, international networks of firms can facilitate the diffusion of technology and the flow of capital and services, thereby increasing the effectiveness of welfare-enhancing industrial policies and making restrictive and discriminatory industrial policies less effective.

Subcontracting, international procurement and sales

Apart from their role in FDI, MNEs also contribute to the growth of trade and manufactured exports in developing East Asia through a variety of non-equity arrangements and relationships linking suppliers and buyers across countries. As domestic manufacturers in the region enhance their production capability, the importance of non-equity participation by foreign MNEs in exporting and marketing can be expected to rise. One such type of non-equity arrangement is subcontracting, which involves arm's length transactions between buyers and suppliers.

In the industrial structure of developed countries, the development of supporting industries and ancillary services tied to large firms has traditionally been important. Manufacturers often prefer subcontracting to in-house production because it gives them access to specialist knowhow, increases their flexibility and helps reduce costs. As products and processes increase in complexity, many large firms concentrate on what they know best and subcontract the rest to specialist firms. In an environment of uncertainties in demand and rapid technological change, manufacturers are also better able to diversify when final products are manufactured in short runs by outside suppliers. The increase in demand for Just-in-Time (JIT) production systems (in which the delivery of parts is coordinated to meet the immediate demands of production) has imposed a change in the relationship between buyer firms and their subcontractors; rather than being driven purely by price, buyers need to develop closer and more stable relationships with a smaller number of local suppliers. Subcontractors also find such a relationship beneficial as it gives them access both to a high volume of business and to large firms' technology without the substantial costs of marketing and technology acquisition.

Subcontracting has been particularly important in the Japanese industrial system, with dependence on subcontracting being especially high in the electrical/electronics and machinery industries. The distinctiveness of the Japanese subcontracting system has been highlighted in a number of studies (Wong 1991). First, unlike the 'flat' procurement structures of American and European corporations, Japanese corporations typically have a pyramid-like structure of multitier subcontracting. This hierarchical structure appears to be very efficient in minimising communication and monitoring costs. Second, both large corporations and their core subcontractors have a strong commitment to long-term relationships. Most small to medium sized subcontractors are highly dependent on a few corporate buyers. These subcontracting relationships last a long time, minimising transaction costs and allowing for long-term investments in human resources and capital equipment. The Japanese subcontracting system is under threat, however. The subcontracting relationship functioned well in the past when cooperation and trust coexisted in a growth environment that enabled both large firms and subcontractors to grow together. This was supported by the ready availability of long-term bank loans at low interest rates to finance subcontractors' technological upgrading. With the appreciation of the yen and the increase in competition from Asian NIEs, production has tended to move offshore, disrupting traditional buyer–supplier relationships. In addition, a growing number of subcontractors now possess independent advanced technological capabilities. Such firms have become increasingly reluctant to depend only on the procurement requirements of traditional large buyers.

The trend towards globalisation of production and the integration of manufacturing-related activities in a few regional centres has increased the potential of East Asian developing countries to participate in subcontracting. To shorten the production lifecycle and increase speed of response to changing market conditions, many MNEs are integrating several stages of the production process in one or more locations, implementing JIT management systems and using local subcontractors. The appreciation of the yen since the mid 1980s in particular has forced many Japanese MNEs to establish offshore production facilities, source locally and reduce their dependence on supplies from Japan.

In the East Asian developing economies, the subcontracting strategies of foreign MNEs vary according to the nature of their technology and their overall manufacturing strategies, as well as local supplier conditions and host government policies. In the production of standardised products using mature, non-proprietary process technologies, the emphasis tends to be on open and arm's length procurement policies because of the large number of suppliers available. An MNE may also choose to subcontract parts production and service provision where it lacks in-house specialist process knowhow, or where the product or service is peripheral to the firm's core business. It is likely to emphasise long-term subcontracting relationships when the procured product or service is highly specialised, often requiring significant, asset-specific investment in the relationship by the buyer. An MNE buying a relatively standard product may also emphasise long-term relationships if a stable subcontracting system is considered necessary for responding flexibly to future changes in technology and the market. Another MNE for whom subcontracting is a temporary measure, undertaken only until demand expands enough to justify in-house production, may prefer not to commit itself to a long-term subcontracting relationship. The subcontracting relationship is also influenced by the market structure of the supplier industry. The market power of MNE buyers increases when there are few buyers and many suppliers and when there is considerable scope for buyers to import but limited scope for sellers to export. While globalisation of competition has caused a trend towards convergence of procurement strategies and buyer–supplier relationships among large MNEs of different nationalities, major differences remain among host countries in the availability and quality of supporting industries.

To promote local industry and maximise the domestic linkages from FDI, most East Asian developing countries impose local content requirements. Singapore, which in 1986 opted instead to improve the supplier base through the establishment of a Local Industry Upgrading Program, is the exception. The scheme aims to upgrade the capabilities of local supporting industries by tapping the technical and managerial expertise of MNEs. Singapore's Economic Development Board brings selected MNEs and local small and medium sized enterprises together in partnerships, attaching experienced engineers from the former to the latter for a specified period, and providing government financial assistance to the latter to assist them to upgrade. The Local Industry Upgrading Program focused first on operational upgrading to improve the quality and reliability of vendors' products; this has since progressed to collaboration with buyers in product and process development. The scheme gives MNEs access to high-quality and cost-competitive products on a timely basis, while enabling the Singaporean partners to improve their business capabilities and gain a potential world market for their products. From initially covering MNEs and local enterprises in the electronics sector, the program has been extended to include other industries and services, and large local firms.

Case studies on East Asia show that, apart from the electrical/electronics industry, subcontracting arrangements have been important in the garment exports of Hong Kong, Singapore, Taiwan and Thailand, and in the bicycle and footwear exports of South Korea and Taiwan (UNTCMD 1992). In their initial stages, such arrangements usually involve production of components with low value-added, but in many cases progress to the production and export of more sophisticated products with higher value-added. Many local firms in the Philippines and South Korea, for instance, now undertake subcontracting work for MNEs in the semiconductor industry.

Wong (1991) surveyed the subcontracting practices of Japanese, American and European MNEs in the electrical machinery industry in Singapore, Malaysia, Korea and Japan. The author found a clustering of related production processes in a few regional centres, with many MNEs integrating the stages of production using the JIT parts supply system and local subcontractors. In Singapore, Wong found that the presence of a large, MNE-dominated electronics industry had generated strong demand for a local supply of parts and manufacturing services. This had resulted in the rapid growth of various supporting industries, including such activities as printed circuit board (PCB) assembly, manufacture of electronic components, metal stamping, mould and die making, plastic injection, automated equipment design and manufacturing, paper and plastic packaging, and printing. These supporting industries were characterised by a relatively large number of local small and medium sized enterprises selling to a much smaller number of foreign MNEs.

Singapore's local supporting industries shared some common characteristics. First, they were very dependent on MNE operations in both Singapore and Malaysia and increasingly dependent on the international procurement activities of MNEs in Singapore. Second, the implementation of JIT systems and the consolidation of the supplier base in Singapore had led to a greater demand by MNEs for a more flexible response capability from suppliers. Third, MNEs tended to form long-term subcontracting relationships with local suppliers, even for some standardised items. Fourth, demand by MNEs was increasing particularly rapidly in the areas of subassembly and box-built manufacturing. However, unstable demand had raised the risk profile of suppliers and made it more difficult for them to achieve economies of scale and scope in production. Fifth, the more labour-intensive activities were under increasing competitive pressure from suppliers in Malaysia, Thailand and Indonesia. Local subcontracting industries were responding by relocating low-tech production offshore, seeking cheaper sources of supply through regional and international procurement, upgrading local suppliers through greater technology specialisation and participation in early product development and design, and participating in joint supplier–buyer R&D. Finally, the use of long-term relationships by buyers did not vary by nationality; instead, factors such as product quality, cyclical variations in demand, the technological sophistication of products and corporate philosophy had a greater impact on the tenure of the relationship between buyer and seller.

Subcontracting arrangements would also seem to be dynamic and evolving. A study of Taiwan by Chi (1990, cited in Wong 1991) showed that well-established firms bought more local products than did newcomers; only after some time were newly arrived firms attracted by the demonstrated capabilities of local suppliers.

Trading companies, distribution networks, and international procurement and sales

The overseas distribution subsidiaries of MNEs also contribute to the trade of home and host countries through downstream marketing of home/host country exports and upstream sourcing of home/host country imports. Overseas distribution networks are especially important in markets characterised by marketing barriers to entry and tightly controlled distribution systems. Overseas distribution subsidiaries may be established by MNEs in the manufacturing sector or by independent multinational trading companies, the latter including the well-known Japanese trading companies.

According to UNTCMD (1992), trading MNEs handled about 20 per cent of world exports and imports in the mid 1980s. In Western countries, trading companies have declined in importance as manufacturers have acquired the skills to procure raw materials and sell products in foreign markets. In the early 1980s, US trading affiliates accounted for a 39 per cent share of total exports by all affiliates in host countries (Table 11.5). This share had dropped to 25 per cent by 1989 owing to the declining export share of petroleum trading affiliates. Not all trading affiliates are established by trading MNEs. Of 3,986 trading affiliates of US MNEs worldwide in 1989, for example, only 691 were established by 191 parent trading companies; in the developing economies, 80 per cent of the assets of trading affiliates were owned by non-trading

Table 11.5   Role of trading affiliates of US MNEs in exports of US majority-owned affiliates in host countries, 1977, 1982, 1988 and 1989

	Total exports of all affiliates (US$ billion)	Share of trading affiliates in total exports (%)			Share of other trading affiliates in non-petroleum exports (%)
		All trading affiliates	Petroleum trading affiliates	Other trading affiliates	
All host countries					
1977	194	33	19	14	28
1982	252	39	20	19	30
1988	322	28	9	19	23
1989	318	25	6	19	22
Host developing countries					
1977	92	–	–	5	35
1982	84	–	–	7	24
1988	65	–	–	15	23
1989	68	–	–	17	24

Source: UNTCMD, 1993, Table VIII.5.

parent firms. Japanese overseas sales subsidiaries, including both those established by trading companies such as Itoh, Mitsui and Mitsubishi and those established by manufacturers such as Sony, Matsushita, NEC, Toyota and Nissan, market about half of Japan's global exports and nearly three-quarters of the country's exports to the United States.

In Japan, the large trading companies (*sogo shosha*) continue to play an important role in international procurement and marketing. *Sogo shosha* perform the role of intermediaries. Through their extensive global networks, they provide a wide range of the services importers and exporters require, including financing, transportation, warehousing, distribution and marketing; they have access to and provide their clients with a wealth of market intelligence, expertise and contacts. In 1991, *sogo shosha* handled 42.6 per cent of Japan's total exports and 79 per cent of the country's total imports (JETRO 1993c). About 90 per cent of the exports of Japanese MNE affiliates in developed economies, and 54 per cent of those in developing economies, were handled by Japanese trading affiliates in 1989. In contrast, trading affiliates accounted for less than one-quarter of the total exports of US subsidiaries in developing economies (UNTCMD 1992). By 1990 the nine largest *sogo shosha* had more than 3,000 foreign affiliates, 55 per cent of which were located in developing countries. In their efforts to diversify, *sogo shosha* have increasingly used their large financial resources to become involved in investment activities. Upstream, they have moved into large-scale resource development projects — mining, oil and gas, for example — infrastructure projects such as industrial parks and land transport networks, and manufacturing. Downstream, they have moved into service activities such as retailing, catering and recreational facilities. By March 1991, their direct investment abroad amounted to US$19 billion, or 6 per cent of total Japanese FDI.

Difficulties in penetrating the Japanese market have led US MNEs to establish sales subsidiaries in Japan. Encarnation (1992) found that American MNEs sold some 10 per cent of all US exports to Japan in 1988, or double the contribution of US subsidiaries manufacturing in Japan. Outside Japan, however, manufacturing subsidiaries have played the more important role, selling about 20 per cent of US global exports in 1988, or triple the share sold through US sales subsidiaries. The US wholesaling subsidiaries that supply third country markets have been of particular significance to American MNEs. Their role as purchasing agents for shipments back to the United States has been more limited, however, and they supplied less than 2 per cent of all US imports in 1988. In contrast, Japanese wholesaling subsidiaries have played an important role in helping Japan secure overseas supplies. In 1988 they shipped home about 40 per cent of all Japanese imports worldwide, and about 60 per cent of Japanese imports from the United States. These shipments consisted largely of agricultural products, metals and other raw materials.

In the East Asian developing countries, trading MNEs help promote host country exports by providing marketing services and access to international distribution networks, as well as information on product design and quality standards. The trading function of MNEs has undergone a sectoral transformation, with their importance in primary commodity exports declining sharply as a result of changes in host government policies and improvements in the competitiveness of local commodity traders. They now operate mainly in the manufacturing sector, where they perform a variety of functions, particularly in the initial stages of export-oriented manufacturing. Japanese trading companies have at times teamed up with Japanese manufacturers. By 1974, for example, Itoh, Marubeni and Mitsui had invested aggressively in East Asian textiles, typically through multiparty joint ventures with Japanese manufacturers. While *sogo shosha* were often crucial to Japanese investments in East Asian textiles, they have remained notably absent from the electronics and most other industries.

Singapore as a centre for international procurement

Since the late 1960s many component manufacturers have shifted their operations to East Asia, including Singapore, to take advantage of the region's low labour costs. Host countries, encouraged by these MNE investments, developed support industries capable of supplying precision parts and components, to the thriving electronics industry in particular. OEMs have in turn established international purchasing offices (IPOs) at the source of supply. The role of IPOs was given a boost in 1986 when the sharp appreciation of the yen prompted Japanese OEMs to source components offshore.

Singapore emerged in the 1980s as a major base for IPOs in the Asia Pacific region, with Japanese and other manufacturers establishing purchasing offices there to source parts and components for their regional and worldwide plants. The Singapore-based IPO could be a buying office having procurement as its main activity, a buying agent or procurement services firm purchasing parts on behalf of various overseas clients, or a manufacturing plant with the expanded task of procuring parts for overseas affiliates. IPOs with trading company status not only issue purchase orders for goods to be shipped, they also handle vendor qualification and quality assurance, business planning, international logistics, after-sales service support and finance. IPOs with representative office status have lower administrative overheads; their functions are restricted mainly to vendor qualification and mediating between customers (usually affiliates in other countries) and local suppliers by collecting and coordinating purchasing orders.

In the mid 1980s, as part of an overall strategy to develop Singapore as a total business centre, its government introduced tax incentives to encourage major foreign MNEs, particularly in the electronics industry, to establish IPOs in Singapore. As well as supplying the electronics industry with parts and components, these IPOs buy a wide range of other products, including primary commodities, chemicals, furniture, garments and a variety of consumer goods. Many American, Japanese and European MNEs, including Alcatel, AT&T, Robert Bosch, Epson, Fujitsu, Hitachi, IBM, Mitsubishi, Motorola, NEC, Oki, Seiko, Sony, Toshiba and Xerox, set up IPOs in Singapore to source products and services for their worldwide manufacturing needs. In 1992, 106 IPOs established under the government's tax incentive scheme — mainly MNEs from Japan, the United States and Western Europe — purchased S$7 billion worth of products (Table 11.6), including Winchester disk drives, computers, turnkey electromechanical assemblies, PCBs, active and passive electronic components, wire and cable harnesses, power supplies, metal stamped parts, die-cast parts, engineering plastic parts, tools and dies, and precision machined parts. As shown in Table 11.7, American IPOs accounted for over half the value of goods purchased in Singapore. Nearly half of total IPO purchases were sourced from Singaporean vendors; external sourcing was mainly from other ASEAN countries, the Asian NIEs and Japan. Of these total purchases, 38.3 per cent were for use in Singapore, with most of the remainder destined for the United States, Europe, Malaysia, Thailand and Japan.

Phua (1991) conducted a case study of three IPOs in Singapore: one American (Xerox), another European (Alcatel) and the third Japanese (Sony). The first two are overseas manufacturing plants; the last is Sony's regional headquarters and has full decision-making powers. These IPOs performed the role of gatekeeper and buyer during the procurement process. While the procurement process did not deviate much from past purchasing practices before offshore purchasing, IPOs were able to expedite the time taken for the initial stages of procurement owing to their managers' familiarity with the local supplier base, business practices and language. The location of the IPOs in Singapore, close to the source of procurement, also lowered procurement costs compared with direct purchasing by a distant MNE.

Table 11.6   **Purchases of Singaporean IPOs by source country and destination, 1992 (Singapore dollars, per cent)**

Source country/ destination	Purchases		Destination	
	S$ million	%	S$ million	%
Singapore	3,120	44.6	2,715	38.8
ASEAN	1,108	15.8	965	13.8
Malaysia	680	9.7	422	6.0
Thailand	306	4.4	485	6.9
Indonesia	87	1.2	22	0.3
Philippines	35	0.5	36	0.5
Asian NIEs	1,033	14.8	96	1.4
Hong Kong	242	3.5	5	0.1
Taiwan	570	8.2	40	0.6
South Korea	221	3.2	51	0.7
China	45	0.6	–	–
Japan	990	14.1	342	4.9
United States	462	6.6	1,385	19.8
Europe	60	0.9	991	14.2
Australia	–	–	16	0.2
Other	176	2.5	484	6.5
Total				
S$ million	6,994	100.0	6,994	100.0
US$ million	4,293		4,293	

Source: Based on unpublished data supplied by Trade Development Board, Singapore.

Table 11.7   **Purchases of Singaporean IPOs by origin of IPO, 1992 (no., Singapore dollars, per cent)**

Country of origin	IPOs		IPO purchases	
	No.	%	S$ million	%
United States	30	30.0	4,037	57.7
Japan	33	33.0	2,060	29.5
Europe	23	23.0	790	11.3
Other	14	14.0	107	1.5
Total	100	100.0	6,994	100.0

Source: Based on unpublished data supplied by Trade Development Board, Singapore.

The criteria for supplier selection were generally similar among the three IPOs, although weighted differently by each. In the initial selection process, such factors as firm size, production capacity, manufacturing capability, financial strength, quality standards and the ability to deliver on time were important. These selection criteria tended to favour larger MNE vendors, who had better track records and business reputations. Smaller local suppliers were placed at a disadvantage. Alcatel and Sony practised multiple sourcing to hedge against the risk of dependence on a single supplier who might be unable to handle rising procurement volumes. Xerox alone was engaged in single sourcing, with the best suppliers being awarded contracts to supply parts and components to the company's plants. The procurement process was not centralised in the case of Xerox and Alcatel; their overseas plants could ask any IPO in the firm's purchasing network for a quotation. In Sony's case, the process was centralised, with corporate headquarters in Japan deciding on the source, type and quality standard of the parts to be procured. All three IPOs viewed the development of the buyer–seller relationship as an important part of their buying strategies. The type of the relationship varied with the size of the supplier base, which in turn was dependent on the sourcing strategy of each IPO. Due to the distance between purchasing office and plant, neither Xerox nor Alcatel practiced JIT purchasing, although Sony had partially implemented the concept.

The advantages of centralised procurement in Singapore are several. First, central-ised procurement gives firms access to the advantages of a large supplier base, including competitive prices, a wide range of engineering and product design capabili-ties, stringent quality control, quick access to market intelligence and information, and increased awareness of changing market conditions. Most of the world's MNEs in the electronics industry have an office in Singapore. Singapore is itself a major manufac-turing and trading centre for electronic products, components, parts and supporting services; it has over 1,500 firms supplying electronic parts and components alone. The electronics industry is the largest manufacturing sector in terms of output, value-added and employment. In 1992, Singapore's total trade in electronics reached S$73 billion (US$44.8 billion), of which re-exports amounted to S$10.5 billion (US$6.4 billion).

Second, Singapore is strategically located close to offshore suppliers. This makes it possible for firms to achieve the benefits associated with JIT inventory systems — lower inventory costs, fast response to changes in engineering and design specifica-tions, and lower capital requirements. Singapore also offers low-cost financing, good land, air and sea transportation and warehousing facilities, efficient and simple import and export procedures, well-developed financial and legal services, a highly skilled workforce, widespread English-language ability, and political and social stability. These are crucial attributes for time-sensitive products with short lifecycles and JIT systems, which depend on the uninterrupted flow of supplies.

Third, IPOs receive strong official support in Singapore. Applications for repre-sentative or liaison office status are reportedly approved within a couple of weeks. The

Trade Development Board publishes trade directories, as well as monthly updates on new vendors and new products and services available in Singapore and the surrounding region. This helps IPOs reduce the time they spend vetting and selecting suppliers. An electronic data interchange facilitates communications and transactions between IPOs and vendors, and gives firms the capability to support JIT systems. IPOs can also test parts and components sourced in the region at an electronic testing centre. Because samples need not be sent to corporate headquarters for testing, the qualifying process for parts approval is shortened. The Local Industry Upgrading Program assists Singaporean vendors to improve their technical capabilities and meet IPO requirements. Fiscal support is also provided to approved companies in the form of tax concessions. These are available to firms establishing regional headquarters and IPOs in Singapore, or conducting warehousing and trading activities there. The concessionary tax rate is generally 10 per cent, compared with the standard corporate income tax rate of 27 per cent.

Singapore also benefits from being a centre for IPOs. Apart from bringing direct employment and income benefits, IPOs generate demand for a wide range of services, including transport and telecommunications, banking, insurance and legal services. Although the procurement activities of Singapore's IPOs are not limited to Singapore, their presence has improved technology transfer and strengthened the manufacturing base. The stringent quality and delivery requirements of MNEs have exposed local small and medium sized subcontractors and vendors to internationally competitive market environments. IPOs also provide an immediate and direct export channel for Singapore's electronics manufacturers, a channel which is particularly important for local small and medium sized enterprises. Export sales through an IPO offer substantial savings in marketing costs. As IPOs meet the needs of manufacturing plants in various countries, local vendors are able to gain access to multiple markets through their linkages with IPOs.

Business networks and international procurement and sales

Increased competition from offshore producers, the pace of technological innovation and shortened product lifecycles have in the past decade led to changes in the nature of the buyer–seller relationship. Study has focused on behavioural differences between arm's length trade on the one hand and intrafirm trade, strategic alliances, partnerships and business networks on the other, and on the implications of these differences. With the rise of the East Asian economies and intraregional trade and investment, interest in Chinese business networks and the Japanese *keiretsu* system, which are commonly perceived to be exclusionary, has grown.

Although there is a large body of anecdotal evidence about Chinese business networks in Southeast Asia, owing to the scarcity of quantitative data, little systematic documentation or analysis has been done. Chinese business networks are known to rely extensively on social relations, with family-owned business empires and enterprises commonly being based on communal ties, ancestral roots and extended family relationships. Business transactions are often based on trust rather than on a formal, contractual relationship, and are typically less transparent than Western-style business transactions. Chinese business networks have contributed to the sharp growth of ethnic Chinese businesses and investments in China and ASEAN countries, where the risk of operating in a different political, economic and legal environment has been reduced by dependence on trust relationships. The rapid growth of FDI in Southeast Asia by ethnic Chinese from Hong Kong, Taiwan, Singapore and elsewhere has given rise to concerns in some host countries about the exclusionary behaviour of Chinese business networks. The tendency of ethnic Chinese foreign investors to seek local Chinese rather than indigenous businesspeople as joint venture partners has aroused political sensitivities. In view of the growing importance of ethnic Chinese capital and investments in East Asia, more rigorous research is urgently needed on the characteristics of Chinese business networks and their implications for host countries.

In the growing global and regional competition between American and Japanese businesses, the role of *keiretsu* in determining Japanese competitiveness at the national level and their perceived extension to the rest of East Asia have drawn increasing academic interest. The Japanese corporate culture, based on the *keiretsu* structure, is characterised by networks of firms closely connected by cross-shareholdings, production links and long-term supplier–customer relationships. Because suppliers and customers become very familiar with each other's requirements, transaction, inventory and production costs can be held down. The *keiretsu* system is perceived to be exclusionary, and also as inefficient when loyalty dominates price and quality in procurement and sales criteria. The American corporate culture, in contrast, is perceived to emphasise the independence of companies and arm's length procurement and sales behaviour.

Dobson (1993) found that the production relationships of manufacturing affiliates in East Asia varied according to the investing country and the industry. US affiliates in the electrical industry were well established in East Asia and oriented to the home market in their sales, while the newer, Japanese affiliates were more heavily oriented to local and third country markets. Evidence from firm-level surveys and interviews supported the view that Japanese firms were indeed less open to outside suppliers than American firms, for a number of reasons. Japanese investors were late-comers to East Asia compared with American and European companies. Under Japan's system of lifetime employment, these firms have tended to rely on Japanese managers, reducing their exposure to alternative non-Japanese suppliers. Because of the ready availability of Japanese suppliers, the use of non-Japanese alternatives has also entailed relatively higher transaction costs. Dobson argues that the behaviour of Japanese and US networks will converge in the longer term. On the one hand, networking will increasingly characterise the behaviour of non-Japanese globalising MNEs as they respond to the lowering of tariff barriers, the emergence of dynamic new competitors in East Asia, and the rapid international diffusion of technological capability which has eroded their monopoly power. On the other hand, host governments are pressuring Japanese affiliates to adopt more open procurement behaviour, including increased sourcing from local suppliers. Porter (1990) downgrades the role of *keiretsu* in Japan's competitive advantage, stressing instead the importance of a well-developed network of supporting industries and small and medium sized subcontractors providing backward and forward linkages, and the use of trade associations and trading companies to collect and disseminate market information.

Concern has been expressed that Japanese MNEs are replicating the *keiretsu* structure abroad, creating what are in fact exclusive production networks. A UNCTC study noted that some Japanese affiliates in Asia (and Europe) are part of self-contained regional networks in which affiliates in the East Asian economies are linked operationally to Japanese parents and to other affiliates in North America and Europe (UNCTC 1991). These networks serve local markets, sell finished goods in the United States and Europe, and act as low-cost suppliers to other affiliates. Dobson, however, using 1990 data on Japanese manufacturing affiliates in the United States, the European Union and Asia, found little evidence to support the exclusive network hypothesis (Table 11.8). She found that the electrical industry in Europe had the highest levels of internalisation of all Japanese affiliates, with 36 per cent of local inputs and 24 per cent of local sales remaining within the group. In Asia, although Japanese component suppliers were active in providing inputs, internalisation was less pronounced, and suppliers sold to any buyer. On the sales side, the local linkages of Asian affiliates were more mature than those in Europe and the United States, and sales were spread evenly among local, Japanese and third country markets. Dobson argues that Japanese networks in East Asia functioned in more exclusionary ways than American firms, not because the Japanese *keiretsu* structure was being replicated, but because firms tended to rely on Japanese managers who lacked local contacts and were wary about using non-Japanese products. Where local suppliers met quality standards, they were used by Japanese MNEs.

Procurement and sales behaviour of Japanese and US firms

The international procurement and sales behaviour of MNEs can be studied in greater detail using firm-level surveys of the trade behaviour of the foreign affiliate — specifically, its exports, the imports displaced by its local sales, and the direct and indirect effects of its investments and purchases of intermediate goods. Unfortunately data on US and Japanese MNEs only are readily available. A number of recent studies have examined the sales and procurement behaviour of affiliates of US and Japanese MNEs in East Asia using data from surveys carried out by the US Department of Commerce and Japan's Ministry of Trade and Industry (MITI).[3] The following discussion draws heavily on the work of Dobson (1993), Encarnation (1992), Urata (1993) and OECD (1993) in this field.

Urata (1993) examined the procurement and sales patterns of Japanese manufacturing affiliates in Asia in the 1980s (Table 11.9). He found that the value of both procurement and sales more than doubled between 1980 and 1989, from ¥4.9 trillion to ¥11.6 trillion in the case of the former and from ¥6.1 trillion to ¥14.3 trillion in the

Table 11.8 Sales, inputs and intragroup transactions: a comparison of Japanese affiliates in the United States, the European Union, Asia and the NIEs, 1990 (per cent)

	All manufacturing				Electrical				Transport				Chemicals			
	US	EU	Asia	NIEs	US	EU	Asia	NIEs	US	EU	Asia	NIEs	US	EU	Asia	NIEs
Inputs																
Total	100	100	100	100	100	100	100	100	100	100	100	100	100	100	100	100
Intragroup	48	55	27	26	76	77	36	40	38	44	21	16	5	16	34	48
Local intragroup	2	4	2	3	2	8	2	1	4	0	1	4	1	0	2	2
Local sources	47	34	55	61	19	22	42	44	53	47	59	70	95	79	56	49
Intragroup	5	11	4	5	13	36	5	3	7	0	2	6	1	0	3	4
Japanese imports	50	42	35	28	73	50	46	48	47	52	41	29	5	15	35	47
Intragroup	88	91	63	71	97	96	65	74	72	84	49	41	80	84	84	93
Third country imports	4	23	11	12	9	28	12	8	0	2	0	1	0	6	9	5
Intragroup	35	57	24	27	32	75	30	41	8	0	1	0	100	52	34	49
Sales																
Total	100	100	100	100	100	100	100	100	100	100	100	100	100	100	100	100
Intragroup	10	35	19	15	6	38	38	32	15	46	7	8	5	17	11	10
Local sales	95	66	70	74	97	73	37	37	95	51	92	81	96	52	78	74
Intragroup	7	20	7	5	4	24	13	5	14	1	6	7	1	0	4	1
Sales to Japan	4	2	14	11	2	1	28	30	4	1	2	4	4	0	10	12
Intragroup	66	59	59	56	98	14	60	54	30	100	36	14	100	90	40	32
Third country sales	1	32	16	15	1	26	36	33	1	48	7	15	0	48	12	14
Intragroup	38	63	37	36	48	79	44	41	8	92	9	12	57	36	35	39

Source: Wendy Dobson, 1993, Table 7.

case of the latter. Encarnation (1992) showed that Japanese and US MNEs behaved similarly in East Asia, investing in majority-owned subsidiaries whose sales exceeded home country exports. These subsidiaries traded extensively with their parent firms and other affiliates. While US MNEs were more actively engaged in offshore production, Japanese MNEs conducted more intrafirm trade, but both differences

Table 11.9 **Procurement and sales of Asian affiliates of Japanese firms, 1989 (per cent)**

	Local market	Japan	Other Asia	Non-Asia
Procurement				
All manufacturing	49.8	38.9	6.1	2.4
Food	87.7	3.3	4.3	5.2
Textiles	43.1	22.4	6.4	28.1
Wood and pulp	92.8	2.3	4.4	0.5
Chemicals	56.3	34.7	1.9	7.1
Iron and steel	36.0	56.1	4.3	3.6
Non-ferrous metals	59.3	18.1	4.3	18.3
General machinery	53.6	42.5	3.2	0.7
Electrical machinery	42.4	44.6	12.5	0.5
Transport machinery	57.7	41.8	0.1	0.4
Precision machinery	42.1	45.2	11.0	1.7
Petroleum and coal products	89.5	10.5	0.0	0.0
Other	36.0	48.4	7.3	8.3
Sales				
All manufacturing	63.9	15.8	9.7	10.6
Food	66.9	16.1	9.8	7.2
Textiles	70.5	14.9	8.1	6.5
Wood and pulp	34.4	35.9	20.2	9.5
Chemicals	78.1	10.3	8.8	2.8
Iron and steel	87.7	4.2	4.2	3.9
Non-ferrous metals	73.3	12.1	12.8	1.8
General machinery	56.9	18.2	5.9	19.0
Electrical machinery	37.4	26.9	16.7	19.0
Transport machinery	92.1	1.6	2.2	4.1
Precision machinery	55.0	22.2	7.8	15.0
Petroleum and coal products	100.0	0.0	0.0	0.0
Other	78.5	12.1	4.3	5.1

Source: Urata, 1993.

251

were narrowing over time. Dobson (1993) also compared the procurement and sales patterns of Japanese and US affiliates. She found that US manufacturing affiliates were more closely tied into the production structure of the US parent, relying more heavily on the US home market for both inputs and sales than did Japanese affiliates.

Procurement and sourcing

In 1988 American and Japanese subsidiaries in East Asia absorbed 14 per cent and 17 per cent respectively of their home countries' exports to the region. Most of Japan's exports to its subsidiaries in East Asia were channelled through trading and distribution subsidiaries, while the majority of the United States' exports to its East Asian subsidiaries were directed to manufacturing subsidiaries.

US subsidiaries in East Asia exported more to the United States than they imported from it. Japanese manufacturing affiliates in East Asia likewise exported more to Japan than they imported from it, as did Japanese distributors. In the electronics industry, exports back to Japan accounted in 1988 for 25 per cent of the total sales of Japanese subsidiaries, a ratio well above the East Asian average for Japanese manufacturers as a whole. Another 17 per cent of the total sales of Japan's East Asian manufacturing subsidiaries was exported to third countries in East Asia. In contrast to the diversity of the Japanese export environment, exports back to the United States accounted for over 60 per cent of total sales reported by US electronics subsidiaries in East Asia (Encarnation 1992).

In his examination of the procurement pattern for parts, components, and semifinished goods purchased by Japanese manufacturing affiliates in Asia, Urata (1993) found a rise in the local procurement ratio from 42.2 per cent in 1980 to 49.8 per cent in 1989. The extent of local sourcing depended on the length of time the affiliate had been in operation as well as on the capabilities of supplier industries in the host country. In the 1980s, the local procurement ratio rose for most industries, reflecting a rise in the production capability and quality standards of local firms. Surprisingly, however, the electrical machinery industry experienced a decline in its local procurement ratio. Urata suggests that this may have reflected an inability by local producers of parts and components to keep up with the rapid expansion of demand in the industry and the pace of technological change. Japanese manufacturing affiliates depended mostly on Japan for their import needs: for over 40 per cent of total procurement in the case of the machinery industry and the iron and steel industry.

Based on 1990 data, Dobson (1993) found differences in sourcing behaviour among Japanese affiliates in the United States, Europe and Asia, and among the electrical, transport and chemicals industries. Local sourcing of inputs was highest in the Asian NIEs — as much as 60 per cent, compared with only 30–50 per cent in Europe and the United States — reflecting high local content requirements. Among industries, local sourcing of inputs was highest in the chemicals and transport industries, and lowest in the electronics industry, which imported key high-priced technical components from Japan. In the electrical industry, local sourcing was higher in Asia (around 40 per cent) than in Europe or the United States (about 20 per cent). The degree of local sourcing by the automobile industry was roughly the same among affiliates in Asia, Europe and the United States. In chemicals, affiliates in Asia tended to rely more heavily on supplies from Japan.

Dobson conducted a case study of four MNEs in the electrical/electronics sector in Singapore, two Japanese and two American. Three had several manufacturing and sales affiliates in East Asia, while the fourth had a large manufacturing presence in Japan and used its regional operations to procure parts and components. All four MNEs were cost driven. Free trade zones enabled them to ship parts and components around the region without being subject to trade tariffs. Attitudes towards, and the use of, local suppliers varied by firm rather than by home country. By volume, none of the four relied on locally controlled suppliers for more than 20 per cent of parts and components. In most cases MNEs sourced key components in Japan or the United States, acquiring the remainder from locally based Japanese firms. One Japanese affiliate had achieved 80 per cent local content, importing its other requirements, mainly high-tech components, from Japan. The source of much of this local content (70 per cent) was local Japanese suppliers. An American affiliate said that its use of local suppliers varied with the length of time it had been producing the product locally. In the case of start-up production, all parts would be imported from the original suppliers for the first year; regional sourcing would then rise to 25–30 per cent, with simpler parts and components being obtained from local suppliers and more sophisticated ones from the United States, Korea, Taiwan or Japan. By the end of the second year, regional sourcing would have risen to 50–60 per cent, with home sourcing still accounting for 30 per cent. All four MNEs required that local suppliers meet standard criteria on delivery, quality, price, availability of product information, and reliability. Because local Japanese suppliers were well able to meet these requirements, the American MNEs relied on them just as heavily as did the Japanese.

Sales and exports

Although US and Japanese MNE affiliates in Asian developing countries experienced rapid growth in the 1980s, their combined share of these countries' total exports of manufactures actually declined from 12 per cent in 1982 to 9 per cent in 1989; in Asia their share declined from 13 per cent to 8 per cent (UNTCMD 1992). This relative decline may be attributed to the faster export growth of domestic firms in response to the shift in industrial policy from import substitution to export-oriented manufacturing. The exports of domestic firms could also have been stimulated by the presence of trading MNEs, and by subcontracting arrangements. In 1988, the total sales of Japanese subsidiaries in East Asia amounted to US$85.5 billion, or about 30 per cent more than comparable sales by US subsidiaries (Encarnation 1992). Data deficiencies make it difficult to compare rigorously the export behaviour of Japanese and US affiliates. In the 1970s Japanese affiliates contributed less to exports than their US counterparts. More recent evidence suggests that the export share of Japanese investors is rising as firms target offshore production as a means of maintaining their export competitiveness (UNESCAP 1993).

Encarnation (1992) found that in 1988 the ratio of exports to total sales of US subsidiaries reached one-third, up from one-quarter in 1957. Japanese subsidiaries also experienced a rise in this ratio, from one-quarter in the early 1970s to one-third in the 1980s. In East Asia, US manufacturing investments have traditionally been more export oriented than Japanese investments. Whereas US manufacturing affiliates in East Asia exported back to the home market as well as to third markets, Japanese affiliates were more likely to target host country and third country markets, with limited exports going back to Japan. In the 1980s Japanese manufacturing affiliates became more export oriented. UNTCMD (1992) found that the export ratios of US MNEs in Asia exceeded 50 per cent in the early 1980s, to stagnate during the decade in part because of strong domestic demand. In contrast, the export ratios of Japanese affiliates in Asia increased rapidly to about 40 per cent. Urata (1993) showed that Japanese affiliates worldwide had higher export ratios than their US counterparts, mainly because of the exporting activities of Japanese trading affiliates. In the manufacturing sector, however, US affiliates, with an export ratio of 37 per cent in 1988, appear to have been more export oriented than Japanese affiliates, which had a ratio of 21 per cent in 1989. Although the export ratios of Japanese manufacturing affiliates were rising in the late 1980s, in the absence of more recent data it is not possible to say whether this trend continued into the early 1990s.

Dobson (1993), in the comparison referred to earlier of Japanese affiliates in the electrical, transport and chemical industries, found that Japanese manufacturing affiliates in Asia were less export oriented than those in Europe but more export oriented than those in the United States. The export ratios for these three regions were 30 per cent, 34 per cent and 5 per cent respectively, with the ratios for the United States and Europe reflecting the huge size of the US market and the integration of European economies. Export orientation varied among industries. In the electronics industry, Japanese affiliates in Asia had an export ratio of 63 per cent, compared with 27 per cent for affiliates in Europe and 3 per cent for those in the United States. The ratio for the chemicals industry was 22 per cent, while that for the automobile industry was only 8 per cent.

In the case of US electronics subsidiaries in East Asia, exports home accounted for 60 per cent of sales in both 1977 and 1988. Much of this trade was generated by offshore production in search of low-cost labour, and by the US tariff schedule (section 807), which imposes import tariffs only on value that is added offshore, and not on US components that are reimported in the assembled product. The investments of American semiconductor manufacturers in labour-intensive assembly operations in East Asia placed them close to their powerful buyers. Competition from imports from Japan, oligopolistic rivalry and US trade policy pushed other US MNEs to invest in East Asia in search of low-cost sources of supply. US affiliates soon went beyond importing and assembling US-made components into low-tech products for re-export back to the United States, and began to diversify their sources of supply by purchasing from other countries in the region.

Japanese MNEs have been less inclined than their US counterparts to use offshore production bases in East Asia to supply the home market. Encarnation (1992) found that Japanese manufacturing affiliates sold nearly one-quarter of their East Asian production in third country markets in the United States and East Asia in 1977, more than twice as much as they exported back to Japan. Urata (1993) found a growing export orientation toward Japan. Export sales to Japan as a proportion of Japan's total manufacturing sales rose from 9.8 per cent in 1980 to 15.8 per cent in 1989. Export orientation intensified in the electrical machinery industry in particular, with the export/sales ratio rising from 48.4 per cent in 1980 to 62.6 per cent in 1989. This rise in the export ratio can be attributed to the increase in the share of exports going to the Japanese market: in the same period, Japan's share of total electrical machinery sales rose from 16.2 per cent to 26.9 per cent. Other sectors that experienced large increases in the export/sales ratio included textiles, non-ferrous metals, general machinery and precision machinery. Urata attributed the shift in export destination toward Japan to two factors: the appreciation of the yen, and host government policies aimed at gaining better access to the Japanese market.

Export sales to third countries stood at one-fifth of total sales for Japan in 1988 (a share that has remained roughly constant), and increased moderately to nearly one-quarter of total sales for the United States. The exports to third markets of American affiliates in East Asia increased from one-sixth of total sales in 1966 to one-quarter in 1977, with Japan becoming the largest third country market, especially for US subsidiaries in the wholesale trade and petroleum industries. US manufacturing subsidiaries, meanwhile, exported only 5 per cent of total sales to Japan. Outside Japan, US manufacturing subsidiaries typically exported to other affiliates of the same multinational corporation.

Intrafirm trade

As stated earlier, data on intrafirm trade are available only in the form of firm surveys published mainly by the US Department of Commerce and MITI. US data for 1989 (Table 11.10) show that over one-third of US merchandise trade was intrafirm, accounting for 24.5 per cent of total US exports and 15.4 per cent of total US imports. Contrary to expectation, the share of intrafirm trade in total US trade did not show a significant increase in 1977–89; it declined until 1982, to recover after that. A possible explanation of this U-shaped curve for intrafirm trade is found in exchange rate fluctuations and the slow growth of foreign affiliates' sales in the early 1980s due to adverse economic conditions in many countries (OECD 1993). In the intrafirm trade between parents and their overseas affiliates, imports by US parents fell from 20.3 per cent of total US imports in 1977 to 16.3 per cent in 1982, then further to 15.4 per cent in 1989. This decline was due to the sharp fall in the share of oil and mineral imports in total US merchandise imports in 1977–89. If these sectors are excluded, US firms' imports from their overseas affiliates fall in 1977–82 but recover in 1982–89; in manufacturing industry, the share of intrafirm imports by US parents showed moderate gains between 1982 and 1989.

Table 11.10 Comparison of procurement and sales behaviour of Japanese and US affiliates, 1980 and 1990 (per cent)

	All manufacturing				Electrical				Transport				Chemicals			
	US		Japan		US		Japan		US		Japan		US		Japan	
	1982	1988	1980	1990	1982	1988	1980	1990	1982	1988	1980	1990	1982	1988	1980	1990
Inputs																
Total intrafirm share	na	na	37	29	na	na	40	35	na	na	4	22	na	na	22	34
Home country	na	na	42	50	na	na	45	42	na	na	51	58	na	na	31	56
Intrafirm share	91	na	67	63	97	na	78	65	45	na	56	49	92	na	24	84
Sales																
Total intrafirm share	80	36	41	21	8	10	12	37	0	na	4	7	4	7	4	12
Home country	48	41	10	16	65	60	16	27	65	0	2	2	2	1	4	10
Intrafirm share	na	na	77	59	na	na	73	60	na	na	46	36	na	na	84	40
Third country	22	22	26	20	23	27	32	36	33	0	6	6	10	23	5	12
Intrafirm share	66	na	24	37	na	na	32	44	na	na	62	9	na	na	2	35
Local	na	36	64	64	19	13	52	37	na	100	89	92	92	76	35	78
Intrafirm share	na	na	9	7	na	na	10	13	na	na	9	6	na	na	3	4

Source: Wendy Dobson, 1993, Table 6.

256

Unlike the more definite trend for imports, the share of intrafirm exports of US parents in total US merchandise exports fluctuated widely in the 1980s. Intrafirm trade between the United States and other OECD countries comprised mainly parents' sales to affiliates rather than affiliates' sales to parents. US affiliates in Canada, however, tended to buy as much from their parents as they sold to them, while US affiliates in developing countries sold more to their parents than they bought from them. Canada and Europe were the two main destinations of intrafirm trade between US parents and their foreign subsidiaries, together accounting for about 70 per cent of the total intrafirm exports of US MNEs in 1989. Intrafirm imports by US MNEs from Canada grew sharply in 1977–82, with growth moderating in 1982–89. Large increases were also registered in Mexico and Europe at the expense of 'other' areas. US intrafirm trade is heavily concentrated in the more technology- and capital-intensive industries, particularly transport equipment, machinery (including electrical/electronic equipment) and chemicals; these three industries together accounted for about 70 per cent of total intrafirm exports. Fuels declined in relative importance, reflecting the switch to arm's length imports for petroleum.

Intrafirm trade between US-based affiliates and their foreign parents fluctuated during 1977–89. While intrafirm exports remained at around 10 per cent of total US exports, intrafirm imports rose from 19.2 per cent of total US merchandise imports in 1977 to 26 per cent in 1989. This was the only component of US intrafirm trade to show a significant increase in 1977–88, in part because wholesale trade in motor vehicles and equipment by Japanese firms rose while the share of intrafirm imports of European and Canadian affiliates in the United States declined. Almost 95 per cent of affiliates' imports from Japanese parents was classified as wholesale trade in 1989, compared with 48 per cent of imports from European parents, 31 per cent from Canadian parents and 17 per cent from other foreign parents. Wholesale trade accounted for over 78 per cent of the total imports of affiliates in the United States from their foreign parents, with wholesale trade in motor vehicles and equipment being the major contributors. Exports by US-based affiliates to their foreign parents were concentrated more in metals and agricultural raw materials. The intrafirm trade (sales and purchases) of manufacturing affiliates in the United States with their foreign parents was concentrated in the chemicals and machinery industries (OECD 1993).

Japan's share of intrafirm trade in total trade is unknown, as MITI's survey data show only the share of intrafirm trade in the total trade of surveyed firms. The data do show a noticeable rise in the offshore/domestic sales ratio of Japanese firms — estimated at 7 per cent for Japanese manufacturing industries in 1991 — reflecting the rapid growth of Japanese outward FDI. The corresponding ratio for the United States was far higher: 24 per cent in 1989. The data also show the importance of wholesale trade for Japan. This type of trade accounted for 36 per cent of intrafirm exports and 72 per cent of intrafirm imports in 1989, indicating the importance of corporate networks of Japanese trading firms and the relatively recent history of Japanese FDI. The role of Japanese trading firms thus contrasts sharply with that of US trading firms in US intrafirm trade. The MITI data also show that intrafirm trade in manufactures in Japan, as in the United States, tends to be concentrated in industries that are relatively intensive in human capital and technology. Japan's intrafirm exports are heavily concentrated in electrical machinery and transport equipment, and involve the export of parts and components from Japanese parents to foreign affiliates for assembly within a vertically integrated international production structure. Intrafirm imports into Japan of these two industries are of minor significance, suggesting that final products assembled by foreign affiliates are either sold in host markets or shipped to unrelated buyers in third country markets (OECD 1993).

Conclusion

The growth of international procurement and sales reflects the rapid rise in FDI in the 1980s and the increasing globalisation of production by MNEs. In the face of technological change, intensified international competition and the emergence of new competitors from East Asia, MNEs of various nationalities have rationalised production, procurement and marketing in order to lower production and transaction costs. FDI has created intrafirm trade between parent and affiliate and among affiliates. Traditional arm's length trade involving independent buyers and suppliers is giving way not only to intrafirm trade but also to other forms of non-equity relationships between buyers and sellers. These new arrangements involve international trading companies, distribution subsidiaries and networks of MNEs, business networks such as *keiretsu* and the Southeast Asian networks of ethnic Chinese, and international and domestic subcontracting arrangements between MNEs and local parts, components and specialised service suppliers.

The FDI–trade nexus has enabled host developing economies in East Asia to embark on export manufacturing without having to undergo a lengthy and costly period of building up exporting expertise and channels. Subcontracting arrangements have also facilitated the transfer of technology and industrial knowhow from foreign MNEs to local small and medium sized enterprises supplying parts and components.

The nexus is not, however, without its problems. First, an initial high dependence on FDI to secure and then expand host country exports in world markets may not lead to the development of a domestic export capability if foreign MNEs adopt restrictive practices and if there are no complementary domestic policies aimed at building up efficient and competitive local supplier industries. Without a domestic export capability, growth is unlikely to be self-sustaining. The host country's problems would be exacerbated if subsequent rises in production costs, infrastructure and skills bottlenecks, or general labour shortages enticed foreign MNEs to relocate to other emerging low-cost production centres. Some host governments, such as Singapore, are engaged in the development of local supporting industries, not so much by prescribing local content requirements, but by providing technical and financial support to local small and medium sized enterprises and encouraging foreign MNEs to share their technical expertise.

Second, the intensified competition for FDI among East Asian developing countries and between East Asia and other developing regions has led host governments to dismantle some of their regulatory rules and performance requirements, thus improving the overall climate for investment. At the same time, however, many of these governments are engaging in an 'incentive war' in which they compete in offering a wide range of fiscal and other financial incentives to attract FDI. There is a need for cooperation among all parties, to avoid a zero-sum game situation, improve the investment climate of host countries, enhance the contribution of FDI to the development process, minimise 'incentive wars' among host countries, and protect the rights of foreign investors.

Third, the growth of non-arm's length procurement and sales, and in particular of intrafirm trade between parents and affiliates and among affiliates of the same parent or business group, could expose host countries to the negative effects of transfer pricing practices. These include the overpricing of imports and the underpricing of exports by MNEs to enable them to evade taxes and exchange controls. Non-arm's length transactions may help minimise the transaction costs of MNEs, particularly those operating across business environments characterised by diverse political, economic and legal frameworks. However, they can also create problems for policy makers in that industrial, trade and exchange rate policies may become less effective when buyer–seller relationships and purchasing decisions are less determined by open market practices and pricing.

Notes

1 The geographical definitions used in this chapter are as follows:

Asian NIEs: Hong Kong, Korea, Singapore and Taiwan;

ASEAN-4: Indonesia, Malaysia, the Philippines and Thailand;

ASEAN: the ASEAN-4 and Singapore;

developing East Asia: China, the Asian NIEs and the ASEAN-4;

East Asia: developing East Asia and Japan.

2 Kojima (1978) has argued that Japanese-style FDI promotes development to a greater extent than US-style FDI because it is labour intensive and more export oriented. This hypothesis has been challenged by several researchers as being unsupported by empirical data.

3 For the United States, benchmark data are available from the US Department of Commerce for 1977, 1982 and 1989 on trade between US companies and their foreign affiliates, and for 1980 and 1987 on trade between foreign companies and their US affiliates. Annual survey data of more limited coverage are also available. Similarly, MITI provides four benchmark surveys, for 1980, 1983, 1986 and 1989, covering the foreign affiliates of Japanese companies. MITI's data are less detailed than those published by the US Department of Commerce and do not distinguish between majority and non-majority owned affiliates. The usefulness of the data for

comparative analysis is strictly limited because of differences in definitions of what constitutes a firm and what percentage of equity constitutes a foreign affiliate. The data are also difficult to interpret because of distortions introduced by transfer pricing.

References

Benvignati, A.M. 1990, 'Industry Determinants and Differences in US Intra-Firm and Arms' Length Exports', *Review of Economics and Statistics*, 72, August, pp. 481–88.

Dobson, Wendy 1993, *Japan in East Asia: Trading and Investment Strategies*, Singapore: Institute of Southeast Asian Studies.

Encarnation, Dennis J. 1992, *Rivals Beyond Trade: America versus Japan in Global Competition*, Ithaca, NY: Cornell University Press.

Helleiner, G.K. and R. Lavergne 1979, 'Intra-Firm Trade and Industrial Exports to the United States', *Oxford Bulletin of Economics and Statistics*, 41, pp. 297–311.

JETRO 1993a, *JETRO White Paper on Foreign Direct Investment 1993*, Tokyo: JETRO.

_____ 1993b, *JETRO White Paper on International Trade 1993*, Tokyo: JETRO.

_____ 1993c, *The Role of Trading Companies in International Commerce*, Tokyo: JETRO.

Kojima, K. 1978, *Japanese Direct Foreign Investment: A Model of Multinational Business Operations*, Tokyo: Charles Tuttle.

Lall, S. 1978, 'The Pattern of Intra-Firm Exports by US Multinationals', *Oxford Bulletin of Economics and Statistics*, 40, pp. 209–22.

MITI (Ministry of International Trade and Industry), various years, *Kaigai Toshi Tokei Soran*, Tokyo: Keibun Publishing.

OECD (Organisation for Economic Cooperation and Development) 1993, *Intrafirm Trade*, Paris: OECD.

Phua May Ling 1991, An Exploratory Study of IPOs in the Electronics Industry in Singapore, Paper submitted in partial fulfilment of requirements for the degree of Master of Business Administration, Singapore: National University of Singapore.

Porter, Michael 1990, *The Competitive Advantage of Nations*, New York: The Free Press.

Siddharthan, N.S. and M. Kumar 1990, 'The Determinants of Inter-Industry Variations in the Proportion of Intra-Firm Trade: The Behaviour of US Multinationals', *Weltwirtschaftliches Archiv*, 126, pp. 581–90.

UNCTAD (United Nations Conference on Trade and Development) 1993, *World Investment Report 1993: Transnational Corporations and Integrated International Production*, New York: United Nations.

UNCTC (United Nations Centre on Transnational Corporations) 1991, *World Investment Report: The Triad in Foreign Direct Investment*, New York: United Nations.

UNESCAP (United Nations Economic and Social Commission for Asia and the Pacific) 1993, *Economic and Social Survey of Asia and the Pacific 1992*, New York: United Nations.

UNTCMD (United Nations, Transnational Corporations and Management Division) 1992, *World Investment Report 1992: Transnational Corporations as Engines of Growth*, New York: United Nations.

_____ 1993, *Foreign Investment and Trade Linkages in Developing Countries*, New York: United Nations.

Urata, Shujiro 1993, 'Changing Patterns of Direct Investment and Implications for Trade and Development', in C. Fred Bergsten and Marcus Noland (eds), *Pacific Dynamism and the International Economic System*, Washington DC: Institute of International Economics.

US Department of Commerce, various years, *US Direct Investment Abroad*, Washington DC: Bureau of Economic Analysis, US Department of Commerce.

Wong Poh Kam 1991, *Technological Development through Subcontracting Linkages: A Case Study*, Tokyo: Asian Productivity Organisation.

12 Direct investment in low-wage and high-wage countries: the case of Taiwan

Tain-Jy Chen, Ying-Hua Ku and Meng-Chun Liu

There are two major schools of thought on foreign direct investment (FDI). The conventional school, pioneered by Hymer (1960) and Caves (1971), argues that FDI is undertaken only by firms possessing some intangible asset. These firms invest in a foreign country in order to exploit the firm-specific advantage embodied in the intangible asset. FDI is therefore seen as an aggressive action to extract economic rent from a foreign market.

The other school, represented by Vernon (1966) and Kojima (1973), portrays FDI as a defensive action undertaken by firms to protect export markets threatened either by competitors in the local market (Vernon 1966) or by unfavourable developments in macroeconomic conditions (wage increases and currency appreciation, for example) at home (Kojima 1973). 'Defensive' FDI is often made in low-wage countries, where cheap labour enables investors to restore their international competitiveness by reducing production costs. 'Aggressive' FDI may be made in any country in which local production is seen as the best mode to enter that market.

Empirically it is difficult to distinguish between these two types of investment because FDI is undertaken for a mixture of reasons. For instance, while Kojima (1973) claims Japanese FDI to be of the defensive type, his example of Japanese direct investment in East Asia has been criticised as being indistinguishable from US investment in Canada or Europe (Mason 1980). Taiwan, however, provides a perfect case study for examining the differences between aggressive and defensive FDI.

Taiwanese firms embarked on a course of active overseas investment in 1986. Concurrent with this wave of FDI, domestic wage rates increased rapidly and the local currency appreciated dramatically. This pattern seems reminiscent of Japanese FDI in the early 1970s. However, unlike Japanese investors in the 1970s, Taiwanese firms have not only invested in countries where wage rates are lower than those in Taiwan, such as the lesser developed Southeast Asian countries, they have also invested substantially in industrialised countries where wage rates are much higher. Although Taiwanese FDI in Southeast Asian countries may have been directed at expanding

262

firms' markets and acquiring cheap labour, in the United States and Europe it cannot possibly have been for the latter purpose. It would appear, then, that Taiwan's FDI in high-wage countries is of the market-oriented kind and that its investment in low-wage countries is a mixture of the two types (though presumably closer to the labour-related type). A study by Taiwan's Council of Economic Planning and Development (CEPD 1992) indicates that the primary motivation for Taiwanese firms to invest in the United States has been to expand local markets, while investment in Southeast Asia has been targeted at taking advantage of low-cost labour. The purpose of this chapter is to compare the two types of FDI: their determinants and their effect on investing firms.

An often asked question is how firms based in developing countries are able to invest in developed countries, given industrialised countries' superior technological capacity and managerial resources (Wells 1983). We will not attempt to answer this question here. Rather, we will adopt the conventional indicators of firms' intangible assets and see how relevant they are in interpreting Taiwanese FDI in industrialised countries. The focus is on how firms investing in high-wage countries differ from those investing in low-wage countries.

Investment pattern of large firms

Since large firms are capable of making multiple investments, their decisions regarding investment in low-wage and high-wage countries reveal the strategic choice between cost reduction and market expansion. This study is based on Taiwan's top 674 private firms, defined as those whose annual sales in 1986 exceeded NT$500 million (approximately US$14 million at the time) and those listed in China Credit Information Service (1987), which contains information on firms in Taiwan for 1986. We excluded state-owned enterprises from the analysis because their FDI decisions are often influenced by political considerations.

We followed the FDI history of these firms from 1986 to 1991. The first question asked was how many of them had engaged in FDI during the period, and this was tabulated by industry (Table 12.1). The FDI literature based on the experience in Western countries suggests that large firms are more likely to venture abroad. In Taiwan, too, the incidence of FDI increases significantly with the scale of the firm.

As can be seen in Table 12.1, of the 674 firms, 150 (22.3 per cent) engaged in some form of FDI during the period studied. In other words, roughly one in five of these firms responded to changing macroeconomic conditions by investing abroad. The tendency to invest differed greatly between industries, however. The plastics industry had the highest propensity to invest: 38.9 per cent of firms in this industry engaged in FDI. It was followed by the electrical and electronic products industry with 32.4 per cent and the chemical materials industry with 31.4 per cent. Coincidentally, these industries also constituted the mainstay of Taiwan's exports prior to 1986. They are also the industries that have attracted the most inward foreign investment to Taiwan. There is little reason to believe, however, that this outward movement of FDI was engineered

Table 12.1   FDI by Taiwan's leading 674 firms, 1986–91 (no., per cent)

Industry	Total number of firms (A)	Number of firms carrying out FDI (B)	Share of FDI (A/B) (%)
Food	74	7	9.5
Beverages and tobacco	10	1	10.0
Textiles	97	17	17.5
Apparel	33	7	21.2
Leather	10	2	20.0
Wood products	14	4	28.6
Paper and pulp products	17	4	23.5
Chemical materials	35	11	31.4
Chemical products	20	4	20.0
Petroleum and coal	0	0	–
Rubber	11	3	27.3
Plastics	36	14	38.9
Non-metal minerals	10	2	20.0
Basic metals	51	4	7.8
Metal products	21	5	23.8
Machinery	14	2	14.3
Electrical and electronic products	148	48	32.4
Transport equipment	29	6	20.7
Footwear	21	4	19.1
Miscellaneous manufacturing	23	5	21.7
Total	674	150	22.3

Source: China Credit Information Service, 1987; unpublished data provided by the Foreign Investment Commission, Ministry of Economic Affairs, Taiwan.

by multinational firms with subsidiaries in Taiwan. Rather, industry characteristics are probably the crucial factor in FDI, regardless of the origin of capital and perhaps even of the characteristics of the individual firms in an industry (Horst 1972).

At the other end of the scale, the basic metals industry was the most apathetic to FDI: only 7.8 per cent of firms in this group had engaged in FDI. Similarly low proportions of less than 10 per cent were observed for the food and for the beverages and tobacco industries. Typically these industries are oriented toward the domestic market and lack export experience. Firms with little exposure to exports tend to be cautious in engaging in overseas production. Buckley (1982) has argued that exporting is a first step in the evolutionary process toward internationalisation; only a successful exporter will commit itself to direct investment. Since these industries are local market oriented, any FDI they do undertake is likely to be primarily to expand their markets rather than to defend exports. Unlike the more export-oriented industries, investment by these sectors tends to go to low-wage countries and usually involves products that command reasonable demand even in these countries. By comparison, market-oriented FDI in high-wage countries usually involves products that cater to high-income economies.

FDI by other major export industries, namely textiles, apparel and footwear, was slightly below, but close to, the industry average. This indicates that even though exports may be a precondition for FDI, actual investment differs widely between export industries. The textiles, apparel and footwear industries are characterised by more or less homogeneous products; price competition dominates the international markets for these products. Product differentiation in these industries is achieved mainly through advertising, and after-sales service is almost unnecessary. Because local production does not facilitate product differentiation, investment is geared primarily toward cost reduction and is therefore destined for low-wage countries. The explanation for the low levels of FDI by these industries compared with the plastics and electronics industries thus lies in their lack of market-oriented investment.

Table 12.2 lists the distribution of FDI in high-wage and low-wage countries in 1986–91. It can be seen that FDI in high-wage countries increased steadily after 1986 to peak in 1989. FDI in low-wage countries also rose steadily, but was still rising in 1991. Although six years is too short a time from which to infer FDI behaviour, the pattern seems to suggest that market-oriented FDI occurs only intermittently and is subject to macroeconomic shocks that disturb the portfolio balance. In Taiwan's case, it was the sudden appreciation of the currency that lowered the cost of acquiring foreign assets. Many firms took this opportunity to establish production-related facilities — including R&D units, distribution warehouses and sales networks — in

Table 12.2   FDI in high-wage and low-wage countries of Taiwan's leading 674 firms, 1986–91 (US$ thousand, per cent)

	FDI in high-wage countries		FDI in low-wage countries	
	US$ thousand	%	US$ thousand	%
1986	3,582	48	3,878	52
1987	15,244	63	8,947	37
1988	49,340	78	13,841	22
1989	362,822	78	104,252	22
1990	142,024	41	205,183	59
1991	98,271	27	259,866	73

Source: China Credit Information Service, 1987; unpublished data provided by the Foreign Investment Commission, Ministry of Economic Affairs, Taiwan.

industrialised countries. On the other hand, labour-related FDI seems to have occurred almost continuously, driven by rising wages at home and the evolution of the product lifecycle. Although the currency appreciation which commenced in 1986 reinforced the effect of wage increases, setting off a boom in this kind of investment, FDI activity has not died down even since the currency stabilised. Although we believe that labour-related FDI will also eventually peak, barring further currency appreciation or other major external shocks, its volume will probably remain above that of market-oriented FDI. Recently, however, China opened its doors to investment in the production of goods, chiefly for local consumption. Access to this lucrative market will probably bring about another wave of market-oriented investment in the coming years.

Determinants of FDI

In an earlier paper, Chen (1992) investigated the determinants of Taiwan's FDI on an *ex ante* basis. Using a data set similar to the one used here, he found that size, export share and recent performance (measured by the average growth rate of revenue in the last three years) were important factors in an individual firm's incentive to invest abroad. In this section, we examine the actual FDI actions of firms, focusing on the different determinants of FDI in high-wage and low-wage countries.

The variables included in the regression analysis are as follows:

> dependent variable: a binary variable equal to one for firms engaged in FDI in 1986–92, and zero otherwise;
>
> SALE: value of sales, in NT$ billion;
>
> LAB: labour intensity, measured by the ratio of the number of employees to the value of fixed assets, the latter in NT$ million;
>
> EX: share of exports, or the value of exports divided by total sales;
>
> EXS: the squares of EX;
>
> AWA: average annual earnings per employee, measured in NT$ million;
>
> RD: the ratio of R&D expenditure to the value of sales;
>
> GROW: average annual growth rate of sales from 1984 to 1986, as a percentage;
>
> ROF: the proportion of equity owned by foreign nationals; and
>
> DIND: an industry dummy, equal to one for the plastics, electronics and chemical materials industries, and zero otherwise.

All variables are measured in terms of 1986 statistics. SALE is a typical variable representing the scale of the firm. The variables LAB, EX, AWA, RD and GROW are designed to capture the intangible asset described by Hymer (1960) and Caves (1971).

LAB (labour intensity) represents the competitive pressure facing a firm when the local wage rate rises, and EX (export share) the export market defence motive. AWA (average wage) represents the level of human capital embodied in the labour force. Helpman (1984) has shown this to be an important ingredient in the growth of multinational firms. RD (R&D) is a typical variable used in the study of Western multinationals (see, for example, Caves 1974) to represent the capability to innovate or the degree of product differentiation. GROW (average growth rate of revenue in recent years) indicates the 'health' of firms and their ability to expand.

In addition, we include ROF (foreign equity) so as to examine the relationship between equity ownership and the decision to invest abroad. This variable represents the 'corporate decision' approach to FDI (Aharoni 1966). According to this approach, competitive pressure and profitable opportunities are not sufficient to produce FDI. The objectives of managers, the limited decision-making horizons of managers, the cost of information and other factors may prevent the firm from engaging in foreign investment even if it is capable of doing so. We suspect that the foreign managers of multinational subsidiaries in Taiwan have little incentive to undertake FDI.

The last variable, DIND, is an industry dummy which captures the three industries that have been observed to be most active in FDI (Table 12.1). The purpose of inserting this variable is to see whether some firm characteristics exist that are conducive to FDI when industry characteristics are controlled.

SALE is expected to favour FDI in both high-wage and low-wage countries; AWA, RD and GROW are expected to be conducive to FDI in high-wage countries; and LAB and EX are expected to be conducive to FDI in low-wage countries. ROF is expected to have a negative impact and DIND a positive impact on FDI in each type of country.

In addition to the statistics available from China Credit Information Service, we obtained data from the 1986 Census of Industry and Commerce. After deleting missing observations, we were left with a sample of 482 firms for the regression analysis.

We began with a single equation PROBIT regression to examine the relationship between the explanatory variables that represent firm characteristics and the dependent variable that indicates whether or not the corresponding firm has invested. At first, no distinction was made between FDI in high-wage and low-wage countries. Dependent variables took the value of one if the firm engaged in any type of FDI. FDI in high-wage countries was then investigated separately; dependent variables took the value of one only if the firm invested in a high-wage country. Next, a similar estimation was conducted for low-wage countries. Of the sample firms, 120 had undertaken FDI: 88 in low-wage countries, 60 in high-wage countries and 28 in both. Korea was used to distinguish high-wage from low-wage countries: countries with per capita income lower than that of Korea were classified as low-wage countries and the remainder, including Korea, as high-wage countries. Note that although wages in Korea are a little lower than those in Taiwan, we believe that this difference is not large enough to attract labour-related FDI to Korea. The demarcation is drawn in such a way that FDI in high-wage countries is dominated by market-oriented aspirations and devoid of the labour-related motive. The results are given in Table 12.3.

Table 12.3 Single equation PROBIT estimates of FDI by Taiwanese firms

Explanatory variable	All countries				High-wage countries				Low-wage countries			
Constant	-1.704**	(5.2)	-1.718**	(5.2)	-2.086**	(5.6)	-2.208**	(5.6)	-1.225**	(3.8)	-1.215**	(3.7)
SALE	0.145**	(4.7)	0.148**	(4.8)	0.136**	(4.6)	0.143**	(4.6)	0.048**	(2.7)	0.043**	(2.4)
LAB	0.136	(1.1)	0.133	(1.0)	0.042	(0.3)	0.014	(0.1)	0.029	(0.2)	0.020	(0.1)
EX	2.876**	(3.6)	2.470**	(3.0)	0.095	(0.3)	0.006	(0.02)	2.710**	(3.3)	2.437**	(2.9)
EXS	-3.040**	(3.5)	-2.648**	(3.0)					-2.781**	(3.1)	-2.520**	(2.7)
AWA	1.815	(1.6)	1.815	(1.2)	2.384*	(1.8)	2.021	(1.5)	-0.211	(0.2)	-0.539	(0.4)
RD	2.381	(0.5)	-0.596	(0.1)	9.703**	(2.0)	7.188	(1.4)	-0.080	(0.02)	-2.568	(0.5)
GROW	0.003	(1.1)	0.001	(0.3)	0.006**	(2.3)	0.004	(1.5)	-0.001	(0.5)	-0.003	(1.0)
ROF	-1.101**	(3.6)	-1.470**	(4.5)	-1.372**	(3.1)	-1.913**	(3.9)	-0.691**	(2.3)	-0.942**	(3.0)
DIND			0.717**	(4.7)			0.877**	(4.9)			0.542**	(3.5)

Notes: Numbers in brackets are asymptotic *t*-statistics.
　　　　** indicates significance at the 5 per cent level,
　　　　* indicates significance at the 10 per cent level.

Source: Chen, Ku and Liu's estimates.

It can be seen from the table that when no distinction is made between FDI in high-wage and low-wage countries, only five variables are statistically significant in explaining Taiwan's FDI, namely SALE (firm size), EX (export share), EXS (export share squared), ROF (foreign ownership) and DIND (industry dummy). Our results show that large firms are more inclined to invest overseas, while foreign owners are uninterested in sprouting overseas investment from their Taiwanese subsidiaries. Export share exerts a positive impact on FDI up to a point (47.3 per cent), and then becomes a disincentive for FDI. This suggests that those firms which are overdependent on export markets may choose to adjust their market orientation before venturing abroad. In fact, when the domestic currency appreciates, the profit margin from domestic sales gains relative to exports if the firm is a price taker in both markets. The presence of the industry dummy, which represents active FDI sectors, does not suppress the significance of these variables.

When FDI in high-wage countries is distinguished from that in low-wage countries, however, the results are different. While firm size, foreign ownership and the industry dummy remain important determinants of direct investment in high-wage countries, export share ceases to be relevant. Furthermore, some variables designed to capture the intangible assets of firms become statistically significant when the industry dummy is absent. Average wage rate, R&D intensity and average growth rate in the previous three years contribute positively to investment in high-wage countries. All three variables become statistically insignificant, however, when the industry dummy is present. In a result similar to that of Horst (1972), industry characteristics are found to be more important than firm characteristics in determining FDI. Labour intensity (LAB) remains an insignificant factor for FDI in high-wage countries.

In contrast, all three variables representing the firm's intangible assets were found to be irrelevant to FDI in low-wage countries. Export share (EX and EXS) does appear to be an important determinant of FDI, however. To some extent firms that depend on the export market are more inclined to invest in low-wage countries. Beyond a certain point (48.7 per cent), though, this export dependency seems to provide an incentive for market reorientation rather than FDI. Firm size continues to contribute positively to FDI in low-wage countries.

While the industry dummy is significant for FDI in low-wage countries, its presence does not suppress the influence of other factors, especially export share. This suggests that export dependency is not industry-specific. In fact, although the plastics and electronics industries are export oriented and active in FDI, there are other industries (for example, textiles) that are equally export oriented but not particularly active in FDI. Therefore, while the intangible asset which is exploitable in high-wage countries tends to be concentrated in certain industries, there are also firms in the same industries that invest in low-wage countries. Whether they are exploiting the same intangible asset remains to be studied. Since the only explanatory variables that are significant in the case of low-wage countries but insignificant in the case of high-wage countries are EX and EXS, the advantage that underlies FDI in low-wage countries may be related to a firm's ability to export.

In carrying out the single equation analysis, the firm's decision to invest in a high-wage or low-wage country was considered to be made independently. In fact, though, the decision to invest in a high-wage country may depend on whether low-wage countries present a better alternative, or whether the firm in question has the managerial capacity to handle another investment project after deciding that low-wage countries are to be the priority investment destination. In other words, whether to invest in a high-wage or low-wage country is likely to be simultaneously determined. We therefore conducted a bivariate PROBIT analysis on these choices using the same set of explanatory variables (Table 12.4).

It can be seen from the table that the results are essentially the same as those for the single equation PROBIT analysis. Only minor variations in coefficient estimates and asymptotic t-statistics are observed. We can therefore conclude that there are different sets of determinants for FDI in high-wage and low-wage countries, implying that investment in each is driven by different forces. In particular, the intangible asset hypothesis seems to be more powerful in interpreting Taiwan's direct investment in high-wage than in low-wage countries. Since the degree of export dependency does not influence Taiwan's FDI in high-wage countries, we may consider Taiwan's investment in these countries to be mainly for the purpose of expanding markets. On the other hand, direct investment in low-wage countries is correlated with export dependency. All indicators of the intangible asset fail to exhibit a significant impact on investment, suggesting that direct investment in low-wage countries is aimed mainly at cutting production costs and restoring competitiveness in the export market. Investment in both country types exhibits an industry bias, indicating that some industries,

Table 12.4   Bivariate PROBIT estimates of FDI

Explanatory variable	High-wage countries				Low-wage countries			
Constant	-2.023**	(5.0)	-2.151**	(5.1)	-1.211**	(3.6)	-1.217**	(3.7)
SALE	0.116**	(3.5)	0.124**	(3.5)	0.048**	(3.6)	0.042**	(3.3)
LAB	0.033	(0.2)	0.003	(0.01)	0.022	(0.2)	0.014	(0.1)
EX	0.067	(0.2)	-0.008	(0.03)	2.486**	(2.6)	2.341**	(2.5)
EXS					-2.519**	(2.4)	-2.403**	(2.2)
AWA	2.302*	(1.8)	1.977	(1.5)	-0.150	(0.1)	-0.467	(0.4)
RD	0.051*	(1.7)	7.395	(1.0)	-0.308	(0.04)	-3.053	(0.4)
GROW	0.006**	(2.1)	0.004	(1.3)	-0.001	(0.4)	-0.003	(0.8)
ROF	-1.319**	(2.6)	-1.828**	(3.1)	-0.699*	(1.8)	-0.950**	(2.5)
DIND			0.856**	(4.5)			0.548**	(3.5)

Notes: Numbers in brackets are asymptotic *t*-statistics.
      **   indicates significance at the 5 per cent level,
      *   indicates significance at the 10 per cent level.

Source: Chen, Ku and Liu's estimates.

presumably those characterised by differentiated products, are more inclined to engage in FDI than others.

FDI in high-wage and low-wage countries has two determinants in common: firm size, which is generally conducive to FDI, and foreign ownership, which is not.

The effect of FDI on performance

Knowing that different types of firms invest in different types of countries with different motivations, we thought it would be of interest to examine how investment affects performance. We therefore traced the performance of the set of firms investigated above; the results are summarised in Table 12.5. We examined four indicators of performance: sales, profit, exports and employment. Since quite a few firms in our sample failed to make the top-firm rankings in 1992, our analysis may be subject to a selection bias in favour of firms that performed well in terms of sales. The bias is particularly serious for the group of firms that did not engage in FDI at all in 1986–91, for out of 362 firms in this group, only 266 made the 1992 rankings. The bias for other groups is relatively minor.

Sales

It can be seen from the table that in 1986 (the year in which sales were used to measure firm size in the regression analysis), firms that did not make any direct investment

Table 12.5 **Effect of FDI on performance, 1986 and 1992 (sales: NT$ million; profit: NT$ million; exports: US$ million; employment: no. of persons)**

	No FDI	Investment in high-wage countries only	Investment in low-wage countries only	Investment in both
Sales				
1986	1,772	4,964	2,418	4,828
1992	2,889	7,325	3,440	7,508
Change (%)	63.0	47.6	42.3	55.5
Sample size	266	30	52	26
Profit				
1986	125	530	211	373
1992	209	817	203	551
Change (%)	67.2	54.2	-3.8	47.7
Sample size	215	29	47	26
Exports				
1986	14.1	33.3	21.4	37.3
1992	24.1	79.5	39.6	88.8
Change (%)	70.9	138.7	85.1	138.1
Sample size	264	29	59	28
Employment				
1986	676	1,736	1,227	2,364
1992	654	2,006	1,150	2,201
Change (%)	-3.3	15.6	-6.3	-6.9
Sample size	266	30	52	26

Note: 1986 and 1992 levels are sample means; change (%) is percentage change in sample means from 1986 to 1992.

Source: Chen, Ku and Liu's estimates.

abroad had the lowest average sales, NT$1,772 million. This group was followed by firms that invested only in low-wage countries. The remaining firms, which invested either in high-wage countries only or in both country types, recorded higher levels of sales revenue. In other words, a size difference is evident between firms investing in high-wage and in low-wage countries. While large firm size is not conducive to all FDI, only the largest firms invested in high-wage countries. If we compare sales revenue in 1992 with that in 1986, it can be seen that the ranking of the groups does not change; however, firms that did not invest overseas had the highest growth rate (63 per cent). This group was followed by firms investing in both regions (55.5 per cent), those investing in high-wage countries (47.6 per cent) and those investing in low-wage

271

countries (42.3 per cent). These differences are not statistically significant, however, owing to large variations between the samples.

Profit

Firms that invested in high-wage countries not only had the highest profit levels (NT$530 million), they also had the highest profit rate (10.7 per cent, calculated by dividing average profit by average sales). The other three groups recorded similar, if slightly lower, profit rates. From 1986 to 1992, all groups except firms investing in low-wage countries experienced an increase in average profits. The group investing in high-wage countries maintained the top position at 11.2 per cent. The group investing in low-wage countries had the lowest profit rate, 5.9 per cent, while the profit rates of the other two groups remained virtually unchanged. The results reinforce the notion that firms investing in high-wage countries are the most profitable and probably enjoy some monopoly rent derived from their intangible assets. Firms investing in low-wage countries are more likely to be under competitive pressure. Despite their efforts to invest abroad, most could not arrest the decline occurring in their profits. Again, this suggests that these firms may have been fighting for their survival.

Exports

The group of firms investing in both high-wage and low-wage countries had the highest level of exports (US$37.3 million). However, the groups that invested in low-wage countries had the highest export ratios. Non-investing firms were at the bottom in terms of both export value and export ratio. Note that although export dependency is shown to be unimportant in determining FDI in high-wage countries, firms that did invest in these countries had an average export ratio of 23.8 per cent. This group also recorded the highest growth of exports: a jump of 138.7 per cent in value from 1986 to 1992. A similar growth rate was observed for firms investing in both high-wage and low-wage countries. Firms investing in low-wage countries and those remaining at home had lower rates of growth. This reinforces the view that direct investment in high-wage countries is undertaken as a means to expand markets. The evidence also suggests that this effort has paid off.

Employment

Employment is another popular indicator of firm size. The employment rankings of the four groups of firms were similar to their sales rankings. Turnover per employee, however, reveals a completely different picture. Turnover per employee was NT$2.86 million and NT$2.62 million respectively for firms investing in high-wage countries and non-investors. By comparison, turnover per employee was NT$1.97 million for firms investing in low-wage countries and NT$2.04 million for those investing in both high-wage and low-wage countries. In other words, although labour intensity does not systematically affect the decision to invest in low-wage countries, firms investing in these countries do have lower per capita turnover.

Interestingly, from 1986 to 1992 employment increased only in the firms that invested in high-wage countries. All other groups experienced a decline in employment of 3–6 per cent. This seems to suggest that only FDI purely for the purpose of expanding markets will lead to an increase in employment at home. All firms underwent a degree of restructuring, whether they invested abroad or not. This can be seen by examining turnover per employee. Turnover per employee increased from NT$2.62 to NT$4.42 million in the case of non-investors, surpassing that of firms investing exclusively in high-wage countries. Turnover per employee for the latter group increased only modestly, from NT$2.86 to NT$3.65 million. In firms that invested only in low-wage countries, turnover per employee increased from NT$1.97 to NT$2.99 million, another impressive performance. If restructuring is measured by per capita turnover, then firms investing in high-wage countries underwent the smallest degree of restructuring. Because of their profitability, they could probably afford not to restructure. Meanwhile, firms that did not seek FDI underwent the most intensive restructuring, presumably by investing in automation and other areas that upgrade labour performance.

In sum, we observed substantial differences between firms in profitability, export performance and per capita turnover. Firms investing in high-wage countries were the most profitable and the most capable of expanding their exports, but the least successful at enhancing per capita turnover. Firms investing in low-wage countries experienced a fall in profit and employment, but their per capita turnover at home improved substantially.

Conclusion

The chapter compared Taiwan's overseas investment in high-wage and low-wage countries. We found that investment in the two types of countries was driven by different factors, and was therefore designed for different purposes. Firms that possessed greater human capital, spent more on R&D and grew more rapidly were more likely to invest in high-wage countries with the intention of further expanding their markets; to some extent, firms that depended more on the export market for their revenue were more inclined to invest in low-wage countries in search of cheap labour. This seems to suggest that market-oriented FDI differs from labour-related FDI in terms of the intangible assets that firms seek to exploit overseas.

While firm size was conducive to both types of FDI, it was especially important for investment in high-wage countries. In general, firms investing in high-wage countries were larger than those investing in low-wage countries, in terms both of sales and employment. This group of firms was also more capable of maintaining its profitability and expanding its export markets after making such an investment. Firms investing in low-wage countries experienced a decline in profit and employment after engaging in FDI. This suggests that market-oriented FDI is an aggressive act aimed at creating monopoly rent and that labour-related FDI is a defensive act aimed at protecting export markets.

References

Aharoni, Y. 1966, *The Foreign Investment Decision Process*, Cambridge, MA: Graduate School of Business Administration, Harvard University.

Buckley, Peter 1982, 'The Role of Exporting in the Market Servicing Policies of Multinational Manufacturing Enterprises: Theoretical and Empirical Perspectives', in M.R. Czinkota and G. Tesar (eds), *Export Management: An International Context*, New York: Praeger.

Caves, Richard 1971, 'International Corporations: The Industrial Economics of Foreign Investment', *Economica*, 38, February, pp. 1–27.

_____ 1974, 'Causes of Direct Investment: Foreign Firms' Shares in Canadian and United Kingdom Manufacturing Industries', *Review of Economics and Statistics*, 56, pp. 279–93.

CEPD (Council for Economic Planning and Development) 1992, Tui Wai Tou tzu Cheng che Ping ku Pao kao [A Study of Taiwan's Foreign Direct Investment], Unpublished project report, Taiwan.

Chen, Tain-Jy 1992, 'Determinants of Taiwan's Direct Foreign Investment', *Journal of Development Economics*, 39, pp. 397–407.

China Credit Information Service 1987, *The Largest Corporations in the Republic of China 1987*, Taipei: China Credit Information Service.

Helpman, Elhanan 1984, 'A Simple Theory of International Trade with Multinational Corporations', *Journal of Political Economy*, 92, pp. 451–71.

Horst, Thomas 1972, 'Firm and Industry Determinants of the Decision to Invest Abroad: An Empirical Study', *Review of Economics and Statistics*, 54, pp. 258–66.

Hymer, Stephen 1976, *The International Operations of National Firms: A Study of Direct Foreign Investment*, Cambridge, MA: MIT Press.

Kojima, Kiyoshi 1973, 'A Macroeconomic Approach to Foreign Direct Investment', *Hitotsubashi Journal of Economics*, 14, pp. 1–21.

Mason, Hal 1980, 'A Comment on Professor Kojima's Japanese Type Versus American Type of Technology Transfer', *Hitotsubashi Journal of Economics*, 20, pp. 42–52.

Vernon, Raymond 1966, 'International Investment and International Trade in the Product Cycle', *Quarterly Journal of Economics*, 80, pp. 190–207.

Wells, Louis 1983, *Third World Multinationals*, Cambridge, MA: MIT Press.

13   Summary of discussion ———

Gordon de Brouwer

The discussion at the Twenty-First Pacific Trade and Development Conference on corporate links and foreign direct investment (FDI) in Asia and the Pacific echoed the main analytical threads of the conference: detailed and specific analysis of the nature and behaviour of the multinational enterprise, and more general analysis of the institutional and cultural environment in which the multinational enterprise operates.

The firm as actor

In discussing the nature and behaviour of the international firm, the participants critically assessed the theoretical tools available for analysis and reviewed recent developments in firm behaviour and strategies, including technological transfer, and trade and investment linkages.

Theories of the multinational firm

The conference was presented with a number of theoretical tools with which to explain the multinational firm. Richard E. Caves used a dynamic transaction cost theory of the firm to explain foreign investment, arguing that multinational firms have proprietary assets from which they seek to gain rents by producing and selling in a variety of markets, with the success of the firm described by a distribution of outcomes. Peter A. Petri drew on 'new economic geography' to describe the clustering of economic activity in countries or regions, highlighting the importance of factor mobility and exploitable economies of scale. Gary Hamilton used the economic–sociological framework of 'embedded networks' to stress the importance of networks and institutional factors in international business activity. Denis F. Simon and Yongwook Jun also used the framework of networks, while Motoshige Itoh and Tain-Jy Chen drew on comparative advantage theory. The interaction of these competing and complementary paradigms of multinational firm behaviour underlay much of the discussion at the conference.

275

A common element in the discussion was the focus on dynamics, and on the limitations of static analysis. Shujiro Urata asserted that it was inappropriate to use static analysis to describe and analyse dynamic processes. By way of example, Caves pointed out that static theory predicts that a reduction in trade barriers should lead to less foreign investment and more exports, which is not consistent with the boost to both foreign investment and exports that occurred with the reduction of barriers within the European Union.

Alan E. Bollard took this further, arguing that the evolution of the firm is not just 'process dynamics' — in which firms are born, grow, stabilise, contract and die — but also a matter of 'biological dynamics': firms metamorphose and adapt to changes in their environment; they form and re-form relationships (which may be symbiotic or parasitic); and their genetic composition alters over time. In this sense they are like forests, with ecological interaction taking place not just within each forest but between them as well. The behaviour of the firm should not, then, be treated as endogenous to the firm's perception of its proprietary assets and to past and current operating environments in home and host countries. In this respect, according to Bollard, the economics literature lags behind that on business management.

In spite of the common focus on dynamics, there was debate about the appropriateness and significance of some of these analytical tools. For example, while Wendy Dobson found the new economic geography debate attractive, Chia Siow Yue and H. Edward English queried its value, arguing that it did not take sufficient account of comparative advantage. While Chia agreed with Dobson, she also noted that many of the clusters in the United States occurred by historical accident. English argued that the crux of investment and trade lies in dynamic comparative advantage, and that clustering does not help to explain investment and trade in the resource sector. He also criticised the new economic geography for not distinguishing between large and small countries. Petri responded that new economic geography did not supplant comparative advantage theory; rather, it highlighted the fact that factor mobility makes a difference to the economic outcome, and that mobility in turn depends on technology, defined by Petri as production, design and marketing. Once clusters form, they have a life of their own. In this sense, the size of the country is paramount since clustering tends to occur in larger and more centrally located countries.

Mari Pangestu took issue with the concepts of 'networks' and 'international engagement' used by Simon and Jun, arguing that they are not really 'theories' at all. Pangestu argued that the basic concept underlying the existence of business networks and linkages is dynamic comparative advantage. Caves noted that, according to the predictions of Simon and Jun's network model, trade by subsidiaries should be more evident in industries with complex marketing or production processes. The network model is, however, only a sufficient rather than a necessary explanation of this phenomenon. It may be rather that transaction costs have fallen and the profitability of such trade has risen, or that demand has become more homogeneous in markets over time, or that markets have matured and traded goods have become more differentiated, or that governments have liberalised markets such that it no longer benefits a parent company which isolates its subsidiary to do so. The implication is that the facts are consistent with a number of theories, and so the burden of proof that one theory is *the* theory is heavy. All theories have some limitations and are difficult to apply universally. No wonder, then, that Bollard described established multinational enterprise theory as highly eclectic and hybrid.

More generally, Kiyoshi Kojima cautioned against the narrow application of theory. He pointed out by way of example that although investment in Korea may initially have been driven by relatively low unit labour costs, this advantage had been well and truly lost, even though recently one did see much divestment occurring. Simplistic or rigid views were, he maintained, inappropriate. Similarly, Farid Harianto and Caves found Chen's low-wage/high-wage categorisation of FDI recipients as the tool for distinguishing between cost-based defensive investment and market-expanding strategic investment oversimplistic. A firm that invests in a low-wage country may, after all, be attempting to enhance its proprietary assets. Hugh Patrick argued that if wages are a key factor in the decision to invest, then the capital–labour ratio in the host country should be statistically significant in investment regression. This was not the case in Chen's statistical analysis, possibly due to overaggregation.

Kojima also warned that theory should not be applied indiscriminately or without due regard to subject matter. He took as an example the new geographic explanation of trade and investment, which focuses on the reduced cost of cross-border trade and the increased mobility of productive capital as underpinning the development of clusters in Asia. Kojima concluded that the language of the debate fitted better with investment in manufactures than investment in services, even though the latter in fact forms the vast bulk of Japanese FDI. He wondered whether theory and analysis would change if the focus was more explicitly on services. Kojima also found rather too simple the argument that Japanese investment in electronics shifted to Asia just because labour there was cheap and close at hand. The true explanation had more to do, he felt, with manufacturers seeking to evade trade barriers in the United States and the European Union.

Caves argued that the failure of a multinational firm may be the result not of poor corporate strategy, but of a 'bad draw' from the distribution of outcomes. Urata noted that while the exit from a market of a multinational enterprise may be a bad draw for the firm involved, this is not necessarily the case for the host country. If production continues and ownership is transferred, transfer of technology and domestic control may increase, and productivity may be boosted by the change in management. Even if the operation is closed down, a developed site remains to be used by others and the local skill level has been enhanced. From the point of view of the firm, Patrick wondered whether the view of random outcomes is relevant: even if the outcome is in general random, individual firms do not regard their success or failure as driven by chance but believe that they have information or proprietary assets which alter either the distribution or their place in it.

More fundamentally, Urata argued that if the outcome for the multinational enterprise were simply random, then analysis of multinational enterprises would become inherently uninteresting. While agreeing that there are random or unexplained elements, Urata said that there is also much which explains the outcome for the firm, such as the strategies it pursues with respect to the structuring of its internal and external networks, level of local procurement, and international division of labour. The discussion returned repeatedly to these factors as the means by which the multinational enterprise re-creates itself in the face of a changing environment. As production and distribution processes become more complex and disaggregated, the possibilities for new strategies and structures are enhanced for the firm.

Simon and Jun stated that technological change had exerted tremendous pressure on Japanese multinationals to focus on time to market, quality and customisation, and to engage constructively with their competitors through the formation of business networks. Dennis J. Encarnation pointed out that North American and European firms were subject to the same forces. Simon agreed, saying that the issue for all firms is how fast they can generate proprietary assets and exploit them. Petri said that the speed of technological change is such that agreements now tend to be of shorter duration and greater variety. Patrick thought that the development of networks and the expansion of interfirm and intrafirm links may lead to less foreign investment. He referred to the case of the US firm, Nike, which purchases directly from overseas suppliers instead of itself investing and producing. Simon agreed again, noting that it was more difficult to capture the true extent of economic influence if statistics on trade and investment were not able to account for this type of expansion.

Discussion of the expansion of networks brought a number of policy issues to the fore. Pangestu said that it is important to understand that the decision to invest in a particular sector is influenced more by the host country's technological capability and level of labour skills than its cost of labour. She also argued that global specialisation means that a country cannot specialise in everything, while English noted that the smaller a country is, the easier it is to identify its dynamic comparative advantage. Bollard and Urata questioned whether the formation of networks was a euphemism for collusion and hence causes a reduction in consumer welfare. Jun thought consumers benefited from the price reductions and greater product mix offered by networks, while Patrick regarded the key issue as the degree of competition in final consumer markets.

The breaking up of the home country's production and distribution processes and the potential for hollowing out also received attention. Participants tended to the view that hollowing out is not a problem for Asian economies. Leonard Cheng noted that in Hong Kong and Japan the shift of production processes offshore had been accompanied by an expansion of the high-wage services sector; hollowing out in these countries had in fact been an enriching process. He contrasted this to the US experience, where labour was forced into low-wage, service sector employment. Simon asserted that Japanese policy makers were not prepared to tolerate the kind of hollowing out that had occurred in the United States. Cheng also emphasised that the part of the production process kept onshore generally had high value-added, but he cautioned that the loss of that part of production which is valuable to goodwill and control does present a problem for the multinational firm since this places at risk its ability to extract rents. Peter Drysdale argued that the process of international production was motivated by pursuing rents, and so was intrinsically enriching. He queried whether the consensus in Japan that internationalised production enhances domestic living standards will hold in the face of domestic recession coupled with an extremely rapid movement offshore of production in key sectors, such as electronics and automobiles.

Technology transfer

Mingsarn Kaosa-ard noted that the debate on technology transfer had changed considerably over the past few decades. In the 1960s, for example, discussion had followed neoclassical lines in focusing on the appropriate technology required for labour-intensive developing countries. In the 1970s the issue was whether multinational enterprises were expropriating rents without providing the spin-off benefit of technology transfer. By the end of the 1980s, debate had shifted to addressing the most effective mechanism for technology transfer. The more difficult policy questions arose, she thought, in the current macroeconomic debate between those who propose free market policies and those who propose structural or industrial policies as the best means to achieve growth. Kaosa-ard, P.K. Lau and Akira Kohsaka emphasised that it is vital for policy makers to be aware of the costs of industrial policies, of what they can expect to gain from the process, and to whom they expect the gains to accrue. Kohsaka said that the most crucial determinant of FDI in the late 1980s was international factors, adding that whether FDI can generate positive net transfers to host countries is not necessarily evident because of low domestic value-added in some industries. Juan J. Palacios, however, argued that host countries should not adopt a purely passive role in technology transfer, as occurs in Mexico, but should rather guide technological upgrading through government policies and development plans, as is the case in Malaysia. He warned against extremes while making the case for the development of an indigenous capacity.

Patrick, Kaosa-ard, Harianto and Carlo Filippini stressed that the quality of domestic human resources affects the extent of the gains to be made from technology transfer. Filippini argued that rising levels of education in developing countries force these countries to compete in new spheres (as they seek to attract investment which fits with their enhanced education/skill levels), and that this might put downward pressure on wages. Filippini and Giovanni Capannelli thought that the absorptive capacity of the host country is important in assessing the value of technology transfer, while Filippini argued that technology now changes so rapidly that some technologies may be too advanced for developing economies to absorb for rather a long time. Cheng rejected the idea of some technologies being more appropriate than others for a developing country as an inherently static concept that ignored training and on-the-job learning. Patrick and Hal Hill regarded the process of technology transfer as dynamic and containing the seeds of a variety of spin-offs for growth.

Kaosa-ard questioned the suitability of the electronics industry as a subject for analysis, given that it is one in which technology transfer is *not* an issue: the industry is export-oriented and foreign investors must transfer technology to remain competitive. She thought the more controversial aspects of technology transfer might better be gauged by examining other less export-oriented industries. Palacios rejected this on the grounds that the product mix in the electronics industry is highly diversified. He said that it is precisely MNE-based, high-tech industries like electronics that are most relevant for assessing technology transfer given the significant effects the transfer has on host country industrial development. Urata also took issue with Kaosa-ard, arguing that technology transfer is better judged as occurring when control of operations is passed to local management. He implied that import-competing rather than export-oriented industries tend to be those with the greatest transfer of technology. Lau bemoaned the inadequate definition of 'technology transfer'.

Trade and foreign investment

The relationship between foreign investment and trade featured in the debate. Petri pointed to the dynamic complementarity of trade and foreign investment, arguing that they are substitutes only when viewed narrowly on a product or static basis. Dobson appreciated Petri's econometric work, although she pointed out that the composition of his sample was unclear. Pangestu wondered whether the relationship between investment and trade had in fact changed during the 1980s, speculating that before deregulation in the mid 1980s they may have been more like substitutes. Demonstrating this could, she thought, make it easier for economists to argue the advantages of open trading systems. Petri agreed that the trade and investment nexus is dynamic and changing over time.

Lee Tsao Yuan regarded the snapshot provided by Itoh and Jun Shibata of Japanese investment in the Malaysian electronics industry as a micro example of how foreign investment generates trade. Encarnation and Petri pointed out, however, that Malaysia's exports to Japan have in fact been declining over time, while the proportion of domestic Malaysian sales has been increasing. Capannelli thought that location theory is relevant in explaining the link between investment and trade, with home and host country policies significantly influencing the outcome.

An associated issue was whether it is necessary for countries to maintain a balance between investment inflows and outflows. Petri and Patrick thought that there was not a case for policy to be concerned with balance on economic grounds. Patrick noted that Stephen Hymer had argued in the 1960s in *The International Operations of National Firms: A Study of Direct Foreign Investment* (1976, Cambridge, MA: MIT Press) that multinational enterprises in globally oligopolistic industries invested in each other's markets in order to send signals to, punish and persuade other firms. The current equivalent is that the multinational enterprise invests in the countries of its competitors in order to monitor technological innovations and business strategies. The relative absence of fresh inflows of inward foreign investment in Japan therefore suggests a diminution of the competitiveness of non-Japanese firms. Patrick thought that this line of argument was not particularly important in the case of Japan, and that the key motivation for balance was political. Mark Mason agreed.

With respect to the issue of FDI in Japan, Patrick thought Japan an unsuitable model for assessing FDI policy in general. Even though Japan restricted inward FDI for much of the postwar period, it had substantial industrial and human capital and its firms were able to unbundle the technological advantages associated with FDI by using the international market place and restrictive government policies. In recent years the situation has changed: Japanese firms are at the frontier of technology, firms are less willing to sell their technology, and high domestic labour and property costs have made FDI in Japanese manufacturing unviable. Simon also argued that Japan uses its outward FDI as a mechanism for technology transfer, though some countries, such as South Korea and China, remain dissatisfied with the pace and depth of Japanese technology exports, whether through licensing or FDI.

Mason, Ryuhei Wakasugi, Patrick, Itoh and Encarnation agreed that while the legacies of past policies have persistent effects, change in Japan will eventually occur since opportunities for profitable investment do exist, particularly in the wholesale and retail sectors and in the financial services industry. Noting that there was no surge in FDI following the liberalisation of the Japanese trading system in the 1980s, Soogil Young said that this indicated the success of the Japanese policy of encouraging domestic industry and deferring liberalisation until domestic firms had become competitive and entrenched. Jun and Vladimir Yakubovsky were more pessimistic about the future, saying that the scope for inward investment is limited since Japanese firms have less need for foreign technology and capital. Drysdale and Patrick cautioned against treating Japan as an isolated case: chauvinism and barriers to investment are present in most countries. Drysdale noted that the concept of the firm as a non-political actor is inappropriate as a basis for theorising about the political economy of the multinational enterprise and its success or failure. The capacity to handle unfamiliar political territory had been important to the success of individual firms. Simon pointed out that the foreign firms which are successful in Japan tend not to broadcast their success, and so the public perception of the foreign penetration of the Japanese market and economy can be distorted.

The firm and its environment

The role of government

The discussion generally tended to the view that governments have played an important, but not always benevolent, role in East Asia's economic growth. The significance of government lies in creating the legal framework for private behaviour and for making interventions market conforming.

It was generally accepted that governments perform a fundamental role in the economy and exert pervasive effects on the choices and actions of private agents. As argued by Caves, the rents that multinational firms attempt to extract on the basis of their proprietary assets are at the hazard of how governments structure taxes and subsidies, devise contract law and determine general policy. Lawrence B. Krause wondered whether and to what extent government support was necessary to develop the multinational enterprise's proprietary assets. Ippei Yamazawa asserted that the policies of both the home and host countries are relevant, and Pangestu and Chia provided an example. There is growing intraindustry and intrafirm trade in electronic components and finished goods between Singapore and Indonesia, reflecting not only the competitive advantages of the two countries but also government policy to promote Singapore as a regional procurement centre. Pangestu argued that the trade link in this case rests not so much on natural comparative advantage as on particular government policies. Simon ascribed the involvement of Taiwan's firms in Subic Bay to that government's policy of strengthening its diplomatic relations with the Philippines. Mason's and Wakasugi's analyses of Japan's relatively low levels of inward foreign investment are also testimony to the importance of government. In the case of Japan, however, the host government created obstacles to *impede* FDI from abroad. Looked at more generally, Urata suggested that location theory is more useful than transaction cost theory in explaining the role of government in determining the behaviour of the multinational firm.

Ross Garnaut argued that confidence in the international trading system is a key public good provided by governments. He took as his examples the explosion of China's trade after the signing of the Sino–UK agreement in 1984, and the jump in FDI in Guangdong province after Deng Xiaoping's visit to the region in 1992. Both events highlighted the importance of political stability and created confidence in public institutions and policy. The public good exists and has meaning precisely because it facilitates the operation of the market.

Indeed, as Young emphasised, the key to Asia's success has been that government policy has been either pro-market or market conforming. Hill and Bollard noted that both the level of intervention and role played by government have changed over time. In the 1970s, for example, foreign investment took place behind high tariff walls and took the form of joint ventures with public enterprises. The general view held by governments at the time towards foreign investment was distrust and diffidence. This can be contrasted with the outward-looking, market-oriented policies that developed in the 1980s and which predominate today.

The absence of good governance does not necessarily preclude economic develop-ment, but it can retard the process, especially over the longer term. The example referred to by Caves, Garnaut and Hamilton was the development of private contrac-tual enforcement mechanisms in China. The strength of the family and the importance of *guanxi* (personal and business connections) in China can be regarded as market-based solutions designed to overcome the problems of trust and retaliation associated with contracting in a society that has only limited enforcement of property and contractual rights. Garnaut argued that the scope and operation of private legal structures are limited; to paraphrase Lee Kuan Yew, for FDI by non-Chinese foreigners to expand further, a credible formal system of commercial law must develop.

The role assumed by government is not always so beneficent, and, as Patrick argued, considerable impediments to trade and investment in the region still remain, particularly in agriculture and manufacturing. Existing policies continue to distort market outcomes and reduce welfare, as evidenced by low foreign investment in the Japanese services sector, for example. Garnaut said that, while it has little direct control over small and medium sized enterprises, the Taiwanese government enjoys considerable influence over the operation of large firms. It has used this power to limit investment by firms in mainland China, as in the case of Formosa Plastic. (Chen, however, disputed the pervasiveness and effectiveness of this policy.) Similarly, the labour-intensive end of Hong Kong manufacturing has shifted to southern China, with the partial exception of textiles, which has remained in Hong Kong only to avoid violating US quotas. Government policies can also be inconsistent and give misleading signals to the market. C.H. Kwan cited the example of MITI, which, while encouraging the relocation of excess capacity in the Japanese petrochemicals industry to China, is at the same time threatening to impose antidumping measures on Chinese textile exporters. Krause argued that if changes in the structure or control of the firm boost productivity, as proposed by Caves, then it is important that financial markets be developed and fully functioning. There was, Krause said, scope for improvements in policy in this respect in Korea and Japan.

Young highlighted the need for a multilateral or regional investment agreement. While concurring, Pangestu argued that such an agreement should not be in a binding legalistic form but rather a set of principles towards which countries in the region could progress. Yamazawa noted that there was already a voluntary investment code on APEC's agenda, which he thought would be implemented. Florian A. Alburo, in commenting on the trade-related investment measures in the Uruguay Round, argued that quick action on imperfect agreements was preferable to slow implementation of perfect agreements. Both Alburo and Krause questioned the applicability of GATT rules when much trade is 'managed'. Alburo suggested that the promotion of competition and openness was the key to improving national welfare and resolving conflict on trade and investment related issues.

Alburo, Patrick and Young also pointed out that even if a policy is 'right', it has little chance of success if government bureaucracies are opposed to reform — especially in the lower echelons where policies are actually implemented. Young argued that the only way to overcome this problem is to reduce the size of the bureaucracy. Sir Frank Holmes pointed out that bureaucracies are not always opposed to reform; in New Zealand, for example, reform policies were strongly supported by the public service.

The discussants emphasised that government action and policy do not occur in a vacuum, but are themselves intimately and dynamically linked to and affected by market forces. The pressure on ASEAN countries to liberalise foreign investment rules, for instance, is largely market-driven as governments seek to ensure that their economies remain internationally competitive as a location for foreign investment.

Culture, Chinese subregional integration and implications for Asia

Yun-Wing Sung, Mee-Kau Nyaw, Hamilton and others argued that a common language and culture, derived from geographical proximity, underpins the integration of Hong Kong and South China. But the extent to which culture is more generally important in explaining East Asian corporate structure and behaviour was the subject of considerable debate.

Lee identified an increasing recognition that Asians do things differently; indeed, that there may be peculiarly Asian values and forms of capitalism and democracy. Given the relative economic performance of East and West, some have argued that the East Asian way is superior. According to Lee, however, the evidence is far from unambiguous. For example, the sustained and strong growth of East Asia is consistent both with the proposition that Asian business structures perform well and with the standard prediction that growth results from sound fiscal policy and high savings. Similarly, she noted that business networks in Asia are of diverse types.

Overall, participants were circumspect about the role of cultural factors. Caves, Hamilton, Nyaw, Garnaut and others argued that Asian forms of organisation and behaviour are determined by the same sorts of forces and principles that determine organisation and behaviour elsewhere. Caves, for example, said that the emphasis on family and *guanxi* in Chinese organisation derives from the fact that, in the absence of official enforcement of contracts, these are natural internal governance mechanisms. There is an underlying cohesive logic to relations regardless of culture, though culture is important in determining the particular form of the relation.

This was analysed further. Patrick argued that while the family may be important as an economic grouping in China, family-based big business groups are also typical of developing economies and were common in the earlier stages of development in Europe and North America. In discussing the role of networks of Overseas Chinese, Patrick and Chia argued that the existence of minority groups and discrimination of itself tends to engender minority-based networks. As the environment in which these groups operate changes, so does the form of the organisation.

While agreeing with the thrust of this, Bollard warned that there is much in the behaviour and performance of a firm that is firm- or entrepreneur-specific, although he, Sung and Chia thought that this was less relevant in the case of multinational enterprises. Bollard argued that holistic and encompassing theories of the firm are, of their very nature, unable to capture the richness and dynamism of firm behaviour. This leaves a proper role for regional and cultural analysis.

Some participants also took exception to generalisations about certain groups. Nyaw challenged generalisations made about the Chinese, arguing that there are significant regional differences between Chinese on the mainland as well as among Overseas Chinese between and within countries. Garnaut broadened the scope of the discussion, challenging the idea that there is a single Asia and a single West. He pointed out that elements of structure and corporate culture in banks in Germany and Japan, for example, have more in common than corresponding elements in Germany and the United States. Jun and Simon's analysis of Japanese corporations was questioned on similar grounds. Encarnation argued that it is not just Japanese firms that are undergoing internal transformations, forming networks or engaging in local procurement. North American and European firms are also seeking such transformations, but little is done to compare these groups. He cautioned against the premature use of regional or country labels. While Simon agreed, he also emphasised that network building by Japanese companies was proceeding at a much faster and more comprehensive pace.

Nyaw warned against naivety in analysing the motives of overseas Chinese in investing in mainland China: often they invest not in their home town but in other towns; they place more importance on good relations with local party officials than on family connections; and they are generally motivated more by money than by altruism. Kaosa-ard also argued that the importance of the Overseas Chinese network is overstated, drawing on the example of the Chinese in Thailand. She said that fewer and fewer Thais of Chinese origin speak or read Chinese, and that English is the language of international business. She argued that much of the Chinese investment in Thailand — such as that by the Hong Kong firm, Honeywell — has nothing whatsoever to do with the fact that there are ethnic Chinese there. She also commented that some people prefer Japanese to Chinese connections because, even if Japanese firms are skilful at negotiating contracts which are advantageous to them, they tend also to be more reliable and resilient than Chinese firms.

Chia and Bollard recognised that the form and behaviour of the firm is dynamic, and that there may be a tendency for national differences to become smaller as markets become more global. For example, as capital integration increases throughout East Asia and as Asian firms make greater use of share markets, standard Western forms of organisation, such as the separation of ownership and control, will tend to dominate. Asian forms are, then, changing.

A recurring topic in the discussion of common culture was the subregional integration of the three Chinas, a process described by Garnaut as the biggest story in regional economic integration of the past decade. While Sung provided substantial detail on the integration of mainland China, Hong Kong and Macau, and Taiwan, stressing the importance of common language and geographical proximity, the discussion brought forward additional information. Garnaut pointed out that Chinese statistics tend to understate income and hence the economic importance of regions and the scale of integration. Estimates of consumption patterns in Guangdong indicate the region has a per capita income of about US$2,000. This is three times the official figure, and places Guangdong higher than Hong Kong on the scale of total income. Zhu Naixiao also highlighted the extent of monetary integration between Hong Kong and Guangdong, with both currencies circulating in each area. Patrick warned that trade statistics overstate the degree of integration because they are based on sales rather than domestic value-added; much of the trade between Hong Kong and Guangdong is just a shuffling between production processes. Simon pointed out that a significant amount of Hong Kong investment in China is in fact investment from the mainland redirected through Hong Kong to take advantage of tax benefits.

Chinese subregional integration has important implications for policy. Garnaut used the term 'market integration' to describe the market-driven integration process in China. He contrasted this with government-driven processes such as the European Union and NAFTA, which he called 'institutional integration'. According to Patrick, the market-driven process works and should be encouraged to continue to do so. The more flexible goods and factor markets are, the deeper and faster is the ability of the economy to adapt to change. Garnaut agreed, saying that in response to a decline in domestic manufacturing and rising real wages, Hong Kong had been able to respecialise rapidly. Kwan argued that the governments of more mature economies should distinguish more clearly between GDP and GNP and target the latter, including net factor income earned overseas.

The process of integration was also seen as carrying seeds of tension and conflict. Simon and Chia both pointed to the deficiencies in the legal framework and conflict resolution mechanism in China. This created problems for firms in Taiwan and Hong Kong, especially with respect to intellectual property rights and contract enforcement. Sung noted that there had been many cases in which negotiations that initially took place in China were subsequently formalised in Hong Kong to ensure the rule of law. Chia observed that subregional integration may also lead to trade diversion from Hong Kong and Taiwan and to the hollowing out of domestic industry in these economies. Garnaut noted that, except for the period between the 1949 communist revolution and the start of the Cultural Revolution, Overseas Chinese and their networks had not been regarded as a threat in their adopted countries. He warned that the development of China may change this perception.

Some participants were doubtful about the wider policy relevance of Chinese subregional integration. Moktar Tamin warned that, in general, experiences in one region are not readily emulated elsewhere because there is much that is not replicable over time or space. Lee argued that the process of integration between Hong Kong and South China does not provide a primer for other countries because Hong Kong reverts to mainland Chinese control in 1997 and so does not negotiate and contract as a sovereign country. Sung agreed that the policy implications of integration are not readily applied elsewhere if Hong Kong is to be regarded, not as an autonomous entity, but as the 'Manhattan' or regional headquarters of the Pearl River Delta region. Chia stressed that Chinese subregional integration is of the South–South kind, and so cannot form a closed or exclusive system. Dobson argued that this is true of East Asian integration in general, and that greater interdependence does not imply that either the Chinese subregion or East Asia is decoupling from the rest of the world; these economies will remain dependent on North American and European markets because of their high incomes and sophisticated consumer preferences. In short, the specific policy implications of regional integration are limited to the economies directly involved.

In this respect, there was optimism about the future role of the Hong Kong economy. The putative problem of the de-industrialisation and hollowing out of the Hong Kong economy would become an internal Chinese issue after Hong Kong's economic and political integration with mainland China in 1997. Garnaut suggested that Hong Kong would in future play an increasingly important intermediary role in southern China, in step with the greater complexity and differentiation of production, goods, services and business structure in the region. Kwan thought that rapid development in China would see Hong Kong threatening Singapore's position as the procurement centre of East Asia. Steve Parker wondered whether the process of development in China could be described as a pushing back of the market frontier, from Hong Kong to Guangdong, and then in time further back into the mainland. Garnaut thought that policy formulation would follow similar lines, speculating that the increasing integration of Hong Kong and Guangdong would progressively force the central authorities to relax controls in China as a whole and adopt more market-oriented policies. He also wondered whether an easing of restrictions on labour movement would ease the decline of local manufacturing production and employment in Hong Kong, though he thought that high property prices might prevent this.

The optimism about Hong Kong's future was not shared equally by all. Simon argued that the very diversity and heterogeneity of China limits the importance of Hong Kong both as an entry point to the mainland and as an intermediary. Common language, family connections and contiguous borders may underpin the role of Hong Kong in Guangdong province, but would not extend much beyond southern China. Indeed, he argued that in Beijing and Shanghai, for example, there is resistance to Hong Kong. If the bulk of the penetration of Guangdong by Hong Kong is by small and medium sized firms for whom cultural affinity is important — as discussants thought it may be — then one would expect less penetration of the rest of mainland China to come from Hong Kong.

What, then, are the implications of Chinese subregional integration for growth and development in the Asian region? The question is important in two respects. In the first place, the development of China, with its huge population, carries with it the prospect of substantial export growth for both developed and developing East Asia. Tamin, for example, reported that detailed micro analysis of Sino-Malaysian trade predicted growth in a variety of Malaysian exports as a consequence of China's development. He also spoke of the new interaction in East Asia, whereby the NIEs and ASEAN had in turn become suppliers of FDI to China, as a welcome opportunity for deeper integration in East Asia. Min Tang hailed the development of the Singapore Industrial Park in Suzhon City in eastern China as an example of ASEAN interaction with China and as a model for FDI in developing countries. Singapore's experience in foreign investment promotion and regulations will be applied in the park. This should help to attract multinational corporations to China by creating a familiar and secure environment. It can also provide the Chinese government with a good example of how to administer investment arrangements.

Second, concern was expressed that the wave of investment into China may be occurring at the expense of investment and development in developing East Asia, particularly ASEAN countries. To illustrate this, Kwan referred to a 1993 JETRO survey of the investment intentions of 625 Japanese firms in light of the severe yen

287

appreciation. The striking and surprising result of the survey was that 60 per cent of investment by these firms was targeted for China (and about 15 per cent each for the European Union and the United States), with the general outcome holding for all industries regardless of factor intensity. The implication is that Japanese investment in China is about to boom. Kwan argued that the attractiveness of China lies not so much in its inexpensive labour and natural resources, but in its large population, rapid growth and huge potential domestic market, especially given the prospects for extended slow growth in mature markets. This suggests that current events are not so much a diversion of investment from ASEAN as an independently motivated flow into China.

Conference participants were relatively sanguine about investment diversion and the unwinding of clusters in ASEAN. Dobson reasoned that the unravelling of a cluster would be associated with actual disinvestment, such as had occurred in the US auto and electronics industries, but both she and Urata said that there was no evidence as yet of this occurring in East Asia. Much more industry-specific study needs to be done before the hypothesis of diversion can be accepted, according to Dobson. Chia said that there is limited evidence of investment diversion. In the first place, the apparent decline in new investment into ASEAN occurred *before* the wave of new investment into China. This downturn was associated with similar falls in investment in Japan and elsewhere, and was therefore more likely to be a cyclical phenomenon than a trend. Second, the data quoted by Kwan refers only to new investment — investment yet to eventuate — and not to reinvestment, which remains relatively strong. She also argued that ASEAN remains important as a platform for entry into China. The scope for investment diversion is limited while the opportunities for investment and trade creation are considerable. Moreover, Chia and Chen both noted that official Taiwanese policy favours investment in other parts of East Asia over investment in mainland China. Pangestu commented on the significant problems encountered with data on foreign investment. Taking Indonesia as the example, she noted that the apparent decline in FDI in 1993 had more to do with the fact that data are lumpy and were 'artificially' boosted by three big projects in 1992. Jun suggested that the increased interest in China of Japanese business interests is explained by the Japanese 'pack' mentality and predicted that the bandwagon effect will be shortlived. Pangestu and Chia welcomed competition from China as a discipline on ASEAN governments to implement market-conforming policy and to further liberalise domestic markets.

Chinese subregional integration was also discussed in the context of the potential for future conflict with competing business networks, especially those of Japan. Japanese networks were characterised by Jun as being highly vertically integrated, subject to bunching and follow-the-leader behaviour, focused on bilateral networks, and motivated by market share and long-term profit. Chinese networks were characterised by Hamilton as being family oriented, horizontally integrated and flexible, more amenable to multilateral networks, but concerned with maintaining control over key assets. Simon queried whether both types of network could coexist over time in their present form, since they are not fully complementary. Garnaut and Chia also noted that the development of China could create tension and unease in non-Chinese East Asia about ethnic Chinese networks. Young wondered whether the emergence of China as an economic superpower would destabilise East Asia, notably by inducing political and economic friction between China and Japan. Drysdale and Young argued that it is imperative that regional and global arrangements and organisations remain open, and that China (and Taiwan) join the World Trade Organisation. They saw the link between an open, non-discriminatory trade regime and welfare-enhancing FDI activity as being particularly important for the region. A discriminatory or preferential approach to trade policy, with rules of origin and other problems, would erode both confidence and expanding regional integration.

Conclusion

The discussion focused on the multinational firm as actor, and how the firm re-creates itself in the light of interaction with other firms and its changing environment. Change and development are ever more rapid, and so the need to reappraise analysis and techniques is greater. The discussants saw the area as rich with potential for further analysis, particularly with respect to microeconomic and industry developments, internal networks and parent–subsidiary dynamics, and the welfare implications of changes in business organisation and behaviour.

Index ————————————————————

Printed in the United States
by Baker & Taylor Publisher Services